For Peter Ashton
with happy memories
NMMP 78
George Fodg

Also by George C. Lodge

The
New
American
Ideology

The
New
American

George C. Lodge

Ideology

How the ideological basis
of legitimate authority
in America is being
radically transformed—
the profound implications
for our society in general
and the great corporations
in particular.

Alfred · A · Knopf · New York · 1976

THIS IS A BORZOI BOOK
PUBLISHED BY ALFRED A. KNOPF, INC.

Portions of this book appeared in slightly different
form in the *Harvard Business Review*

Library of Congress Cataloging in Publication Data

Lodge, George C
The new American ideology: how the ideological basis
of legitimate authority in America is being radically
transformed.

Includes bibliographical reference and index.
1. Economics—History—United States.
2. Industry and state—United States—History.
3. Political science—History—United States.
I. Title.
HB119.A2L63   1975   301.5′0973   75–8242
ISBN 0–394–49227–7

Manufactured in the United States of America
Published September 25, 1975
Reprinted Twice
Fourth Printing, July 1976

For
N. K. L.

New times demand new measures and new men;
The World advances, and in time outgrows
The laws that in our fathers' day were best;
And doubtless, after us some better scheme
Will be shaped out by wiser men than we
Made wiser by the steady growth of truth.

(James Russell Lowell's
tribute to Cromwell)

CONTENTS

Oddly enough, I know exactly when this book was begun. It was with my first memory: New York City, 1930. I was three years old, waiting in a chill rain on the sidewalk of Fifth Avenue for my uncle to pick us up for an outing. A car came down the avenue. It was a limousine, like the one in which the Little King of the comic strips used to ride, a great, long black thing with no roof over the chauffeur. I saw a figure in the enclosed rear—a woman, I think, muffled in fur. The question for me was: Why was the chauffeur outside in the wet and the woman inside? What set of ideas made this legitimate?

Of course, I was not alone in worrying about legitimacy in the United States of 1930. It was a time, very like the present, when great institutions—the government of Herbert Hoover, the banks and big corporations—had failed to cope with crisis. The Great Depression was shaking America's roots.

This book is about the legitimacy of great institutions. It is about the ideas which once gave them authority but which now no longer do; about their justification and purpose, their structure and behavior. It concerns the distance between what they are and are becoming, and the myths and ideas which have justified them. It is about the transformation of American ideology and its consequences for the future. And it also contains a prescription for the preservation of life, liberty, and the pursuit of happiness.

To understand the transition through which the United States is passing, it is necessary to go back to the birth of Western civilization and to examine the philosophical soup in which American ideology was brewed; and at the same time, to demonstrate historically the utility of the ideological method for integrative analysis. Furthermore, the perspective of history is helpful in conveying a proper sense of what is inexorable and an awareness of the parameters within which we have choice.

While this may seem a pretentious effort for one individual mind, there are mitigating circumstances. It seems to me that this is a book which the times demand; somebody had to write it. If it only serves to stimulate someone else to do the job better, it will have been entirely worthwhile. The reader will note that there is little here which is original except for the synthesis. It is a new arrangement of ideas and of significant developments related to those ideas, designed to explain America's difficulties and to draw attention to the choices confronting its leaders.

I have relied on the knowledge acquired through many specialties—economics, history, sociology, political science, philosophy, and the physical sciences. The reader should, however, be skeptical because I am properly disciplined in none of these. This book is—and could only be—the work of a generalist. As such, it will be regarded with suspicion; superficiality, ignorance, and irresponsibility are only the most obvious dangers.

The list of those who have helped me with parts or all of the manuscript at various stages of preparation is very long, and I shall here express my gratitude only to those who contributed the most. Let me hasten to point out that none of them should be contaminated by what is erroneous even though they deserve credit for whatever is good and true.

First of all, I want to thank those in the Master's and Advanced Management programs of the Harvard Business School, who for the past ten years have been patiently stimulating me.

Professors Joseph R. Strayer of Princeton University and F. A. M. Alting Von Geusau of the University of Leiden were most helpful with Chapter 2, as was Professor William M. Welty of Pace University with Chapters 4 and 5.

At Harvard University my thanks go to Professors Robert Austin, Alfred D. Chandler, Jr., James P. Baughman, John D. Glover, Louis Hartz, Milton Katz, Warren A. Law, Renato Tagiuri, Richard E. Walton—who as Director of the Division of Research of the Harvard Business School gave me his generous support as did his predecessor, Dean Lawrence E. Fouraker—and to Lee Auspitz, Emanuel G. Mesthene, and Robert Post.

I owe very special thanks to Walter McBeth, who during the past four years has pushed my thoughts harder and further than anyone else. As senior editor of the *Harvard Business Review,* he helped me greatly with two articles which appeared in the *Review,* and the organization and clarity of this book have benefited greatly from his assistance.

In addition, I am grateful to several outstanding editors: Max Hall at Harvard, and Ashbel Green and Ann Adelman of Alfred A. Knopf.

Three research assistants also have my thanks: Bruce Krag for his work on the ancient and medieval world; Jeffrey Madrick for his help on America; and Tom Johnston for general bibliographical assistance. My mother and father, Emily Sears and Henry Cabot Lodge, have read many versions of this book and have been kind enough both to encourage and to criticize most usefully.

Profound thanks for typing countless drafts, making sense out of many scribbles, and checking footnotes go to Jackie Foott and especially to Patricia Potter.

Finally, I must thank my wife, Nancy, whose passionate respect for all that lives and deep outrage at all that inhibits life have inspired me more than she knows.

GEORGE C. LODGE

Boston, Massachusetts
June, 1975

The
New
American
Ideology

1 The Importance
of Ideological Analysis

America in the mid-1970's is an apprehensive nation, lacking a
sense of direction and control on the part of politicians, business
managers, and the American people at large. Inflation resists government efforts to contain it. Food, fuel, and other critical commodities are in short supply. Malaise in the work place cuts down
productivity. Our sense of morality grows more obscure as each
morning's newspaper brings new revelations of illegal actions by
business and government leaders. The structures of government
themselves are bloated and inefficient, manipulated by powerful
interest groups whose clear-cut ends seem to justify almost any
means. We are finding it difficult to grasp—far less resolve—such
pressing problems as ecological imbalance, urban and general environmental deterioration, troublesome population distributions,
and the persistent phenomenon of unemployment. The allocation
of our wealth, power, and control is being called into question.
And in all these areas there seem to be few criteria to judge
whether or how changes should be made.

For the United States is in the midst of a great transformation,
comparable to the one that ended medievalism and shook its institutions to the ground, making way for what we now call modernity.
The old ideas and assumptions that once made our institutions
legitimate are being eroded. They are slipping away in the face of
a changing reality, being replaced by different ideas as yet ill-
formed, contradictory, and unsettling. We stand in an age of uncertainty, a time in which the old guides are unreliable, the old
institutions seamy, a time when many, particularly the young, seek
solace in fantasies, often induced by drugs and occasionally suici-

dal in effect. What is new and different about today is that it so directly challenges those beliefs we have always assumed to be unquestionably good—the importance of economic growth and the efficiency of America's economic machine, for example. Furthermore, the mood is pervasive, cutting across age, race, and region. The nation is riddled with the sense of illegitimacy; consequently, its institutions lack authority.

Large corporations, the backbone of the nation's economy and the mainstay of its employment, are in the grip of a many-sided squeeze. These organizations feel the scarcity of resources, the pressures for environmental protection, the imposition of many new and sometimes contradictory definitions of community needs. As the chief executive of General Motors commented: "I am concerned about a society that has demonstrably lost confidence in its institutions—in government, in the press, in the church, in the military—as well as in business."* The relationships of such corporations to the communities they affect are increasingly regulated in the name of some collective good, but the regulation is often planless and incoherent. At the same time, competition mounts from more ordered societies, such as that of Japan.

Internally the corporation also faces irresolution, shown in weakened motivation on the part of workers, increasing absenteeism and unrest, rising wage and labor costs. There is a growing dissatisfaction with both the formal and the informal arrangements that connect top management people to those beneath them in the corporate hierarchy, and as a result new, "participative" forms seem to be evolving.

The question of ownership of large publicly held corporations is causing even sharper doubts about the role of stockholders and boards of directors, as well as about the authority, legitimacy, and responsibility of corporate management itself.

America's universities, organized traditionally to serve the specialized interests of the community's institutions, are finding it difficult to rearrange the old structures of scholarship to provide students with ways of grappling with the changing whole. They seem unable either to reveal or to explore the ties that bind genetics to politics, government to psychology, or ecology to philos-

---

* Richard C. Gerstenberg, *1973 Report on Progress in Areas of Public Concern* (Detroit: General Motors Corp., Feb. 8, 1973), p. 87.

ophy and economics. The old categories of knowledge frequently resemble straight-line tangents to the circle of reality, while the demands for integration are increasing. The traditional institutions of religion and culture are likewise in difficulty—they are splintered, and the splinters are rotting. Sects, often exotic, are multiplying. The resounding truth seems to be that of the Katha Upanishad: "Who sees the variety and not the unity, wanders from death to death."

It is therefore urgent for us to clear our heads, inspect our old assumptions, identify as precisely as possible what is happening, and weigh the choices that remain open to us. The old ideas are hard to discard, to be sure; they have glorious attributes, springing as they did out of the revolutionary transition from hierachical medievalism during the sixteenth and seventeenth centuries to modern forms of democracy. We are troubled also because the old ideas are what in many instances make legitimate the seats of power. They justify the status quo, and it is uncomfortable to look at the weakness below.

But the stakes are high. Some institutions may be able to adapt to the new ideas that are emerging, survive, and prosper. Others —notably corporations—may flee, searching the world for more hospitable ideological surroundings where the old structures are still acceptable. Still others will crumble and die, unwilling or unable to change or move. We are in crisis, but unlike the great wars or depressions, this particular crisis is far from unifying. The community has immediate pressing needs, but they are ill-defined, and we seem unable to pull ourselves together. Planning we must have, but whom can we trust to do it? A growing discrepancy between distrust of government on the one hand, and the enlargement of what we know it must do on the other, marks the problem.

Fundamentally, we seek new political and social constructs that can encompass our economic and technological activity, setting our society and its institutions back onto some kind of firm base and guiding us to a new vision of the American community. But what are to be the terms of this transition? And by what criteria shall we define the "good" community? How many people do we want, where should they live, what are their rights? There are no pragmatic answers to these questions. Experimentalism by its very nature presupposes a floundering from crisis to crisis. Broad conceptions are both essential and inexorable. They may come cruelly, with bloodshed, repression, and waste, or humanely, efficiently, and with a maximum of freedom. If we perceive the nature of the crisis sooner rather than later and do not shrink from its implications—however threatening to our existing assumptions and interests those implications may be—the transition could be relatively benign. If, on the other hand, we wait, confident of muddling through, we are likely to lurch from one crisis to another until large-scale depression and disruption cause us to welcome the orderly relief of dictatorship. At the beginning of World War II Karl Mannheim, the German sociologist, wrote from exile in England:

> Only if we know why Western society in the crisis zone is passing through a phase of disintegration, is there any hope that the countries which still enjoy a comparative peace will learn to control the future trend of events by democratic planning, and so avoid the negative aspects of the process: dictatorship, conformity, and barbarism.*

He spoke of the loss of a sense of mission, a sudden impotence, in those to whom society has traditionally looked for leadership. And he warned of the dangers of piecemeal control, a visionless flailing, laissez-faire weakly propped by rhetoric.

To manage change on the staggering scale we are witnessing, establish broad conceptions for the community, and redesign our institutions appropriately, we must have more information about ourselves and more techniques with which to manipulate that information. Far more important, we need a different way of looking at things, one that will reveal the critical keys of change and allow us to perceive the process as a whole instead of as an inexplicable series of unrelated shocks. The traditional scientific method cannot be particularly helpful here; taking things apart for analysis and measurement is insufficient. The crisis lies in the whole, in our society's very foundations, the assumptions which permeate it, in the relationships within it, man-to-man and man-to-matter, and in our perception of all this. So far the preferred American approach has been the optimistic one: "I need not worry about the whole; the whole will take care of itself." But that is exactly what it will not do.

---

* Karl Mannheim, *Man and Society in an Age of Reconstruction* (New York: Harcourt, Brace & Co., Inc., 1940), pp. 6 and 40.

As a means of understanding what is going on around us, rationalism has several limitations; much is emotional, intuitive, and mystical. Indeed, those very factors which are the most important are also perhaps the least susceptible to formal isolation and rational analysis. There are few hard data. How, for example, do we measure resentment? And there are few facts on which to base authoritative predictions. How does one predict the influence of Eastern religions in this country? Or how would one have assessed the effects that finally flowed, say, from the establishment of the early Christian communities in the Roman world?

This book attempts to outline a mode of thought, not exclusively rational, that can lead us to the unifying vision we so badly need. It is concerned with a way of understanding the past, the present, and the future that will make the transformation through which we are now passing more comprehensible and controllable. I shall argue that a useful way to understand and deal with what is happening is through the concept of ideology. This concept allows us to perceive the vital relationships between the social, political, economic, cultural, and scientific factors affecting our institutions; to inspect the old assumptions upon which the legitimacy of those institutions has rested; and to foresee the alternatives we have for the future. I shall first trace the evolution of several ideologies in Western society from antiquity to the present day and then present in detail my own analysis of the shape the new American ideology is assuming. This introductory chapter is intended to explain my general course and to suggest the kinds of topics that will be taken up along the way.

The Nature of Ideology

An ideology is a collection of ideas that makes explicit the nature of the good community. It is the framework by which a community defines and applies values, such as survival, justice, self-respect, fulfillment, and economy (the efficient use of resources). All communities everywhere have treasured such values; in themselves they are timeless and essentially noncontroversial. However, different communities define them differently. In ancient Egypt, justice and self-respect involved lugging stones to glorify the god-king. For a time the Pharaonic ideology provided an acceptable consensus, coercive as it may have been; then it eroded and collapsed. Likewise, the medieval Christian view of justice was quite different from our view of justice today, and both differ from Plato's view of it, but the value, justice, has remained a constant. The equality promised in the Declaration of Independence is not a value, as I define it, but rather a specific ideological element, an interpretation of several values for a specific time and place, and one that was essentially harmonious with the definitions of justice and self-respect which obtained in the United States at the time the Declaration was written.

Ideology is thus a living structure, a bridge by which values are given specific meaning in various cultures at different points in space and time and conveyed into the life of the community. It is a dynamic system of objectives, priorities, and criteria for the life of a community in all its aspects—social, economic, and aesthetic. Ideology legitimizes the existing order and its patterns of action. It is formed and nourished by the circumstances and experiences of the community, by such factors as geography and demography, by traditional science, philosophy, and religion, and by institutional practice and behavior; and it, in turn, affects each of these factors. For example, the framework for making values explicit in Japan, a relatively small country sustaining a great many people, will plainly differ substantially from the ideology of nineteenth-century America, a large continent with a relatively small population.

The concept of ideology assumes that a community is an organic whole influenced largely (although not necessarily exclusively) by a dominant set of coherent ideas. An ideology is thus a framework of interrelated ideas drawn both from within and outside the society—a framework that is used to articulate, develop, and sustain the consensus upon which a community lives, acts, and takes direction.*

By definition, no community is without an ideology. Sometimes such ideology is sharp and clear, sometimes obscure; certain of its

---

* This definition and what follows draws from Carl J. Friedrich, *Man and His Government* (New York: McGraw-Hill Book Co., Inc., 1963), pp. 91–2; Karl Mannheim, *Ideology and Utopia* (New York: Harcourt, Brace & Co., Inc., 1953) and *Man and Society in an Age of Reconstruction, op. cit.;* and George Lichtheim, *The Concept of Ideology and Other Essays* (New York: Random House, Inc., 1967).

elements may be conscious and explicit, others unconscious and implicit; today it may be vital and relevant, tomorrow dead. But whether a community is large or small—nation, neighborhood, or factory organization—its existence depends upon a common approach to values and some agreement as to how those values are to be made explicit in the real world. Ideology serves as the collective unconscious of the community, comprising the underlying bases of its motivation.

Ironically, we in America have had the notion that "ideology" is basically a European commodity; a bag of theoretical confusion, whether tagged as socialism, communism, or fascism, which we left in the old country with our ancestors and from which hardheaded Americans are happily free. This, as I shall show, is nonsense. No community has been more deeply imbued with ideology than ours. Our neglect of it is partially responsible for its current state of disrepair. Its renovation, with which this book is ultimately concerned, will be our most important task for years to come.

For some time in America we have been moving from one ideological framework to another; or to put it more precisely, the old structure has been disintegrating and a new one is—for better or worse—being put up in its place. It is this transition which causes our institutions to tremble.

Any ideology can be conveniently divided into five basic components. The first has to do with the individual human being, his rights and his place in society, and the definition of his fulfillment and self-respect, as well as of the means by which these are to be achieved. The second concerns the means by which his rights are guaranteed. The third relates to mechanisms and criteria for controlling the exploitation of material resources. The fourth comprehends the role of the state and the function of government. The fifth pertains to the nature and organization of knowledge, and, more specifically, the function of science.

The Traditional American Ideology

The traditional ideology of America is composed of five great ideas which correspond to these five components. They first came to America in the eighteenth century, having been set down in seventeenth-century England by several men, notably John Locke, as "natural" laws. I refer to this ideology as "Lockean" because of Locke's central contributions to it, recognizing that this may be an oversimplification, that many others contributed to it, and that we have significantly departed from the original formulation over time. (We speak of Marxism, after all, to denote the whole body of ideas assembled after Marx's death, some of which were only embryonic in his thought and writings.) Briefly stated, then, the five components of the traditional Lockean ideology are these.

FIRST, *individualism*. This is the atomistic notion that the community is no more than the sum of the individuals in it. It is the idea that fulfillment lies in an essentially lonely struggle in what amounts to a wilderness where the fit survive—and where, if you do not survive, you are somehow unfit. Closely tied to individualism is the idea of *equality*, in the sense implied in the phrase "equal opportunity"; and the idea of *contract*, the inviolate device by which individuals are tied together as buyers and sellers. In the political order in this country, individualism evolved into *interest group pluralism*, which became the preferred means of directing society.

SECOND, *property rights*. Traditionally, the best guarantee of individual rights was held to be the sanctity of property rights. By virtue of this concept, the individual was assured freedom from the predatory powers of the sovereign—the Stuart monarchs for Locke, and Hanoverian monarchs for our revolutionary ancestors.

THIRD, *competition*. Adam Smith most eloquently articulated the idea that the uses of property are best controlled by each individual proprietor competing in an open market to satisfy individual consumer desires. This principle of competition is still the intellectual linchpin of our economic system.

FOURTH, *the limited state*. In reaction to the powerful hierarchies of late medievalism, the conviction grew that the least government is the best government. We do not mind how big government may get, but we are reluctant to allow it authority or focus. And we resist the idea of planning by government, preferring instead that it respond to crises and to interest groups—whoever has the clout can call the tune.

FIFTH, *scientific specialization and fragmentation*. This is the corruption of Newtonian mechanics which says that, if we attend to the parts, as experts and specialists, the whole will take care of itself.

This traditional ideology took firm root in wilderness America. The separate ideas have developed through history; at times one or another of them has been distorted or set aside so that our leadership could deal more effectively with a particular problem. What is most remarkable and significant, however, is that (distortions, modifications, and exceptions notwithstanding) this ideology has never been explicitly inspected, renovated, or replaced. It remains pervasive, a quasi-religious entity which must not be called in question. However distorted or eroded, it has remained unassailably the primary source of legitimacy for our institutions, whether economic, political, or social. And this is so even though our most powerful institutions, large corporations in particular, have in fact departed substantially from it. Its resilience is formidable.

The power and cohesion of this Lockean constellation and its peculiar suitability for the rugged early societies of wilderness and frontier America to a large extent explain the religious reverence in which we have held it. Furthermore, the phenomenon has reinforced itself, generating myths, some of a downright romantic quality, that have held us spellbound, while making us reluctant to consider whether the original power and efficacy of the constellation is still operative. There is the myth of the founding fathers, the initial and potent champions of organized America and its ideology, who are seen as men of superhuman wisdom and courage, and whose writings and deeds are taken as reflections of revealed truth. There is the myth of manifest destiny, that the Lockean order is to be established from sea to shining sea, and then worldwide for good measure—so that we feel we have a mission to save Indochina from communism and to plant our flags on the moon. John Wayne personifies the Lockean hero, and we pass from rags to riches with Horatio Alger.

Most fundamental of all is the myth of material growth and progress. This has stemmed directly from the traditional ideology, for implicit in individualism is the notion that man has the will to acquire power, that is, to control external events, property, nature, the economy, politics, or whatever. Under the concept of the limited state, the presence of this will in the human psyche meant the guarantee of progress through unfettered competition, notably when combined with the Darwinian notion that the inexorable processes of evolution are constantly working to improve nature.

Scientific specialization has been part of this "progress," fragmenting knowledge and society while straining their adaptability. Such splintering has brought us at least one hideous result: an amoral view of progress "under which nuclear ballistic missiles definitely represent progress over gunpowder and cannonballs, which in turn represent progress over bows and arrows."* This treacherous myth places no apparent limit on the degree to which man can gain dominion over his environment, nor does it stipulate any other ideological criteria for defining progress.

Our reluctance to examine our ideology, or even to admit that we have one, appears particularly ironic when one considers how very distinctive the American version of Lockeanism is in comparison with its ideological results elsewhere. Even within the community of Western Europe, the ideological differentials that grew from the "natural" laws noted by Locke and his contemporaries are quite sharp. In one sense this should not be surprising, since Locke did not invent the principles on which he based his vision of community. The ideas had been around for a number of years as both consequence and cause of the breakdown of the organic, hierarchical ideology and structure of medieval Europe, and were the common inheritance of the communities which emerged from that decline. In England itself the discrepancies of ideology from the distinctive American version are as striking as the parallels so frequently noted. There the ideas of Locke were quickly augmented and altered by the spirit of Jeremy Bentham's utilitarianism and the somewhat later thought of John Stuart Mill. Their formulations were more useful to the requirements of modernizing England than were the earlier ones set down by Locke. In accordance with these formulations, a Briton today is prepared to credit

---

* Gunther S. Stent, *The Coming of the Golden Age: A View of the End of Progress* (Garden City, N.Y.: The Natural History Press, 1969), p. 90.

his government with considerably more prestige and authority than is an American; and he cares far less about competition than he does about productive effort to serve the country's needs, as these are defined by government.

In France, the Lockean notion of individualism that emerged in the seventeenth century was overtaken by the idea of the General Will that evolved in the eighteenth, with the French Revolution and Rousseau:

If you would have the General Will accomplished, bring all the particular wills into conformity with it; in other words, as virtue is nothing more than this conformity of the particular wills with the General Will, establish the reign of virtue.*

Further, in understanding the institutional differences between France and the United States properly, we must acknowledge the two quite different uses to which Locke and Rousseau put the notion of contract. For Locke it was an individualistic device; for Rousseau, a communitarian one. In France, the individual was to be fused into society, the General Will becoming the embodiment of private desires and entirely superior to them. The French state thus became an instrument of intervention in the interest of the General Will, to plan and guide the nation's institutions. From the very beginning America rejected this strain of collectivism, toward which it is now inexorably drifting. Ironically enough John Rawls, the American philosopher, now seeks to legitimize this drift by employing a variation on Rousseau's notion of social contract.**

In Japan even wider ideological divergencies are apparent. The Japanese motifs of harmony, cooperation, and sacrifice of the individual to communal aims reflect a profoundly different cultural framework, based on different philosophic and religious roots as well as particular geographic and demographic conditions. The Japanese ideology deserves our attention here since one of its important effects is a deliberate symbiosis between business and government. This has led to serious competitive difficulties for American free enterprise in world markets, and in the early 1970's

---

* Jean Jacques Rousseau, *The Social Contract and Discourses,* translated and edited by G. D. H. Cole (New York: E. P. Dutton & Co., Inc., 1956), p. 297.

** John Rawls, *A Theory of Justice* (Cambridge, Mass.: Belknap Press, 1971); see also Robert A. Nisbet, *The Sociological Tradition* (New York: Basic Books, Inc., 1966), pp. 35–41.

we seemed half-inclined to emulate the efficacy and perhaps even the methods of their system. Whether such change is possible can be judged only after the ideologies on which the American and Japanese systems are based have been understood in all their dynamic characteristics and objectively compared.* (The Appendix contains a brief attempt to set out the Japanese counterparts of traditional American ideology.)

I have suggested how an ideological analysis can serve us today. Such analysis lays bare the ideas that have dominant influence on a community. And since these ideas are often regarded as un-questionable assumptions within a community, the particular value of ideological analysis stems from the fact that it fixes attention on those dominant influences, which might otherwise remain ob-scure or pass wholly unnoticed.** Ideological analysis addresses the problem of *man's knowing,* bound as he is by his location in time and place and culture. Like a didactic psychoanalysis or a training in anthropology, it helps to make explicit the local con-ditions that structure perception and direct the synthesis of knowl-edge. This must be beneficial, because the person who is most ignorant of these dominant factors and conditions is the least free and the most predetermined in his conduct. Conversely, the study of ideology liberates us from the blinders of implicit culture; by becoming aware of the determinants that dominate us, we remove them from the realm of unconscious motivation into the domain of the controllable. Such liberation is particularly important for those in positions of leadership, since they carry an extensive responsibility for timely innovation; but it is also a particularly

---

* For an excellent analysis of how traditional Japanese ideology has been reflected in the structure and conduct of Japanese business institutions, see M. Y. Yoshino, *Japan's Managerial System: Tradition and Innova-tion* (Cambridge, Mass.: The M.I.T. Press, 1968). Franz Schurmann of the University of California at Berkeley has used the concept of ideology brilliantly to describe the nature and purposes of Chinese organizations. See especially Chapters I and IV of *Ideology and Organi-zation in Communist China* (Berkeley and Los Angeles: University of California Press, 1968). In the Chinese case, ideology becomes a singularly useful tool with which to discern and understand the differ-ences between China and the Soviet Union, as well as some of the similarities between China and Japan.
** Louis Wirth in Introduction to Mannheim, *Ideology and Utopia,* p. xiv.

difficult state for the members of a ruling group to attain. As Mannheim has pointed out, these leaders

in their thinking [can become] so intensively interest-bound to a situation that they are simply no longer able to see certain facts which would undermine their sense of domination. There is implicit in the word "ideology" the insight that in certain situations the collective unconscious of certain groups obscures the real conditions of society both to itself and to others and thereby stabilizes it.*

As we consider the cultures of the past 5,000 years from which we have inherited our ideological concepts, we will be struck by the extent to which our atomistic, individualistic ideology constitutes a fundamental aberration from the historically typical norm. It stands as a radical experiment that achieved its most extreme manifestation in America in the nineteenth century. Since that time our ideology has been steadily deteriorating in the face of various challenges—wars, depressions, new economic and political systems, the concentration and growth of populations, and institutional as well as environmental developments. America now appears to be heading into a return to the communal norms of both the ancient and medieval worlds. A historical analysis of ideological trends should therefore help us to understand the process we now face. And although this book is mainly concerned with the United States, much of it is relevant to the West in general. For example, France and Italy today exhibit different versions of the return to communitarianism. In Italy particularly, it is a mistake to regard communism as a radical movement; it is rather a form of neomedievalism in a country where Lockeanism never really became implanted. In this sense it is a conservative impulse, a return to a more comprehensive set of ideas. The drift toward collectivism in the West obviously poses a severe problem for democracy—a further dilemma with which I shall be concerned.

The New American Ideology

Pursuing the technique of ideological analysis to understand events today, I believe it is possible to identify new elements in our ideological set—vague in outline, to be sure, but clear in general direction. Very briefly, these are my impressions of the emergent American ideology (see Figure 1):

---

* *Ibid.,* p. 36.

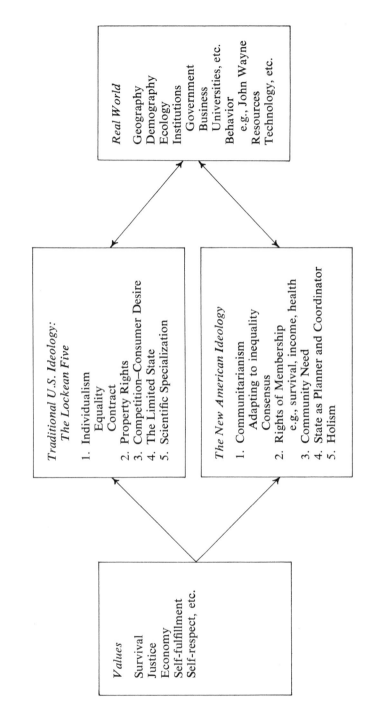

FIGURE 1

First, *communitarianism* is augmenting and replacing individualism. For most people today, fulfillment occurs through their participation in an organic social process. The community as we conceive it is indeed more than the sum of its individuals. It has special urgent needs, and the survival and self-respect of the people within it depends on the recognition of those needs. There are few who can get their kicks *à la* John Wayne, although many may try. Fulfillment for most depends on their place in a community, their identity with a complete social process. And, further, we know that if the community—factory, neighborhood, nation, or world—is well designed, its members will have a sense of identity with it. They will be able to make the maximum use of their capacities. But if it is poorly designed, people will be correspondingly alienated and frustrated.

In the complex and highly organized America which has evolved, few can live in the ruggedly individualistic state Locke had in mind. Both corporations and unions have played leading roles in creating circumstances that have eroded the old idea of individualism and induced the new communitarianism. In an increasing number of corporations, this communitarianism is becoming the source of managerial authority in a consensus of the managed rather than in the old contractual relationship between employer and employee. Paradoxically, both management and unions have lingered with the traditional, individualistic idea of contract long after the contract itself became collective. The old notion of equality is also being transformed. Traditionally, we have attempted to guarantee that each worker have equal opportunity. The young lawyers who are enforcing equal opportunity legislation, however, argue that discrimination of various kinds has become institutionalized, endemic to the corporate community; and to avoid prosecution a corporation must now ensure equality of result and equality of representation, as opposed to the former equality of opportunity. AT&T, for example, has had to pay substantial reparations and restructure itself in order to ensure that women and minority groups are fairly represented in its hierarchy. Thus a corporation must adapt itself as a whole to take account of inequalities in the community around it, and a new criterion for the legitimacy of corporate conduct is upon us.

Second, *rights of membership* are augmenting and replacing property rights. A curious thing has happened to private property—it has stopped being very important. After all, what difference does it really make today whether a person owns or just enjoys property? He may get a certain psychological satisfaction out of owning a jewel or a car, a TV set or a house, but does it really make a difference if he rents them? Today a new right has clearly superseded property rights in political and social importance: the right to survive, to enjoy income, health, and other rights associated with membership in the American community or in some component of that community, including a corporation. As of January 1, 1974, for example, all U.S. citizens who were sixty-five years old, or blind, or disabled, had an absolute right to a minimum income of $140 a month. Richard M. Nixon's Family Assistance Plan would have guaranteed an income to all. Health legislation guaranteeing medical care to all is likely in the future. The membership rights represented in such planning are communitarian rights that public opinion holds to be consistent with a good community. They represent a revolutionary departure from the old Lockean conception, under which only the fit survived.

The value of property as a legitimizing idea and basis of authority has eroded as well. It is now obvious that our large public corporations are not private property at all. The 1.5 million shareholders of General Motors do not and cannot control, direct, or in any real sense be responsible for "their" company. The best we can say is that the corporation is a sort of collective, floating in philosophic limbo, dangerously vulnerable to the charge of illegitimacy and to the charge that it is not amenable to community control. Consider how the management of this nonproprietary institution is selected. The myth is that the stockholders select the board of directors, which in turn selects the management. But in truth management selects the board, and the board, generally speaking, blesses management.

Managers thus get to be managers according to some mystical hierarchical process of questionable legitimacy. Under such circumstances, it is not surprising that "management's rights" are fragile and its authority waning. Alfred Sloan, the great organizer of GM, warned of this trend in 1927:

There is a point beyond which diffusion of stock ownership must enfeeble the corporation by depriving it of virile interest in management upon the part of some one man or group of men to whom its success is a matter of personal and vital interest. And conversely at the same point the public interest becomes involved when the public can no longer locate some tangible personality within the ownership which it may hold responsible for the corporation's conduct.*

Third, our method for controlling the use of property is changing radically. Where once we entrusted this function to open competition in the market place, we are more and more applying the criterion of *community need* to the utilization of resources. It was to this notion of community need, for example, that ITT appealed in 1971 when it sought to prevent the Justice Department from divesting it of Hartford Fire Insurance. The company lawyers said, in effect: "Don't visit that old idea of competition on us. The public interest requires ITT to be big and strong at home so that it can withstand the blows of Allende in Chile, Castro in Cuba, and the Japanese in general. Before you apply the antitrust laws to us, the Secretary of the Treasury, the Secretary of Commerce, and the Council of Economic Advisers should meet to decide what, in the light of our balance-of-payments problems and domestic economic difficulties, the national interest is."**

Note that here, as so often happens, it was the company that argued the ideologically radical case. The suggestion is obvious: ITT is to be a partner with the government—indeed, with the cabinet—in defining and fulfilling the communitarian needs of the United States. There may be some short-term doubt about who is the senior partner, but partnership it is. This concept differs radically from the traditional idea underlying the antitrust laws— namely, that the public interest emerges naturally from free and vigorous competition among numerous aggressive, individualistic, and preferably small companies attempting to satisfy the needs of the consumer.

Fourth, the role of government is inevitably expanding to embrace the concept of *the state as planner*. Government is becoming the setter of our sights and the arbiter of community needs. Inevitably, it will take on unprecedented tasks of coordination, priority setting, and planning in the largest sense, and for better or worse will become far more authoritative as it moves to make the

---

* Quoted in Herman E. Krooss and Charles Gilbert, *American Business History* (Englewood Cliffs, N.J.: Prentice-Hall, Inc., 1972), p. 264.

** See *Hearings Before the Committee on the Judiciary, United States Senate, 92nd Congress, Second Session on the Nomination of Richard G. Kleindienst of Arizona to Be Attorney General* (Washington, D.C.: U.S. Government Printing Office, 1972).

difficult and subtle trade-offs which now confront us—between environmental purity and energy supply, for example.

Government is already big in the United States, probably bigger in proportion to our population than in those countries which we call socialist. Some 16 per cent of the labor force now works for one or another governmental agency, and by 1980 the percentage will be higher. Increasingly, American institutions live on government largess—subsidies, allowances, and contracts to farmers, corporations, and universities—and individuals likewise benefit from social insurance, medical care, and housing allowances. The pretense of the limited state, however, means that these huge allocations are relatively haphazard, reflecting the crisis of the moment and the power of interest groups rather than any coherent, objective plan. To give one example, the web of interrelated factors which together constitutes the "energy crisis" is at least in part the result of governmental ad hocism and the lack of integrated planning.

Finally, and perhaps most fundamentally, comes the growing acceptance of *holism,* or the theory that nature tends to group units of whatever kinds into wholes, and into a single, great integrated whole. The perception of reality now demands that we perceive entire systems, not only the parts thereof. The old idea of scientific specialization has given way to a new consciousness of the interrelatedness of all things. Spaceship earth, the limits of growth, the fragility of our life-supporting biosphere have all dramatized the ecological and philosophical truth that everything is related to everything else. Harmony between the works of man and the demands of nature is no longer the romantic plea of conservationists; it is an absolute rule of survival and thus of profound ideological significance, subverting in many ways all the earlier Lockean theory.

I shall argue for the accuracy of these particular transformations of our traditional ideological beliefs. But whether or not one agrees with my specific perceptions and arguments, it must be clear that an ideology is not a lifeless dogma. It is a collection of ideas or principles which is subject to continuing flux. It may, of course, appear dogmatic as reflected in the behavior of certain individuals or institutions at given times and places—for example, in Oliver Cromwell or Chairman Mao or these archetypal Lockean individualists, the robber barons. But an ideology itself over time undergoes constant modifications and distortions; and when these are so extreme as to flaw dramatically the original logic and consistency of the design, the ideology changes in nature. A period of chaos ensues, from which a new ideology emerges.

The Preservation of Values

The transition from the Old Five to the New Five has to a great extent already taken place. There can be no going back. The choices we have left concern the ways in which we decide to implement the new ideology while preserving what is most valuable in the old.

In general, as I have said, an ideology should provide a community with social, political, and economic definitions for values at any one time. In this sense, ideology is the foundation of public opinion upon which law and institutional practices are erected. Thus, by distinguishing between the transitory framework of ideology and the timeless, universal, and noncontroversial values of which it is an interpretation, it is clear that values can be sustained only when the ideological framework that connects them to the world of experience is solid and coherent. If change in the real world—in the revelations of science, the functioning of institutions, the organization and characteristics of people—is not reflected in ideological change, values tend to lose their meaning. The danger here is that the interests of the status quo will encourage a community to retain an outworn ideology, supposing it to be equivalent to values, with the result that the real values are misapplied and suffer. An undue loyalty to traditional ideology can actually kill values.

A community unmindful of its ideology is liable to be misled by it. This is a special problem for Americans, whose pragmatic preference has caused them to neglect their ideology. I have already noted our tendency to relegate it to the dusty shelves of myth. We have failed to inspect its component ideas or to note explicitly their deterioration in the face of reality; we have discarded them pragmatically; but they have not been replaced and thus they continue to affect our decisions long after their utility has declined.*

Our great reluctance to see our history as the expression of an ideology is partly due to the traditional connotations of the word. Ideologies have always been particularly visible and influential at times of revolutionary transformation. They are the distilled ideas around which change turns. Administrative bureaucracies which depend on routines established upon the basis of the old ideas feel threatened by the new ones. Those in authority, whose powers and legitimacy are sanctioned by the old theory, sense subversion in the new. It is not surprising that in every revolutionary situation the status quo seeks a remedy in arbitrary decrees based upon the old ideology and is reluctant to meet the changing situation realistically. The status quo regards revolution, Mannheim says, "as an untoward event within an otherwise ordered system and not as the living expression of fundamental social forces on which the existence, the preservation, and the development of society depends."**

Two meanings of ideology have arisen because of this sensitive connotation. The first meaning I have already given, and it is the sense in which I shall use the term. The second, derogatory meaning connotes the false consciousness or doctrinaire characteristics of those who are unaware or unmindful of political reality. It is exemplified by Marx, for whom economics was either "scientific" or "ideological," depending on whether or not it gave what he felt was an objective and true account of the socioeconomic process.

The term "ideology" was first used around 1800 in post-revolutionary France by a group of philosophers who were interested in the science of ideas, which is what the word literally denotes. The group's founder, Destutt de Tracy, defines this science as follows:

The science may be called ideology, if one considers only the subject matter; general grammar, if one considers only the methods; and logic, if one considers only the purpose. Whatever the name, it necessarily contains these three subdivisions, since one cannot be treated adequately without also treating the two others. Ideology seems

---

* See Edward S. Mason, "The Apologetics of 'Managerialism,'" *The Journal of Business,* The School of Business of the University of Chicago XXXI (January 1958):9.
** Mannheim, *Ideology and Utopia,* p. 105.

to me to be the generic term because the science of ideas subsumes both that of their expression and that of their derivation.*

Rejecting metaphysics, these philosophers sought the derivation of ideas in anthropological and psychological sources.

Napoleon was responsible for initiating the derogatory meaning of the word when he found that this group was opposing his imperial ambitions and so contemptuously labeled its members "ideologists." In effect, he judged them to be unrealistic, in terms of what he regarded as the practical requirements of his political environment. Thus was set up the dichotomy between ideology and the world of experience or pragmatism. The "pragmatic point of view was already implicit in the accusation which Napoleon hurled at his adversaries," writes Mannheim.** Since then Americans have taken a somewhat Napoleonic view of the word and the concept, in spite of the fact that the United States has probably been more ideologically controlled than most other communities. We have tended to view ideology with some suspicion, as unrealistic, impractical, irrelevant to our real problems. Americans prefer to think of themselves as pragmatists who do what needs to be done—if it doesn't work, we can undo it and try again.

Because of the importance of pragmatism in American life, it is necessary to sharpen its distinction from ideology. William James first used the term "pragmatism" in 1898, although the pragmatic theory had been developed a decade earlier by C. S. Pierce. Pragmatism is difficult to define precisely, partly perhaps because James, as both psychologist and philosopher, wrote simultaneously at several different levels.† Pragmatism says that the truth of a proposition can only be measured by its experimental results and its practical outcome. Truth changes, and is relative in both space and time. In twentieth-century America, as we shall see later, pragmatism took on two quite distinct meanings. First, it was a body of philosophy which reflected a radical departure from the Lockean ideology, saying, in effect, that Locke no longer

---

* Destutt de Tracy, *Les Eléments de L'Idéologie*, 3rd ed., p. 4n., as quoted in Mannheim, *Ideology and Utopia*, pp. 63–4n.

** Mannheim, *ibid.*, p. 65.

† See Ralph Ross, Introduction to William James, *The Meaning of Truth*, (Ann Arbor: The University of Michigan Press, Ann Arbor Paperbacks, 1970).

worked in contemporary America and that the country needed something new and different. In that sense, this book is a continuation of the pragmatic tradition. But pragmatism also came to stand for a form of experimentalism that amounts to opportunism: Whatever works is good and true. It is easy to see how pragmatism could in popular usage be taken as opportunism, if not expediency, particularly since James himself wrote: "The true . . . is only the expedient in the way of our thinking. . . . The truth of an idea is not a stagnant property inherent in it. Truth *happens* to an idea. It *becomes* true, is *made* true by events."* (Emphasis added.) It is in this second sense that pragmatism has caused difficulty, by distracting us from the essential task of ideological inspection and renovation. Whatever James had in mind, his thought served admirably as an articulation of American distrust for those whom James called "intellectualists," European philosophers and their ilk, of the same sort probably that bothered Napoleon. Pragmatism as experimental opportunism was wonderfully harmonious with traditional American ideology, particularly individualism: What works for you is good for you, what works for me is good for me. Pragmatism in this sense was indeed the natural, if unruly, child of Locke. But once one has reached this individualistic formulation, one must face the question of how a community of pragmatists is to be kept together. How is it to achieve consensus and purpose? Spurning ideology as artificial, rigid, and confusing, the pragmatist appears to feel no need of an explicit framework of ideas to carry values into application in the real world and to define their temporal meaning. He must therefore assume that a sufficient number of individuals in the community somehow intuitively agree closely enough about the definition and application of values in the real world to allow the community to function. In our terms, then, for pragmatism to work, the pragmatist must assume the existence of a valid ideology, even as he denies the need for its existence. Indeed, during the heyday of this mode of thought in the nineteenth and early twentieth centuries, such an assumption was acceptable, although logically absurd.

So pragmatism is useful as a method of philosophy only when a valid ideology serves to provide an adequate community con-

---

* Mannheim, *Man and Society in an Age of Reconstruction,* p. 206.

sensus. If a community's problems derive from ideological failure, then there is no pragmatic remedy, and to seek one only delays the necessary ideological inspection and renovation. The danger of pragmatism is that it leads to the delusion that truth, and even thought, is entirely determined by the situation at hand. It makes us unmindful of the context of ideas which affects thought and decisionmaking and which also is a determinant of the situation.

Nevertheless, it is important to recognize the positive significance of the pragmatic process to ideological development. Ideology depends upon pragmatism for a design which is appropriate to the real world of experience at any given time. Pragmatic thought has made us aware of that organic process by which every act or idea is essentially a part of conduct; it rejected the older, artificial distinction between action and pure theory which certain philosophers, isolated from the world, had invented. As Mannheim said:

Only to those who live a cloistered life can the nature of thought appear as purely contemplative, i.e., as self-contained and not as an instrument of life and action. In life as it was originally lived there was no thought which was not directly linked with action. To overlook or deny this integration of thought in conduct is to deny that thought in its very nature is determined by the situation.*

The Scientific Example

Perhaps the neatest and best-documented pragmatic process we can witness today is that of science. On the positive side, science digests and synthesizes its growing mass of data into remarkable general formulations that contribute greatly to ideology. One might cite vaccination, which has changed our entire thinking about plagues; or the principles of genetic engineering, now emerging and certain to affect our concept of individual rights. (Of Newton's and Einstein's formulations I shall say more later.) On the other hand, the experimental mode and opportunistic side of scientific work have tended to promote specialization; this is the negative effect of pragmatism. Science has come naturally to pursue an infinity of narrowing searches for how things are in practical detail. Mannheim even speaks of the defense mechanisms which scientists devise to shield themselves from one another as

* *Ibid.*, pp. xi, xvi.

a kind of professional ideology. And he goes on to point out the danger of this:

Once a single branch of knowledge is studied in isolation it becomes unreal, and paradoxical as it may sound, the only person who is acting realistically is the theorist, who pieces these fragmentary observations together to form a coherent scheme.*

The worst of it is that such theorizing may be the work of mere amateurs who lack either the sense of discipline or the responsibility the specialist is trained to employ.

As well as indicating both the good and bad points of the pragmatic process, science as it has developed historically offers an excellent explanatory model for the evolution of societal ideology. Ideology uses the science of the day to support its contentions. Far from opposing science, as Marx contended, it builds itself with scientific bricks and mortar. The force of Locke, for example, derives in large part from his consistency with the science of Newton. Equally, an ideology fails when its scientific underpinnings become passé; to take one example, the science of ecology has fundamentally altered Lockean conceptions of property rights as they relate to land use.

Ideology is also, of course, rooted in religion and philosophy, amongst a host of other factors; but generally it is most directly connected to and affected by the "real" world of a culture. In this sense it is a bridge between the abstract and the concrete, between the theoretical and the experiential. It is inspired by and constructed from both ends—the world of science and ideas at one end, and the world of institutions, people, earth, air, and water at the other. Hence the analogy between the evolution of science and the evolution of ideology.

Further, the nature, power, and importance of the concept of ideology in the development of society becomes clearer if we apply it to the history of the development of scientific knowledge and technique. Thomas S. Kuhn of Princeton University has done just this in *The Structure of Scientific Revolutions.*** Instead of

---

* *Ibid.,* p. 29.
** Thomas S. Kuhn, *The Structure of Scientific Revolutions* (Chicago and London: University of Chicago Press, 1962); see also Werner Heisenberg, "Tradition in Science," *Science and Public Affairs,* December 1973, pp. 4–10.

speaking about the ideologies of science, however, he uses the very comparable notion of paradigms. By a "paradigm," he means the collection of ideas within the confines of which scientific inquiry takes place, the assumed definition of what are legitimate problems and methods, the accepted practice and viewpoint from which the student prepares for membership in the scientific community, the criteria for choosing problems to attack, and the rules and standards of scientific practice.*

Kuhn looked at such major transformations in the development of science as those associated with Copernicus, Newton, Lavoisier, and Einstein. Each of these required "the community's rejection of one time-honored theory in favor of one incompatible with it." Each caused scientists and others to view the world in a new way, with a different focus of attention, noting different things with different consequences. Each revealed new problems to be solved and suggested new means to their solution, making legitimate new methods and new assumptions. Each was controversial and revolutionary.** And each involved a shift from one paradigm to another.

One of the most striking features of a paradigm is the extent to which it insulates and preserves the status quo and so prevents major changes, whether conceptual or phenomenal.† It does this largely by controlling the criteria for choosing problems to be solved:

To a great extent these are the only problems that the community will admit as scientific or encourage its members to undertake. Other problems . . . are rejected as metaphysical, as the concern of another discipline, or sometimes as just too problematic to be worth the time.††

A paradigm can thus prevent a community from perceiving and attacking many important problems which are not reducible to the appropriate puzzle form. In this way we become the prisoners of our instruments and our specialties, which have themselves emerged from a particular way of looking at problems and the world. And it is only when anomalies confront the old model that new scientific theories emerge. These theories are preceded by a time of dramatic professional insecurity as loyalists to the old paradigm repeatedly fail to make the puzzles of normal science come out as they should:

---

* *Ibid.,* p. 11.   ** *Ibid.,* p. 6.   † *Ibid.,* p. 35.   †† *Ibid.,* p. 37.

The state of Ptolemaic astronomy was a scandal before Copernicus' announcement. Galileo's contribution to the study of motion depended closely upon difficulties discovered in Aristotle's theory by scholastic critics. Newton's new theory of light and color originated in the discovery that none of the existing pre-paradigm theories would account for the length of the spectrum, and the wave theory that replaced Newton's was announced in the midst of growing concern about anomalies in the relation of diffraction and polarization effects to Newton's theory.*

Kuhn identifies some other characteristics attending the emergence of these new theories and the new paradigms they entail: the novel theory seems a direct response to crisis; the breakdown of the old paradigm takes a long time and centers on long-recognized problems; the solution of these problems has been at least partly anticipated during a period when there was no crisis in the corresponding science; and, in the absence of crisis, those anticipations are ignored. He concludes that while crises are a necessary precondition of novel theories, the response to crisis is slow and confused because the community does not renounce the old paradigm until a new one is available to take its place:

The decision to reject one paradigm is always simultaneously the decision to accept another, and the judgement leading to that decision involves the comparison of both paradigms with nature *and* with each other.**

When do anomalies produce a crisis? Kuhn sets three conditions: If the anomalies inhibit some development of great practical importance, as, in the case of Ptolemy's paradigm, calendar design and astrological practice; if there is some new technology available which does not fit the old paradigm; and, finally, if the general inconvenience in living with the anomaly rises high enough.† Today we may wonder whether the revelations of ecology are not forcing the anomalies of the contemporary scientific paradigm into a situation of crisis. The specialization of contemporary science reminds one of the complaint of Copernicus about the scientists of his day:

With them it is as though an artist were to gather the hands, feet, head and other members for his images from diverse models, each part excellently drawn, but not related to a single body, and since they

---

* *Ibid.*, p. 67.   ** *Ibid.*, p. 77.   † *Ibid.*, p. 82.

in no way match each other, the result would be monster rather than man.*

As with ideological change, paradigm change does not so much entail new knowledge as looking at the old knowledge in a new way, placing the data in a new system of relations. There are other specific analogies worth noting. The search for assumptions is often an effective way to loosen the grip of the traditional paradigm (or ideology) and to suggest the basis for a new one. Invariably, the men who invent new paradigms have been "either very young or very new to the field whose paradigm they change."** And Kuhn himself drew the critical analogy between the political and scientific:

Political revolutions aim to change political institutions in ways that those institutions themselves prohibit. Their success therefore necessitates the partial relinquishment of one set of institutions in favor of another, and in the interim, society is not fully governed by any institutions at all.†

In short, what a man sees scientifically or ideologically depends upon both what he looks at and what his previous experience has taught him to see. Why did Galileo see a swinging, falling stone so differently from Aristotle? Because, Kuhn says, Aristotle was concerned with a change of state and Galileo with a process. They proceeded from different paradigms.†† Equally, why do we see a slave so differently from the way we did three hundred years ago? Because we are employing a different paradigm of the good society, a different ideology.

But new ideologies, like new paradigms, emerge from old ones. When confronted with anomalies, politicians and businessmen, like scientists, will devise ad hoc modifications, pragmatic devices, to make do within the context of traditional ideas. And the transition can often be made more comforting by the camouflage of old language and concepts. President Nixon, for example, was prepared in 1971 to impose state intervention to control technology, production, wages, and prices, but at the same time he

---

* Quoted in T. S. Kuhn, *The Copernican Revolution* (Cambridge, Mass.: Harvard University Press, 1957), p. 138.
** Kuhn, *The Structure of Scientific Revolutions*, pp. 88–9.
† *Ibid.*, p. 92. †† *Ibid.*, pp. 112 and 123.

felt it necessary to affirm repeatedly his loyalty to the traditional ideology of individualism, private enterprise, competition, and limited government. True, a system, scientific or otherwise, can often withstand high levels of irritation before its underlying theories are in need of renovation. But can we any longer tolerate such a degree of ideological schizophrenia? I believe the crisis of which I have spoken is real, is indeed upon us. If this is correct, we cannot wait too long before resolving it or we risk losing the valuable achievements of the past in an uncontrolled upheaval. For ideological revolutions are society-wide and they are carried out in life itself, not in the luxurious peace of the laboratory, the journal, or the specialist's study. That is the significant difference between ideologic and scientific revolution, otherwise so closely analogous. It is fair to say that the more quickly we get a new paradigm of society into place, the shorter and calmer will be the transitional period, and the more we shall be able to salvage from the past. We shall find it helpful to keep this image of scientific evolution before us as an aid to understanding the contributions that science makes to ideology in a substantive sense and also as a model for the ideological change that is occurring in our community and its institutions.

Organizational and National Ideologies

Until now I have used the term "ideology" in relation to social and political communities. I shall also use it to describe and to understand the behavior of business communities—specifically corporate organizations, which are the central nongovernmental institutions of our society. The concept is of further value in dealing with the relationships between business communities and the surrounding communities of which they are a part. Normally, we should expect that the ideology of an organization would derive from and be at least roughly harmonious with that of the surrounding national community. In surer days, the statement, "What is good for General Motors is good for the United States," was considered acceptable. Today it is somehow discordant. Such discordance may arise because the deterioration or renovation of organizational ideology has moved faster than the national ideology, causing tension and friction. It follows that the management of an organization can perform its function better if it is aware of the condition of ideology, both in the organization and in the relevant community. Thus the ideology of an organization is the collection of ideas which combine to form and control the following things:

ONE, the organization's conception of its purpose and direction.

Two, its external relationships with the communities it affects and of which it is a part.

THREE, the internal relationships between the various components of the organization itself, such as stockholders, upper and lower management, supervisors, and workers.

But ideology as a method of thought forces us to take an integrative view of the organization; hence the purpose of a business is inseparable from its external relationships and its internal composition. The three must therefore be approached together.

A variety of methods can be used to probe this ideological combination. First, one can analyze the motivation of the head man, whether entrepreneur or manager. It may be useful to emphasize the distinction between the two.

The entrepreneur can be seen as a prototype of Lockean man. He seeks individual fulfillment in an individualistic way, doing what is new or unknown or putting together what is known in a new way. His activities tend to be unplanned, exploratory, and experimental; his organization is generally small so that he personally can know and control it. He is often engaged in introducing change.

The manager, as I define him, is primarily an administrator, concerned with doing what is known and preoccupied with planning, efficiency, and organizational harmony. He is the head of a bureaucracy or technostructure, to which he is loyal. For him, change or transformation, while important, tends to be unsettling, unnatural, and difficult.

Both the entrepreneur and the manager are subject to the same varied set of motives: to acquire money, power, or prestige, to satisfy an intellectual need, to obtain influence and status in the community, to acquire security, and so forth. But each will behave quite differently under the stimulus of the motive. The entrepreneur will tend to be individualistic, competitive, and aggressive; the manager more communal and bureaucratic. Obviously, different organizations at different times require and normally receive different types of leadership. What is less obvious, perhaps, is that the organization will tend to take on the ideology of its leadership. If leadership changes drastically, it may be difficult for the organization to catch up ideologically.

Roger Harrison writes of another distinction between types of leadership, a distinction that affects the nature and purpose of the organization. He says that some managerial groups are task-oriented and others power-oriented. Americans, he found, tend to be more concerned about organizing to get the job done, with everyone who is capable of contributing doing what he can. Europeans are more preoccupied with organizing to maintain certain power relationships: where one stands in the hierarchy is important, those in authority tend to ignore the suggestions of those who are not, those not in authority tend to keep quiet, and so on.* These are some examples of different ideologies, reflecting different managerial types, which may have quite varied effects on the purpose and relationships within the organization.

Stanley Udy undertook an extensive analysis of the interaction between the community and its needs and the ideology of work organizations, distinguishing between those forms of work which are production determined, technologically determined, and socially determined. A striking example of the first is buffalo hunting by the Plains Indians of America:

At certain times of the year, entire communities organized themselves to hunt buffalo. The hunt was a general social goal in that it was culturally defined as part of the yearly round, and not subject to discretion by the community as a work organization. . . . Hunting was simply institutionalized as a community activity.**

Furthermore, the community reorganized itself for hunting, assigning roles, authority, and power with the idea of the hunt in mind rather than other general criteria such as age, kinship, and

---

* Roger Harrison, *Organisation Ideologies* (mimeo., Manpower Development Unit, BOC Staff College, Chartridge Lodge, Chesham, Bucks., England, June 1971), p. 3. This paper describes the experience of the author, a professional consultant, in applying the notion of ideology to organizational behavior in several corporations in Europe.

** Stanley H. Udy, Jr., *Work in Traditional and Modern Societies* (Englewood Cliffs, N.J.: Prentice-Hall, Inc., 1970), pp. 9 and 10.

the like. It should be no surprise that the ideology of organizational leadership—whether individualistic, communal, task-oriented, or power-oriented—will be affected by the ideology of the surrounding community and its needs.

Second, the concept of organizational ideology can be approached by defining the function of the organization. For what purpose does it exist and by what right? Peter Drucker says that the basic purpose of business is to satisfy consumer desire, to make or provide goods or services people will want to buy*—a conception plainly consistent with Lockean ideology. Under this approach, the individual consumer's behavior, desires, and expectations become of paramount importance. This idea either fails to distinguish between the satisfaction of consumer desires and community needs, or says that the former are more important and sufficient. Others assert that the function of business is to organize and meet the needs of the community—as, for example, with Pharaohs' pyramids, America's railroads, and France and Britain's Concorde supersonic airplane. Implicit in this formulation is the idea that a community exists, that it is more than the sum of the individuals in it, that it has needs which presumably are identified by the state, and that the community through the state assigns priorities to those needs and plans their fulfillment.**

A third way of analyzing the ideology of a business organization is to view the organization, not in terms of what it makes or does or provides, but in terms of its end results. Here again the national ideology is a crucial determinant. One traditional American response is that the purpose of a large, publicly owned business

---

* Peter Drucker, *The Age of Discontinuity* (New York: Harper & Row, 1969), p. 52.

** It is this conception of business purpose which most nearly approaches that of Philip Selznick, who is concerned, as Joseph Bower says, with "the definition of organizational mission or purpose. Selznick argues for the need to structure the interaction of the organization and its environment." Bower quotes Selznick: " 'Beyond the definition of mission and role lies the task of building purpose into the social structure of the enterprise, or . . . of transforming a neutral body of men into a committed polity.' " Joseph L. Bower, "Descriptive Decision Theory from the Administrative Viewpoint," *The Study of Policy Formation*, edited by Raymond A. Bauer and Kenneth J. Gergen (New York: The Free Press, 1968), p. 128, quoting Philip Selznick, *Leadership and Administration* (New York: Harper & Row, 1957), p. 90.

is a financial return to individual investors. More recently many in America, as elsewhere, would probably say that the purpose of business is the employment of workers. In black America, however, the answer might be that business is one tool for the introduction of political and social change; it is a way to reallocate power and must serve that end. In the United Kingdom, on the other hand, the purpose of business might be regarded as the glory, prestige, and welfare of the British nation, as it certainly would be in Japan. In each case, the ideology of the larger community has a dominant influence on the ideology of the business organization.

Finally, business can be seen purely as an ideological representation. One can imagine, for example, two extreme, contrasting ideological models. The first we might call individualistic or Lockean; the second, Japanese, Chinese, Buddhist, Confucianist, or, more simply, communal.

In the individualistic model, (a) the tone is highly individualistic. Relationships among and between managers and workers are determined by informal and formal contracts. (b) Authority derives from a rigid and explicit hierarchy. (c) The primary recognized work incentive is wages. And (d) each member of the organization can easily quit. There are few inhibitions against opting out if the individual is dissatisfied or sees a better opportunity elsewhere.*

In the communal model, on the other hand, (a) the emphasis is on the organization as a whole, as a community of which the individual becomes a part. As a result, he may lose some of his individuality. (b) Authority rests upon a continuing consensus. Considerable effort is spent in developing a sense of participation throughout the organization. It is reported, for example, that the Chinese factory manager performs menial tasks regularly to maintain a sense of community—as if the chairman of the board of GM were to work on the assembly line one day a month. (c) The primary incentive is a strengthening of the nation—for example, building a "better" Japan. And (d) loyalty to the organization is important. Quitting is difficult, if not impossible, and security is high.

---

* Albert O. Hirschman, *Exit, Voice and Loyalty* (Cambridge, Mass.: Harvard University Press, 1970).

I trust it is now clear that organizations and specifically corporations have ideologies, and that these are inextricably tied up with the larger national ideology. I shall make considerable use of this notion of corporate ideology later, but for the moment, a short critique of one company should suffice to illustrate the value of the concept.

The Anomaly of Size

If we were to extract General Motors from its ideological context, it would appear merely as a collection of men and machines which receives certain inputs, works on them, and discharges them for sale to a variety of world consumers. Starting fresh, so to speak, these men and machines could be put together in a variety of ways, depending on our objectives and how we think we could best achieve them. We could combine them in large or small units; we could govern the units in an authoritarian or a participative fashion; we could connect men to other men with a contract, or by means of a cooperative structure; we could place a certain value on profits, both short- and long-term, on market growth, on environmental pollution; and so on. In short, we could design General Motors according to an ideology of our own choosing.

However, whatever else the result of such an operation might be, it would not be General Motors. Alfred P. Sloan, GM's president from 1923 to 1946 and the man who created the company's extraordinary bureaucracy, put it well:

General Motors could hardly be imagined to exist anywhere but in this country, with its very active and enterprising people; its resources, including its science and technology and its business and industrial know-how; its vast spaces, roads, and rich markets; its characteristics of change, mobility, and mass production; its great industrial expansion in this century, and its system of freedom in general and free competitive enterprise in particular. . . . If in turn we have contributed to the style of the United States as expressed in the automobile, this has been by interaction.*

---

* Alfred P. Sloan, Jr., *My Years with General Motors* (Garden City, N.Y.: Doubleday & Co., Inc., 1964), p. xxi.

But while GM may be American in its essence, it does not follow that today it is an expression of the traditional American ideology. The national ideology is changing, after all; and it is this evolving ideology that GM reflects. In some ways it is lagging; in others it appears to be forging ahead, bearing a flag whose color is profoundly disturbing to the traditionalists among us. True, General Motors was born and weaned in the traditional ideology of America. But as it grew in strength and size, from 1908 to the present, pragmatically probing and testing its expanding environment, GM has changed institutionally and so has the environment around it. Today, the corporation constitutes a radical departure from the traditional ideas upon which it at first rested so solidly. At the same time, the surrounding ideology of America has become quite different. America is no longer so caught up with the glory of the automobile itself as an instrument of personal power, nor with the intrinsic worth of efficient technologies of production, nor with the unquestioned benefit of material growth.

The traditional ideology says that General Motors is the result of the initiative of individuals; that it is private property; that it is owned by its shareholders; that private property is a natural right; and that the owners should therefore be given maximum freedom to develop GM efficiently for economic growth and the satisfaction of consumers. To be sure, over the years the community has found it necessary to place constraints on this freedom as a result of a changing consensus about such matters as safety, child labor, union rights, minimum wages, and unemployment. But these are exceptions to the rule of freedom. The primary control over the relationship between GM and the community is competition, the idea being that if GM competes with other automobile companies in meeting the desires of individual consumers, a satisfactory community is ensured. Again, within the corporation, the idea of individualism has led to the most desirable relation between employer and employee being seen as one of contract. For this purpose, under the law, the corporation—the employer—is held to be an individual contracting for the work of another individual—the worker or, as it has evolved, a collection of workers in a union. Finally, GM as originally constructed caused no difficulty to the concept of the limited state. The principal role of the state is to protect the individual, his property, and his right to contract; and to safeguard all individuals by ensuring competition. So far, so good—under the traditional ideology, GM as described above was a legitimate institution.

But these traditional legitimizing concepts have eroded in the case of GM—and, of course, in the 2,000 or more other large, publicly held corporations like it in America. During the first two decades of this century, the entrepreneur W. C. Durant forged GM out of a number of small companies which were private property in both a real and philosophical sense. Their owners were for the most part their founders; they were clearly identifiable; and they were plainly responsible for and interested in the uses to which their property was put. There was no question that Louis Chevrolet and his counterparts at Buick, Oldsmobile, Oakland (now Pontiac), Cadillac, Hyatt Roller Bearing, and so on were owners of property. They raised money for their operations from others, but the others were few in number and were clearly represented among the company's directors. The legitimacy and authority of the direction of such property was plain.

But by 1970 this remarkable organization which Durant created and which Sloan had molded into one of the world's most formidable institutions, with gross sales larger than the total product of most countries, had some 1.4 million stockholders.* And almost 90 per cent of GM shareholders owned two hundred shares or less.

Of course, GM's "owners" are not really owners at all. They do not control the company; they do not direct it; they are not responsible for it. These characteristics of ownership lie with a self-perpetuating managerial hierarchy, which itself largely controls the board of directors. GM's shareholders are investors, whose sole interest in the company is the return it pays on their investment. Under our traditional scheme, then, the company—and every company like it—is an anomaly.

And what of its relation to the state? In examining the relationship between GM and the community it affects and of which it is a part, we must ask: What is the relevant community? There is the state of Delaware, from which the nation has allowed GM

---

* "The owners of GM stock come from every state of the United States, from each of the Canadian provinces and territories and from more than 80 other countries"—*Annual Report 1970* (Detroit: General Motors Corp.), p. 25.

to obtain its community charter; and there is Detroit, the state of Michigan, Brazil, France, South Africa, and most of the rest of the world, where the company operates. The most authoritative of these communities is the United States, which, according to its dominant ideology, has given considerable freedom to a variety of forces inside GM to determine the company's activities. These forces include the shareholders, the directors, the governing management, middle and lower management, scientists and technologists, supervisors, production workers, distributors, and salesmen. Whether GM is actually to be considered chartered to *any* single state or nation, weak or otherwise, is unclear. Of course, the same remark can be made about any large multinational company.

Given these extraordinary conditions, by what means and according to what criteria are relationships to be determined between this nonproprietary, or para-proprietal,* collective and the community which it affects? One answer, according to the traditional ideology, is competition for the dollars of the individual consumers in the market place. Because of GM's global scope, we should have to construe "market place" to mean "international market place," of course, and then puzzle over the question whether trading in that enormously complex domain can be competitive in the sense we have traditionally given the word. But even domestically, just as the idea of property has become eroded and distorted, so has the idea of competition. Today we are increasingly concerned with community needs, and competition is exceedingly clumsy in distinguishing between consumer desires and community needs. In the early 1960's, when the automobile companies began to wonder whether they should not do more about auto safety, they undertook a survey to find out what individual consumers wanted. The returns indicated that power, performance, and physical beauty were the things that sell cars to consumers, not safety. Given the conception GM had of itself and of its ideological context, the company continued to serve consumer wants. Obviously, it did not entirely neglect safety; rather, the idea and practice of competition had assigned to safety a relatively low order of priority among the criteria that determined GM's relationship to the com-

---

* Paul P. Harbrecht, S.J., *Toward the Paraproprietal Society: An Essay on the Nature of Property in Twentieth Century America,* Introduction and Commentary by Adolf A. Berle, Jr. (New York: Twentieth Century Fund, 1959).

munity. That those criteria were at least partly formed by the company's own advertising, and that they might bear no relation to community needs, did not enter the company's philosophical scope at the time.

What happened is now well known. Ralph Nader, made famous by his revelations of danger in *Unsafe at Any Speed* and his subsequent encounter with GM detectives, went to the community and said in effect: "It doesn't make any difference what consumers want. The community needs safety." The community, speaking through government, answered, "You're right," and so, with the passage of the National Highway Safety Act in 1965, safety moved up the criteria ladder to a place of higher priority.

This same result could have been achieved another way if the dominant ideology had been different. The automobile companies could have counselled among themselves. They could have decided that there was a need to make cars safer, and agreed to do so uniformly. It would have been clear that no one company could afford to "go safe" alone because the consequent economic loss would cause unfair discrimination against its stockholders. Such counselling and conspiracy, however, would almost certainly have involved a violation of the antitrust laws, enacted to preserve competition.

Or, as an alternative, any company that wondered about the safety problem could have gone to the community—that is, to government—and said, "As technical experts in the field of automotive transport, we believe that the community should consider the matter of safety and should set national standards accordingly. Tell us *how* safe you want us all to be." The end result in either case would have been much the same as that induced by Nader. The means might have been less costly; certainly, they would have been less shocking. At the very least, it would appear, we must revise our old positions on competition for the future. As large issues relating to the community as a whole—safety, air pollution, the most desirable form of transportation or communications, the utilization of open space—become more pressing, competition will be an increasingly unsatisfactory means of controlling the corporation's relationship to the community. And to the extent that the corporation operates on both a national and an international scale, we shall have to accept criteria for control that transcend national boundaries.

There are, of course, other ways of determining the relationship between GM and the community. GM could decide to maintain maximum control over the relationship; in so doing, the company would be emphasizing its political as well as economic characteristics. It would continue to assert that it is private property and seek to perfect its legitimacy. It might pursue one of two alternatives here. First, it could seek to make the myth of shareholder ownership a reality, and design a nonstatist, legislative process whereby shareholders are in fact involved in the decision-making. Or it could argue that it is a collective, a cooperative of sorts. In this case, it would activate the internal human components of the company—managers, workers, technicians, dealers, and shareholders. Through a process of corporate democracy, these groups would establish the authority by which management would function and the criteria by which decisions would be taken on such matters as the ecological effect of the GM conversion system and the political effects of elements of the system on this country, South Africa, or any other place.

The consequences of either of these options are troublesome. The first would seem to lead to continued fruitless attempts by small traditionalist minorities of shareholders—Campaign GM, the Episcopal Church, etc.—to behave as though they were owners of GM and to seek to make decisions accordingly. It would also encourage a wide variety of outside interest groups to force GM's management to act according to their individual interests, whether angry consumers, angry dealers, or angry environmentalists. This option provides for the perpetuation of traditional myth at the expense of an increasing loss of rational and predictable control over the relationship between the community and GM by either GM or the state. In principle, it is merely reactionary and nonconstructive.

The second option would inevitably lead to a shift in the basis of management authority from the present one of diluted property rights to one of consensualism. If workers, shareholders, and other groups were naturally to participate in management, a number of thorny consequences would result. The traditional contractual relationship between management and labor would be altered—which might, incidentally, improve morale. Questions would arise about the rights of one human component over another. For example, a small shareholder who has invested his savings presumably has a set of rights which are different from those of a worker in a Detroit plant. Should there be weighted voting in the GM legislature? Questions would arise, too, about the balance of internal/external relationships of the company. Does a shareholder of GM have any greater interest in or rights regarding GM's community relationship than a nonshareholder? If GM cars are unsafe or polluting, is the interest of a shareholder or some other GM human component any greater than that of any other member of the public?

Alternatively, relationships between GM and the community could be determined by the political order, following upon *its* conception of objectives, priorities, and needs.

This approach implies that the community through its political processes already possesses a well-defined conception of objectives, priorities, and needs; the state must be seen, therefore, as having a more explicit visionary function than has generally been the case in peacetime United States. It would tend to lead to the chartering of GM by the national government as opposed to Delaware, and perhaps at some point to the subjection of the company to international governmental regulation. This changes the traditional concept of ownership, making of GM a privately managed, privately financed creature subservient to the state's planning.

In practice, this approach is impeded by a number of factors: our ideological resistance to state planning, the condition of American political leadership, the national suspicion that government is constructed for the benefit of big business, and so on. However, some combination of these options is obviously possible. On what that combination might be I shall speculate later. My point here is to demonstrate the use of ideology as a method of thought and analysis in approaching GM's problems.

One remaining idea from the Lockean Five needs mentioning in the context of General Motors, and that is individualism. There is some evidence to suggest that many workers' needs are not being met through the conventional relationships between company and union. Six per cent absenteeism at General Motors and an even higher rate at other auto companies, disruption and sabotage, flagging productivity, lagging motivation, division within the union, and the decreasing effectiveness of supervisory leadership are all symptoms.* It appears the worker on the assembly line is painfully aware that he is not fulfilling the grand idea of individualism, about which he was informed early in life.

Furthermore, the ideological companion to individualism, the contract, is suspect. The contract was a useful device for connecting an employer and an employee when both were distinct and known to one another. The authority of Louis Chevrolet or W. C. Durant was clear; they were individuals who had taken great risks and demonstrated creativity. When a worker was employed by them, he knew for whom he was working, and where he belonged. Today, the management of GM rests on myths and fictions. Its authority is murky; it has lost its individuality, as has the worker, having immersed himself in the union. Thus GM is a gigantic, impersonal collective composed of two increasingly enormous but faceless bodies joined together in a hesitant and ephemeral relationship by collective contract.

Is individualism faltering as an idea? Is the contract of questionable value? If so, what replacements can be considered? And what are the implications for the size and nature of business organizations, for their administration and management?

There is, of course, nothing new or strange about such questions. The history of business from the most primitive times to the present is one of tensions between economic activity and the community as a whole. There is always an ideological context, whether it be the principles of generosity governing the trading system (Kula) of the Trobriand Islands,** the principles of national interest which governed business activity in sixteenth- and seventeenth-century England, or the ideas of competitive and possessive individualism and materialism which have governed us more recently. "The hard facts of economics," perceived through the conditioning of time and place, have always existed and frequently grated against the ideology. In our own case, now that

---

* Judson Gooding, "Blue Collar Blues on the Assembly Line," *Fortune,* July 1970, pp. 69ff.; and "Young Workers Disrupt Key G.M. Plant," by Agis Salpukas, *The New York Times,* Jan. 23, 1972. In spite of the massive unemployment attending the collapse of the automobile industry in 1975, these problems of productivity and motivation continued.

** Bronislaw Malinowski, *Argonauts of the Western Pacific* (New York: E. P. Dutton & Co., Inc., 1953).

we and our central institutions have grown so immense, the Lockean shoe is beginning to pinch. The fact is we are in a period of ideological transformation; the old ideas need inspection. And no amount of pragmatic groping will do any good so long as it is confined within the limitations of ideas whose vitality has passed.

Business is only a part of a whole. Serenity in the business-community relationship depends upon the definition of the whole, its purpose and direction. Once that is clear, business can conform. Such definition will be difficult, for we are sure of little except that we have outgrown the old forms. Ideological analysis can at least inform us of what we are and what we have been, thus making it a little easier to decide where we can and want to go.

If we in America are to save what is best, avoid tyranny, and provide for the self-respect of each person, then we must be alert to the ideological transition which is upon us.

CHAPTER 2 Economic Activity and the Political and Social Order in the West

A central function of ideology is to define the criteria by which a community relates economic activity to its surroundings. In my scheme of things, economy is a *value*. It entails the efficient, purposeful use of human and material resources. The definition of what "efficient" and "purposeful" shall mean, however, is a matter of *ideology*. Ideology prescribes and crystallizes the relationships that ought to exist between the economic, social, and political elements of a community.

Over the last 2,500 years, the several successive ideologies of the Western world have imposed clear limits on man's economic activities, and indeed have generally subordinated them to social and political priorities and objectives. The significance of what I call Lockeanism is that, particularly as practiced in America, this ideology has tended to sever economic activities from their political and social context, allowing economic ends to dominate. Political and social institutions have thus come to be assigned the task of cleaning up the mess left in the wake of economic undertakings.

The relative freedom of the economic sphere from social and political constraints constituted a historic reversal—a kind of revolutionary blip—that could not even have been imagined throughout most of the course of Western development. This reversal emerged from an ideological storm, long abrewing, which burst upon Western civilization three or four hundred years ago, with the result that instead of economy being embedded in its social relations, social relations came to be embedded in the economic system.* The question facing the West today is: Can any ideology endure which subordinates the political and social to the economic?

The Ancient World: The Community and Its Needs

The dominant ideologies of the ancient world were communitarian; the community and its needs were of transcendent importance. Individuals derived fulfillment and self-respect by serving those needs as members of a rigid hierarchical structure, extending from the loyal slave to the wise statesman. Property was needed to promote the community welfare, to preserve and enhance the political and social order, and to provide the economic goods the community needed. For its part, the government of the state was responsible for defining community need and governing all to ensure that the need was satisfied. This governance was sometimes dispersed and more or less democratic, as in Greece, and sometimes centralized and authoritarian, as in Rome.

The communitarian ideology worked well for a long time to legitimize the institutions of the various ancient societies. Then a variety of events occurred which eroded the traditional ideology and caused the disintegration of those societies. First, institutions, especially business, departed from the old ideas and undermined them. Second, the old ideas were no longer clearly tied to the real world; for example, having been created for a rural and agricultural world, they served less well the needs of cities and empires.

Traditionally, the big business of the ancient world was undertaken directly by and for political and social institutions—the city, the state, religious organizations, the manorial estate. In some Greek and Phoenician trading cities, big business may have run the state, but in general there was a symbiotic relationship between business and the state; economic activity was clearly subservient to social and political ends. To glorify deities, pyramids and temples were built. To make war, roads and fortresses

---

* Karl Polanyi, *The Great Transformation* (Boston: Beacon Press Paperback, 1944), p. 57.

were constructed. To establish the economic self-sufficiency of localities (a necessity in a world lacking civilian transport), the manorial system was created. In those relatively rare instances where public food supplies were maintained, the task fell to political and sometimes religious authorities, as in Egypt, Mesopotamia, and early Rome.

Smaller business—what we would today call private enterprise —operated for the most part in the shadowy interstices of society. Merchants, bankers, artisans, and the like were tolerated as useful but were rarely accorded power or prestige by the political and social order. Always suspect, vigilantly watched, the businessman was regarded as the servant of that order, acceptable as long as he was dutiful.

The merchant was neither aristocrat, serf, nor slave. Aristotle could not even envision a proper place for him. The production or exchange of goods for gain was not, he thought, either natural or good, the legitimate reason for production being consumption, not profit. Aristotle's objection to business lay in its inconsistency with what he felt was the good life, the natural social order, and a proper political and social perspective. On the other hand, he found farming for urban consumption and rural self-sufficiency quite natural, necessary, and admirable.

Aristotle's ideology, of course, fitted the exigencies of the times, and thus worked for a while to sustain and justify the institutions of the status quo. Only when markets were well established was there a continuing and firm justification for producing beyond the requirements of consumption; only through the need of the community for such markets could the merchant's role be legitimized. Since markets played a peripheral role in the agrarian society of the ancient world, the business function was regarded as of minimal use and the entrepreneur even constituted a threat to the existing order. The notion that the man of commerce should be set free of the overarching constraints of the political and social order was, of course, unthinkable.

Plato commented explicitly on the necessity for economic activity—trade in particular—being held tightly in the strong embrace of community need and the social good. Retail trade he found, was a corrupting occupation, to be tolerated only because of its usefulness in assigning exact values to commodities and redistributing them. It must be closely watched and regulated according to the judgment of the aristocracy, for the good of the whole community.*

The ideas of Plato and Aristotle served to justify and legitimize important institutions of the ancient world. In the economic sphere, they worked tolerably well as long as society remained essentially agricultural. But when Athens had become a great commercial center and its wealthy landlords were producing wine and oil for profit, the Athenians ridiculed the farmer and his ways; the traditional ideology eroded and disintegration set in.

Similarly, in the latter days of Rome, cartels of grain merchants reaped huge profits by manipulating the food supplies of the great cities of the empire. It became increasingly difficult for the political authorities to control such practices. Augustus, Claudius, Julian, and other emperors experimented with various forms of price regulation, but they had neither the understanding nor the power to control the merchants' manipulation of the market. Desperately, through various ad hoc interventions, they sought to cope with each crisis as it came along, but the economic system had effectively impelled itself beyond their reach.

The aristocracy of the ancient world, the keepers of the traditional ideology, belonged to the ruling class of a stratified slave-owning society. Their power and the social order was inseparably tied to a certain conception of property. In Sumeria, all productive property was regarded as belonging to one or another god in whose name the king ruled. In Egypt, virtually everything belonged to the Pharaoh, who was both god and king. Indeed, broadly speaking, until the revolutions of the seventeenth and eighteenth centuries, holding clear and outright title to property automatically placed a man in the ruling or priestly class. For the ancient world (and for medieval society, too), a severance or distinction between economic power and political and social power could be nothing but dangerous—a menace to both public and private virtue, a threat to established concepts of property, to the established structures of authority, in short, to the prevailing ideology and all its institutional reflections. And the almost

---

* Cf. Aristotle, *Politics,* Book I, 9, §§ 1–11, in Benjamin Jowett, *The Politics of Aristotle* (Oxford, England: The Clarendon Press, 1885), pp. 15–16. See also Benjamin Jowett, *The Dialogues of Plato,* Laws XI: 918, 919 (Oxford, England: The Clarendon Press, 1953), pp. 488–9.

unceasing efforts of various types of businessmen to obtain independent power, to acquire and maintain ownership of property for production, was indeed a continuing source of tension in those societies.

There was tension too around the issue of work. According to the traditional ideology of the ancient world, manual labor was the contemptible task of slaves. During the periods when societies were essentially agricultural, this notion was a practical one. But as the institution of work changed—as freedmen, artisans, and many other sorts of people became engaged in it—the contempt for work had to weaken. Even in ancient Greece, philosophers had attempted to give meaning and virtue to work in its own right. In the eighth century B.C., Hesiod maintained that the peasant gained dignity by knowing his place, performing his duty, and doing his work. The virtuous peasant, however, did not live to work; he worked to live.* Similarly, Plato conceded that even the merchant could achieve virtue through the performance of his work if he made life itself and not the pursuit of wealth his central aim.

Fundamentally, the ancient world held that money was sterile. Wealth—money and property—was regarded ideologically as being purely means for consumption. Its productive capabilities, which, of course, were exemplified in the exported produce of a vineyard or the building of a ship, were not comprehended in the traditional ideology. Aristotle argued in the *Politics* that the profits of the merchant were without justification since he merely used money to make more money. And fittingly, the Greek god of money and profits was Pluto, ruler of the underworld. This god, mythology had it, was blind. And if it is too much of an anachronism to charge him with the sin of greed, at least it can be said that once he had something in his possession, it required

---

* Werner Jaeger, *Paideia: The Ideals of Greek Culture,* translated from 2nd German edition by Gilbert Highet, vol. 1 (Oxford, England: Basil Blackwell, 1939), pp. 67–9, 71–3. Hesiod in *Works and Days* opposed the aristocratic ideals of Homer. His views developed under the impact of changing social and economic conditions, as the Greeks abandoned their agrarian base and turned increasingly to the sea, commerce, and trade for their livelihood. The ideal of justice (*Areté*), defined by Homer as attainable only by the nobility through art, intellect, and physical prowess, was converted by Hesiod into an ideal attainable by all through work.

a hero to take it from him. It was as if the thing were lost to the living world. This preoccupation with blind and infernal greed pervaded the medieval ideology also. Not until the England of the seventeenth century was wealth finally transformed into a thoroughly respectable entity and endowed with symbols of cultural dignity.

Another concept generic to the slave-owning cultures of the ancient West was the differential value of individual men, assigned by class. Inexorably, however, the ancient argicultural system based on slavery declined; concomitantly, the needs of the community became diversified and extended. Political changes resulted, of which the establishment of written law, such as Solon's codification of the laws of Athens, was one of the most important. So long as the law had remained a matter of oral consensus, precedent, and assumption, the aristocratic class was able to maintain the favored treatment and the societal status quo which was its base and source of power. But after the formalization of the code, all men were embraced within its dictates. The true concept of citizenship had been born; and even if the slave and merchant were not admitted to the highest status of citizenship, they nonetheless had to be assigned some fixed status within the social context so that the codified law might operate with some consistency and uniformity. In the case of the merchant, the diversification and extension of the community's needs and the codification of its laws were twin levers by which his business became more necessary and his social position strengthened. He gained a value within society's framework, but his legitimacy was still questioned.

This particular trend in the ancient world reached its zenith when the Romans began the practice of admitting commercially and politically important provincials from the territories they had conquered to full citizenship—eventually even to the Senate itself —and thereby to the full protection of the Roman legal code. In this case, political and economic developments had worked a great social change: the concept, not merely of citizenship but of *universal* citizenship had been invented and established as real and legitimate. Herodotus may have been a citizen of the world, in an intellectual sense; but the Gallic senator in Rome was a citizen of the world in a social sense, a political sense, and an economic sense to boot.

The society of the Empire was, of course, still a class structure; the concept of equality in the modern sense had not yet been born. However, the seeds or conditions of the modern ideological concept of equality had been established. So had the concept of a universal empire. These ideas, in combination with a new religious dynamic that stripped away some of the strength of the persisting vision of class hierarchy, evolved into a magnificently strong new conception that lay at the roots of the ideology of medieval Europe.

In the decay of the manorial ethic, the expansion of society, the codification of law, the adjustment of the concept of the state and its membership, one can observe a sequence that will become very familiar in the course of this book. Under the pressure of new needs and circumstances, old institutions begin to rupture, new institutions are devised to meet those needs, the old ideology that had legitimized the old institutions lingers on after the old institutions have changed, and the new institutions are left vulnerable, in philosophic limbo, without a clear ideological basis.

It is significant that the role of the commercial sector is still today ambiguous and mysterious in many ways, millennia after its rise began; and that the concept of a universal citizenship, while applauded and pursued from age to age, is still one that has not been entirely integrated into the great ideologies of the West, although in the medieval world and again in later Europe and America the idea played an increasingly powerful ideological role.

The result of this sequence of institutional and ideological evolution is tension between the new institutions, their practices and behavior, and the old ideology. Crisis attends the weakening of the institutions that claim still to be its legitimate expressions; and the entire framework of society trembles.

Finally, it should be noted that in the ancient Mediterranean world, the submergence of material and economic considerations to social and political priorities is made very clear by the attitudes of those cultures toward invention and technology.

Hero at Alexandria invented a steam engine, but the prevailing ideology determined that it should be used not for the generation of power but for the amusement of temple crowds. Augustus ordered the execution of one inventor because his work would have caused unemployment.* Invention was a positive menace to the social edifice of the static societies, and most notably to that of Rome; thus business, itself the cause and effect of so much innovation, was also a menace.

Although the far-flung needs of the Roman Empire provided the commercial element with a somewhat happier role than had earlier societies, the fundamental prejudice against it remained nonetheless. Cicero wrote: "Trade, if it is on a small scale, is to be considered vulgar; but if wholesale and on a large scale, importing large quantities from all parts of the world and distributing to many without misrepresentation, it is not to be greatly disparaged. . . ." He went on, however, to reflect the fundamental Aristotelian respect for the householder and landowner: "Nay, it even seems to deserve the highest respect, if those who are . . . satisfied with the fortunes they have made, make their way from the port to a country estate, as they have often made it from the sea into the port."**

Business was acceptable only if it met the needs of the community. The great difficulty for Rome, however, was that its definition of "needs" and its designation of legitimate means of fulfilling those needs were limited and conditioned by prevailing ideology. And so too today. The United States needs energy resources; our ability to manage that need is limited and conditioned by traditional ideology. In the Roman case, the power of traditional ideology proved disastrous.

Rome's need as she saw it was the maintenance of her Empire. This required efficient means of production and transportation, which in turn required innovation, which was discouraged. Agricultural methods remained much as they had always been; neither deep plows nor effective pulling harnesses for horses had been developed. The Roman road system, while admittedly a marvel, could not be used for distributing bulk products because the maximum load that could be pulled by a horse was only about 500 pounds. This caused an increased reliance on water transportation

---

* Arnold Toynbee, "How Did We Get This Way—and Where Are We Going?", *Management's Mission in a New Society,* edited by Dan Fenn (New York: McGraw-Hill Book Co., Inc., 1959), pp. 3–17.

** Cicero, *Deofficiis* 1. 150–1, translated by Walter Miller (Cambridge, Mass.: Harvard University Press, 1947), p. 155.

for such bulk items as wine, grain, and lumber. Rome however did not develop good sailing ships or adequate rudders with which to steer them.

So, in spite of all its achievements and high civilization, the Empire allowed a level of technology that only scarcely surpassed that already reached in Hellenistic Egypt.* At the least, the Empire might have declined more slowly if its society had had an effective means for exploiting the possibilities of technology. But, inhibited by an outdated ideology, the victim of a once-glorious paradigm, the Empire could neither accept nor manage essential change. It fell apart. And, of course, business fell apart with it.

The Medieval World: Christianity and the Individual

In the ashes of Rome grew the seeds of a new ideology which was to shape the institutions and the nature of life henceforth in Western civilization. The driving force was the figure of Christ and the rules of those who attempted to follow Him. Two new conceptions were paramount: the intrinsic worth of each individual, and the apocalyptic vision of the coming of the Kingdom of Heaven on earth. Both were revolutionary developments compared to the ancient ideological conceptions; both contributed to the uniqueness of the West.

The tremendous force of these new concepts and the high degree to which they were integrated and given vitality can be seen par excellence in a letter, dated 1145, describing the construction of the cathedral at Chartres. Archbishop Hugo of Rouen wrote to Bishop Thierry of Amiens:

The inhabitants of Chartres have combined to aid in the construction of their church by transporting the materials; our Lord has rewarded their humble zeal by miracles which have roused the Normans to imitate the piety of their neighbours. . . . Since then the faithful of our dioceses and of other neighbouring regions have formed associations for the same object; they admit no one into their company unless he has been to confession, has renounced enmities and revenges, and

---

* Frank W. Walbank, "Trade and Industry Under the Later Roman Empire in the West," *Cambridge Economic History of Europe,* vol. II, *Trade and Industry in the Middle Ages,* edited by M. Postan and E. E. Rich (Cambridge, England: Cambridge University Press, 1952), pp. 49–50. See also pp. 52–4, 59–66, and 84–5.

has reconciled himself with his enemies. That done, they elect a chief, under whose direction they conduct their waggons in silence and with humility.

Who has ever seen!—Who has ever heard tell, in times past, that powerful princes of the world, that men brought up in honour and in wealth, that nobles, men and women, have bent their proud and haughty necks to the harness of carts, and that, like beasts of burden, they have dragged to the abode of Christ these waggons, loaded with wines, grains, oil, stone, wood, and all that is necessary for the wants of life, or for the construction of the church? But while they draw these burdens, there is one thing admirable to observe; it is that often when a thousand persons and more are attached to the chariots—so great is the difficulty—yet they march in such silence that not a murmur is heard, and truly if one did not see the thing with one's eye, one might believe that among such a multitude there was hardly a person present. When they halt on the road, nothing is heard but the confession of sins, and pure and suppliant prayer to God to obtain pardon. At the voice of the priests who exhort their hearts to peace, they forget all hatred, discord is thrown far aside, debts are remitted, the unity of hearts is established.*

These two new ideas—one of the individual and the other of the community—both almost infinitely removed from the societies of antiquity and yet their ideological descendents, must be examined next. We begin with the role of the individual, the single member of this "unity of hearts."

The words of the Rule of St. Benedict outlining the treatment of guests are significant here:

Let guests, after their reception, be conducted to prayer, and then the prior, or any one he may order, shall sit with them. Let the Divine Law be read in the presence of the guest for his edification, and after this let all courtesy be shown to him. For the guest's sake the prior may break his fast, unless it be a strict day when the fast may not be broken. The brethren, however, shall keep the accustomed fasts. Let the abbot pour water on the hands of the guests, and let him and all the community wash their feet. After this let them say the verse, *We have received Thy mercy, O God, in the midst of Thy temple.* Let special care be taken of the poor and pilgrims, because in them Christ is more truly received, for the very awe of the rich secures respect for them.* *

---

* Henry Adams, *Mont-Saint-Michel and Chartres* (Boston: Houghton Mifflin Co., 1904), p. 104.
** *The Rule of Saint Benedict*, translated and with an Introduction by Abbot Gasquet (London: Chatto and Windus, 1909), p. 91.

This makes a fascinating comparison—in tone, sensibility, and point of view—with Aristotle's vision of the individual as demonstrated in his comments on slavery:

A piece of property is like a part taken from a whole, it is completely the property of the whole, whereas the converse does not hold; so that a slave is his master's property in an absolute sense, whereas the slave cannot belong to the slave in any sense.

Throughout all medieval doctrine runs the idea of the absolute and imperishable value of the individual. In the later Middle Ages, the Aristotelian notions of class structure and of an organic social order returned to submerge the early egalitarian Christian idea. The latter rose again, however, in the Reformation and in the libertarian revolutions thereafter to undermine medieval institutions, which by then had become socially stratified, and to foster the institutions of our own day.

It is important to look more fully at this early Christian idea of individualism. It is, as Gierke wrote,

That every individual by virtue of his eternal destination is at core somewhat holy and indestructible . . . that the smallest part has a value of its own, and not merely because it is a part of a whole: that every man is to be regarded by the Community, never as a mere instrument, but also as an end. . . .*

This is not the élitist individualism of the pre-Christian Stoics. Troeltsch made a distinction that clarifies the special political and institutional effects which early Christian thought was to have. The Stoics lacked any conception of world renewal, any notion of a coming Kingdom of God on earth. Theirs was the individualism of a virtuous élite, bound up with existing institutions. Their hope, like Plato's, lay in a highly trained group of individuals who could lead the masses. "Christianity on the contrary," says Ernest Troeltsch, "was a movement of the lower classes, who are able to hope for and expect something quite fresh, and who in their Myth and their Hero, have at their disposal energies of a very different kind which can exert a proper influence by mass psychology." Christianity stood for a spiritual revolution, for the creation of a

* Otto Gierke, *Political Theories of the Middle Ages,* translated with an Introduction by Frederic W. Maitland (Cambridge, England: Cambridge University Press, 1927), p. 82.

new type of community which gave to every believer the promise of being permanent.

Obviously the Christian utopia has been a long time coming, but the slow percolation of these new ideas of the goal of human existence and of individuality has plainly helped to shape the institutions of the West. For all their meanderings and corruptions, these concepts have constituted a continuing revolutionary force down to the present day, when it is seen, for example, in the radical pursuits of the young priests and bishops of Latin America and the efforts of American clergymen such as Martin Luther King, Jr., and Jesse Jackson.

Also inherent in the Judeo-Christian view of the individual is the idea of personality. The word comes from the Latin for mask, *persona,* and was first used by the early Church to connote the three masks or modes of being of the Trinity. It came to mean a discrete person, possessed of full individuality and capable of a complete and independent existence. This view of man is clearly far removed from those of the ancient world, where the matter of character was theoretically a function of class. Such a concept of personality is also clearly distinct from the later, Lockean version of individualism, which tended to sever man from every other man and from the community. By connoting his participation in the interaction and drama of life, the idea of the personality emphasized the social nature of man and his place in a community as basic to a man's separate life. The whole man and his fulfillment depended not merely upon the individual self but upon the many relationships between the individual and those around him. It was this communitarian element in Christianity which dominated the political, social, and economic institutions of the early Middle Ages and which is inherent in utopian forms of contemporary communism.

Finally, embedded in the Judeo-Christian conception of the individual is the notion of man as the world's master. "God blessed them, saying to them, 'Be fruitful, multiply, fill the earth and conquer it. Be masters of the fish of the sea, the birds of heaven, and all living animals on the earth.' "* This conception also

---

* Genesis 1:28. Bertrand de Jouvenel, the French futurist, has said: "Western man has not lived with his natural environment. He has merely conquered it"—*Time,* Dec. 19, 1969, p. 25.

permeated the medieval world. In contrast, the non-Christian cultures of the ancient Mediterranean world had generally envisioned man as an integral part of the universe. In Egypt and Mesopotamia, as in the Hindu and Buddhist world, man was a part of, not separate from, other modes of existence. Virtue lay in harmony with the world of nature. And this ideal was also central in Greece; when Aristotle stated that slavery was "natural," he meant that the institution was part of the created world, the natural social order, which man could not and should not try to change. Man's mastery of other men was accepted implicitly, but the notion that he is the proper master of the world would have been absurd or even meaningless to the Greeks.

The Judaic and the early Christian concepts gained strength in the medieval order, driving underground the older religious views of the Mediterranean world and of Europe, which had been based primarily on natural harmonies and on man's role within the harmonic system. Except insofar as Aristotle influenced the Scholastic philosophers, notably St. Thomas, natural law re-emerged as a potent concept only in the days of Newton and Locke, when the medieval structure was in full decline.

In the medieval view, the individual—this imperishable and precious soul of God's most valued creature—was to be joined with all his fellows into an eternal community, a paradise on earth. Again, this was the second great idea of early Christianity: the confident expectation of the parousia, the apocalyptic coming of the Kingdom of God on earth.

Combined with the idea of the individual, the concept of the Kingdom gave to Christianity a revolutionary and utopian quality, arousing believers to dangerous and adventuresome activity to prepare themselves and the world for the fulfillment of God's promise on earth. This basic faith in and drive toward the Kingdom was strengthened by the memory of the Roman concept of the universal state and citizenship, which constituted a kind of subconscious precedent and demonstrated the secular feasibility of the notion.

There was, of course, a good deal of backsliding; social institutions inconsistent with the Christian vision prevailed, but they were under the threat of eventual destruction, and believers could comfort themselves with that.

This notion of the Kingdom distinguishes the West from all

other civilizations. It establishes the critical—if tremulous—principle that one can never accept existing institutions as final. In consequence, the West has been in a continual state of search. This idea was a major cause of and justification for the West's preoccupation with exploration and invention.* Fifteenth-century China had better boats than Europe, more resources, more experience with the sea, and a more powerful central government, yet did not attempt to explore the unknown world; it was already in its final state, at the center of the universe. The questing spirit of medieval and Renaissance Europe is with us still, as is the concept of the individual and his unique value.

A Positive Idea of Work

The ideas of individual worth, the whole personality, and the coming of the Kingdom of Heaven were critical to the development of another new ideological element—a positive ethic of work. An appreciation of labor in a Benedictine monastery is revealing:

Labor was to be man's greatest joy and the instrument of his union with God. Industry was the key to the upbuilding of the new world that Benedict created within the precincts of his monastic establishment. Everything was seen as an aspect of work. The singing of the divine office in church was the *opus Dei*, the work of prayer to God that is peculiar to the monk. It had to be done well. Manual labor was in its way, however, no less important in the life of the monastery, which could only exist through the support of the monk's hands. . . . Christ has redeemed human toil, making the humblest "chore" a labor of love. The dignity of labor was proved in the joy of a good monk's life. Work was but the highest expression of love.**

Christ was a carpenter, Paul a tentmaker, other apostles were fishermen; and the early followers of the primitive Church found their fulfillment in manual labor. In this same spirit, monks working in the fields with their hands made this heightened valuation of work an everyday reality for the Middle Ages. Benedict's concept of a lay community, in which each member should labor with his hands, evolved into a twofold division: a group of priests,

---

* See Myron P. Gilmore, *The World of Humanism, 1453–1517, The Rise of Modern Europe,* edited by William L. Langer (New York: Harper & Brothers, 1952).
** Geddes MacGregor, *The Hemlock and the Cross: Humanism, Socrates, and Christ* (Philadelphia: J. B. Lippincott Co., 1963), pp. 91–2.

upper-class in origin, who worked with their minds; and a group of brothers, lower-class in origin, who worked with their hands. Both kinds of men, and both kinds of work, were equally precious, for both were dedicated to God and the coming of the Kingdom. The vitality of this concept precluded any return to the contempt in which Aristotle and the other Greeks held work. Even now it has great impact: the Peace Corps and such programs as Crossroads Africa early discovered that perhaps their greatest effect in underdeveloped countries came from exposing the intelligentsia to the spectacle of young students working with their hands, enjoying the experience and not feeling demeaned by it.

Time, however, was also precious for the medieval mind; the way to the Kingdom must be prepared quickly. Thus, early Christian ideology also created a fertile ground for technological innovation and its employment for earthly improvement. The Benedictine monks, in particular, used every device they could to escape backbreaking toil, in order to free their time for worship, private prayer, and reading. Today we have the same pressure for time-saving productivity, but somehow the purpose or vision has changed.

One medieval monastery's use of machines is described as follows:

The river enters the abbey as much as the wall acting as a check allows. It gushes first into the corn-mill where it is very actively employed in grinding the grain under the weight of the wheels and in shaking the fine sieve which separates the flour from the bran. Thence it flows into the next building, and fills the boiler in which it is heated to prepare beer for the monks' drinking, should the vine's fruitfulness not reward the vintner's labour. But the river has not yet finished its work, for it is now drawn into the fulling machines following the corn-mill. In the mill it has prepared the brothers' food and its duty is now to serve in making their clothing. This the river does not withhold, nor does it refuse any task asked of it. Thus it raises and lowers alternately the heavy hammers and mallets, or to be more exact, the wooden feet of the fulling machines. When by swirling at great speed it has made all these wheels revolve swiftly it issues foaming and looking as if it had ground itself. Now the river enters the tannery where it devotes much care and labour to preparing the necessary materials for the monks' footwear; then it divides into many small branches and, in its busy course, passes through the various departments, seeking everywhere for those who require its services for any purpose whatever, whether for cooking, rotating, crushing, watering, washing or grinding, always offering its help and never refusing. At last, to earn full thanks and to leave nothing undone, it carries away the refuse and leaves all clean.*

The example set by the monks in organizing labor and utilizing machines was soon emulated. Harnesses were developed that would not choke a horse when it drew a wagon; plows that cut deeply into the soil, thereby increasing productivity; stirrups that allowed a heavily armored man to sit upon a moving horse; new systems of three-field cultivation that increased food production by nearly half and, significantly, added greatly to the production of protein. The first great advances in power generation were made; for example, in 1066 England alone had 8,000 watermills, together providing twice as much energy as the manpower of the 100,000 persons who built the Great Pyramid. This increased power was probably twenty times as great as the Egyptian work force, given the different population levels of the two countries.** Even rudders appeared for steering boats. And it was, in fact, this spirit of technological innovation that allowed the big business of the eleventh and twelfth centuries—castle and cathedral building —to proceed, to the greater glory of God, his vicars and regents, and ultimately, to the Kingdom of Heaven.†

Many, if not all, of these new devices and techniques were borrowed from Eastern sources—Persia, China, Mongolia—but the uses to which they were put in the West demonstrates the influence of Christian ideology upon the society. The crank, for example, which is alien to human physiology, was invented in Tibet and was used in Buddhist countries to drive prayerwheels. The West adapted the idea for power generation by the windmill, necessary in the cold North where watermills had limited usefulness in winter. Once their effectiveness as power sources had been demonstrated, windmills spread from Northern Europe to the Holy Land in less than twenty-five years. In contrast, perpetual motion machines were common in the East, and represented perhaps the

---

* Migne's account of St. Bernard in the *Patrologia Latina,* as quoted in Lewis Mumford, *The Myth of the Machine: Technics and Human Development* (New York: Harcourt, Brace & World, Inc., 1967), p. 270.
** *Ibid.,* pp. 263–71.
† Eugen Rosenstock-Huessy, *The Driving Power of Western Civilization: The Christian Revolution of the Middle Ages* (Boston: Beacon Press, 1949), pp. 96–7, and elsewhere.

furthest refinement of mechanics in the static cultures, in which life itself was conceived as a cycle of perpetual motion. Even in the Mediterranean world, what scientific impulse the Hellenic culture possessed had been crushed by the fixed-world concept of Roman civilization. Christian civilization renewed it and surpassed anything previously dreamed of:

[Medieval men] were coming to think of the cosmos as a vast reservoir of energies to be tapped and used according to human intentions. They were power conscious to the point of fantasy. But without such fantasy, such soaring imagination, the power technology of the Western world would not have been developed. When Peter of Maricourt's friend Roger Bacon wrote, c. 1260, "Machines may be made by which the largest ships, with only one man steering them, will be moved faster than if they were filled with rowers; wagons may be built which will move with incredible speed and without the aid of beast; flying machines can be constructed in which a man . . . may beat air with wings like a bird . . . machines will make it possible to go to the bottom of seas and rivers," he spoke not alone but for the engineers of his age.*

Here, then, is a constellation of medieval ideas—the absolute value of the individual, the extension and enhancement of his contribution through technology, the goal of building toward and preparing for the Kingdom—that suggest clearly the route the institutionalization of the times was bound to take. The principal role fell naturally to the Church, remained with it by and large, and grew within it. The Benedictines led in the organization of productive labor and the development of technology. From the monks also came "the political language" which was essential for institutional organization, and most especially from those who gathered in the monastery at Cluny in Burgundy, founded in 910. In general, early Europe's capacity for effective institutionalization was attributable to the Roman Catholic Church and especially to "united monasticism," which established what became the political, social, and economic fabric of medieval Europe.**

The elements of unity and universality in a culture determine in large measure its distinctive genius. In the Middle Ages, political authority attained a certain degree of homogeneity; the feudal system was supranational. But economy could not remotely be

---

* Lynn White, Jr., *Medieval Technology and Social Change* (Oxford, England: The Clarendon Press, 1962), pp. 133–4.
** Rosenstock-Huessy, *op. cit.*, p. 42.

considered an agent of universality. The unity of Europe arose from claims of religious faith and the memory of the Roman Empire. The process by which these both came to be institutionalized in large measure constituted the first revolution of the Christian era: "One great ocean of creed and an archipelago of economic islands—that was the situation in the year 1000."* The primary allegiance and power belonged to the religious, that is, the social system; the subsidiary allegiance belonged to the political system, that is, to the structure of feudalism and the free cities. These allegiances were the more compatible, and could share a common vocabulary the more easily, because the religious and political sectors developed parallel structures and hierarchies. The question of a third allegiance, an economic allegiance, arose only slowly, in ideological isolation from the other two.

Great institutions gather great power, however, and it is a cliché that power corrupts—corrupts even institutions of distinctive genius. The monastic foundation at Cluny began as a reform movement to purify a decadent monasticism in an even more corrupt Church, to revive the early Christian ideology. In the year 998, St. Odilo of Cluny instituted All Souls Day, a profoundly democratic feast, during which prayers are said for all souls, both born and unborn, saved and unsaved, noble and commoner. All are equal in death. All must come to the Lord on the Last Judgment.

All Souls objectified for the West a tradition not only of equality but also of militancy in its spirituality—an army of Christian soldiers. Undoubtedly, without All Souls and the Last Judgment, the Church would have found it much more difficult to enforce its will on barbarian, emperor, and noble.

The centralizing force of Cluny was no less important. The Church's corruption during this period was pervasive and far-reaching, so much so that people looked to the Holy Roman Emperor for universality. The masses and nobles alike sought in the Empire the power which could end ceaseless strife and bring about peace. Contemporary engravings show the emperor holding the oil of baptism and a dove—the symbol of the Holy Spirit. The motto on the engraving was in fact the motto of the Empire: *Jerusalem visio pacis.***

Cluny rose during this time. It grew to a "super-abbey," and

---

* *Ibid.,* p. 43. ** Jerusalem vision of peace.

purified the monastic movement.* It enforced its rulings on other monks initially by power of example, eventually by constitutional rule. All monasteries in Europe came under the abbot of Cluny. It instituted reform standards for worship, liturgy, and monastic life. Under its leadership, monasteries became not only centers of spiritual activity and thus of policy formulation but also leaders in the organization of large-scale production. Both in thought and in institution, Cluny became in the tenth century the first corporation to transcend time and place in medieval Europe.

It is significant that Gregory VII, who began the Papal Revolution (1073) and took back from the emperor the keys of Jerusalem, was elected to the papal see out of Cluny. He proclaimed the papacy successor of both St. Peter and St. Paul. He reformed the clergy. He used investiture as a device to regain control of bishops and priests from the secular authorities. And through the administration of oaths, he tranformed vassals into theurgic knights.

Gregory asserted:

that the Roman Church was founded by God alone
that the Roman pontiff alone can with right be called universal
that he alone can depose or reinstate bishops
that he alone may use (i.e., dispose of) the imperial insignia
that it may be permitted him to depose emperors
that he himself may be judged of no one
that he may absolve subjects from their fealty to wicked men.

These assertions add up to the proclamation that the Church is the universal political institution.

It should be remembered that all this took place during the beginning of the power revolution of the early Middle Ages symbolized by the harness, the watermill, and the windmill. These technical innovations had begun to render obsolete the old manorial system. Lords were restricted in their power by Gregory from claiming all the benefits of the new technology. When excess population developed in the 1000's because of the innovations, lay lords, stimulated by monastic examples, began to farm their swamps and woodlands. The power of the monasteries forced lords to compete for settlers by loosening the ties of serfdom. The renewed Church and monastic movements, together with technical

---

* Rosenstock-Huessy, *op. cit.*, p. 54.

innovations encouraged by those movements, began the revival of economic life in Europe.

Ideological Degeneration and the Loss of Legitimacy

The ideological power of the early revolutionary Church was thus sufficient to establish it as a pervasive force in the development of medieval social, political, and economic institutions. In the process, however, the Church departed institutionally from its legitimizing ideology until, by the later Middle Ages, Christian practice as well as thought, far from being revolutionary, had become the embodiment of the status quo.

Three factors were of central importance in this process. First was Constantine's recognition of the Roman Catholic Church as the official Church in the fourth century. This was the beginning of the Church's inseparable connection with the established order, which led to its overwhelming concern with the legitimization of and finally social control over that order. Second was the acquisition of territory starting in the ninth century, which made the Church not only a spiritual entity but a political state, a property owner, and an economic enterprise of substantial proportions. Third were the battles for supremacy between the pope, the Holy Roman Emperor, and later the other rulers of Christendom. The Church was obsessed not only with sustaining the existing political structures but with controlling them as well. It became committed to the feudal class structure and to its permanence. Poverty was blessed. The old apocalyptic vision of the Kingdom of Heaven on earth was replaced by a fearsome concentration on sin in this life and salvation in the next, sin being often equated with violation of the established norms of the status quo. In the process of gaining earthly power, the Church outstripped its legitimizing ideology and, ridden with corruption, eventually broke apart. Although monastic orders made repeated efforts to cleanse the Church and to bring it back to its original virtues, even the monks themselves became rich, powerful, and corrupt. The Church's catastrophe reached an extreme stage in Europe during the French Revolution when anti-clericalism drove men "to throttle the last king in the bowels of the last Jesuit."*

---

* John Herman Randall, Jr., *The Career of Philosophy,* vol. 1 (New York: Columbia University Press, 1962), p. 851.

Ideological and institutional decay brought with it decadence and violence, two of the most terrible effects of ideological dissolution. Huizinga describes some of these effects:

> The Church, on the one hand, had inculcated gentleness and clemency, and tried, in that way, to soften judicial morals. On the other hand, in adding to the primitive need of retribution for the horror of sin, it had, to a certain extent stimulated the sentiment of justice. . . . Torture and executions are enjoyed by the spectators like an entertainment at a fair. The citizens of Mons bought a brigand, at far too high a price, for the pleasure of seeing him quartered, "at which the people rejoiced more than if a new holy body had arisen from the dead." . . . So violent and motley was life, that it bore the smell of blood and roses. The men of that time [the fifteenth century] always oscillate between the fear of hell and the most naive joy.*

In the history of man, such periods as these have more often than not been stamped with violence, destruction, and cruelty. Indeed, it is still unclear whether we have yet learned to manage the crisis of ideological transformation without the wholesale disintegration, waste, and inhumanity that overtook Rome and the late Middle Ages or characterized the revolutions of France, Russia, and China.

The Rise of Private Enterprise

Even while the pious were laying the foundations at Chartres, the Venetians were sending fleets of as many as one hundred ships to trade in the Levant; lords were seeking political privilege for economic gain; and in the not-too-distant future, popes and monasteries would be borrowing from bankers at interest. The economic order, always present but hitherto forced into the background by the political and social ethics of the early Middle Ages, was beginning its rise.

The slow fermentation of commerce and industry, which eventually did so much to break the power of the hierarchies of the medieval world (and especially that of the ecclesiastical hierarchy),

---

* J. Huizinga, *The Waning of the Middle Ages: A Study of the Forms of Life, Thought and Art in France and The Netherlands in the XIVth and XVth Centuries* (London: Edward Arnold and Co., 1924), pp. 13, 15, 18–21.

took place for the most part in towns, the natural centers of business and markets from antiquity to the present day.

The breakdown of the Roman Empire had speeded an already serious decline in commercial and business life. The manorial institutions aimed at self-sufficiency reasserted themselves as trade came to a virtual halt. Most artisans worked as parts of these institutions. Cities withered to a small fraction of their former size.

Some trade and some markets had persisted, of course—one thinks of the great trade fairs of the Middle Ages in such towns as Toulouse. And with the second millennium trade began to revive more strongly, although it was a dangerous undertaking because of inadequate police protection on the roads and rivers. By the twelfth century, trade was clearly the chief instrument of economic revival and partly responsible for the rebirth of cities.*

The people of the cities of that period were in one way or another "business people," outside of and free from the feudal order.

In order to be professional and to conduct trade all the year around merchants and artisans had to be exempt from the ties and liabilities which restricted the liberty of movement and freedom of contract of the lower orders of feudal society. Their houses and tenements with their shops had to be free from the obligations which burdened rural tenures; their transactions had to be judged by a law better suited to dealings between merchant and merchant than were the feudal customs and common law.**

Hence the expression of the period, "the city air makes free."

However, there were very definite strictures on this freedom, none set more stringently than the Church's admonition against the sin of greed. "A furious chorus of invectives against cupidity and avarice rises up," says Huizinga.† St. Thomas Aquinas, following Aristotle, laid down strict rules concerning usury, the vile evidence of the sin of greed: "To take usury for money lent is unjust in

---

* Henri Pirenne, *Economic and Social History of Medieval Europe* (New York: Harcourt, Brace & Co., Inc., 1937), pp. 97–103.

** M. Postan, "The Trade of Medieval Europe: The North," *The Cambridge Economic History of Europe*, edited by M. Postan, *et al.*, vol. 2 (Cambridge, England: Cambridge University Press, 1963), pp. 168–74, 171.

† Huizinga, *op. cit.*, pp. 18–21.

itself, because this is to sell what does not exist, and this evidently leads to inequality which is contrary to justice."* He admitted certain significant exceptions: if a man received late payment of a debt, or financed a dangerous and risky venture, such as a sea voyage, or acted as an agent in international currency exchange, he might justifiably charge interest. Interest was justifiable when money was to flow as the lubricant of constructive commerce. As a practical man, Thomas would not have contravened "common sense" so far as to prohibit such investment.

In the twelfth and thirteenth centuries, in fact, the Church was active in assisting the growth of those who were to become the merchant princes and bankers of the Renaissance. Ideologically, this assistance was justified by the positive value which the Church ascribed to work and to the profit which flowed from work. St. Thomas did not despise profit; he merely set conditions to its just creation and limits to its just size (usually 5 per cent return on investment). Martin Luther had a similar conception: he coupled wealth with work and profits with the risk of loss as well as the chance of gain. Eventually profits were held illegitimate only if they were made on a deal in which the lender took no risk. And banking grew so unexceptionable that a younger son of the Medici actually became pope.

One can speculate that the civic pride and political contributions of the Medici somehow ameliorated the inherent sin of their business. Many other merchants who were solely preoccupied with business fared far less happily. Iris Origo has given a vivid picture of the plight of the usurer:

In the depositions during the trial of some usurers in Pistoia at the end of the thirteenth century, one of them was referred to as a heretic (twice branded as such with a cross, on his chest and thighs) and others as blasphemers, liars, drinkers and whore-mongers. True or false, these accusations show the usurer as he appeared to his contemporaries: Shylock with his pound of flesh, the personification of cupidity and avarice. . . . Fra Filippo delgi Agazzari told . . . the horrifying tale of a usurer whose corpse was placed in a mortuary chapel that his heirs had built for him but on the night after the funeral "all the devils of Hell surrounded the chapel wherein he lay,

---

* St. Thomas Aquinas, *Summa Theologica,* translated by the Fathers of the English Dominican Province, Part II (New York: Benziger Brothers, 1918), pp. 329–40.

with so much noise and clamour that for miles around no man could sleep; and in the morn it was seen that the chapel had been uprooted and cast into the river near-by."*

Origo relates a particularly enlightening story about one Italian merchant of the fourteenth century, a man who seems to have devoted himself wholly to trade. Francesco Di Marco Datini (1335–1410) was a merchant of humble background who accumulated a considerable fortune. Not only was he forbidden by the Church to take excessive interest on money lent, he could take no interest at all. Francesco's most trusted adviser, Ser Lapo Mazzei, wrote that he would have no part of one of Datini's transactions, "for I think it would be against the laws and statutes of God— which are, that no interest should be taken on a loan of money." A few days later he added: "I believe you are bound to give back that money to Ludovico, as arising from a *contratto usuralo*; and I think I, too, should confess and make penance."

Datini's remarkable archives do not show him to have been dishonest or especially greedy. Yet clearly in all his letters there is an undercurrent of uneasiness and guilt. His hard work and dogged persistence caused his mother to cry out, "Crave not for all! In Christ's name beware of rising too high: that snare has caught some very big birds." Again his friend, Lapo Mazzei, counsels:

It grieves me that you should take these enterprises of yours . . . with so great an avidity, desire, solicitude and anguish. It is not good. A wise man should learn to bridle himself. . . . You know men are not pleased with a house wherein the maid rules the mistress; even so the soul wherein reason is ruled by the will, is displeasing to God.

Despite their increasing importance to the society, then, the merchant and the financier, insofar as they attended to business and only to business, were generally inferior characters, essentially illegitimate under the prevailing ideology. Even enormously successful banking families, such as the Fuggers, were never accorded the power that their wealth suggests they might have acquired. Eventually that particular family disappeared from finance because the grandsons felt pressed to buy estates and return to the

---

* Iris Origo, *The Merchant of Prato: Francesco Di Marco Datini* (New York: Alfred A. Knopf, Inc., 1957), pp. 153–61.

orthodox social order—to turn respectable, as Cicero had advised centuries earlier. Chastellain, historian to the Duke of Burgundy, remarked in the early 1400's:

Coming to the third estate, making up the kingdom as a whole, it is the estate of the good towns, of merchants and labouring men, of whom it is not becoming to give such a long exposition as of the others, because it is hardly possible to attribute great qualities to them, as they are of servile degree.*

The merchant class was suppressed because its labor was fundamentally suspect in the eyes of the established institutions; and suppressed classes evolve rules and procedures—private ideologies, if you will—to ensure their own solidarity and survival. The most detailed and ultimately the most harmful regulation of business in the Middle Ages emanated in fact from business circles themselves. The mercantilist regulation of the medieval town is well known. Rules forbidding outsiders to sell at retail, rules requiring wandering merchants to display their goods for sale even if they were merely passing through, rules forcing local producers to bring all their goods to the public market—all these were imposed by the townsmen to protect their own interests and to ensure that what trade there was benefited their town and not another. The towns were governed by businessmen and owners of urban real estate; their regulations were established by merchants and artisans, and consequently restricted in both scope and vision. So far as political regulation from the nobility was concerned, Pirenne asserts they ". . . made no attempt to control the movement of commerce and we should seek in vain for traces of an economic policy deserving of the name."**

Such political and social control as there was, was exercised according to the tenets of an outmoded ideology—as in the case of restriction of the condition and terms of interest. Where any policy was made, it was on an ad hoc basis, merely temporizing to solve a current problem.

Just as merchants and financiers were directed by a rigid ideology, so the early corporations and guilds grew up in accordance with prevailing ideas of society and structure. Corporations initially were formed by groups within the several class categories,

---

* Huizinga, *op. cit.,* pp. 48–52.   ** Pirenne, *op. cit.,* p. 92.

never between. This meant that corporations, at least in their early forms, fitted with the surrounding political and social structure. Again we see the submission of economic structure and motives to the all-embracing whole. City industries were composed of groups of knights, free peasants, artisans, or whatever, and each possessed laws of its own. Within each corporation there was a spirit of solidarity, cooperation, and helpfulness. It was a world of personal relationships, a collective world, with little mobility and little rationalism.

But there was blood as well as roses within the economic sector itself. The big merchant did not want to be bound by local regulations, and often fought free of them; hence he was frequently at odds with the guild, the small shopkeeper, and the artisan. The profit seekers—bankers who lent money to the princes, international businessmen, textile entrepreneurs—were in conflict not only with the ethos of the ecclesiastics and nobility, but also with the small businessmen, who feared the fluidity of major economic activity at least as much as the orthodox hierarchies did. And, although the landed interests often fulminated at the profits of the merchant, they rarely if ever took the side of the journeyman against the master. To do so would have been ideologically inconsistent with the notion of hierarchy, which by then had shown itself stronger and more desirable in practice than the concept of the Kingdom of Heaven. Naturally, toward the end of the era, major financiers and merchants had established monopolistic or semi-monopolistic positions. Whether this outcome was good or bad is not to be debated; the point is that it was the result of circumstance and of the existence of a fast-weakening, irrelevant ideology that effectively precluded the formulation of new and redeeming long-range economic policy. The economic sector just grew.

The ideological implications of the monetary economy itself began to be felt in Northern Europe from as early as the thirteenth century. Troeltsch describes its impact, speaking of it as "the spirit of gain for the sake of gain" . . .

Where this spirit predominates it makes all values abstract, exchangeable and measurable; it mobilizes property and, in a way of which no one hitherto had dreamed, advancing beyond the merely natural dependence of life, it groups together the economic values and the possibilities which they contain. The economic system based on money depersonalizes values, makes property abstract and individualistic, creates a rational law of trade and possessions, raises men above the natural conditions of life, unites its fortunes with forethought, intelligence, and calculation, replaces the idea of Providence and the spirit of mutual help and solidarity of those who are bound together in loyalty to one another, by products which are at all times ready for use. . . . It is the cause of the development of formal abstract law, of an abstract, impersonal way of thinking, of rationalism and relativism. . . . [It leads to] restless and changing social differentiation.*

As in the writings of Plato and Aristotle, we sense a culture fearful that its established definitions of value are slipping away, its institutions falling prey to sterile gods. And medieval society was as little able to deal with the fact that caused its fears—the emergence of a potent economic sector—as the reactionaries of Athens had been. Many in the modern world continued to regard economy, and specifically profit, in exactly this light.

Our present confusion about monetary theory and the ideology appropriate for the economic sector stems, in fact, from medieval and ancient times—we have never clarified the value of money and profit in scale against our other values. Karl Polanyi has asserted that "most of the confusion existing in monetary theory [i.e., regarding the theory as (merely) economic] was due to the separation of politics and economics, this outstanding characteristic of market society."** Throughout his work, Polanyi insists that this separation is due to the Industrial Revolution, which thrust all land, people, and resources into a market to be bought and sold. But in fact, the distinction antedated the Industrial Revolution by centuries; the growth of industry only completed a process begun in the later Middle Ages, by expanding the importance of the market economy in relation to the other institutions of Western Europe. One can even speculate that if the economic sector had not cut the cord that bound it to the early medieval ideology and flourished on its own, the Industrial Revolution would not have taken place when or as it did. However that may be, the differentials inherent in that industrial expansion

---

* Ernest Troeltsch, *The Social Teachings of the Christian Churches,* translated by Olive Wyon, vol. 1 (New York: The Macmillan Co., 1931), pp. 246–51.
** Polanyi, *op. cit.,* p. 195.

were, of course, so great as to create a qualitatively different society.

In the forefront of institutional innovation during the later Middle Ages were new conceptions of landed property and business enterprise, especially in Northern Europe and England. The fact that these innovations were accompanied by new and revolutionary religious impulses was not accidental. And along with all of this came a gradual separation of the economic from the political and social, a divergence between economic power and political authority. In the early Middle Ages, the two were clearly combined in the feudal prince. Over time, he relinquished authority in the interests of order to the king to whom he swore loyalty. Eventually his possessions of land, once considered temporary according to the will of the sovereign, became permanent. His obligations to the king were met if he provided goods, men, arms, and taxes. Gradually, contracts replaced personalities, and law the spirit of mutual loyalty.

The separation of political authority and economic power was, of course, by no means made complete in the Middle Ages; it lay at the roots of the English civil wars and subsequent revolutions. But its beginnings lay in the breakdown of the feudal world.

Further, in the fifteenth century, the separation was abetted by the needs of kings for revenue. Kings contracted out exploration rights to groups of merchants and soldiers of fortune. One of the principal reasons that Europe and not China undertook great explorations lay in the property/authority distinction in the West:

Similar incentives were largely absent in the case of the Chinese. The great expeditions of the Ming in the fifteenth century were characteristically enterprises financed by the government and staffed by the bureaucracy. Even when merchants were permitted to participate for their own gain, institutional guarantees for private property did not exist on the same scale as in Europe. The opportunity for expansion occurred for both China and Europe; indeed, from the point of view of technological achievement as measured by the size and range of expeditions, the opportunity presented to China was far greater. Yet the European society whose rulers were far less wealthy than the Chinese emperor was in reality in a much better position to seize that opportunity. In the absence of comprehensive monolithic government control the European system allowed for a greater measure of individual incentive and broader basis of participation.*

---

* Gilmore, *op. cit.*, p. 37.

The European rulers also attempted to increase the wealth of their nations by taking the typically feudal regulations of the town and applying them *vis-à-vis* the outside world. Mercantilism was but feudal city regulation writ large, and for the most part it failed. The France of Louis XIV never had the necessary administrative power to enforce free trade throughout France. In England the regulations collapsed of themselves. (That they did so sooner in England than on the continent provides part of the explanation for England's early success in industrialization.) The inability on the part of governments to regulate economic life to any measurable extent and the power of business and commerce, beginning particularly in the seventeenth century, were important factors in the breakup of medieval institutions and the rise of the modern nation-state.

To summarize the interaction between ideology and institutions in the Middle Ages so far: A powerful and revolutionary collection of ideas emerged from the ashes of Rome. Emphasizing the worth of the individual human being, his personality, and his exploits on earth, these represented a radical departure from the static cultures of Greece and Rome. Upon these ideas the institutions of the Roman Catholic Church were erected, binding together and legitimizing the chaotic world of early Europe. Inexorably, the Church's power and influence dominated all political, social, and economic life. At the same time, the secular power of the feudal lords and their kings grew. Compromise between Church and State became necessary, and both institutions became preoccupied with maintaining their own power and structure. They turned to the static ideology of the classical world, thus implicitly renouncing the ideology that had given them birth and becoming corrupted and illegitimate in the process. Chaos, confusion, and abuse abounded. New institutions, notably of a commercial nature, began to emerge. Searching for legitimacy, they eventually found it, as we shall see, in the seventeenth century in variations of early Christian thought, new conceptions of "natural law," and in the revelations of science.

By that point, indeed, a new ideology was both necessary and inevitable. Medieval Europe had become unmanageable. Lawlessness, corruption, and brutality were rampant—the complex world of feudalism was breaking down, its components pulling apart. The monarchy and the authority of the centralized state gained ascendancy over the disparate power of the feudal lords on their estates and gradually forced the Church from its position of supremacy. The old feudal aristocracy was increasingly threatened by the new forces of business, and business itself required increasing state control.

As Sir George Clark put it,

It is misleading to summarize in a single phrase any long historical process, but the work of the monarchy in the seventeenth century may be described as the substitution of a simpler and more unified government for the complexities of feudalism. On one side it was centralization, the bringing of local business under the supervision or control of the government of the capital. This necessarily had as its converse a tendency toward uniformity.*

Samuel Huntington has pointed out a distinction between England and the continent in this transition which is of crucial importance to America. In seventeenth-ceuntry England, as on the continent, the Church was subordinated, authority centralized, and sovereignty asserted; but it was not long before these phenomena provoked a constitutional struggle between the king and Parliament, from which Parliament emerged the victor.** America, however, was plucked ideologically, as it were, out of the early stages of this process—from late-sixteenth-century Elizabethan England. Its founding ideas, later set down by Locke, originated in an England in transition from medievalism, an England in which the natural law of the medieval period continued to hold sway, a pluralistic England in which authority was still diffuse and government far from centralized:

In seventeenth century Europe the state replaced fundamental law as the source of political authority and within each state a single authority replaced the many which had previously existed. America, on the other hand, continued to adhere to fundamental law as both a source of authority for human actions and an authoritative restraint on human behavior.†

---

* Sir George Clark, *The Seventeenth Century,* p. 91, as quoted in Samuel P. Huntington, *Political Order in Changing Societies* (New Haven, Conn.: Yale University Press, 1968), p. 95.
** Huntington, *ibid.,* pp. 95–6.   † *Ibid.,* p. 98.

In America, as in transitional Tudor England, and in the medieval period before it, authority or sovereignty was not concentrated in a single institution or individual but "remained dispersed throughout society as a whole and among many organs of the body politic."*

The founding fathers of the United States, following the Lockean ideology, rejected the authoritarianism of eighteenth-century Europe, preferring the decentralization, dispersion, and division of power characteristic of an earlier period. Fundamentally suspicious of government, America employed Lockean thought almost as a religion to justify the most extreme divorce of economic activity from political controls, a divorce which has continued to trouble us up to the present day.

---

* *Ibid.*, p. 99.

3 The Lockean Paradigm and Paradox

The Lockean ideology clearly reflected some elements of medieval ideology. Locke's individualism and egalitarianism are reminiscent of early Christian thought. His assertion of the right to property was rooted in natural law, although his interpretation of that law differed substantially from that of Aristotle and Aquinas; he made it universal and thus theoretically, at least, democratic. In one sense, Locke's conception of the limited state and of dispersed political power was medieval in tone; clearly, he rejected the idea of the authoritative modern state as it eventually evolved in Europe and England. In another sense, he was obviously associated with those who were eager to sweep away what Robert Nisbet has called "the communal debris of the Middle Ages."* His individualistic view of society which, taken to its extreme, borders on anarchism, contrasted sharply with the conceptual unity of medieval thought. Further, he was plainly repelled by the medieval notion that the uses of property were to be subsumed within the general social and political order, employed as a means of sustaining that order.

Whatever Locke's theory may have been, his ideology in the hands of its users became the means for radical change. Above all, this was an atomistic ideology that tore down the very concept of a divinely based organic whole, accentuating the individual in aggressive competition rather than the relationships between that individual and the surrounding community (hence clearly distinct from the early Christian notion of personality). Admirably suited

---

* Robert Nisbet, *The Sociological Tradition* (New York: Basic Books, Inc., 1966), Chap. 3.

to the needs of the rising commercial class, it justified the divorce of economic activity from social and political relationships. Such activity began to be seen as good in itself—a notion that was literally anathema to medieval society—and the motives of man were assumed to be largely if not exclusively economic. Thus, the development of society came to be regarded almost exclusively in economic terms.

Before launching into a detailed exposition of how the Lockean paradigm was first noted down and then expanded during the last few centuries, it may be helpful to consider some contemporary examples of interaction between the medieval and Lockean ideologies. These examples—taken first from Latin America and then from the large publicly held American corporation—demonstrate the relevance of the preceding analysis to the ideological problems that confront us today.

The Myth of "Development":
Economic Man and Medieval Man

For the past twenty years or more, the United States has been engaged in promoting the "development" of poor countries. Our conception of development and that of those whom we have influenced has been generally represented by the phrase "economic development." Nothing could emphasize more poignantly the validity of Polanyi's observation (noted earlier) that modern Lockean man has indeed separated economic activity from its political and social setting and endowed that activity with supreme importance. We now have ample opportunity to see the impossibility of achieving anything definable as development by employing this ideological conception in areas of the world in which medieval traces continue to predominate. The northeast of Brazil is such an area.

The application of Lockean principles and assumptions about "economic man" here has been strikingly unsuccessful. One of a number of stories illustrating the continuing failure of America and of American-influenced Brazilians to "develop" the northeast concerns a shoemaker in Recife. Like the medieval artisan, he made a small number of good-quality shoes. Although in Recife the price of his shoes was high, in New York it was low. A visiting economic developer, seeing his work, was certain that his little shop could be modernized and expanded and that the shoemaker, drawing on the inexhaustible supply of cheap labor, could become a thriving exporter to the United States. Arrangements were made with several large American outlets to buy the man's product. All went well until one day the shoemaker said he had had enough. He didn't want to make any more money; he wanted to go back to his old ways. He was not an "economic man."

The efforts to change Brazil's northeast have been based upon assumptions of entrepreneurialism which we have virtually taken for granted. They have also assumed that the large-scale construction of dams, roads, and the like will somehow produce the social change inherent in any definition of development. It was believed that the principal obstacle to development in the northeast was the regular drought which the region suffered and that if its effects could be mitigated, "development" would follow. Celso Furtado, the Brazilian economist who was for a time a leader in northeast development, saw that material and technological injections in fact made matters worse. They increased the prosperity of the large farms, thus strengthening the status quo. More peasants were encouraged to remain in the region or came there for seasonal work. In consequence, when the droughts did occur or when agricultural commodity markets softened, the poverty of the masses was intensified.* The droughts were, as Furtado said, "a smokescreen," hiding the real and much larger problems of change and development in the northeast.

These real problems were the political, economic, and social structure of the region, the pattern of land ownership, and the allocation of and participation in power. It became apparent that little change could occur so long as the region was controlled by a handful of men who were able to isolate the peasant from any countervailing power and regulate his economic and political relationship with the environment. So long as this small group could command and channel government intervention, economic and technical injections by government were likely to solidify rather

---

* Celso Furtado, *Diagnosis of the Brazilian Crisis*, p. 148, as quoted in G. C. Lodge, *Engines of Change* (New York: Alfred A. Knopf, Inc., 1970), p. 167.

than alter the existing structure.* As long as medievalism thrived, in other words, the assumptions and institutions of a different ideology—entrepreneurialism—were invalid.

Sporadic revolutionary efforts, spearheaded by the Roman Catholic Church, have unsuccessfully sought to dislodge the old structures. In 1972, a movement began in the state of Piaui which appears to be offering better hope for change. Alerted to the need for reformation, all elements of the political and social order in Piaui became engaged in an effort to renovate the community. The governor and his wife, the Church, the military, and representatives of all occupational groups and economic classes were involved; it was an organic effort somewhat reminiscent of the building of Chartres Cathedral in the twelfth century, when economic activity was plainly seen as inseparable from the political and social order.

Other efforts in Latin America popularly associated with Marxism may be more precisely seen as profoundly traditional, a form of neomedievalism, directed at breaking down the separation of economic activity—whether of foreign firms or domestic capitalists—from the social and political context. Invariably the cooperation and support of the Church has been central to the fulfillment of political and social change.

Here we see an interesting possibility. The development of Brazil, and more generally of Latin America, has been presumed by the United States and U.S.-trained Latin American specialists to depend upon the introduction of aspects of traditional Lockean ideology, particularly as they have been interpreted by American economists. These efforts have encountered impressive opposition from the entrenched élites; they have also been discordant with the powerful vestiges of medieval ideology.**

Latin America never underwent the Lockean revolution of Europe and the United States, so development there may well leapfrog Lockeanism, passing directly from a traditional medievalism into a new organic sociopolitical form. The Peruvian industrial relations law, for example, which requires eventual ownership of companies by the workers, can perhaps best be seen as a

---

* Lodge, *ibid.* See also Stefan H. Robock, *Brazil's Developing Northeast: A Study of Regional Planning and Foreign Aid* (Washington, D.C.: The Brookings Institution, 1963), p. 48.
** See the discussion of *"arielismo"* in Lodge, *op. cit.,* pp. 102–3, 104.

transition from sixteenth-century norms rather than from those of the twentieth century. If this law is indeed carried out, it would obviously be most short-sighted to credit Marx or "the Communists."

There are a variety of lessons to be learned here if the United States is to "assist" the development process. First, the Lockean model may not be the best for communities still steeped in medievalism. The Japanese method could be considerably more useful, Japan having demonstrated a remarkable ability to adapt a medieval ideology to the demands of modern times.* Second, the ideological basis of some of our most important institutions—in particular the transnational corporation—needs clarification and explication. Here the Lockean model no longer serves. We have considerable work to do at home, straightening out our own ideological base, before we can confidently set out to do good works abroad. Similarly, it would seem that an essential prerequisite for the development of any community is to clarify its own ideological past, present, and future. Development requires ideological confidence. Without it there can be no consensus, no sense of purpose. The central problem of India and of many other ex-colonial countries may well be ideological bastardization, generally reflecting itself in a thin veneer of nineteenth-century European ideology pasted over deeply rooted but confused ancient ideas.

The Public Corporation as a Medieval Institution

Medievalism, in the sense of the dispersion of power and authority, has lain deep in the American experience. Its presence has been blurred by the anti-medieval emphasis on economic activity during the last few centuries and by the general pervasiveness of the American brand of individualism and individualistic conception of private property. Recently, however, there have been signs that we are moving back from our Lockean aberration toward a more natural form, which can be seen as a sort of neomedievalism. Economic activity is clearly becoming increasingly and explicitly embedded in the political and social order according to criteria that are, in some ways at least, religious in nature.**

---

* See the Appendix, On the Japanese Ideology.
** Samuel P. Huntington might argue that we are instead emerging from medievalism to become at last a nation-state. The two views are not necessarily divergent.

Recalling the description of General Motors in Chapter 1, we must ask ourselves: Can it be that such large institutions are, like the feudal domains, becoming satrapies of the state, their managers vassals loosely tied to the sovereign? Surely those who control our large corporations do not own them as did the business leaders of fifty years ago. They have power, but the legitimacy upon which that power rests has grown as tenuous as the myth of stockholder ownership and is increasingly subject to the will of the political order. But where is the binding force of the Church in the new medievalism? From whence comes the unifying mystique, the ideology? Not from the formal religions, so far as one can see. Perhaps the religion of today lies in the protest movements, Ralph Nader, Cesar Chavez, Jesse Jackson, and the ecologists; perhaps it rests with the educational élite, an amorphous group as yet without unity. Might it not be that the Roman establishment would have looked upon the early Christians much as today's establishment looks at this collection?

In the 1930's, Adolf A. Berle and Gardiner C. Means reported the extent of the divorce between the two aspects of ownership of economic activity in the United States: risking collective wealth in the ownership of profit-seeking enterprise on the one hand, and controlling and managing such enterprise on the other.

The translation of perhaps two-thirds of the industrial wealth of the country from individual ownership to ownership by the large, publicly financed corporations vitally changes the lives of property owners, the lives of workers, and the methods of property tenure. The divorce of ownership from control consequent on that process almost necessarily involves a new form of economic organization of society.*

Berle questioned whether an owner who has surrendered control of his property and wealth has a right to the protection traditionally accorded him by Lockean ideology and the law based thereon. He rightly stated that the answer to this could not be found in the law itself but "must be sought in the economic and social background of the law," that is to say, in what we are calling ideology.**

---

* Adolf A. Berle and Gardiner C. Means, *The Modern Corporation and Private Property*, rev. ed. (New York: Harcourt, Brace & World, Inc., 1967), pp. vii–viii. See also A. V. Dicey, *Law and Public Opinion in England* (London: Macmillan and Co., Ltd., 1963).

** Berle and Means, *ibid.*, p. viii.

Berle made a useful distinction between two categories of property: that which is consumed, and that which is "devoted to production, manufacture, service or commerce, and designed to offer, for a price, goods or services to the public from which a holder expects to derive a return."* The problem, as Aristotle and Aquinas saw, lies with the second form of property, which in modern times has itself come to be divided into two categories—that part which is managed and controlled by its owner; and the larger part, controlled by managers who are in reality independent of owners and who, partly as a result of this independence, are increasingly subject to control by the political order. The enormous influence of the political order in encouraging and fostering enterprise managed by nonowners cannot be denied. It led Berle in *Power Without Property* to call the manager of a modern large corporation a "non-statist civil servant," a vassal of the king. Large quantities of technical information have been gathered by government and thrust into nonstatist enterprises in such fields as nuclear energy and nuclear physics, electronics, space science, and aviation. "Like it or not," said Berle, "these assets are social and statist in origin." The state, like St. Thomas, has also moved resolutely into the administration of wages and prices and thus profits, determining increasingly what a just profit shall be.

There are many other ramifications of this phenomenon which we shall consider later. Suffice it here to stress that the gap between economic activity and its political and social context is closing; increasingly, large corporations are becoming adjuncts of the state. We are experiencing a "massive collectivization of property devoted to production, with accompanying decline of individual decision-making and control . . . [and a] massive dissociation of wealth from active management."**

The evolution of the nation's economic activity, notably in the corporate form, has also introduced a radical change in the allocation of power in our society. Deep in the ideological foundations of the United States was the notion that dispersion of wealth and property through the pursuit of profit would guarantee a dispersion of political power. This was essentially the case in 1910, say, when profit truly connoted an identifiable individual or group of indi-

---

* *Ibid.*, p. xi. ** *Ibid.*, p. xxv.

viduals who sought and got it.* And those individuals and groups, by virtue of their wealth and property, did indeed possess power in the political and social order, much like the feudal lords in the early Middle Ages. Today, however, profit suggests rather "a flow of revenue derived from a large group of customers generally known as 'the public,' part of which is destined for distribution to an even larger group of stockholders, pensioners, insurance policy-holders and others. . . ."** It is tempting to suppose that such dispersion would be accompanied by a comparable dispersion in political power and influence, but this is not the way it has worked. Because of the divorce of wealth and ownership from the control of property, the right to control has become concentrated in large blocks and control itself has been increasingly centralized.† Further-more, the competitive dynamics of the market place have been blurred by the emergence of powerful corporate structures and institutional investors, oligopolies, and conglomerates.

Paul Harbrecht has drawn a direct analogy between the condition of the large modern corporations and the feudal domain. He begins with the fact that both are characterized by a separation of control from ownership. The feudal domain emerged in the eighth century when Charles Martel apportioned Church lands among his fighting men in parcels large enough to support armored troops and horses in the field whenever they should be needed.††

In time the owners of the great estates perceived the value of this use of landed wealth which was entirely in the interest of the grantor who turned over control of his lands to others "on condition that the concessionaire served him, not only with his own person, but with a number of vassals in proportion to the importance of the benefice conceded.‡

The system worked well, performing a clearly recognized function; it spread throughout Europe, and the great feudal domains became the centers of economic and political life. Those who resided on the

---

* Adolf A. Berle, Jr., Introduction to Paul P. Harbrecht, S.J., *Toward the Paraproprietal Society: An Essay on the Nature of Property in Twentieth Century America* (New York: Twentieth Century Fund, 1959), pp. 7–8.
** *Ibid.*, p. 8.   † Harbrecht, *op. cit.*, p. 17.   †† *Ibid.*, p. 19.
‡ *Ibid.*, quoting Henri Pirenne, *Mohammed and Charlemagne* (New York: Meridian Books, 1957).

self-sufficient domain had no cause to leave it; there was nowhere else to go. Profit did not exist since the absence of trade prevented a man from selling his product if he produced more than he needed for himself.

There are other analogies between the feudal domains and the large corporation. First, profits were surely the driving force of American enterprise during the nineteenth and early twentieth century. Today, as Harbrecht has pointed out, this is far less true. The typical corporate American is a salaried employee or a wage earner, a component of what John K. Galbraith calls the techno-structure. The 15 million or so Americans who are stockowners are certainly interested in profit, but the return they receive on their investment is more like the rent the lord received from his vassal than the entrepreneurial profit of earlier American periods. The small businessmen for whom the old notions of enterprise may still be valid are steadily diminishing; Harbrecht estimated that they make up only 13 per cent of our working population.*

Second, as in feudal times, the managements who control large pieces of corporate property such as General Motors are increasingly devoting their energies to maintaining their domains as social and political entities. Corporations are, in fact, the institutions which give our society its dominant characteristics.

Their research and innovations transform our lives, quietly with home appliances or dramatically with atomics and space flight, brashly with TV advertising or culturally with subsidies for education. A corporation can invest a billion dollars in "America's future" and create a climate of confidence or spread an air of pessimism by laying off thousands of workers. Corporations have built towns and destroyed them. Their decisions in these matters are perhaps never taken without regard to other social pressures, but then neither was the domain entirely independent of the crown, the church or popular feeling.**

If there is truth in this historical comparison, it leads to several important considerations. In medieval society, a man's position was determined by his place in the domain. Many today are similarly bound to the corporation. A man's security, his financial condition, his social status, and often his politics are conditioned by his place in and connection with a large corporation. It has been argued

---

* *Ibid.*, p. 21. ** *Ibid.*, p. 22.

that the corporation is more than an organization for processing goods to satisfy consumers; it is a way of life, an integrated center of economic, social, and political activity.

Also, we must consider those individuals who are not absorbed into the corporation or some comparable organization—the young, the old, the minority groups, all of whom have found assimilation difficult or its prospect repellent. In the early Middle Ages, such persons were virtually all embraced in the feudal system, but as time passed and cities formed, more and more moved outside the orthodox order. These dissenters became a prime force in the erosion of the old institutions. An analogous process is occurring today. At issue, then, are two problems for the individual—or in early Christian terms, the person. What should his relationships be as a part of a corporate organization? And what should they be outside those organizations? Questions of status, contract, and consensus emerge, much like those that surfaced in fifteenth- and sixteenth-century Europe.

Finally, there is the matter of control. The vassals of the great domains had control of their property, but the ownership remained with the king, their feudal lords, or the Church. The service upon which the vassal's tenure depended was not always clearly defined, yet there was a standard of performance below which he could not fall without incurring the owner's wrath. His main responsibility was to house troops and horses until they were needed. Like General Motors, Lockheed, Boeing, and many other large companies today, the domain served a communitary interest, roughly hedged by various legislated regulations. But what then of ownership? The analogy would be complete if it were the community—the government—which owned these corporations. *Is this perhaps not the case*, in fact, by any reasonable definition of ownership? Which has more influence on the direction and behavior of General Motors, its 1.5 million shareholders or the United States government? In 1910, no doubt, it was the shareholders; but in 1975, the question is arguable. Perhaps imperceptibly and pragmatically, as a result of its wide-ranging capability to affect the allocation of resources both through subsidization and taxation and by virtue of the demands of the community for increased regulation, government is in fact moving into a position of quasi-ownership of corporations. During the transition, the vassal managers are in a troubled state because they are in practice the real owners—but without authority or legitimacy, and without knowing where to find their lords, Church, or king.

Harbrecht rightly notes: "Observation of the function of property in society leads us to the conclusion that power does follow property, as has often been said, but the power really attaches to him who controls the use of property."* Shareholders may be legal owners of property, yet they have little control over its use and thus little power in society. No increase in the number of shareholders, as some have suggested, will change this. On the other hand, managers derive considerable power from their control of property but such control is being progressively curtailed by the demands of the community and the state.

We see here an ebb and flow of power much like that which occurred between the king, the Church, and the vassals of feudal times. In contemporary America, there is a coalescing of power into the hands of a relatively small number of corporate vassals whose sovereign is inevitably becoming, not the shareholding public, but the political order: the state and the interest groups around it.

Harbrecht also argues that the control of property gravitates to those who can, by the use of property, perform a function valuable to society.** This too appears to be a useful proposition. Charles Martel needed military might to withstand the Moslem invasions. His soldiers and their horses had to eat, so he stationed them on domains which they came to control. Nineteenth-century America needed growth, expansion, invention, and production. Business entrepreneurs were thus given maximal freedom and numerous incentives to control and use property accordingly. Today, control over property has gravitated away from the entrepreneur to a variety of agents and agencies: the market place, financial institutions, various interest groups such as the United Automobile Workers, Ralph Nader and his followers, the environmentalists, and, most importantly, government.

Perhaps our quibbling about ownership is as irrelevant as monks arguing about angels on the head of a pin. "Ownership," says Buckminster Fuller, "is obsolete. The telephone company doesn't

---

* *Ibid.,* p. 24.   ** *Ibid.,* p. 28.

know it, but in the end it is going to be the progenitor of our entire economy and life-style."*

We are continually forced to return to certain vital questions. What does society value? What is the collection of ideas on the basis of which these agents and agencies determine the criteria for control of the uses of property? What is the binding mystique? What the ingredients of the consensus, the purpose of the community? We have seen that in medieval times the Church was of dominant importance in providing the governing ideology—to the point, indeed, that most law was Church law. In the eighteenth and nineteenth centuries, the Lockean ideology and the varieties of religious beliefs which came with it held sway: the Protestant ethic, Daniel Boone, Ralph Waldo Emerson, Walt Whitman, Andrew Carnegie, Henry Ford, J. P. Morgan, and the ever-larger consuming public. These were in effect the bishops of the Lockean age.

Today a new mystique, a new ideology is emerging, with new bishops. The list of names is long and what each represents is by no means clear: Ralph Nader, Charles Reich, Philip Slater, William Irwin Thompson, the Berrigan brothers. Like the prophets of old or the monks of tenth-century Europe, they are calling for and sometimes, in strange ways, railing against ideological transformation. Nader's plaintive cry is especially poignant:

Where is the free-enterprise system? I'm trying to find it. Is it the oil oligopoly, protected by import quotas? The shared monopolies in consumer products? The securities market, that bastion of capitalism operating on fixed commissions and now provided with socialized insurance? They call me a radical for trying to restore power to the consumer, but businessmen are the true radicals in this country. They are taking us deeper and deeper into corporate socialism— corporate power using governmental power to protect it from competition.**

Our probe into the past of Western civilization seems to indicate that the separation of economic activity from its political and social context is an aberration from the norm. In medieval days, the domain was an integrated entity and the power of the vassals

---

* Buckminster Fuller, quoted in "The Next Decade: A Search for Goals," *Time*, Dec. 19, 1969, p. 22.
** Richard Armstrong, "The Passion That Rules Ralph Nader," *Fortune*, May 1971, p. 219.

was continually checked by Church and king. Although modern times have seen an unprecedented separation, the gap is plainly closing. Whether one looks at banking, environmental protection, safety, health, or "the quality of life," social and political pressures are forcing economic activity to be realigned in accordance with their criteria. Kingman Brewster replied to those concerned about interference with the prerogatives of management by saying that "it is a political and social corporate system we are faced with, not just the organization of industrial economy."*

In particular, we hear a great deal about corporate social responsibility. But what does this really mean? Surely it relates to the function that society wants its corporations to perform, whether it be feeding horses or making napalm, spaceships, or lipstick. And no corporate manager, however noble and sensitive, has the right or capability to resolve that question single-handed. It is a task of definition which can only be performed by the political process, through a representative democracy, despotism, tyranny, theocracy, or whatever. But to do its job well, the political process itself depends upon a relevant, vital ideology.

The New Science

The institutions and hierarchical unity of the medieval world were a long time in passing; the critical turning point, once again, was the seventeenth century, when the ideological bedrock of our times was formed. The Counter Reformation was in full swing; the Roman Catholic Church was defending itself against the rising tide of Protestantism, free thought, science, and the entrepreneurial drive of the middle class. Francis Bacon, although a devout Anglican, spoke of "minds washed clean of opinions"; and Descartes, a good Catholic, sought to "unload himself of all the teaching which had been transmitted from the ancient world," looking to science for the means of rendering "ourselves the lords and possessors of nature."**

---

* Quoted in Edward S. Mason, *The Corporation in Modern Society* (Cambridge, Mass.: Harvard University Press, 1960), p. 80.
** Herbert Butterfield, *Origins of Modern Science, 1300–1800,* p. 83, as quoted in Thomas F. O'Dea, "The Role of the Intellectual in the Catholic Tradition," *Daedalus,* Spring 1972, p. 153.

Earlier, the Church had been hospitable to the new science. In 1531, Pope Clement had approved an outline of Copernicus's revolutionary declaration that the earth revolved around the sun and not the other way round. But by the beginning of the seventeenth century, an embattled and thin-skinned Church emphasized discipline, loyalty, and dogma. The Jesuits, for example, were directed "to shun ideas that would weaken Aristotelianism with which so much theology had become entwined."* Galileo delivered perhaps the heaviest blow to the old theological ideology, contending that it was through the language of mathematics that the structure of the world could best be grasped.** In 1629, he finished his dialogues on *The Two Principal World Systems*, which was a general attack upon Aristotelian science and gave support to Copernicus's heliocentric hypothesis. After a trial in 1633, the Holy Office pronounced Galileo to be "vehemently suspected of heresy, namely, of having believed and held the doctrine—which is false and contrary to the sacred and divine scriptures—that the Sun is the center of the world; . . . and that an opinion may be held and defended as probable after it has been declared and defined to be contrary to Holy Scriptures."†

Such spasms of irrational reaction were in a way justified, because the old ideology was indeed crumbling. The idea of one dogmatic Church, whose role was properly to order thought and activity according to its interpretation of the will of God, was losing ground to concepts of religious freedom and toleration. The idea of the absolute monarch, legitimized by God, was being replaced by conceptions of individual liberty, representative government, and the natural right to property irrespective of the sovereign's wishes. And the idea that an understanding of reality lay in perceiving and accepting a spiritual and material whole designed by God was giving way to the notion that any man can perceive reality by applying his senses and reason to the component parts of nature through observation and experiment. In short, the old cosmic glue had lost its gripping power. The collective, the or-

---

    * Giorgio De Santillana, *The Crime of Galileo*, p. 118, as quoted in O'Dea, *ibid.*, p. 155.

  ** John Herman Randall, Jr., *The Career of Philosophy*, vol. 1 (New York: Columbia University Press, 1962), p. 359.

    † Santillana, as quoted in O'Dea, *op. cit.*, p. 155.

ganic, the holistic had given way to the individualistic, the atomistic, the components.

These new ideas arose from a synthesis of thought and events by an extraordinary collection of minds, who saw the real world around them in a new and fresh light. They retained enough of the medieval tradition so that they were not only concerned about a more realistic understanding of the parts of nature, but also attempted to relate the parts to each other and to the whole: Galileo in Italy, Grotius and Spinoza in Holland, Descartes in France, and Hobbes, Newton, and Locke in England. Western civilization even now turns for legitimacy to their ideas. We are still living, as Whitehead put it, upon the accumulated capital laid up by the scientific and philosophical pioneers of the seventeenth century.* Of these men, Newton and Locke are particularly important to the present analysis.

Newton and Locke

Newton, in his studies of particles in motion, of masses in the universe, of fluids and gases, optics and colors, inaugurated the method of reductive analysis—explaining the whole in terms of the behavior of its separate parts. This method contrasted sharply with the traditional Aristotelian analysis, which attempted to explain the parts in terms of the ways they functioned in the whole as the latter was perceived. Newton's procedures followed three stages. First, analysis of observed facts to discover the principles involved in their behavior; second, incorporation of all the relevant phenomena of the field under investigation into a mathematical system depending on those principles; and finally, verification of the reality of those principles by experiment. Newton described the purpose of his method in the *Opticks*: "To derive two or three general principles of motion from phenomena, and afterwards to tell . . . how the properties and actions of all corporeal things follow from those manifest principles."**

Scientifically, this approach represented an immense innovation, of course; its philosophical implications, sometimes neglected, were

---

* Randall, *op. cit.,* p. 565.
** Newton, *Opticks,* p. 377, as quoted in Randall, *op. cit.,* p. 576.

also immense. Newton was deeply concerned with the causes of motion, in an ultimate sense, as well as with mathematical description of how and why motion occurs. He was, after all, born into an England where magic, astrology, and old wives' tales were still prevalent, and he was enough a creature of his time to be preoccupied with establishing a metaphysical foundation for what he discovered. It is significant that most of the letters between Newton and Locke, his contemporary, concern interpretations of the Bible, especially the Book of Daniel.* John Maynard Keynes called Newton "the last of the magicians . . . the last great mind which . . . looked on the whole universe and all that is in it as a riddle, as a secret which could be read by applying pure thought to certain evidence, certain mystic clues which God had laid about the world. . . ."** He was searching for the key to the universe, a grail of knowledge that could be his if only he could find the right path, the right method, the true way.

Newton believed profoundly in the existence of a total causal plan, but try as he might, he was unable to discover it in his examination of the mathematical relations between material bodies. Ultimately, he concluded that the causes of these relationships were tied up in the unknowable essences of material objects. He had tugged several links of the chain of knowledge, but his chosen method would carry him no further; unable to proceed, he accepted a mystery. This mystery, even in his own thinking, was a religious quantity; Newton gave all his absolutes, his unknowable essences, a source in the mind of God. As J. H. Randall puts it,

This Divine Sensorium or Mind sustains the entire field of physics, just as the Divine Will, or ether, the vehicle of force, holds the system of moving masses together. . . .
. . . Newton's procedures implied that the concern of science was with mathematical relations in the experienced world. Yet his empirical logic drove him to assume that the terms of those relations [the causes] are not in the experienced world at all, and yet are the only reality. The absolute masses of classical mechanics, instead of being

---

* See MS 140, c. 31, fol. 99, in the Bodleian Library, Oxford. Among other religious works, Newton left behind him a manuscript entitled *Observations on the Prophecies of Daniel and the Apocalypse of St. John.*

** "Newton the Man," *The Royal Society,* Newton Tercentenary Celebrations, 1947, p. 29, as quoted in Giorgio De Santillana and Hertha von Dechend, *Hamlet's Mill* (Boston: Gambit, Inc., 1969), p. 9.

taken as mathematical abstractions or isolates, were regarded as the sole components of nature. Here is a cardinal illustration of what Whitehead called "the fallacy of misplaced concreteness."*

Locke, who was born into the same world as Newton, lacked any concept of such a fallacy. Quite the contrary. He saw reflected in Newton's physics a radically new and, for him, entirely correct concept of the nature of individual man and of his relation to nature, religion, and the state. According to this physics, nature was a system of physical objects, located in an infinitely extending, absolute space and related in their motions by empirically investigable and verifiable laws. The two men complemented each other in the construction of an epistemology and a metaphysic to sustain this new concept of a physical universe inhabited by man.

Newton called the objects of his physics "material substances." The qualities of these objects, their colors, sounds, odors, and warmth, do not belong to the material objects themselves, but rather are "mere appearances projected back upon the material object by the observer."** These objects, he continued, in some sense exist in two different kinds of space and time:

ONE, that which he called "absolute . . . true and . . . mathematical" space and time: the single, public space of nature, which has the same mathematical and geometrical properties always and everywhere; and a public time, which "flows equably without relation to anything external."

TWO, that which he called "relative . . . apparent . . . sensible" space and time; the space and time that frame the sense-experience of the individual.

The critical question for Newton and Locke (and indeed for us) was: What is the relationship between the sensed qualities in sensed space and time, and physical objects (material substances) in absolute space and time?

Newton gave a controversial answer:

The warmth which we sense in the stove, the fragrance which we smell in the rose, and the red which we see on the flag, do not belong to the material objects at all, independently of the presence of the observer.

---

* Randall, *op. cit.,* pp. 591 and 589.
** F. S. C. Northrop, *The Meeting of East and West* (New York: The Macmillan Co., 1946), p. 75.

. . . Nature is composed only of colorless, odorless physical atoms located in a public mathematical space and time which is quite different from the relative private space and time which one immediately senses.*

For him, sensed qualities in relative space and time depended entirely on the observer and ceased to exist if he was removed; the real, absolute material substances in absolute space and time could be known by man only via these sensed and relative qualities.

As a result of this debate, Newton propounded a three-termed relationship. First are the real, rationally conceived, absolute physical objects persisting in absolute, mathematical space and time. These are known directly by God alone and only theoretically by man. They are revealed only through the second term—the observer—who perceives them as sensed qualities in relative, apparent, private space and time, which is the third term in the relationship. It follows that the public world of absolute space, time, and matter is the same for everyone; the private world of apparent sensed qualities is different for everyone, since it depends upon the observer. The nexus between private space and time and public space and time seemed to Newton and Locke to be man himself, who participates in both, touching the relationship with his senses and the absolute with his mind.

This formulation had an important consequence: Locke redefined man in such a way that he *does* participate in both the public and private worlds. Man is composed of two parts, he said. The first is his body and the property he owns, which are made up of many material substances or atoms. The second is a single, indestructible, immortal, mental substance, a "tabula rasa" or consciousness, his soul, his political person. Furthermore, he said, one man's mental substance is as good as another's. Through this consciousness, material objects in absolute space and time make their impression, become perceived and known, and one man's impressions and knowledge, again, are as good as another's.

This definition of man led to new concepts of religion and the state. It clearly required complete religious toleration, for example. In his *Letter Concerning Toleration,* Locke wrote:

The only narrow way which leads to heaven is not better known to the magistrate than to private persons, and therefore I cannot safely take him for my guide, who may probably be as ignorant of the way

* *Ibid.,* pp. 76–8.

as myself, and is certainly less concerned for my salvation than I myself am. . . . The care, therefore, of every man's soul belongs unto himself, and is to be left unto himself.*

Since religion has to do only with the

introspectively given personal, private mental substance, the care of souls cannot belong to the civil magistrate, because his power consists only in outward force. . . . Nor can any such power be vested in the magistrate by the consent of the people, because no man can so far abandon the care of his own salvation as blindly to leave to the choice of any other . . . to prescribe to him what faith or worship he shall embrace.**

Lockean scientific and philosophical theory says nothing about the relation between the many mental substances or persons. It therefore drew out no prescribed social laws, either of God or nature. It concluded that the laws of ecclesiastical or civil governments were mere conventions, deriving their sole authority from the private opinions of the independent atomic individuals and their joint majority consent. Locke shows none of the organic social principles of Aristotle, for whom man is in his essential nature a political animal.† There is none of the idealism of Kant, who fought his way through the distinctions between private relatives and public absolutes to a vision of community, the Kingdom of Ends, and to a moral philosophy based around that concept. In Locke, indeed, there simply are no criteria for communitarian existence.

Locke's view of Newton's three-termed relation thus led him to conclude that the individual person is absolutely free and independent, and that there are no principles grounded in the nature of mental substances that allow the state anything more than conventional status. The two basic premises of Locke's theory of government and the American Declaration of Independence arose from this: All men are born free and equal; and the origin and basis of government is in the consent of the governed.††

When Locke spoke of equality of persons he was referring to their mental substances. The obvious inequalities between Einstein and a moron arise, he would have said, from the different structures of the bodies or material substances of the two. This

---

* John Locke, *A Letter Concerning Toleration,* edited by C. L. Sherman (New York: Appleton-Century Co., 1937), pp. 186–7.
** *Ibid.,* pp. 185–6.   † Northrup, *op. cit.,* p. 88.   †† *Ibid.,* p. 93.

difference in no way alters the legal relationship of man to the state. "Here lies," says Northrop, "in considerable part, the basis of modern man's conviction that regardless of his brain, his social status, his birth, or his accomplishments—even though, in a given instance, all these be negligible—he is as good as anybody else."*

Newton's philosophy and Locke's derivations from it were shortly challenged by the utilitarian onslaughts of Bishop Berkeley. Berkeley attacked Newton's three-termed relationship directly. He argued that if one accepts Locke's conclusion that all meanings derive from sensed data or their association, then an absolute material substance—a physical object, say—is nothing more than an *association of certain sensed data* in a mental substance— someone's mind. It is therefore quite different from the absolute, colorless entity that Newton and Locke had described. Yet Newtonian physics and Lockean theory assume the absolute reality of material substances. Hence the fundamental philosophical assumptions of Newton and Locke are faulty.

David Hume saw Berkeley's point but disagreed with his method; Hume also understood the obvious values in Newton's and Locke's theories. So he attempted a reconstruction of their epistemology. Kant thought Hume guilty of procedural errors in his thinking, and deplored the lack of an ethical dimension; he set out to construct a parallel but improved view of the universe. Bentham, Fichte, Mill, Hegel, Marx, and eventually every other European philosopher joined the fray in one way or another, but none was entirely successful in presenting an acceptable view of man in the world.**

The New Individual

It was this inadequacy which led the pragmatists, particularly in America, to abandon the philosophy of Europe as a basis for action in the real world. The pragmatists failed, however, to perceive three critical factors: the lingering aura of Newtonian metaphysics which surrounds his scientific method, so central to our society; the resilience of Lockean ideology, which has survived without much explicit argument in this country; and the

* *Ibid.*, p. 94. ** *Ibid.*, p. 113.

inadequacy of pragmatism to help us meet the need for ideological change today. To be sure, Newton would be shocked and dismayed to see the narrow specialization of the modern scientist, a man concerned with pure objects and objective, experimental truth. Locke would be amazed that a society of equals, as we proclaim ourselves, devotes much communal wealth to welfare programs. Both would doubtless be taken aback by the pragmatic principle that concentration on the parts will do well enough, that the whole will somehow take care of itself. Yet it is through this principle that their legacy has lately evolved, with all the consequent distortions I have noted. In fact, it has taken the hydrogen bomb and a general ecological crisis to alert us to the error in this beloved principle and to compel us to return to Newton's search for a means to grasp the whole.

Pragmatically, we have ignored the need for an integrated or holistic view of the world. The time has now come when we can no longer do so. The scientist cannot be left to devise our undoing, however unwittingly. Government cannot be left a fragmented collection of parts inadequate either to define or to meet the needs of the community. Academe cannot wash its hands of the need for synthesis; physics, genetics, biology, psychology, and more must be coordinated and somehow "brought to bear." These are only a few of the cries of our time, and to answer them we need a renovated ideology. We may choose to discard Newton's conception of absolutes, or of God, or of a Divine Plan, but we must substitute a workable equivalent. And whatever this alternative turns out to be, it must clarify the role of the individual within the new structure of his political, social, and economic universe. The question of his role was raised in the critical moments of the seventeenth century; it has never been resolved. Today, as in the seventeenth century, thoughts and events are again coinciding to force a transformation. Today, as then, the relation between economic life—business and technology—and its sociopolitical context are central issues. Today, as then, new institutions and structures are upon us and countless consequent events and circumstances in the offing.

These new structures are perceived as useful, as were those of the new middle class in the sixteenth and seventeenth centuries. They are also inconsistent with, and even shocking to, the traditional ideology. Large organizations have, for example, been efficient in utilizing technology and exploiting resources; large concentrations of people in cities are a convenience if not a necessity; modern society demands complexity, and complexity in turn requires political institutions capable of analysis, planning, and choice. These structures and their halo of effects represent a radical departure from the ideas with which our age was born, particularly the Lockean notions of individualism, property, and the limited state. No one man—Lockean, Darwinian, economic, or otherwise—can possibly analyze, plan, and choose on such a scale, even for himself. And yet it is still to those very ideas of individualism, private property, and a weak central government to which we look for explanation, justification, legitimization, and control of our structures and institutions.

At the same time, the promised land of the Lockean ideology is for most remote indeed. For the poor, the black, the Mexican-American, the assembly-line worker, for many women, most city dwellers, and many young people, old-style individualism isn't working. Some call for the alteration of our institutions to make individualism work: break up the large organization, they say; splinter and disintegrate the political order, return to the country-side and nature, renounce government planning as an authoritarian menace. Appealing as such a call may be, it strangely resembles the futile protests of a medieval pope against the rise of science. And while such a concept has occasionally worked for us, in pure form, its time has passed. John Wayne represents a fitting myth for wilderness America, but walking down a city street, his six-guns blazing, he would be something of a menace. If the needs of society are inexorable and the trends of social organization inevitable, then we must change the institutions through which those needs are met.

In his remarkable history of Western thought, J. H. Randall sees a new structure being built within the ruins of the old. But he has found this structure "quite irrelevant to the whole ideology of freedom and individuality." We have, he said, "to buck the whole current of our long intellectual tradition to retrace our steps and recover a new form of collectivism adequate to our industrial age."*

---

* John Herman Randall, Jr., *The Career of Philosophy*, vol. 1, paperback ed. (New York and London: Columbia University Press, 1970), p. 18.

By "collectivism," Randall presumably meant that sense of community, that recognition of the organic nature of society and of the interaction of all things within the whole, which marked the pre-Lockean era. To contemplate such a communitary way, to discard the old individualism, causes understandable dismay among many: young and old, conservative and liberal. Anomie, alienation, confusion, and frustration mark our era. And if we look at the last time such a transformation took place in Western thought, in the seventeenth century, we can see comparable unrest. Heretics were burned, the stubborn racked, revolutionaries imprisoned and exiled. We may be in for the same. Hopefully, we can make the transition less painfully. Certainly the sooner we recognize its dimensions, the better off we shall be. There is much in the individualism of the Enlightenment which is glorious, just as there is much about Randall's collective which is odious; our task is to find a new synthesis that, as much as possible, saves the glorious and excludes the odious.

We have to unravel the roots of our traditional ideology, examine its assumptions and the context of its making, inspect its evolution through history, test it, and seek a new set of assumptions upon which to base our changing social order. And for a start, we must turn again to the thoughts of Locke, particularly as they relate to the real world and the institution of property.

John Locke (1632–1704) appears in his papers and in Peter Laslett's biography as a man most unlikely to have marked the world so deeply. And yet in many ways he is the typical paradigm changer described by Thomas S. Kuhn (see Chapter 1). Maverick, amateur, neither committed to nor accepted by the institutions of his time, Locke was no more a part of the ruling group than he was one of the ruled. He was a lonely, timid, introverted, asthmatic bachelor, described in Laslett's words as "an independent, free-moving intellectual, aware as others were not of the direction of social change."* Not a great man in the heroic sense, Locke lived during extraordinary times and was peculiarly well suited and situated to observe, understand, and record what was happen-

---

* Peter Laslett, *Locke's Two Treatises of Government: A Critical Edition with an Introduction and Apparatus Criticus* (Cambridge, England: Cambridge University Press, 1967), p. 44.

ing. He was both a doer and a thinker, involved in the hurly-burly of revolutionary English politics and at the same time capable of standing apart from it. He described the events, interpreted them, and integrated them philosophically with the scientific insights of his contemporary and friend, Newton. He was able to serve as the instrument through which the experience of change in the world of post-Cromwellian England could be clarified and explained, and as the synthesizer through whose mind that experience could be provided with the conceptual foundation needed to make it legitimate and continuing. He found roots for experience in science and philosophy, describing the tree that grew so that it could be planted elsewhere.

Locke came of a middle-class Puritan family; his grandfather had done well as a cloth contractor and, as Cicero advised so long before, had purchased an estate.* His father was a Calvinist attorney who served as a captain in Oliver Cromwell's army. Locke was seventeen when Cromwell beheaded Charles I because of the latter's stubborn insistence on maintaining traditional notions of the monarchy and religion. Three years later, in 1652, he arrived at Oxford, says Laslett, "urbane, idle, unhappy and unremarkable."** He was to spend some thirty years off and on at Oxford, but it was a marginal existence. Not being a very good student, he "found a way out in medicine," taking up botany, and duly received his bachelor's degree. Although even as an old man he was prescribing cures for breast cancer, designing trusses, and advising midwives, he never became a full doctor of medicine.† He hated teaching but somehow managed to "wriggle his way" into a faculty position at Christ Church. It is doubtful that the philosophy department even knew of his existence; not until the next century did Oxford teachers acknowledge his books in the classroom. Even then he must have presented a substantial prob-

---

* Puritanism then was the religion of those whom Michael Walzer describes as "the sociologically competent . . . those who *had* been called." It was also the religion of the economically prosperous, those who were "extraordinarily sensitive to the dangers of disorder and wickedness"—*The Revolution of the Saints: A Study in the Origins of Radical Politics* (Cambridge, Mass.: Harvard University Press, 1965), pp. 218, 225.

** Laslett, *op. cit.*, p. 18.

† See Locke, *Miscellaneous Notes,* Manuscript Room, Bodleian Library Oxford.

lem to the curriculum planners because in truth he was not really a political philosopher at all. He was rather, "the writer of a work of intuition, insight and imagination, if not of profound originality, who was also a theorist of knowledge. . . ."*

Any interest Locke may have had in politics or philosophy seems to have been quite pedestrian until by chance in 1667, at the age of thirty-five, he met Anthony Ashley Cooper. Lord Ashley, later to become the first Earl of Shaftesbury, was Chancellor of the Exchequer and one of the ablest men in England at the time. Charles II was on the throne, attempting to revive the authority of the crown as well as to reinstate the power of the Roman Church. Cromwell had been dead eight years and Ashley represented the leader of the forces of Parliament, Puritanism, and toleration.

Fire and plague had swept London and Ashley had come to Oxford with an ailing liver to take the waters.** The physician who was to have brought them to him in twelve bottles was unavailable, and so the job fell to Locke. One thing led to another, and Locke directed an operation on Ashley's abdomen, involving the insertion of a silver pipe, which miraculously seemed to do him good. So a famous friendship developed without which it is doubtful that Locke's works on *Toleration* and *Government* would have been written.

Benefiting from many conversations with Shaftesbury, Locke had a first-hand view of England's transformation from monarchical absolutism to parliamentary democracy. He lived with Shaftesbury for fifteen years, acting as his speech writer and pamphleteer, turning out long notes on the issues of the day: religion, the rights of Parliament, the nature of the individual, questions of property, and the like. Both he and Shaftesbury were prominent in a variety of plots and conspiracies, including the efforts to force Charles to exclude his Catholic brother, James, from the succession.† Shaftesbury was arrested for sedition in 1681 and died in exile in Holland the following year. In 1684 Locke, also in exile, was expelled from Christ Church by Charles II for "factious and disloyal behavior."†† In a complaint to the Earl of Pembroke written from Amsterdam and dated December

---

* Laslett, *op. cit.,* pp. 23, 24, and 85.
** *Ibid.,* p. 25.   † *Ibid.,* pp. 27, 31.   †† Christ Church MS 375.

8, 1684, Locke denied the charge and thought it hard that "having reaped so little advantage from his association with Shaftesbury in the latter's lifetime he should suffer so much on that account now he is dead."* This is perhaps one of history's more blatant displays of ingratitude, even though self-preservation in a dangerous time may have justified it. In any case, with the Glorious Revolution of 1688–9, Locke returned from exile something of a hero, his ideas having been taken as the foundation for the reforms that were introduced by the new government of William and Mary.

It is important if we are to understand the role and function of such a person in our own day to note that Locke was not an inventor, hardly even an innovator. He was a perceptive and reasonably profound recorder of what had actually occurred ideologically in seventeenth-century England. The purpose of his *Treatises of Government* was to vindicate what had happened— the Convention Parliament, the English Revolution, and the refutation of absolute monarchy. His *Letters on Toleration* likewise set down what had come to be accepted after one hundred years of bloody struggle—liberty of conscience and religious toleration. Incidentally, he made two important exceptions: atheists are not to be tolerated, since "the taking away of God dissolves all"; and the Church of Rome must be repudiated, because of its unnatural allegiance to a foreign sovereign. He was more than a historian, however, because he established the connecting links between events and values so that the events became legitimate. In this sense he was, by our definition, an ideologist. That he was so successful a one is perhaps partly due to the fact that he was greatly helped by the liberating ideas which came from the new science. Voltaire said of him, "He is helped everywhere by the torch of physics. . . ."**

Locke's originality as ideologist lay in his extreme use of the doctrine of natural rights: the rights of the individual, the natural right of private property, and the notion that government existed solely to guarantee those rights. These ideas found their way into the law through Sir William Blackstone (1723–1780), and into economic activity through Adam Smith (1723–1790). "The prin-

---

* *Ibid.,* p. 31.
** Lettres philosophiques, Lettre XIII; Lanson, I, pp. 168–9, as quoted in Randall, *op. cit.,* hardbound ed., p. 866.

cipal aim of society," wrote Blackstone, whose influence in America was to be enormous, "is to protect individuals in the enjoyment of those absolute rights which are vested in them by the immutable laws of nature. . . . The first and primary end of human law is to maintain and regulate these absolute rights of individuals."* Locke's individualism was shortly reinforced by Smith's emphasis on man's self-reliance, his "constant effort to better his own condition," which if allowed to progress in a free, competitive environment, would insure a good community.** This belief was at the root of Smith's labor theory of value: "The property which every man has is his own labor, as it is the original foundation of all other property, so it is the most sacred and inviolable."†

Locke's own proclamation of these natural rights was in large part polemic, designed to counter the monarchical theories of Sir Robert Filmer and the Tory court for the purposes of Shaftesbury and his Whig movement. However, that fact does not diminish his commitment to them, nor does it diminish the honest acceptance which they received from the Whigs. These were middle-class businessmen and relatively small landholders.†† The guarantee of their property, both of body and estate, was of dominant importance to the assurance of their political rights as individuals independent of the king, just as it was a safeguard of their economic independence. Locke's dictum that "The great and chief end . . . of Men's uniting into commonwealths, and putting themselves under Government, is the Preservation of their Property,"‡ became an article of faith for many of his contemporaries, and was one of the significant formulations exported to the colonies. Some one hundred years later, Madison echoed it in *The Federalist Papers* in these words: "The protection of these faculties [the diversity in the faculties of men from which the rights of property originate] is the first object of government. From the protection of different and unequal faculties of acquiring property, the possession of different degrees and kinds of property immediately results."

This was a doctrine designed to justify the rights of a rising

---

* *Commentaries,* Book I, Chap. i; as quoted in Randall, *ibid.,* p. 661.
** Randall, *ibid.,* p. 792.
† Adam Smith, *Wealth of Nations,* Book I, Chap. x, Part 2, as quoted in Randall, *ibid.,* p. 661.
†† Laslett, *op. cit.,* pp. 45 and 59.   ‡ *Ibid.,* Second Treatise, Sect. 124.

group of acquisitive entrepreneurs against monarchy. It was, as Polanyi said, "a revolution of the rich against the poor," of aggressive individualism against medieval communitarianism; it was the same drive that would reach such hideous proportions in the Industrial Revolution of the next century. Locke's social philosophy should not be mistaken. He was a determined enemy of beggars and the idle poor, believing that an impoverished family had no right to expect leisure for its children after they passed the age of three.* The conflict between king and Parliament was in part at least based on the desire of the crown to slow down or regulate economic progress until it became socially bearable.** Locke intended that the able among economic men should be given immediate free rein.

The central difficulty with Locke's extreme individualism for us has come to be its possessive quality. No one has revealed this problem more clearly than the Canadian political philosopher C. B. Macpherson. In his enthusiasm to escape medievalism, says Macpherson, Locke developed a "conception of the individual as essentially the proprietor of his own person or capacities, owing nothing to society for them. . . . Society becomes a lot of free equal individuals related to each other as proprietors of their own capacities and of what they acquired by their exercise."† The poor, the deprived, the propertyless, the incapable, the lazy, and the shiftless were set aside. What Locke had done was to base his individualistic conception of property rights on natural right and natural law. Well and good, but he then removed all the old limits inherent in natural law.††

It is instructive to examine how this was done. Locke starts with

---

* Laslett, *op. cit.,* p. 43. It is worth recalling that Locke lived in a day of intense social dislocation. Rapid population growth, the enclosure of rural land, and sheep farming had disrupted the old rural society, sending thousands of beggars onto the roads. Michael Walzer recounts that these beggars "formed a distinct social group, completely alienated from the work-a-day world on whose fringes they dwelt"—*op. cit.,* pp. 199–231. Many poured into the cities, creating problems of crime and unemployment.

** Karl Polanyi, *The Great Transformation* (Boston: Beacon Press Paperback, 1944), pp. 34–8.

† C. B. Macpherson, *The Political Theory of Possessive Individualism: Hobbes to Locke* (Oxford, England: Oxford University Press, 1962), p. 3.

†† *Ibid.,* p. 199.

the medieval position that the earth and its fruits were given originally to mankind in common. Yet, said Locke, "being given for the use of Men, there must of necessity be a means to appropriate them some way or other before they can be of any use . . . to any particular Man." A man must own a piece of earth before it can be any good to him. Locke derives this right from the postulate that "every Man has a Property in his own Person. This no Body has any Right to but himself. The Labour of his Body, and the Work of his Hands, we may say, are properly his." A man obtains a right to property if he mixes his labor with it. Macpherson notes that no consent is needed to justify this kind of appropriation, for, as Locke wrote, "If such a consent as that was necessary, Man had starved, notwithstanding the Plenty God had given him."*

There were, however, limitations which Locke believed natural law imposed on the right to appropriate property:

First, one can own only so much as leaves "enough, and as good . . . in common for others." This limitation is inherent in each man's right to self-preservation. Second, "As much as any one can make use of to any advantage of life before it spoils; so much he may by his labour fix a Property in." There is no justification for waste. Barter of the surplus product of one's labor was, however, permitted by Locke within this limitation.** Third, he limited the right to property to the amount a man can use with his own labor.

In so defining the natural right to property and its limitations, Locke was using primitive agrarian economy as his context. Simply stated, these limitations are open to many objections, some purely logical and others deriving from the political, social, and economic context in which Locke was writing. To meet such objections, Locke devised a number of modifications to his rules. The rule that one must leave "enough and as good in common for others" is clearly rendered inapplicable if population increases sufficiently rapidly in relation to available land. Hence Locke's remark that anyone could exercise his right to property if he were to go to the "vacant places of America."†

In addition, the rule that spoilage of produce and product poten-

---

* See Laslett, *op. cit.,* Second Treatise, Sects. 4, 26–8.
** *Ibid.,* Sects. 27, 31, and 46.   † *Ibid.,* Sect. 36.

tially limits ownership, although provided with the cumbrous safety latch of barter, was a hopelessly agrarian and outdated notion in the England of his time; so Locke unearthed Pluto and supplied property with the attribute of liquidity. Noting that gold and silver do not spoil, he countenanced the "Invention of Money and *the tacit Agreement* of Men to put a value on it . . ."* [Emphasis added].

Furthermore, the accumulation of money is useful to "drive trade" and to serve as capital.** But this modification of a second rule has troublesome consequences. As Macpherson rephrased Locke's argument, "Now that it is possible to exchange any amount of produce for an asset which never spoils, it is neither unjust nor foolish to accumulate any amount of land in order to make it produce a surplus which can be converted to money and used as capital." In other words, money makes possible the ownership and private use of large tracts of land and great property—within the framework of tacit consent—a consequence that would seem to invalidate the natural provision that everyone should have as much as he could make use of.†

In so justifying the capitalist appropriation of land and money, Locke recognized the inevitable inequality in the distribution of wealth that would follow from it, but wrote this off simply to "the necessity of affairs and the constitution of human society."†† Note that this extended right to property and its uses has nothing to do with the community or the state; it derives simply from the natural purposes of men, from their natural rights, and from the "tacit agreement" which they have given to the use of money (an agreement which, it will be remembered, was hardly tacit in the Middle Ages).

Locke overcame the sufficiency limitation on property—that whatever a man appropriates, he must leave as much and as good for others—by using essentially the argument of productivity. In a revision to the third edition of the *Treatises,* he added a new argument:

---

* *Ibid.*
** Locke, "Some Considerations of the Consequences of the Lowering of Interest and Raising the Value of Money," 1691, *Works,* 1759 edition, vol. ii, pp. 22–3, as quoted in Macpherson, *op cit.,* p. 205.
† Macpherson, *op. cit.,* pp. 208 and 204.
†† *Works,* 1759, vol. ii, p. 19, as quoted in Macpherson, *op. cit.,* pp. 206–7.

. . . he who appropriates land to himself by his labour, does not lessen but increase the common stock of mankind. For the provisions serving to the support of humane life, produced by one acre of inclosed and cultivated land, are . . . ten times more, than those, which are yielded by an acre of Land, of an equal richnesse, lyeing wast in common. And therefore he that incloses Land and has a greater plenty of the conveniencys of life from ten acres, than he could have from an hundred left to Nature, may truly be said, to give ninety acres to Mankind. For his labour now supplys him with provisions out of ten acres, which were but the product of an hundred lying in common.*

Locke apparently assumed here that the distribution of benefits gained from the cultivation of large tracts would benefit "mankind," but he is far from explicit as to how this would come about.

The third limitation, that a man shall appropriate only so much as he can tend with his own labor, seems to be the most difficult to reconcile with economic reality then or now, but Locke overcame it with remarkable ease through a reformulation of the wage concept. Since a man's property includes his own person, he has a natural right to alienate (sell) his labor in return for wages. Furthermore, once it is so alienated, that labor becomes the property of him who pays the wage. As with other natural rights, this right of alienation does not depend upon the consent of others. A man's right to property is thus established just as much by the work of labor he has purchased as by his own:

Thus the Grass my Horse has bit; the Turfs my Servant has cut; and the Ore I have digg'd in any place where I have a right to them in common with others, become my Property, without the assignation or consent of any body. The labour that was mine, removing them out of that common state they were in, hath fixed my Property in them.**

This view of a man's labor as a commodity he has an unqualified right to sell was plainly a radical departure from the medieval view that a person's work should be a holy endeavor. With it, Locke laid the basis for the introduction of the idea of contract into the employer-employee relationship and gave it a natural legitimacy—indeed a sanctity—which was beyond the jurisdiction of civil powers.

Locke's exposition and qualification of natural law was, as

---

* Laslett, *op. cit.,* Second Treatise, Sect. 37.

** *Ibid.,* Sect. 28.

Macpherson points out, an achievement of radical significance. In effect, it undermined the traditional view that labor and the ownership of property were social functions; in so doing, it legitimized the break between economic activity and its social and political relationships.

The Emergence of the Lockean Paradox

The breakup was responsible for a paradox that emerged in the Lockean paradigm: that while the only legitimate function of the political and social authorities was to ensure the natural rights of individual citizens, these authorities must, as a practical matter, adjust and control these supposedly primitive and absolute basic rights from a perspective of justice and equality. Hence either there must be a moral viewpoint implicit in these rights, which is to be interpreted by the political and social authority, or there is one that is more basic and more primitive than these rights. The paradox develops in Locke's own writings, for example, when he discusses the lower classes and the unemployed.

In his view, unemployment was an aspect of moral depravity caused by "nothing else but the relaxation of discipline and corruption of manners."* The unemployed had forfeited their rights to full and free membership in the political community and were clearly subject to state action. Such action consisted of commitment to workhouses or worse.** Locke's attitude toward members of the laboring class was similarly condemnatory and severe; he withheld from them the right to revolution which he gives to the majority. To him, they seem almost incapable of reason. For "the day-labourers and tradesmen, the spinsters and dairy-maids . . . hearing plain commands, is the sure and only course to bring them to obedience and practice. The greatest part cannot know, and therefore they must believe."† The poor might deserve help in the

---

* H. R. Fox Bourne, *The Life of John Locke* (New York: Harper & Brothers, 1876, vol. ii), p. 378.

** E. B. Cheyney records in his *History of England* that men and women "strong and fit for labour, but having neither masters nor lawful vocations whereby to get their living" were ordered whipped and then "burnt through the gristle of the right ear" (London, 1926, II), p. 333, as quoted in Walzer, *op cit.*, p. 227.

† *Works*, 1759, vol. ii, p. 580, as quoted in Macpherson, *op. cit.*, p. 225.

form of charity, but it must obviously be administered from a superior moral position.

In general, it is thus apparent, the man without property (whether his body or estate) is without the political rights which Locke normally ascribes to individuals. In fact, he is hardly an individual at all. This ambiguity raises the question whether the Lockean ideology is truly individualistic or whether in fact it is not collectivist, dedicated to a political collective of the acquisitive, the entrepreneurial, and the propertied. Locke saw society as composed of individual proprietors related separately to one another, contracting with one another, buying and selling competitively. Society is thus a market place in which the political order functions in morally (i.e., ideologically) appropriate ways to protect the body and estate of the participants. In certain cases, this means the political order shall function to erase a man's inalienable natural rights. Hence the paradox.

Locke's loophole was the notion of equality, to which he reduced the whole moral dilemma. If a coherent system of political obligation and rights is to be developed from the needs and capacities of individuals without imposing some will or purpose from outside, we must assume that the individuals are capable of acknowledging such obligations and rights; that is, we must assume the individual will exchange his natural rights for political and social rights, just as he can exchange his right to property for a right to wages. "This condition can be met if the society is one in which individuals are capable of seeing themselves as equal in some respect more important than all respects in which they are unequal," writes Macpherson, arguing Locke's brief. "Only in such a society can it be said, and accepted, that there is no reason why any man should claim superior rights. For if men do not acknowledge such equality, they can claim unlimited superiority; claiming this, they cannot be morally bound by any non-supernatural system of obligation."*

And elsewhere,

This condition was fulfilled in the original possessive market society, from its emergence as the dominant form in the seventeenth century until its zenith in the nineteenth, by the apparent inevitability of everyone's subordination to the laws of the market. So long as every-

---

* Macpherson, *op. cit.*, p. 83.

one was subject to the determination of a competitive market, and so long as this apparently equal subordination of individuals to the determination of the market was accepted as rightful, or inevitable, by virtually everybody, there was a sufficient basis for rational obligation of all men to a political authority which could maintain and enforce the only possible orderly human relations, namely, market relations.*

A second condition is

that there be a cohesion of self-interests, among all those who have a voice in choosing the government, sufficient to offset the centrifugal forces of a possessive market society. This condition was fulfilled, in the heyday of the market society, by the fact that a political voice was restricted to a possessing class which had sufficient cohesion to decide periodically, without anarchy, who should have the sovereign power.**

Both conditions were crudely fulfilled in America until the end of the nineteenth century. Then they collapsed, because of the democratic franchise and the formation of interest groups (Macpherson mentions the "working class"), which suppressed individualism and defined and gave expression to intolerable inequalities. Cohesion then came to depend upon the ability of a possessor class (or a coalition of powerholders) to keep effective control in spite of universal suffrage. Macpherson adds, "A temporary substitute for the old cohesion has sometimes been provided in our century by war."† But this has become prohibitively dangerous and costly.

So we come to the dilemma of our society. We are organized around the assumptions and central institutions of possessive individualism. All our institutions are made legitimate by those assumptions, but the evolution and maturation of market society has produced changes in the nature and behavior of those institutions —business, government, interest groups—as well as demographic changes in the organization of people. These changes have dissolved the old cohesion upon which a valid theory of obligation to the political order must rest.

Can we win back the old cohesion by finding some new basis for fundamental equality which would be consistent with the maintenance of what have come to be called liberal institutions and ideology? Need we modify or abandon the ideology—possessive individualism—and seek a new basis for cohesion? Macpherson

---

* *Ibid.*, pp. 272–3. ** *Ibid.*, p. 273.   † *Ibid.*, p. 274.

sees a possible answer in the new "equality of insecurity" which has been created by the techniques of modern war. This may, he says, produce a new supranational sense of obligation to a world order for the sake of survival. But that way lies the powder keg, and so we have to turn elsewhere.

The problem is ideological; I suggest we consider an ideological solution. From the way Locke treated property rights, we can see that he was primarily concerned with outcomes and the justification of outcomes—in other words, with the efficient use of land, with natural rights. It is easy to see how such a view could degenerate into one in which each pursues his own interests with no common standard existing above or guiding the pursuit of those interests. As the sociologist Alvin W. Gouldner points out, such a situation either requires a fundamental harmony of interests among all men or it results in irreconcilable conflict.*

Unfortunately, there are severe tensions inherent within Lockean ideology. In affirming the importance of utility, particularly individualistic and possessive utility, it stresses the importance of the consequences of action. But at the same time, it contends that man has natural rights which are unrelated either to the community or to the consequences of action.** The Lockean position regarding property rights, for example, has led us to a most nonutilitarian conception, namely, that since property is sacred in its own right, men of property deserve power and honor. The appeal such a position may have had when it was used in polemics against aristocratic uselessness and an arbitrary monarch has worn thin. Gouldner speaks of a resulting "drift toward an anomic normlessness. In some part, 'utility' was always a thinly disguised rationalization for avarice and venality and the uninhibited pursuit of self-interest."†

It is not difficult to see how the Lockean paradigm evolved into a set of norms which identified success with the individualistic production of wealth and income. It was further bolstered in the United States by the Protestant dictum that God's blessing was reflected in success in the market place and by the Darwinian notion that it is the fit who survive. In such a context, unemployment is failure, unwillingness to work an outrage, and sheer

---

* Alvin W. Gouldner, *The Coming Crisis of Western Sociology* (New York and London: Basic Books, Inc., 1970), p. 68.

** *Ibid.*, p. 70.   † *Ibid.*, pp. 71, 70.

wealth, earned or unearned, a badge of distinction.* In the market place, emphasis is placed on quantity of sales rather than on the utility of what is sold. Poetry and art are dubious pursuits unless they sell. The disposal and control of useless people is left to the judgment of the state as part of its function in protecting the climate for the individualistic pursuits of the propertied.**

It was these Lockean tenets with their inherent paradox which became the national ideology of America. Time and circumstance have distorted them, but even today they remain remarkably resilient.

Oddly enough, the notion that we have an ideology is a surprise to some. So overwhelming has been the Lockean influence that we have tended to regard its teaching as revealed truth. Americans like to think of themselves as a pragmatic people, doing what needs to be done to meet the problems at hand, objectively analyzing the difficulties, approaching their solution experimentally, doing what works. We regard ideology as something abandoned with the old country, something which serves to trammel up the works of socialists, Communists, and such, but from which we are blessedly free. This attitude has been unquestionably useful; it has allowed for considerable experimentation and flexibility, a high order of social and political change, relative stability, and considerable technological innovation and material achievement.

But it is also basically false and this falsity plagues us. America has been profoundly ideological. In fact, in the history of world communities, it is hard to think of one whose ideology has been more pronounced or powerful. Pragmatism worked only so long as the assumptions of the traditional ideology were intact, providing a coherent, acceptable basis from which to make our pragmatic jumps. Those assumptions have been steadily deteriorating for the last century, and today are in a state of disarray. The institutions which derived legitimacy from the old assumptions have outstripped and subverted them. Consequently, our institutions—political, economic, and cultural—are unstable and unsure, lacking in legitimacy and thus in authority. They have lost the confidence of the community.

It would be simpler to move forward were it not for the fact that, despite its dissolution, the old ideology retains enormous

---

* *Ibid.*, p. 74.   ** *Ibid.*, pp. 76–8.

influence. It lives on as myth, profoundly affecting the decision-makers. As with medievalism, it has lingered on long after the institutions it supported have either fundamentally changed or been found critically wanting. The rooting out of the old ideology thus becomes the necessary first step in the transformation to a new one. The task cannot be deferred. There is revolt in our time, revolt which is deeply divided and contradictory.

On the one hand, it is a romantic plea for the promises of the Enlightenment, for a return to individualism in its purest and most extreme form: Do your own thing now. Go where you please. Indulge yourself. Addict yourself. Escape . . . This is a suicidal cry, doomed to extinction, causing blight on a segment of an entire generation.

On the other, it is a call for a new community, for Randall's collective, for new religious or quasi-religious norms by which to measure the goodness of that community. There is in this movement the hope of resurrection, but it is tinged with the dreadful memories of collective movements in history.

A synthesis of these two extremes is, of course, possible. The philosopher John Rawls, for example, has suggested an approach to synthesis in *A Theory of Justice.* For Rawls, justice is the primary value which must be defined and guaranteed by any society; the organization of the community and its institutions must, therefore, be designed to achieve it. He describes justice as fairness.* Its overriding guarantee is that of self-respect. Justice rests upon two principles. The first is that each person has a right to as much liberty as is consistent with the liberty of others—freedom of speech, freedom to determine one's political and economic environment, and the like. He points out that this first principle is nonutilitarian, since it could well fail to result in the greatest good for the greatest number. Utilitarianism suggests that a society should seek the greatest overall balance of satisfaction, and this could well constrain liberty. Rawls's first principle is also non-Lockean, in that it places individual liberty above property in the ideological hierarchy by which justice is defined.

Rawls's second principle relates to the distribution of wealth and the arrangement of power. Here he disposes of Locke's stran-

---

* John Rawls, *A Theory of Justice* (Cambridge, Mass.: Belknap Press, 1971), pp. 11–17.

gling loophole of equality by recognizing the necessity and justice of inequality. He argues that inequalities of wealth and power are just, but only when they can be reasonably expected to work to the advantage of those who are worst off. He says, "the higher expectations of those better situated are just if and only if they work as part of a scheme which improves the expectations of the least advantaged members of society."* Inequalities, to be just, must also be "attached to positions and offices open to all."** This argument has the great merit of recognizing the fact that we are born with unequal capabilities and qualities and always will be. It establishes the necessity, however, that this natural inequality be put at the service of the community of the whole. As Marshall Cohen said in his review of Rawls's book: "Justice does not require equality, but it does require that men share one another's fate."†

---

* *Ibid.,* p. 75; see also pp. 3, 12, 26, 29, 60, and 150.
** *Ibid.,* pp. 60–1.
† Marshall Cohen, "A Theory of Justice," *The New York Times Book Review,* July 16, 1972, p. 16.

CHAPTER 4 Locke in America—
Public Policy and the Corporation
to 1900

As John Locke was writing in England, an almost perfect laboratory for his ideology was opening up on the shores of America. The circumstances were ideal for the reception of his thought: boundless land, unlimited resources, a ready challenge to the ingenuity, initiative, and self-reliance of individuals, huge rewards, and a population of diligent people for whom work was sacred.

To start with, the several American communities were rooted in various reformed versions of medieval ideology. In Massachusetts, for example, there was a communal society, pre-Lockean, governed by a Puritan magistracy, which was committed to the foundation of a religious utopia freed from Old World corruption. Strict laws banned strangers from the pristine settlements of Massachusetts and the champions of God did daily battle with Mammon. The battle lines became somewhat blurred, however, as the teachings of Calvin moved inexorably to bestow God's blessing upon those who were diligent and successful in the market place.

Business was good, and by 1700 the merchants of Boston and roundabout had broken the lines of the older order. Trade and commerce required access to Europe; shipyards and other production facilities required workers. The new entrepreneurs—like their counterparts abroad—resented the strictures of the traditional religious hierarchy. As Bernard Bailyn puts it, "Persecution, a growing number of merchants discovered, was simply bad for trade. It 'makes us stinke every wheare,' the business-minded George Downing wrote to [John] Winthrop, Jr."*

---

* Bernard Bailyn, *The New England Merchants in the Seventeenth Century* (Cambridge, Mass.: Harvard University Press, 1955), pp. 105–6, 134–9.

The Ideology:
Five Seeds on Fertile Ground

During the next two hundred years, largely as a result of the workings of economic enterprise, Locke's ideology came to be a most useful, complete, and precise rationale for synthesizing thought and circumstances in America and for legitimizing the institutions which grew from that synthesis. To tame and exploit the vast, lonely wilderness in which only the fit survived was a task that meshed perfectly with Locke's idea of individual fulfillment through aggressive and self-reliant struggle. Society was an atomistic and egalitarian construct, following the findings of Newton in the physical world; it was not the organic, hierarchical whole of the Middle Ages, and the very nature of the colonial environment tended to guarantee, by selection, that those who came to these shores and survived would be those who were willing and able to live by the ideas of individualism. Buttressed by a supernatural faith in the rightness of the Puritan cause, individualism became a cherished principle; it was rooted deep in both the Declaration of Independence and the Constitution, where it was strengthened by the sanctity of the contract and the guarantee of equality.

The natural right to private property, handmaiden to individualism, assumed transcendent importance early in our history as a guarantee both of political independence and power and of economic subsistence. John Adams spoke for all in the Massachusetts Bay Colony when he said that people were free "in proportion to their property." In a proposed constitution for the colony, he suggested that a restriction be placed on the amounts of land an individual could acquire in order to broaden the base upon which economic and political power rested. He took Locke in his purest and most literal form, confident that if "a division of land into small quantities" enabled all to hold property, "the multitude will take care of the liberty, virtue, and interest of the multitude, in all acts of government."* The fact was that in early America there was land enough for virtually everyone to hold it—unless, of

---

* John Adams, *Works,* IX, 377, as quoted in Oscar Handlin and Mary Flug Handlin, *Commonwealth* (Cambridge, Mass.: Belknap Press, 1969), p. 29.

course, one was indentured, black, and Indian, or a woman.* The notion of equality could thus be sustained without difficulty; private property for all became, not just a rebellious cry, but a noble reality. St. John de Crèvecoeur's *Letters from an American Farmer* provides rhapsodic evidence of its importance:

> The instant I enter on my own land, the bright idea of property, of exclusive right, of independence exalts my mind. Precious soil, I say to myself, by what singular creator is it that thou hast made me to constitute the riches of the freeholder? What should we farmers be without the distinct possession of the soil? It feeds, it clothes us, from it we draw even a great exuberancy, our best mead, our richest drink, the very honey of our bees comes from this privileged spot. No wonder we should thus cherish its possession, no wonder that so many Europeans who have never been able to say that such portion of land was theirs, cross the Atlantic to realize that happiness. This formerly rude soil has been converted by my father into a pleasant farm, and in return it has established all our rights; on it is found our rank, our freedom, our power as citizens, our importance as inhabitants of such a district. These images I must confess I always behold with pleasure, and extend them as far as my imagination can reach: for this is what may be called the true and only philosophy of an American farmer.**

Implicit in early America's conception of property rights was the assumption that if each individual used his property for his own self-interest, a good community would result. Adam Smith formulated this notion best in the *Wealth of Nations* (1776). In effect, Smith said, what is good for the individual is good for the community. He combined the ideas of individualism and property with economic profit and demonstrated their advantages for the community as a whole. The main device to assure this happy outcome was competition: staunchly self-interested property owners were to use their property to compete to satisfy individual consumer desires in the market place. From such a process would come an efficient economy and a good community—such was the law of nature.

Thus the first three components of our Lockean-based ideology, individualism, the right to private property, and the mechanism of competition to control the uses of property, fell naturally into place.

---

* Quoted in Clinton Rossiter, *Seedtime of the Republic* (New York: Harcourt, Brace & World, Inc., 1953), pp. 70–1.
** De Crèvecoeur, *Letters from an American Farmer,* 1782, pp. 24–5, as quoted in Rossiter, *ibid,* p. 75.

The fourth of the Lockean components, the limited state, also followed naturally. In such a setting, the role of government was clearly to protect a man's body and property. Moving beyond this limitation would constitute an interference with the natural working of things and so curtail freedom and liberty. The Federalist Paper No. 51 spoke of the need to design controls over the power of government so "that the private interests of every individual may be a sentinel over the public rights."

And it is obvious that the fifth component, scientific specialization, would also flourish in such a setting. The need for inventions, new techniques, and ingenuity to exploit the vast resources of America with only a handful of people was a powerful natural spur to the urgent pursuit of science for practical ends. Americans followed the Newtonian way and took nature apart to learn how to use and control it. There was a clear belief that one could tinker at will with the parts and that somehow the whole would still be there, miraculously taking care of itself.

Locke's ideas came to America in extreme form through the hands of both English and American pamphleteers and essayists. His personal importance in revolutionary America can scarcely be overestimated. "Most Americans had absorbed Locke's work as a kind of political gospel," says Carl Becker.* Josiah Quincy, Jr., in his last will, dated 1774, left Locke's works to his son, "when he shall arrive to the age of fifteen years," adding, "May the spirit of liberty rest upon him!"** Thomas Jefferson in a letter to Dr. Benjamin Rush named Bacon, Newton, and Locke as "the three greatest men the world has ever produced. . . ."† Locke's influence is clear in the Declaration of Independence; so clear in fact, that Richard H. Lee was led to charge that Jefferson had copied from Locke's treatise on *Government.* Jefferson denied the charge of copying but added: "I did not consider it as any part of my charge to invent new ideas altogether and to offer no

---

* Carl Becker, *The Declaration of Independence* (New York: Alfred A. Knopf, Inc., 1964), p. 27.
** *Last Will and Testament of Josiah Quincy, Jr.,* 1774, as quoted in Bernard Bailyn, *The Ideological Origins of the American Revolution,* (Cambridge, Mass.: Belknap Press, 1967), p. 22.
† Adrienne Koch and William Peden, eds., *The Life and Selected Writings of Thomas Jefferson* (New York: The Modern Library, 1944), p. 609.

sentiment which had ever been expressed before."* Locke and his theories were part of the air the founders of this country breathed.

As we have seen, much of the power of Locke derived from the contention that the rights he asserted were in and of the nature of things. They were in fact God's law. Furthermore, in America they were energized by the Calvinist notion that hard work represented the holy life, that a man's predestined place in heaven was indicated by his material well-being on earth. The poor man was poor because of himself, his laziness or avarice or prodigality; the individual and the will were responsible, not the community.**

Traditional American ideology was thus fused with religion. It constituted a single, integrated, and synthetic body of belief for which the new country was a providential testing place. It became the driving force behind the sense of mission which until very recently has been such a compelling force in sustaining America's conception of herself in the world. It provided the criteria for the design of our institutions, especially business, and gave to the United States a sense of confidence and security rarely duplicated in modern history. The closest comparison perhaps is Mao's China. There too we see an enormously powerful ideology, born in struggle and revolution, suffused with religious fervor, providing the cohesive force for the design, creation, and legitimization of organizations and institutions.†

Nevertheless, the tensions between God and Mammon which marked our Puritan beginnings were clearly still present some two hundred years later when Andrew Carnegie wrote: "Thirty-three and an income of $50,000 per annum! . . . Whatever I engage in I must push inordinately. . . . To continue much longer overwhelmed by business cares and with most of my thoughts wholly upon the way to make more money in the shortest time, must

---

* Letter to John Adams, as quoted in Becker, *op. cit.,* p. 25.

** John W. Clark, S.J., *Religion and the Moral Standards of American Businessmen* (Cincinnati: South-Western Publishing Co., 1966), pp. 4–7. See also Max Weber, *Essays in Sociology,* translated and edited by H. H. Gerth and C. Wright Mills (New York: Oxford University Press, 1946), pp. 302–22; and R. H. Tawney, *Religion and the Rise of Capitalism* (New York: Harcourt, Brace & Co., Inc., 1926).

† See Franz Schurmann, *Ideology and Organization in Communist China* (Berkeley and Los Angeles: University of California Press, 1968), Introduction and Chap. 1.

degrade me beyond hope of permanent recovery. I will resign business at thirty-five."* Carnegie overcame his inhibitions, but not without an ideological struggle. He had to convince himself that his work and the institutional forms which grew from it were consistent with God's law. Locke's version of that law was exactly what he needed for the purpose, especially as it was expanded in the *Wealth of Nations* which came to America in full force in 1825 with the publication of John McVicker's *Outlines of Political Economy.* This version served to legitimize the general laissez-faire upsurge following the Civil War, building on the already deeply planted Lockean themes of individualism, property rights, competition, division of labor, and the limited state. It was in this period that Polanyi's gap between economic activity and its political and social relationships became most manifest. The corporation and the entrepreneur became by natural right the sacred agents of economic growth, which was in and of itself good.

Their medium was competition. The principle of competition was for E. L. Godkin an impermeable economic law, "the law by which Providence secures the progress of the human race. . . . It is a law of human nature."** And the pursuit of profit is the immutable law of individualistic incentive. Some, of course, benefit more than others, and this depends upon certain qualities: intelligence, thrift, postponement of gratification, hard work. But these are qualities which, as Horatio Alger's heroes were to demonstrate, can be developed by even the most humble. Here again, thanks are due to the beautiful workings of natural law. Charles Elliott Perkins, president of the Chicago, Burlington and Quincy Railroad, whose formal education ceased short of college but who by the age of twenty had read and assimilated Locke, Smith, Ricardo, Malthus, Darwin, and the Bible, took to task those who in the name of social justice complained about the inequality of the distribution of the fruits of industry:

They are not equally distributed, but it does not follow they are unjustly distributed. Is the rainfall unjustly distributed when an honest

---

* B. J. Hendrick, *The Life of Andrew Carnegie*, vol. 1, pp. 146–7, as quoted in Edward Chase Kirkland, *Dream and Thought in the Business Community, 1860–1900* (Ithaca, N.Y.: Cornell University Press, 1956), pp. 9–10.

** E. L. Godkin, "Cooperation," *North American Review* CVI, January 1868, p. 173, as quoted in Kirkland, *ibid.,* p. 20.

farmer loses his crop by drouth? Is the law of gravitation unjust when a child accidentally falls out of a second-story window and is injured for life? . . .*

In principle, as Locke had noted two hundred years before, government was an unfortunate interference with the working of these natural laws. It introduced uncertainty. Politics and politicians were a disturbance, and an expensive one at that. "Our governors, all over the world, are at Sisyphus's work," lamented Carnegie, "ever rolling the stone uphill to see it roll back to its proper bed at the bottom."** The great defect of government is that it seeks to impose statutes upon the workings of the economy instead of relying upon the divine inexorabilities of the natural law.

During the 1880's, the Lockean basis for laissez-faire capitalism received an important boost from the notion of natural selection revealed by Charles Darwin. Darwin's discoveries were translated into human terms by the English sociologist Herbert Spencer, who argued that, as with animals, so with men—the fit survive. Here was further proof of the natural rightness of a society ruled by competition without government interference in which each individual fends for himself. Any deviation from the ideological party line was put down with nearly hysterical indignation.

Spencer was indeed the ghost of Locke, but he spoke in such extreme terms that he might have shocked his earthly ancestor. His *Social Statics,* first published in America in 1865, had such influence that forty years later Justice Holmes felt obliged to remind the Supreme Court (in the Lochner case) that "the Fourteenth Amendment does not enact Mr. Herbert Spencer's *Social Statics.*" His trip through America in 1882 was a triumphal tour, his doctrine greeted with religious enthusiasm. Railing against social legislation as an infringement upon individual rights and the sanctity of the contract, Spencer feared for the worst. "We are on the highway to Communism, and I see no likelihood that the movement in that direction will be arrested."†

---

* As quoted in Kirkland, *ibid.,* p. 23.
** Andrew Carnegie, *Triumphant Democracy; or Fifty Years' March of the Republic,* p. 48, as quoted in Kirkland, *ibid.,* p. 122.
† Max Lerner, "The Triumph of Laissez-Faire," in *Paths of American Thought,* edited by Arthur M. Schlesinger, Jr., and Morton White (Boston: Houghton Mifflin Co., 1963), pp. 147–66. See also Ralph Henry Gabriel, *The Course of American Democratic Thought* (New York: The Ronald Press Co., 1940), pp. 162–75.

The cry of "socialism" was frequently used to scare off those who would interfere. Edward Atkinson, a pioneer in industrial insurance and cotton textiles, argued in 1877 that legislation regulating the terms and conditions of labor, hours of work, interest rates, and the like was part of "the hardly disguised socialistic movements of the present day."* Government had no business, for example, interfering with the God-given right of a twelve-year-old girl to sell her labor to a mill owner for ten or twelve hours a day. This was an individualistic right of contract ordained by nature. The purpose of government, again as Locke said, was to remove obstructions to the operation of natural laws.

In this context, it is clear that the Sherman Antitrust Act (1890) was ideologically completely different in spirit from such social legislation as the child labor laws or the Pure Food and Drug Act. The antitrust laws indeed were quite consistent with Lockean principles, permitting government to ensure market competition so that the satisfaction of individual consumer desires might itself regulate business activity. Social legislation, on the other hand, represented direct intervention by government to regulate economic activity according to some communitarian vision of justice.

As the attacks on the abuses of big business mounted toward the turn of the century, business leadership answered in some ways much as it does today, reminding America that business is the temple of our traditional ideology, from where all blessings flow. The iron-master Abram S. Hewitt, Peter Cooper's son-in-law, protested popular hostility to business:

It is curious that the mass of the people of this country should fail to recognize their best friends, because corporations have been the only barrier between the despotism of ignorance and the invasion of the rights of property. Doubtless they abuse their privileges at times, but they alone have the ability and the courage to resist attack, and they are doing the work which was done by Jefferson and Madison in the early years of the Republic.**

Implicit here is the belief that business is the embodiment and protector of the American ideology. It is thus as important po-

---

* As quoted in Kirkland, *op. cit.,* pp. 124–25.
** Letter to R. D. Haislip, June 16, 1898, as quoted in Kirkland, *op. cit.,* p. 127.

litically and socially as it is economically: What's good for General Motors is indeed good for the United States. By being efficient, profitable, and competitive, business is by definition socially responsible because it is the very embodiment of what is socially good.

Business was generally successful at that time in persuading elected officials of the rightness of this myth of omnipotence. But there was always the nagging tension from the folks at home. As Senator W. B. Allison of Iowa told Edward Atkinson, when the latter sought to pressure him on a money bill, "I always like to vote, if I can, so as not to be called upon to explain too much at home."* Businessmen tended to regard such "spinelessness" as "pandering to the caprices" of constituents.** Given the unwieldiness of legislatures, businessmen have found governors and presidents generally more open to their arguments and less ruled by "narrow interests." Judges too, being a well-educated lot, were presumed capable of understanding and sustaining the logic of the natural laws.

American businessmen's concern for legitimacy and their conviction of the prominence of their institution in the American scheme of things has tended to make them singularly aware of the need to educate people about business. The United States is the home of the business schools, and businessmen have as a rule resented resistance to the truth of their teachings. In 1907, for example, Charles Elliott Perkins wrote: "How much good has been done by the talkers? [James J.] Hill has been talking and telling the truth for the last two or three years, but it has not produced any good effect."† One cannot help but be reminded of Richard C. Gerstenberg's complaint in *The New York Times* in 1972 that "the average American has only a hazy idea of what free enterprise means, and much less how it works." Gerstenberg, then chairman of General Motors, went on to attribute to the public's ignorance the lowering ratings of business in public opinion polls,

---

* Letter from W. B. Allison to Edward Atkinson, Atkinson Papers, March 8, 1867, as quoted in Kirkland, *op. cit.,* p. 128.
** Letter from J. E. Horr to Edward Atkinson, Atkinson Papers, 1867(?), as quoted in Kirkland, *op. cit.,* p. 129.
† Letter to H. L. Higginson, March 20, 1907, as quoted in Kirkland, *op. cit.,* p. 134.

poor productivity, and increased government regulation. He suggested that more and better education about "free enterprise" was needed.*

Businessmen, of course, have never been reluctant to call in the political order to protect, promote, and insulate their interests. Governmental commissions have been a favorite tool for such work. The Chicago Board of Trade, for example, caught between agrarian agitation and the pricing practices of railroads running to the seaboard, called for such a commission in 1884, citing the need for "high minded and competent men, wielding the strong arm of national authority, to prevent a reckless competition for traffic, and to adjust the interests of commerce with those of railways." The idea was to terminate "intemperate and ill considered discussion."** But at the same time, businessmen have been unwilling to grant authority to such commissions to interfere with the freedom of business operations. In Massachusetts, the president of an important railroad informed the Railroad Commission:

> I had supposed that your honorable corporation was created to, in some measure, stand between the railroad corporations and their patrons. . . . I have not supposed, and do not now suppose, that the commission intends to go outside of this high position, or to seriously attempt advising the trained and experienced managers of the roads in this Commonwealth upon the details of their duty.†

These reports from the nineteenth century reveal the attitudes of businessmen in a period when the traditional ideology was more vigorous, coherent, and acceptable than it is today, and when, therefore, business's declarations about its legitimacy could be more forthright. Now the old ideology is a less reliable crutch, and while the secret attitudes and assumptions of business leaders may in many cases be similar to that of their forebears, they are less likely to be so outspoken.

Then, the mood was one of confidence. The business leaders of the nineteenth century did little apocalyptic dreaming, although

---

* *The New York Times,* Dec. 29, 1972, op. ed. page.

** *Twenty-seventh Annual Report of the Trade and Commerce of Chicago,* compiled for the Board of Trade, p. xxvii, as quoted in Kirkland, *op. cit.,* p. 138.

† *Third Annual Report of the (Massachusetts) Board of Railroad Commissioners,* January 1872, p. xxxiv, as quoted in Kirkland, *op. cit.,* p. 138.

Charles Elliott Perkins wondered how it all would end: "When we have two or three times as many voters as now and few owners of property in proportion to the whole, there may be troubles which will upset the whole scheme. . . ."* But most exulted in Carnegie's *Triumphant Democracy*, which began:

The old nations of the earth creep on at a snail's pace; the Republic thunders past with the rush of an express. The United States, the growth of a single century, has already reached the foremost rank among nations, and is destined soon to outdistance all others in the race. In population, in wealth, in annual savings, and in public credit; in freedom from debt, in agriculture, and in manufactures, America already leads the civilized world.**

It is clear that the Lockean ideology provided the terms in which business has argued the legitimacy of its organization and behavior as well as its relationship to its environment.

Dean Lawrence Fouraker of the Harvard Business School said not long ago: "If you ask a business student . . . 'Who are your heroes?' . . . the names will come out of the nineteenth century."† This is not surprising, for since then big business has become increasingly estranged from the traditional ideology, from the fabric of orthodox heroism. In mouthing its phrases, business leaders have become increasingly unconvincing. In failing to provide a new ideology, the community has left big business increasingly unattached, vulnerable, and insecure.

The Paradigm Undermined

To remain vigorous, coherent, and acceptable, an ideology must fit harmoniously with the characteristics and needs of the community it is supposed to serve. It must be appropriate to the surrounding geography, population, technology, and history, and to the community's hopes and fears. The ideology of Japan, for example,

---

* Letter to E. F. Perkins, April 7, 1886, as quoted in Kirkland, *op. cit.,* p. 142.
** As quoted in Kirkland, *op. cit.,* p. 167. See also David P. Gagan, "The Railroads and the Public, 1870–1881: A Study of Charles Elliott Perkins' Business Ethics," *Business History Review,* vol. 39, 1965, No. 1, pp. 41–56.
† Lawrence Fouraker, *HarBus,* Sept. 28, 1972, p. 1.

reflects that country's geography and demographics; it emphasizes cooperation, loyalty, harmony, and community. Individual fulfillment derives from one's place in and contribution to the group, the whole. There is and always has been a close partnership between government and business, and a strong sense of national unity. In part, obviously, this ideology is a result of the fact that Japan is a collection of small islands with a great many people crowded upon them.

It is clear that the aggressive, competitive, possessive individualism which emerged in America was well suited to a society that was during its first one hundred years or so largely rural, agricultural, and dispersed, a nation in which human resources were scarce and natural resources great. In 1800, three-quarters of the labor force was in agriculture. By 1880, it was 51 per cent and by 1960, 8 per cent. Until about a hundred years ago, farming and the life that went with it was the dominant influence in America. The ownership of a piece of land, hard work on that land (which paid off if you had luck and guts), an independent life in which initiative and self-reliance were rewarded—these were realities for most Americans.

Although agriculture set the stage for the acceptance and utility of Lockean ideology, it also proved to be among the most powerful forces in its transformation. And indeed the transformation in this instance, as in others, entailed a variety of ideological self-subversion. It occurred through the application of the fifth Lockean component, scientific specialization, to the technology of agriculture. Machinery replaced labor and increased farm production. Louis M. Hacker writes:

The increase in productivity by the 1890s was sensational. Although in the 1830s (and also into the late 1840s) putting a crop in—plowing and sowing—required 15 to 20 man-hours per acre, in the 1890s, on the large farms of North Dakota and California, the man-hour labor time had been reduced to three hours. As for securing it—reaping, binding, shocking, and threshing—the man-hour time per acre fell from 50 to about 6 hours.*

Towne and Rasmussen have estimated that gross product per farmer jumped from $292 in 1800 to $526 in 1900 (in equivalent

---

* Louis M. Hacker, *The Course of American Economic Growth and Development* (New York: John Wiley and Sons, Inc., 1970), p. 105.

dollars) and the increase has been even sharper since that time. Small farms gave way to large ones. Working the land became less important than investing capital properly.

Simultaneously, manufacturing industries grew in the cities, and the flow of population to urban areas began. In 1800, more than 90 per cent of the American population lived in rural areas; even as late as 1890, two-thirds of our people lived in the countryside; but by 1950, the scales had reversed and two-thirds of the population lived in the cities. City life strained the traditional notions of individualism. It is, after all, impossible to stake out a land claim downtown or build a beef herd in an apartment. The meaning of private ownership as a political and social value changed when many, if not most, of our population became renters and "property" meant the cube adjacent, the air rights above the highway, or a share of AT&T.

Immigration also swelled the cities. Early immigrants often had trades or were able to find land; but by the 1880's, proximate free land had vanished and the vast majority of immigrants were unskilled laborers who could only seek work in the mill towns and industrial cities.* By the turn of the century, the American dream lay not in the private farm but in the large industrial organization.

The markets of the country went through a parallel evolution that was equally drastic. The markets of early America were small and dispersed. Communities were relatively isolated and highly dependent on internal exchange. Barter was common. Canals, turnpikes, and later railroads helped to get agricultural produce to the seaports for export, but other kinds of shipping were relatively rare. Markets were competitive and the price system was truly responsive to the laws of supply and demand. Prices were remarkably stable in the years before 1860, with economic growth apparently benefiting both producer and consumer.** Lockean conceptions of the market worked well, so confidence in its validity flourished. As William Appleman Williams puts it:

---

* U.S. Bureau of Census, *Historical Statistics of the U.S., Colonial Times to 1957,* series C115–132, "Immigrants by Major Occupation Group, 1820–1957" (Washington, D.C.: U.S. Government Printing Office, 1960).

** Ralph L. Andreano, ed., *New Views on American Economic Development* (Cambridge, Mass.: Schenkman Publishing Co., Inc., 1965), p. 128.

The agricultural majority of the country developed, through the interaction of existing ideas and continuing experience, a marketplace image or conception of the world and how it worked—and of how it could be manipulated to attain their objectives. That marketplace outlook defined primary values, such as freedom and equal opportunity, as being necessary and worthy per se, and as being necessary to the proper functioning of the marketplace. The integration of the concern with freedom and the concern with economic profit and welfare led to a central conviction that it was necessary to expand the marketplace, and to expand it as a free marketplace, if freedom, profit, and welfare were to be realized.*

The urban minority of the nation generally accepted the farmer's conception of the market and the world. The businessmen of the cities found that it conformed to their own fundamental premises; the farm majority was a vigorous and effective tutor, and the businessman's daily experience seemed to reinforce the lessons he was being taught.**

The nature of domestic markets changed dramatically after the Civil War. As personal income rose, the demand for food did not increase proportionally—it never does. Markets moved away from agricultural products and toward manufactured goods. They became centralized in the growing cities, with railroads making concentration both possible and efficient. As urbanization increased, national market wholesalers could not cope with the needs of rising consumption, and corporations had to take over. The inevitable result, as Alfred D. Chandler has pointed out, was the large, market-oriented, vertically integrated corporation.† There was a consequent movement from the small, independent manufacturer, dispersed and decentralized, toward the larger, multifunctional organization with its many decisionmakers. This tendency was marked by the first great wave of corporate mergers at the turn of the century.

The organization of large numbers of people into giant corporate enterprises for the pursuit of economic objectives has developed into the dominant force in twentieth-century America. Such collectivization came to be plainly inconsistent with traditional

---

* William Appleman Williams, *The Roots of the Modern American Empire* (New York: Random House, Inc., 1969), p. 450.
** *Ibid.*, p. 450.
† Alfred D. Chandler, "The Beginnings of 'Big Business' in American Industry" in Andreano, *op. cit.*, p. 306.

Lockean conceptions, notably with the first four components of the old ideology. Yet, ironically, corporate development was quite consistent with the fifth idea, scientific specialization—technology—the fruits of which in fact nourished and formed the structure of the American corporation, contributing to its inconsistency both with the other four traditional components and with the more recent changing demands of the environment. Modern technology conditions the organization of the large corporation, with its capital resources, its connections to far-flung markets, and its access to government money. John K. Galbraith put it felicitously: "Size is the general servant of technology, not the special servant of profit. . . . The problem of technostructure . . . is whether it can be accommodated to social goals or whether society will have to be accommodated instead to its needs."*

It is clear that industrialization, urbanization, immigration, changes in the nature of markets, the growth of large corporations, and unprecedented technological innovation all made the America of 1900 a very different place from what it had been in 1800. In 1800, the values of survival, justice, economy, creativity, and self-respect could truly be made manifest in the real world through the Lockean conceptions of individualism, property rights, competition, the limited state, and scientific specialization. Indeed, pre-Civil War America was a near-perfect model of a community with a fully functioning ideology, and its very perfection gave the traditional ideology the strength of a religion. It became the widely accepted means to legitimacy for all institutions and thus the basis for authority and order in society. The institutions which grew beneath its cloak, however, came to subvert and pervert it, pragmatically departing from its tenets, causing widespread changes in the real world, dislocating and rupturing the old root system. Legitimacy, authority, and order gradually deteriorated.

The familiar historical sequence observed in Greece, Rome, and medieval Europe was working its inexorable way in America. From the beginning, there were basic functions which had to be performed; resources had to be processed, goods produced, products distributed; and at the same time, resources had to be controlled and allocated for future production and distribu-

---

* John K. Galbraith, *The New Industrial State* (Boston: Houghton Mifflin Co., 1967), pp. 33 and 104.

tion. For a time, these functions could be performed by institutions which were quite consistent with the traditional ideology. Then changes occurred in the real world—population shifted, and markets were altered. As a result, the institutions required to perform the basic functions changed and the rise of new institutions began. The new ones continued to cling for legitimacy to the old ideology. For a time nobody worried too much about the inconsistencies, but inevitably the tension has grown.

The Political Evolution of the Corporation

Even initially there was a dichotomy in the American concept of the role of the state that is central to an understanding of public policy toward the corporation. Thomas Jefferson wanted to preserve this country in its gemlike philosophic mold, an essentially rural, agricultural place in which the Lockean virtues would be safe. "Those who labor in the earth," he said, "are the chosen people of God, if ever He had a chosen people." Let us export raw materials for manufacture in Europe and keep these pristine shores free of the industrial proletariat. "The mobs of great cities add just so much to the support of pure government, as sores do to the strength of the human body."* Although Jefferson mellowed somewhat in his later years, coming to welcome commerce and manufacturing, his thrust was plainly Lockean. And the Constitution reflected a transcendent concern with the protection of property rights and limitations upon the authority of government.

Alexander Hamilton, on the other hand, followed the lead of European mercantilists like Colbert in postulating a more positive role for the state: government was to be used as a tool for fulfilling a vision of the ideal American community. Economic development was for him a concern of the state; it also required the transfer of capital to those most likely to use it in order to increase the nation's productive capacity. The Jeffersonians envisaged a more or less static economy with an essentially limited and passive government. The Hamiltonians saw government as a benign and

* As quoted in Arthur M. Schlesinger, Jr., "Ideas and Economic Development," in *Paths of American Thought, op. cit.,* p. 108.

indispensable agency assisting in the exciting adventure of acquisition and growth.*

American history represents a mixture of these two positions. In easier times, we have behaved as though we believed in Jefferson; in periods of crisis, we have tended to act as Hamilton would have advised, but we have done so pragmatically, seeking ideological cover in Jefferson. Public policy toward the corporation reflects this schizophrenia.

James Willard Hurst has noted the evolution of the terms under which the political order of the United States has allowed the corporation to exist. We inherited from England the notion that a corporation must result from a positive act by the sovereign; but we then molded the notion of the corporation to fit our own circumstances. Hurst describes the result of this evolution as a shift away from political criteria having to do with the needs of the community, to criteria of economic utility pure and simple.** In early America, the corporation was chartered by the state to serve a specific need; in chartering it, the community, which was by and large Jeffersonian, acted in a Hamiltonian way. Later, the right to incorporate was generalized, the idea being that economic growth was good per se and that the most efficient way to promote it was through the corporation. The corporation then became the embodiment of private property, ideologically, and the state's function, following Jefferson, was to protect it, enhance it, and help it flourish for its own sake. Hamilton's vision had been obscured by Jeffersonian laissez-faire.

The evolution began from a most abstract position. In his opinion for the Supreme Court in the Dartmouth College case of 1819, Chief Justice John Marshall described the corporation as "an artificial being, invisible, intangible, and existing only in the contemplation of law. Being the mere creature of law, it possesses only those properties which the charter of its creation confers upon it, either expressly, or as incidental to its very existence."†

---

* *Ibid.,* pp. 109, 110.
** James Willard Hurst, *The Legitimacy of the Business Corporation in the Law of the United States, 1780–1970* (Charlottesville: The University Press of Virginia, 1970), p. 4.
† *The Trustees of Dartmouth College* v. *Woodward,* 4 Wheaton 518, 636, (U.S.) 1819, as quoted in Hurst, *ibid.,* p. 9.

From that time on, it was largely businessmen—entrepreneurs and managers—who gave flesh, bone, muscle, and blood to Marshall's metaphysical being. They developed its goals, organization, and procedures, working within a context which the community as a whole created. At first, when the Republic was in a critical stage, this context emerged from explicit governmental decisions. Then, increasingly, it emerged from the driving force of business itself interacting more or less freely with consumers in the market place. More recently, this validating context has been the result of the confluence of a wide variety of interest groups working together with government and consumers.

Until about 1780, there was no demand in America for the corporation. At that point, serious need arose for roads, bridges, canals, railroads, banks, insurance, and other public services. Money and manpower were scarce. Government was unable to meet the community's need for public utilities directly, so it sought to encourage private, voluntary initiatives to raise capital and to develop managerial talent.* Corporations were chartered and supported with money raised abroad and procured from state legislatures. Local and state governments, for example, eventually provided more than a third of a billion dollars for the development of American railroads.**

Between 1780 and 1801, state legislatures chartered 317 corporations.† During the early 1800's, it was clear that corporate status in law required an explicit community decision about what community needs were and that this decision be made in legislation by government. The national and state governments were, in fact, economic development planners, allocating scarce resources as they deemed most fit to meet their vision of the community. If they had felt they needed an excuse for this somewhat anomalous behavior—which they did not—they might have pointed to the strategic problem that had to be solved quickly. At the time, we were a young nation in crisis. Foreign powers threatened our intrests; indeed, the British burned our capital. We needed navies, merchant fleets, and harbors. Under such conditions, there was

---

* Hurst, *ibid.,* pp. 23, 24.
** Schlesinger, in *Paths of American Thought, op. cit.,* pp. 111, 112.
† Hurst, *op. cit.,* pp. 14, 15.

little opposition to governmental intervention in economic life.*
As in other times of crisis—the Depression, the great wars, the
cold war, the race to space with the Soviets—America willingly
but only temporarily, set aside her official Lockean view of the
state.

Having defined a public need and approved a group of persons
to organize to meet it, the law gave to this group impressive rights,
duties, privileges, and immunities, such as shareholders' immunity
from liability for claims against the enterprise.**

In the 1830's, an increasing distinction arose between the public
corporation chartered for community purposes and the private
corporation formed for profit to satisfy individual consumers. It
was during this period that the business community started to
develop the Lockean ideology for its own purposes and profits.
Business pressure and changing perceptions of community need
brought about the loosening of state control over the corporation
and the decline of the Hamiltonian view of government in national
planning. Business was making its way into the driver's seat. Corporations were restive under Andrew Jackson's aggressive conception of presidential power and at the same time irritated by his
unwillingness to help them.† Hamilton had been the friend of
business as business had been the instrument of the state; Jackson
began to demonstrate that a strong conception of the state could
well be the enemy of private, profit-seeking enterprise.

So, in the mid-nineteenth century, corporations needed an im-
peccable argument in order to repel state intervention—except
where it served their special interests. They found it in Locke's
ideas, which, of course, had been there all along in the spirit of
Jefferson and the hearts of the people; they had only been
temporarily set aside in the early 1800's for overriding national
reasons. Schlesinger quotes Adams sadly on the change:

it was clear to John Quincy Adams . . . by 1837 that his nationalist
vision was fading away. A decade before, "the principle of internal

---

* See Louis Hartz, *Economic Policy and Democratic Thought: Pennsylvania, 1776–1860* (Cambridge, Mass.: Harvard University Press, 1948),
p. ix, quoting Benjamin Wright.
** Hurst, *op. cit.,* p. 19.
† Jackson's refusal to charter a new Second Bank of the United States,
for example.

improvement was swelling the tide of public prosperity," but now it was vanishing before the . . . appeal to . . . state's rights and laissez-faire. "I fell," cried the old statesman, "and with me fell, I fear never to rise again in my day, the system of internal improvement by means of national energies."*

By the 1850's, corporation law favored the centralization of decisionmaking within the business organization, with active management fixed in the board of directors as representative of the stockholder owners. A high value was placed upon the continuity of management, regardless of changes in shareholders, and on the provision of a reliable frame for investment with limited investor commitment. The corporation was emerging as an ingenious vehicle of economic utility, capable of quick improvisation and ready response to opportunity.**

Predictably, however, the collective character of the corporation did not go unchallenged. Its threat to the Lockean ideology was perceived early. William Gouge wrote in 1833:

Against corporations of every kind, the objection may be brought that whatever power is given to them is so much taken from either the government or the people. As the object of charters is to give to members of companies powers which they would not possess in their individual capacity, the very existence of monied corporations is incompatible with equality of rights. . . .†

Gouge foresaw two continuing problems. First, there was the matter of power and its dispersion: How was corporate power to be allocated and defined? What was to be the relationship between corporate power and the state? The answer, such as it was, came in the form of the antitrust laws enacted at the turn of the century. Corporate power was to emerge from the inexorable workings of competition, which the state would keep free and open. These laws merely reiterated the premise that if numerous small, self-interested, individualistic corporate proprietors sought to satisfy individual consumers, the good community would result; power would be sufficiently disbursed and the people would benefit.

Second, there was the matter of individualism and equality of

---

* Schlesinger, in *Paths of American Thought, op. cit.,* p. 115.
** Hurst, *op. cit.,* pp. 25, 26.
† *Short History of Paper Money and Banking in the United States,* as quoted in Hurst, *op. cit.,* p. 30.

rights: Would not great corporate concentrations suppress these rights? This question was answered in two ways. Corporations were to be regarded as collective individuals. This provided a basis of legitimacy for the huge collectives which, over time, were to lose any of the real attributes of individualism and private property as conceived by Locke. Also, the right of corporate status was to be granted to virtually anyone and for any purpose through simple administrative procedures (as in the standard incorporation acts of the 1880's). The notion of corporate status as a special privilege given to a few to serve an explicit community requirement was thus formally replaced by the notion of the corporation as a generally useful form through which to carry on virtually any economic activity.

The ideological confusion that arose around these two questions of power dispersion and corporate status in the nineteenth century has not yet been neatly handled; it is at the crux of many difficulties today. Nonetheless, the urge to grow and the confidence in the pragmatic utility of the corporate form were so strong that the confusion was glossed over by common consent. We postponed, says Hurst rightly, "coming to grips with the creation of adequate legislative standards and adequate administrative means to deal with problems which the play of the market could not adequately handle."* We left unresolved the issues of power. We evaded more specific definition of the public interest and delayed administrative designs to implement it. We were buttressed in this process by simple faith in the Lockean conceptions of individualism, property rights, and the limited state, and also by our sublime confidence that the impersonal competitive market would prevent abuse by the corporate powers, and thereby legitimize them.

The two questions did not trouble corporate managers at all. They saw their function exclusively as that of searching out and fostering consumer desires and then devising strategies by which resources could be allocated to satisfy the expected demands. Corporate structure and behavior have tended to follow this strategy right down to the present, with great success and impact.

In sum, soon after the corporation was instituted in America, certainly by the time of the Civil War, it had burst out from its political and social bonds and taken advantage of its enormous

---

* Hurst, *op. cit.,* p. 36.

flexibility, to become, by virtue of its usefulness, the dominant institutional force in American life. Its utility legitimized it, and so became an end in itself.* Hence the corporation took on its own political and social significance, which was inseparable from and no less important than its economic activity. Furthermore, the legitimacy of the corporation in the nineteenth century was enhanced by the fourth Lockean component, the limited state. The nation was heavily preoccupied with the legitimacy of government, the possible overgrowth and abuse of government's power. Private, individual, or group economic activity, pursued competitively in the market place, tended to lessen this threat. And the fifth component, scientific specialization, well suited an America where new technology and techniques were unquestioned benefits.

Between the 1880's and the 1930's, the United States saw the corporation as so useful that the principal purposes of law became the enlargement of its maneuverability and the limitation of government's right to regulate its power.** Both the Supreme Court and the state legislatures sought to proscribe legislation which would subvert the corporation's organizational or functional integrity. The roots of this policy extended back to Chief Justice Marshall's opinion in the Dartmouth College case in 1819. The New Hampshire legislature had attempted to change the governing body of Dartmouth, a private chartered college, to convert it into a public institution. Marshall ruled that the statute violated the constitutional clause that forbids a state to pass any bill impairing the obligation of contract.† In finding that a corporation is protected by this clause, the court laid the first step for the independence and individualization of the American corporation. In 1886, the Supreme Court acknowledged that a corporation is a person within the meaning of the Fourteenth Amendment, enacted in 1868, which asserts that no state can deprive any person of life, liberty, or property without due process of law. In the 1890's and on into the twentieth century, the court extended these constitutional principles, giving corporations, in the name of liberty and property, the right to protection from unreasonable or discriminatory state laws.†† As Hurst has said: "These readings of the Fourteenth Amendment materially extended the legitimacy which law conferred on private corporate power and at the same time sub-

---

* *Ibid.*, p. 58.   ** *Ibid.*, p. 62.   † *Ibid.*, pp. 62–3.   †† *Ibid.*, p. 65.

stantially curbed the legitimacy of government regulation of corporate behavior."*

In the court's eyes, then, Locke's ideas of individualism and property, transmuted, were in full force as the legitimizers of the corporation and its considerable autonomy by the late nineteenth century. That Locke would have regarded this transmutation of his doctrine as an abomination seems clear, for the corporation was in fact a collective that was becoming increasingly remote from its owners, and, in the process, suppressing individualism within its structure to suit the discipline of production.

However that may be, the state legislatures quickly got the message that corporations were to be regarded simply as devices for promoting economic activity. From 1900 onward, states competed with one another in offering incorporation on terms of increasing liberality. Several of them, eager for the fees and taxes which corporations promised, competed to serve the interests of the new entrepreneurs, granting among other things unprecedented insulation of managers from the interfering hands of their shareholder proprietors.

Businessmen of great genius took advantage of the generosity of New Jersey and Delaware to assist in the drafting of incorporation laws that would meet the changing needs of the times. New technologies and expanding markets were pointing the way to corporations of unprecedented size. Opportunities for financial maneuvering within and among these growing giants were clear if corporate organizations were properly shaped. J. P. Morgan, for example, perceived an expanding market among the growing affluent middle class for limited-commitment investments. To make the most of the opportunity, however, he had to be able to control large aggregations of capital and he needed protection from rash newcomers causing unsettling competition which might shake investors' confidence. He therefore sought new corporate structures, which allowed the creation of large amounts of capital and centralized internal control of corporation finances. Delaware and New Jersey were glad to oblige with new laws.**

The federal and state governments were willing to assume that the open grant of corporate status raised no substantial question relating to the community good, but increasingly serious questions

---

* *Ibid.,* p. 66. ** *Ibid.,* p. 72.

about the control of private corporate power continued to emerge. Notably, efforts had to be made to control abuses of manipulation and to protect the rights of shareholders. Judges interpreted the standard general incorporation acts of the 1800's as requiring that "effective command of all regular business be in the board of directors and that the board not be structured to represent segmental interests among investors."*

Such rulings made sense for closely held corporations, but for corporations with many shareholders the problem seemed more to be one of oppression of the minority by the majority. Moreover:

. . . there was reason to believe that shareholder agreements expressed true shareholder interests in close-held firms; in contrast, among numerous, dispersed stockholders forms of agreement might only conceal the hand of inside manipulation. Nonetheless, until well into the twentieth century, courts, even in the states of the most business sophistication, would not recognize that different functional problems between close-held and broadly held corporations called for different policies.**

The first statutes to meet these problems appeared in the mid-twentieth century and then only in North Carolina and New York. Laws in these states centered on the issue of investor control of management; they allowed the corporation to buy its own shares, sanctioned the removal of directors by stockholders, and the election and removal of corporate officers by the stockholders. As Hurst writes, "The most striking aspect of the matter was that so much time had to pass to obtain this sensible clarification, and then only in a few states. The fact attested to the difficulty of putting legislatures into motion without the push of an energetic lobby."†

Since the 1880–90 period, we have relied on two principal means to assure the legitimacy of private economic power. Primarily, we have tried to keep the market place free and open by extensions of the Sherman Act ban on monopolies or combinations in restraint of trade (1890) and the Clayton and Federal Trade Commission Acts (1914), aimed at curbing the growth of private power which might develop into restraint and thus threaten the vitality of competition. Secondly, we have relied on the self-interest of investors to ensure that the management of the

---

* *Ibid.*, p. 79. ** *Ibid.*, pp. 79–80. † *Ibid.*, p. 81.

institutions in which they invest is efficient and economically effective. A vivid statement of this reliance is to be found in the ruling of the Michigan Supreme Court in *Dodge Brothers* v. *Ford Motor Company* (1919), in which the court defined management's primary obligation to be the competitive pursuit of profit in the interest of shareholders rather than the promotion of pricing policies designed to advance the interests of wage earners or the wider sharing of new technology by the community as a whole.*

At the same time—often at the urging of important segments of the business community—the political order has found it necessary to depart from these two fundamental but indirect control mechanisms and aim directly through government regulation at a wide variety of problems which have arisen at the intersection of the corporation and society. Among other things, these regulations concern the terms and conditions of work, the safety and quality of products, and more recently, the ecological effects of manufacturing and technology. The tempo of regulation appears to have increased as confidence in the two primary bases of corporate legitimacy—competition and shareholder self-interest—has deteriorated.

The Deterioration of Competition

In 1970, some five hundred large corporations had a dominant effect on large sectors of United States economic activity.** With such concentration of power it appeared likely, without collusion or conspiracy on anybody's part, that competition will no longer operate sufficiently to guarantee the optimum consumer benefit either in terms of price or product.

Furthermore, an increasing number of community needs have emerged which have little if any relevance to consumers in the market place—clean air, pure water, auto safety, and the like. Such needs are not to be met by way of competition; indeed, competitive factors tend to hinder the outlay of money and effort necessary to deal with them.

Then, too, the United States confronts substantial competitive difficulties in world markets where more organic nations such as

---

* *Dodge* v. *Ford Motor Co.*, 204 Mich. 459, 170 N.W. 668 (1919) (cf. Dorfman, 3:21–6), in Hurst, *ibid.*, pp. 82–3.
** Hurst, *ibid.*, p. 83.

Japan take advantage of their close government-business relationship to develop long-range planning. Does not ITT or IBM have to be big and strong at home—even if in violation of the antitrust laws—so that it can promote the national interest in terms of balance of payments and competition with other nations? Generally speaking, can a seventeenth-century provincial ideology be made to govern economic activity effectively in the twentieth-century world of internationalism?

How can we compensate for this deterioration of our competitive mechanism? The obvious answer is through the political order. The political order must first decide what is the community good, but shall this be the task of the executive branch, the legislature, the judiciary? Or of interest groups rampaging through stockholder meetings, or students who seize Harvard's Massachusetts Hall to force Gulf Oil to depart from Angola? Shall ITT become a partner of the U.S. government in the design and fulfillment of America's needs? And if so, who is the senior partner, the chairman of ITT or the President of the United States? Is there not something medieval about such demands for communal organization?

The Deterioration in the Idea of Property

According to nineteenth-century theory, the stockholder was to play two roles in making the corporation legitimate. By placing his money in a corporation, a shareholder declares his belief that he can get a better return on his investment there than he can elsewhere. Also he thereby posits the threat that he may withdraw his share and place it elsewhere if his expectations are not fulfilled. In faith and in practice, the stockholder thus provides the manager with a critical means of measuring the manager's own effectiveness.

Stockholders are also, however, conceived to be owners of the corporate property and as such are supposed to play the supreme role in governing the corporation, electing the board of directors and through it selecting and providing authority to the management of the corporation—the hired hands, as it were.

The second of these two roles has deteriorated the more severely. There are some closely held corporations where a few shareholders do indeed exercise their traditional legitimizing function of governance. But the vast bulk of economic activity is under the control of firms with many thousands of individual shareholders who have no real connection with the organizations they are supposed to own and legitimize, save for receiving whatever dividends managements may issue. Whereas a handful of relatively sophisticated businessmen held shares in the railroads of the nineteenth century or the few corporations of the early twentieth, today's investors are a broad cross-section of the American population who neither know nor desire to know anything about the corporation that holds their shares, and who are less interested in short-term profits and entrepreneurial innovation than in long-term assurance of income. Many millions of them are separated from their fictional property by intermediary institutions such as insurance companies, mutual funds, trusts, and pension funds. Indeed, by the 1960's these institutional investors were the largest buyers of corporation bonds and substantial buyers of stock. Through what mystical web such institutions were supposed to pass along legitimacy to the modern corporation is obscure.

Exacerbating this deterioration, developments in the law seem to have deliberately impeded the stockholder from playing his legitimating role. Three elements are plainly necessary if he is to exert his responsibility. He needs information about the corporation; he needs voting power to act on his judgments about that information; and he needs "leverage in law" by which to overcome the inertia or contrary interests of either management or an indifferent mass of fellow shareholders.

In the 1880's, corporation law in the states did provide for shareholders' needs under these three headings; then there was some substance to their supervisory role. Between 1890 and 1930, however, the law weakened the capability of the stockholder truly to own or oversee his property, on the theory that management autonomy is necessary for the corporation's efficient operation, and there was no real reversal of this trend in the period between 1930 and 1960.*

As late as 1965, Hurst found that only twenty-two states required corporation reports of any sort, and "in only fourteen of these twenty-two were reports available to stockholders, and in three the requirement might be dispensed with by the corporation's bylaws."** We can only marvel at how completely our faith

---

* *Ibid.,* pp. 88, 89. ** *Ibid,* p. 90.

in the ability of the corporate structure by itself to undertake economic action for the good of the community obscured and obliterated the procedures for making that structure legitimate. It is significant that the only really effective pressure for the dissemination of information to stockholders did not arise out of any concern for the legitimacy of the internal governance of the corporation but rather out of an eagerness to maintain market confidence for corporate securities—specifically, as a result of new listing requirements for the New York Stock Exchange.* Federal policy had already taken a similar route: in a series of moves beginning in 1933, the Securities and Exchange Commission required even more strict and extensive reporting by corporations within its jurisdiction. Here we see a "sharp contrast . . . between the regulatory weakness of state corporation law and the positive impact of action taken by a national professional group [accountants] backed by national law."**

The weakness at the heart of the legislative process by which corporations are theoretically governed is the proxy, the device by which a shareholder may name an agent to vote his shares for him. Originally, the proxy was designed to serve the convenience of the shareholder. As events have developed, however, it is now a good deal more. Given the range, extent, and complexity of the corporation's influence, financial and otherwise; given its need for continuity; given its near monopoly on knowledge about its affairs; given the almost total lack of restrictions or disclosure requirements in state law and even in SEC regulations until the early 1970's—given all this, the handful of persons at the center of a large corporation have generally been able to exert full command over the proxy machinery and do exactly what they want. The shareholder, happy to view himself in his investor role and unconcerned about his obligations as a property owner, is generally most willing to have his corporation work smoothly. Although some attempts have been made by the SEC to enliven stockholder participation by regulations on the proxy machinery, the big corporation has remained "typically a one-party system of private government under management direction, given formal legitimacy but no great difference of substance by the more strictly policed proxy machinery."†

---

* *Ibid.,* p. 91. ** *Ibid.,* p. 93. † *Ibid.,* p. 97.

Today what legitimacy the corporation has derives principally from its own self-perpetuating management and from whatever bounds the political order may place around it. Evidence for this lies in the following sets of facts: In 1929, Berle and Means found that management controlled 44 per cent of the two hundred largest nonfinancial corporations in the United States. This control was exerted over 58 per cent of the assets of these corporations.* In 1963, Robert Larner found that management controlled 84.5 per cent of such corporations, embracing 85 per cent of the assets of these corporations. Among the five hundred largest nonfinancial corporations, management controlled 75 per cent of the companies, exercising control over 81 per cent of their assets.**

Thus it appears that whatever may have been the original ideas by which corporations were made legitimate, for utilitarian and pragmatic reasons those ideas have been replaced by the practice of self-perpetuating management. The ideas of individualism, property, competition, and the limited state, which provided the original basis for corporate legitimacy, have been greatly eroded in the process. The instability of the corporation today is therefore not surprising. The manager may search desperately for some means of validating himself and his enterprise, pursuing "social responsibility," perplexing himself with "social audits," but he will find no peace until a new ideological foundation sustains the extraordinary mechanism he controls.

---

* Adolf A. Berle and Gardiner C. Means, *The Modern Corporation and Private Property,* pp. 86ff., as quoted in Hurst, *ibid.,* p. 106.

** Robert J. Larner, "Separation of Ownership and Control and Its Implications for the Behavior of the Firm" (Ph.D. dissertation, University of Wisconsin, 1968), as quoted in Hurst, *ibid.,* p. 106.

CHAPTER 5 The Twentieth Century: Ideological Disintegration

By the beginning of the twentieth century, the large, publicly held corporation had become the driving force of the American economy. Economic activity had split away from its political and social relationships and the corporation had thrust itself forward as a virtually self-legitimizing entity—proven by its own goals of efficiency and growth. The old ideology had in fact been replaced in many ways by practical principles of economic utility, but these principles were unattached to any explicit or coherent vision. They were not converted into a new ideology; in fact, every attempt was made to make them fit the old ideology, which could not be done. Ideologically, the corporation had thus worked its way into something of a vacuum.

It was into this vacuum that the state moved in the twentieth century. And exactly because a decisive, consistent, and coherent vision of what the society ought to be was lacking, the state has moved in without being either decisive, consistent, or coherent. As circumstances demanded action, the government introduced a multiplicity of regulatory boards and commissions and a variety of ad hoc legislative restrictions. After seventy years of application, this approach has led us nearly to chaos, for several reasons inherent in the approach itself. Our lingering affection, of revolutionary origin, for the limited state precluded government from engaging in the systematic planning from which sound regulation must proceed. Our propensity for interest group pluralism and our faith in the notion of economic efficiency often combined to place the regulatory authorities at the mercy of those whom they were supposed to regulate. Then, too, our devotion to diffusion of government has led to a proliferation of structures at all levels, rendering efficient government action most difficult.

As government has for these reasons failed to cope with our problems, it has lost authority and confidence. The result has been a downward spiral. The old ideology became an inadequate base for thinking and action; yet, in mythic form, it remained strong and resilient, damping out whatever direct efforts might be made to replace or rejuvenate it. It lived too deep in the hearts of Americans, served too well the interests of business and others who held power. And for all their attacks on it in the name of a changing reality, the philosophers of the time—the pragmatists— failed to produce an integrated or acceptable replacement. This chapter traces the course of the descending spiral in this century and then goes on to examine the characteristics of ideological reconstruction as they have developed to the present day.

The Rise of Industrialization

As a consequence of the gap between myth and reality, and in the name of the values of survival and justice, powerful new groups arose, organizations seeking a new balance and new criteria for authority and power. Also, the role of the state gradually expanded to allow it to curb and bridle economic activity. The traditional ideology was thus further subverted; individualism became submerged in corporate organization and interest group pluralism, and the limited state gave way to government regulation. But, because the myth remained strong, these changes took place surreptitiously, justified at each stage as the necessary response to crises and specific abuses or in the name of efficiency.

As early as 1888, that perceptive British observer James Bryce noted that while Americans clung to the fantasy of laissez-faire, they were actually living in a society in which government was extending its intervention "into ever-widening fields."* Railroads, banks, grain elevators, insurance companies, labor organizations, and working hours and conditions all were becoming subject to the

---

* James Bryce, *The American Commonwealth* (1888), as quoted in Max Lerner, "The Triumph of Laissez-Faire," in *Paths of American Thought,* edited by Arthur M. Schlesinger, Jr., and Morton White (Boston: Houghton Mifflin Co., 1963), p. 165.

pressure of government regulation. Although some businessmen bitterly opposed such intervention, others were the most important single force supporting it. Small businessmen wanted protection against the predatory conduct of the giants, and many large corporations sought governmental intervention to stabilize and protect their markets and sources of capital, so that their planning could be more reliable. In other words, some businesses wanted to preserve the Lockean mode of small, individualistic, proprietary enterprises, while others wanted to ease the way for large, collective, nonproprietary undertakings.*

The fact remained that while many businessmen unhesitatingly called on government to help preserve the context in which business could operate efficiently, as a class virtually all businessmen expressed unmitigated ideological loyalty to the Lockean notion of the limited state. Government regulation of tariffs, cotton distribution, central banking, transportation, and the like did not seem to diminish the commitment of business to the idea that government is a necessary evil and the less of it there is the better. The Progressive movement of Theodore Roosevelt recognized this schizoid tendency, cloaking increasing government intervention in the terms, if not the spirit, of the old ideology.

The old ideas of individualism and property suffered a very similar deterioration in the real world and a very similar perpetuation in myth. Populism was perhaps the first sustained protest against the forces tending to suppress the Lockean conception of individual fulfillment. Emanating from the increasing plight of rural America, it attacked the phalanx of great impersonal organizations centered on business which was ranged against the individual farmer.** By 1900, for better or worse, America had come to "the end of an epoch." And as the century wore on, business played a crucial role in the transition out of Lockeanism in general and in the erosion of individualism and property in particular. The automobile industry is a clear case in point.

---

* Robert H. Wiebe, *Businessmen and Reform: A Study of the Progressive Movement* (Cambridge, Mass.: Harvard University Press, 1962), pp. 44–9. See also James Weinstein, *The Corporate Ideal in the Liberal State: 1900–1918* (Boston: Beacon Press, 1968), p. x.

** Norman Pollack, *The Populist Response to Industrial America* (Cambridge, Mass.: Harvard University Press, 1968).

In 1900, Detroit was already the manufacturing center of the horseless carriage and the internal combustion engine. Its position was strategic. Surrounded by the Pittsburgh-Youngstown steel mills, the rubber plants at Akron, and the Mesabi iron range, it also lay at the hub of one of the world's great water transport systems. It was the natural place for Henry Ford, Louis Chevrolet, R. E. Olds, Henry Leland, and other pioneers of the American automobile industry to open their shops.

Thousands flocked to Detroit to seek work in the new factories. When, in January of 1914, Ford announced that he would pay $5 a day, 5,000 men lined up outside his gates at 5 a.m. on a bitterly cold morning. By the time the plant opened, there were 12,000 outside, and a riot soon broke out. The Detroit *News* reported: "The crowd stormed the doors of the plant, hundreds forcing their way through, bricks and other missiles were hurled at the officers and buildings, and the rioters were dispersed only after a drenching with ice-cold water."*

But no fire hose was sufficient to stem the flow. From the backwoods of Arkansas, the cotton fields of Georgia and Alabama, the farms of Kentucky, the mountains of Tennessee, they came by the thousands—immigrants, illiterates, young and old. By 1928, more than 150,000 negroes were jammed into Detroit's "Paradise Valley" slums. Racial violence was common. In 1929, about 470,000 men worked in Detroit's auto factories; by 1931, there were 211,000 people on relief and some 150,000 had left the city to wander over the land.**

B. J. Widick has recorded the following interview with John Kelly, an auto worker who recalls the early 1930's:

We used to get out to the employment gates by six in those days and we would build a fire and wait around. If you knew someone inside you stood a better chance of being called in. Foremen used to come out and pick whom they wanted, and seniority didn't mean a thing. My brother was a superintendent, so I used to get some breaks. I felt sorry for the others, but what could you do? When I started to sign fellows up in the union my superintendent warned me I'd get fired and never get another job. He said he couldn't believe I would do anything like that when I had a brother who was a superintendent.

---

* Detroit *News,* Jan. 12, 1914.
** Irving Howe and B. J. Widick, *The UAW and Walter Reuther* (New York: Random House, Inc., 1949), p. 29.

One night my brother came over to the house and begged me to quit. He was afraid of losing his job because I was a union man.*

Another worker, Joe Hattley, recalled:

One day I started to complain about a job. My foreman took me over to the window and pointed to all those guys standing outside the employment gate. "If you don't like your job there's plenty of them outside who want it." What could I say?**

Initially, the automobile industry conformed nicely to the Lockean model. An individualistic, inventive entrepreneur—Henry Leland of Cadillac, for example, one of the founders of General Motors—brought together capital and ingenuity. There was unquestioning admiration for the technology he offered and for its general utility. He set up shop and none doubted his legitimacy or authority: he owned his property with a handful of others who were readily perceptible and present to help control the uses to which it was put. From a pool of plentiful labor, men who needed work in order to survive, he hired a number of individuals, and with each he had a clear, authoritative contract, rooted in the cherished ideas of property rights on the one hand, and individualism on the other.

Several factors eroded this model; taken together they amount to collectivization. Henry Leland and the others like him became "the management" of General Motors, a large and faceless collective, a group of professional administrators who had little if any ownership in the property they were managing and whose legitimacy was thus uncertain. Ownership had passed to a diffuse and impotent collection of anonymous shareholders who lacked any clear control over management. The authority of the idea of property had clearly been weakened, as had that associated with the individualistic, risk-taking, readily identifiable entrepreneur. In addition, the glory of the automobile, indeed of technology itself, has been dampened more recently by ecological reality.

On the worker's side, the individual had become one of a mass, out of touch with the owner. He felt powerless, lacking in identity. With the Depression it was quite clear that his willingness to work hard was not enough. The old model was flawed; it could not adequately define or make explicit the value of survival in the real

---

* *Ibid.*, p. 30.   ** *Ibid.*

world of the 1930's. So the workers fought for a new model, a collective one, in which their individualism was submerged into an interest group, the United Automobile Workers, and the contract became collectivized—almost a contradiction in terms, given the individualistic origins of the idea of contract in America.

Then, too, power relationships changed. No longer was it Mr. Leland or Mr. Ford deciding unilaterally what the terms of the contract were, giving the workers the option only to accept or reject. That authority, which had been rooted in property rights, became replaced by the shocking truth that in effect property had no rights in any absolute sense: the cherished prerogatives of management were only those which they could win in a bargain with labor and government. Property has only the rights which the prevailing ideology prescribes and these were changing. The management of GM said, for example, that it would never agree to a union shop, which it considered an unacceptable invasion of "management's rights." A few years later came the union shop. In 1948, GM's president refused to include pension and health insurance programs in the collective contract, claiming: "Only by defining and restricting collective bargaining to its proper sphere can we hope to save what we have come to know as our American system and keep it from evolving into an alien form, imported from East of the Rhine."* Somewhat less than a year later, the courts ruled that pension and insurance programs were proper subjects of bargaining.

These changes, with their profound ideological implications, did not happen easily. Management, relying on the old ideas which had in fact been undermined, sought to preserve its "rights," conceiving of these as absolute, emanating from natural law as Locke had prescribed. The union contended that such rights no longer existed, at least in absolute form; they were up for grabs, to be determined by negotiation. The sitdown strikes of 1935 and 1936 ensued. Some 2,000 members of the UAW seized several plants. Management called upon the state to protect its property rights from the "political radicals."** Governor Frank Murphy sent 1,200 National Guardsmen to enforce a court injunction against the strikers, but the workers refused to vacate the plant. Their

---

* *The New York Times,* March 24, 1948.
** Alfred P. Sloan, Jr., *My Years with General Motors* (Garden City, N.Y.: Doubleday & Co., Inc., 1964), p. 405.

leader, John L. Lewis, challenged the governor and he backed down. At the time, an editorial in *Business Week* ran as follows:

Great industries, whose operations affect the daily welfare of millions, are confronted with demands to sign contracts with groups which, day by day and hour by hour, demonstrate that they have almost no control over their own people, no conception of the validity or *the sanctity of a contract*, . . . no regard for *property rights* or for rights of any sort except their own.* [Emphasis added]

Not only were individualism and property giving way in the the work place to large-scale organization and collectivization; they were also becoming increasingly unreal in the nation's large industrial cities, such as Detroit, where few owned anything and where whatever they did own provided little in the way of the freedom and independence Locke had ascribed to property rights. In the city as in the factory, in the coal fields of West Virginia, the steel towns of Pennsylvania, and the textile communities of Massachusetts, organization of individuals into groups had become essential for survival. As John Dewey wrote in the 1930's:

The situation has transformed itself since the day when the problem of freedom and democracy presented itself as essentially a *personal* problem capable of being described by strictly personal choice and action. . . .

The comparative helplessness of persons in their strictly singular capacities to influence the course of events expresses itself in formation of combinations in order to secure protection from the destructive impact of impersonal forces. That groups now occupy much the same place that was occupied earlier by individuals is almost commonplace among writers on sociology.**

Interest group pluralism had become the pervasive means of influencing the direction of a community, the priorities it set, its definition of goals and needs. In normal times, when overwhelming crises did not command differently, government resembled a giant organ responding to whatever collection of interest groups trampled most heavily on the keys. The heavies called the tune. Although this procedure was with us all along, it came into its own after the turn of the century, with prohibitionists, suffragettes, consumer leagues, churches, unions, and trade associations. Government agencies were created to answer their demands; each new

---

* *Business Week*, April 10, 1937.
** John Dewey, *Freedom and Culture* (New York: G. P. Putnam's Sons, 1939), pp. 56, 62, and 63.

collection of government regulatory agencies invited a new wave of interest groups to influence it; and so the spiral grew. During the Depression and in wartime, the pressure of crisis was sufficient to allow government to exert its power more independently, becoming a force with which people had to work rather than a set of agencies through which they could seek their special interests.* But when the crises subsided, as in the 1920's and early 1970's, the interest groups prevailed again.

These interest groups were not provoked into existence exclusively by industrialization. Minority groups found it necessary to submerge their individualism in order to promote and protect their interests. Irish, Jews, Italians, and more recently blacks have all had to combine to make their power felt, each in somewhat different ways. All have had a pervasive effect on the structures of urban oligarchies.** What demographic shifts had done to the illusion of Locke's paradigm in the nineteenth century, interest group pluralism did again, much more severely, in the twentieth.

During the 1920's, the Lockean illusion and its handmaiden, the Protestant ethic, were further undermined by new kinds of marketing efforts on the part of business. Although industry continued to demand a Protestant ethic, in the area of production— that is, in the realm of work—it stimulated the opposite in the area of consumption.† The discipline of the production line required the virtues of hard work, delayed gratification, thrift, and the like; but corporate marketing came to depend upon the glorification of pleasure and plenty, an ever-rising standard of living, buy-now-pay-later, the Cadillac, the supervacation, and so on. Business thus tended to subvert its own moral base of legitimacy. In place of the Protestant ethic, which it needed to sustain productivity, it was driven by its ambition for growth to substitute what Daniel Bell calls "a hedonism which promises a material ease and luxury, yet shies away from all the historic implications which a 'voluptuary system'—and all its social permissiveness and libertinism—implies."††

---

* See Wiebe, *op. cit.*, Chap. VIII.
** Christopher Lasch, *The Agony of the American Left* (New York: Alfred A. Knopf, Inc., 1969), pp. 135–8.
† Daniel Bell, "The Cultural Contradictions of Capitalism," *The Public Interest*, Fall 1970, pp. 38 and 39.
†† *Ibid.*, p. 43.

Such a perversion, of course, stems naturally from the primary reliance on satisfying consumers in the market place to govern the uses of property. And indeed, as time went by, it became apparent that there was a sharp distinction between the satisfaction of consumer desire and the fulfillment of community need. The first could perhaps be guaranteed by the idea of competition; the second could not.

Yet even as all this transpired, the Lockean myth continued to bloom. The illusion was sustained by what Max Lerner has called the "sense of possibility"; in America, anything can happen. A flock of writers had already popularized the rags-to-riches theme. In a series of biographies of successful men, William Makepeace Thayer suggested that every young man could make it if he followed their example. Orison Swett Marden's *Pushing to the Front* (1894) went through 250 printings with the message that young Americans needed only "the will to succeed" to enjoy the full promise of life. And Horatio Alger, Jr., convinced boys throughout the country that God and America would smile upon those who resisted temptation, saved their pennies, and kept their noses to the grindstone. It was by no means only businessmen, popular writers, ministers, and other figures of the status quo who fed this confidence in the old ideology; it was also fostered by the poor immigrants who kept pouring in from Europe, sustained by dreams of success and deeply committed to their "sense of possibility."* While there were many who made it, a good many more, of course, did not; and as time went by, the definition of "making it" became troublesome. What is "the full promise of life," anyway? William James's descriptive phrase, the "Bitch-Goddess Success," seems as current today as when it was coined in protest against what Lerner terms "the exasperating facade of the laissez-faire system."**

Communitarian Imperatives

Many thoughtful persons were aware of the discontinuity between what was preached and what practiced in America. They sensed the growing problems of legitimacy, the disintegration of

---

* Lerner, "The Triumph of Laissez-Faire," in *Paths of American Thought,* pp. 164–5.
** *Ibid.,* p. 164.

values and practice, the breaking down of the old links that connected the two. Among the first and most perceptive was Herbert Croly, whose remarkable book *The Promise of American Life* was published in 1909. As Felix Frankfurter said in 1930, Croly's book was "a reservoir for all political writing after its publication. . . ."*

Croly's thesis is worth quoting at some length not only because it was among the first comprehensive critiques of Lockeanism in America but because it represented an important part of the intellectual foundation of both Theodore Roosevelt's New Nationalism and Franklin Roosevelt's New Deal, even though neither Roosevelt actually made Croly's ideological leap.

Croly argued that the fulfillment of the promise of American life depended first and foremost upon a sense of national purpose, an end of fragmentation and individuation, a coming together around the need for more equitable distribution of wealth and power among all Americans. He recognized that large corporations must perform the functions of business and commerce efficiently and economically; indeed, he foresaw their continued growth. He saw no future in attempting to control business through the enforcement of the antitrust laws, which he regarded as ineffectual and "a fatal bar to the treatment of the problem of corporate aggrandizement from the standpoint of genuinely national policy."** And he saw no special virtue in the small competitor, given the needs of the community as a whole.

Although Croly had great respect for the function of business in America and for enhancing its efficiency and capacity to innovate, he was also aware of the need for firm controls over the practitioners of business:

The net result of the industrial expansion of the United States since the Civil War has been the establishment in the heart of the American economic and social system of certain glaring inequalities of condition and power. . . . [The managers of big corporations] have not obeyed the laws. They have attempted to control the official makers, administrators, and expounders of the law. They have done little to allay and much to excite resentment and suspicion. In short, while their work has been constructive from an economic and industrial standpoint, it has made for political corruption and social disintegration.

---

* Felix Frankfurter, *The New Republic* LXIII (July 16, 1930), p. 247.
** Herbert Croly, *The Promise of American Life,* edited by Arthur M. Schlesinger, Jr. (Cambridge, Mass.: Belknap Press, 1965), p. 274.

Children, as they are, of the traditional American individualistic institutions, ideas, and practices [i.e., Lockean ideology], they have turned on their parents and dealt them an ugly wound.*

What was required was a more coherent definition of community need, and that, Croly felt, was a job for federal and state government. He proposed the federal chartering of all corporations except those engaged exclusively in local business, arguing that this would allow for the development of efficient enterprises and at the same time ensure that that development was consistent with national purpose. It would do away with the inconsistencies and abuses inherent in state chartering and would, he thought, provide by statute an escape from piecemeal regulation through administrative commissions, in which he had no faith whatsoever.

Just as there must be large corporations, so there must be large labor unions. Describing the nonunion laborer as "a species of industrial derelict," Croly called in effect for state-sanctioned compulsory unionism.** He had recognized the fact of collectivization in America, and he perceived the enormous question that it created: If Lockean individualism was not possible in modern America, then what would be the means to individual fulfillment and self-respect? His answer, which was offered tentatively and with little satisfaction, was "the technical excellence of the individual's work." He also saw a possibility for fulfillment in disinterested service to the community, in the imitation of "heroes and saints."†

Croly recognized that an important obstacle to the fulfillment of his view of the American promise was the ambivalent attitude about the role of the state which we had inherited from our founding fathers. The Hamiltonians, he said, distrusted democracy, and the Jeffersonians distrusted central government itself. Hamilton

succeeded in imbuing both men of property and the mass of the "plain people" with the idea that the well-to-do were the peculiar beneficiaries of the American Federal organization, the result being that the rising democracy came more than ever to distrust the national government. Instead of seeking to base the perpetuation of the Union upon the interested motives of a minority of well-to-do citizens, he would have been far wiser to have frankly intrusted its welfare to the good will of the whole people. But unfortunately he was prevented from so doing by the limitation both of his sympathies and ideas. He

---

* *Ibid.*, pp. 116–17.   ** *Ibid*, pp. 386–7.   † *Ibid.*, pp. 435, 454.

was possessed by the English conception of a national state, based on the domination of special privileged orders and interests; and he failed to understand that the permanent support of the American national organization could not be found in anything less than the whole American democracy.*

The Jeffersonians, on the other hand, had an even more seriously flawed view of the state, one that in the end was the more significant because it gained ascendance over Hamilton's:

> In Jefferson's mind democracy was tantamount to extreme individualism. . . . There should be as little government as possible, because persistent governmental interference implied distrust in popular efficiency and good will; and what government there was, should be so far as possible confined to local authorities.* *

The result, as Croly saw it, was a weak central government that favored the few and hence led to an unjust distribution of wealth— the root of all our evils:

> The triumph of Jefferson and the defeat of Hamilton enabled [*sic*] the natural individualism of the American people free play. The democratic political system was considered tantamount in practice to a species of vigorous, licensed, and purified selfishness. The responsibilities of government were negative; those of the individual were positive. . . . If a political question arose, which in any way interfered with his opportunities, the good American began to believe that his democratic political machine was out of gear. Did Abolitionism create a condition of political unrest, and interfere with good business, then Abolitionists were wicked men, who were tampering with the ark of the Constitution; and in much the same way the modern reformer, who proposes policies looking toward a restriction in the activity of corporations and stands in the way of the immediate transaction of the largest possible volume of business is denounced as un-American.†

One is reminded of James Roche's attack on Ralph Nader and Campaign GM.

Croly also has some interesting things to say—relevant perhaps to the pleaders for the social responsibility of business today— about reformers. He feels it is superficial and inadequate to blame the wrongs of business exclusively on businessmen, for they are only a piece of the system:

> Under the traditional American system, with the freedom permitted to the individual, with the restriction placed on central authority, and

---

* *Ibid.*, p. 41.   ** *Ibid.*, p. 43.   † *Ibid.*, p. 49.

with its assumption of a substantial identity between the individual and the public interest—under such a system unusually energetic and unscrupulous men were bound to seize a kind and an amount of political and economic power which was not entirely wholesome. They had a license to do so; and if they failed to take advantage thereof, their failure would have been an indication not of disinterestedness or moral impeccability, but of sheer weakness and inefficiency.

At fault are the laws themselves, and more especially "the group of ideas and traditional practices behind the laws." The reformers, he said, were nearly the most despicable because

they adhere to the stupefying rule that the good Fathers of the Republic relieved their children from the necessity of vigorous, independent, or consistent thinking in political matters,—that it is the duty of their loyal children to repeat the sacred words and then await a miraculous consummation of individual and social prosperity.*

Others joined Croly in the revolt against Lockeanism.** John Dewey, in a wide-ranging series of essays, developed a philosophy of experience, looking at America as it really was and not as myth would have it. Using William James's radical empiricism, he proposed a series of redefinitions of aesthetics, logic, education, politics, and society. Like Croly, he urged an increase in national authority, in the capacity of the state to plan, concluding that there was no hope in the piecemeal approach.† Thorstein Veblen, Charles A. Beard, and Oliver Wendell Holmes, Jr., also must be included in what Schlesinger has termed "the intellectual maquis of the twenties."

Holmes's famous dissent in the Lochner case in 1905 will serve as a final example of the criticism of this era. The case arose when New York State passed legislation providing for the ten-hour day and sixty-four-hour week in bakeries. The Supreme Court invalidated the law by a vote of 5 to 4, Justice Peckham writing the majority opinion. He relied on the dominant rights of contract and property guaranteed by the Fourteenth Amendment. If the power of the state were used to validate this legislation, Peckham wrote, "no trade, no occupation, no mode of earning one's living, could

---

* *Ibid.,* pp. 149–50.
** See Morton White, *Social Thought in America: The Revolt Against Formalism* (Boston: Beacon Press, 1957; first ed. 1949, Viking Press).
† Schlesinger, "Sources of the New Deal," in *Paths of American Thought,* pp. 377–9.

escape this all pervading power, and the acts of the legislature in limiting the hours of labor in all employment would be valid, although such limitation might seriously cripple the ability of the laborer to support himself and his family."* Holmes in his dissent directly attacked the philosophical roots of the majority decision, asserting the transcendent power of the community acting through the state to limit the rights of contract and property. He made it quite clear, as we have noted, that he was explicitly rejecting the Lockean extremism of Herbert Spencer:

> The liberty of the citizen to do as he likes so long as he does not interfere with the liberty of others to do the same, which has been a shibboleth for some well-known writers, is interfered with by school law, by the Post Office, by every state or municipal institution which takes his money for purposes thought desirable, whether he likes it or not.**

Since the state had already so far interfered with personal liberty, Holmes believed it justified in going one more step to rescue from their plight those who must sell their labor at the market's price or die.

Implicit in the thought and work of Croly, Holmes, and the others lay the ingredients of a new ideology, centered on the communitarian as opposed to the individualistic vision. In it, the democratic state would play a critical integrating and planning role; competition and property would be subordinated where necessary to community and human needs. This new ideology took from the old a faith in science and the scientific method, confident that through reason nature could be controlled for the benefit of mankind.

Those who felt threatened by the new ideology evoked the specters of socialism and communism, failing to note that there was nothing necessarily totalitarian about it. The progressives of the early twentieth century opposed fascism and communism as brutal and false. But they recognized that the old ideology had subverted itself. Individualism had destroyed individual freedom; property rights had come to diminish, not protect, the political and social rights of millions; competition to satisfy consumers had become increasingly irrelevant to community need; the limited state, sup-

---

* As quoted in Morton White, *op. cit.,* p. 103.

** *Ibid.,* p. 104.

posedly sensitive to individual freedoms, had in fact become the servant of the powerful.

The Depression was a dramatization of what was in fact inevitable—the breakdown of the traditional order. The urgent issue was whether a way out of the crisis could be found and democracy at the same time preserved. The solution, the progressives said, lay in massive planning with some new set of definitions at its base, but what these new definitions were, the reformers left vague. John Dewey welcomed Franklin D. Roosevelt's moves to control and manage capitalism, but asserted "no such compromise with a decaying system is possible."* Other intellectuals of the left took up the theme, warning that we could not by some Rooseveltian sleight of hand avoid a thorough overhaul of the system.

The opposing voices from the right were similarly dogmatic. Hoover's last Secretary of the Treasury, Ogden Mills, spoke for the conservatives when he said: "We can have a free country or a socialistic one. We cannot have both. Our economic system cannot be half free and half socialistic. . . . There is no middle ground between governing and being governed, between absolute sovereignty and liberty, between tyranny and freedom."**

However absolute the alternatives were said to be, Franklin D. Roosevelt found a middle course and took it. Gradually, pragmatically, utilizing crisis but rejecting catastrophe, refusing to make explicit the ideological implications of what he did, he managed at least to hold the country together through action, gesture, and charisma. Fundamentally, he relied on the continuity of the old faith and the traditional ideology. However discordant his actions may have been, he never rejected these forces. Louis Hartz refers to "the experimental mood of Roosevelt, in which Locke goes underground, while 'problems' are solved often in a non-Lockean way. . . . What makes the New Deal 'radical' is the smothering by the American Lockean faith of the socialist challenge to it."† Thus the traditional ideology survived the onslaughts of pragmatism.

---

* Schlesinger, "Sources of the New Deal," in *Paths of American Thought,* p. 387.
** *Ibid.*
† Louis Hartz, *The Liberal Tradition in America* (New York: Harcourt, Brace & World, Inc., 1955), pp. 260, 261.

The face of America had changed, but the old foundations of legitimacy had not.

In retrospect it is obvious that the New Deal failed to solve the problems of the Depression. Some models of planning were erected, such as the Tennessee Valley Authority; some new forms of regulation were introduced; but the structure of things, the criteria for legitimacy, were scarcely touched. The old ideology lay around in bits and pieces. No new basis of consensus had been erected. The disintegration of which Croly and his friends had written was still under way.*

World War II provided a temporary means to purpose and unity —in effect, an ideological surrogate. The objectives were clear: the conquest of Berlin and Tokyo. Government determined the framework within which we were to achieve victory, and business conformed. We could ignore our internal discrepancies and contradictions in the name of patriotic devotion to the destruction of an enemy without. The Korean War, the cold war, and the tragedy of Viet Nam followed. Anti-communism became the means to coherence and integration, the unifying creed, again allowing us to postpone the renovation of our ideology. And we paid a terrible price. Lured by McCarthyism and the dogmatism of John Foster Dulles, we envisaged communism as a worldwide conspiratorial menace out of all proportion to its reality. We became blind to the manifold distinctions within the revolutionary world of the 1950's and 1960's, blurring the legitimate struggle of colonial peoples for independence with the imperialistic ambitions of the Soviet Union, failing completely to perceive the distinctions between Moscow and Peking. We tended to see all communists as alike and all change as a communist plot, an arrow pointed at our heart. We enmeshed our minds and hands in numerous "commitments" to doomed and corrupt relics of the status quo, fighting battles we could not win for causes in which we did not believe.

That is over now. We are left with a good deal of wreckage to clear away. We know that communism as an ideology—nonproprietary communal living—is no threat. As practiced in the Israeli kibbutz or even in China, we can admire some of its characteristics, even as we condemn brutality in Russia. The Soviet Union, with

---

* John Braeman, "The New Deal and the 'Broker State': A Review of the Recent Scholarly Literature," *Business History Review,* Winter 1972.

its missiles in silos and on submarines, is a threat, not for any ideological reason but because it is powerful and potentially predatory.

Our biggest problems remain with ourselves, our vision of the good community, our criteria for legitimacy, our need for new bases of authority and discipline, and the design of our relationship with a shrinking world and the fragile biosphere within which mankind must survive. We must cease to temporize. We must pick up the skeins of thought spun in the opening decades of the twentieth century—skeins that we have set aside during forty years of external threat, real and mythical—and weave them into something we can believe in. We must seek a new synthesis of ideas by which to judge and regulate our community.

In so doing, we cannot take the pragmatist's advice and reject ideology; that is a meaningless pretense. We must accept the fact of ideology, not as dogma, but as the basis of critical assumptions, the unconscious guide to decisions, the justification of the status quo. We must inspect it and renovate it, remembering that there is no such thing as a community without ideology. The choice we have is not whether to have an ideology; it is whether to have an ideology that is vital or dead, integrative or divisive.

Once again, it is useful to recall the example of Locke, who not so much invented a new ideology in the seventeenth century as articulated a timely body of ideas which already had considerable currency, and then rooted them in the new science of Isaac Newton. Locke was a synthesizer, bridging the gap between the real world of revolutionary England and the new science. He was a grand explainer of what was in fact happening, chaotically but inexorably. He was a legitimizer of change, a smoother of the path, a revealer of the issues and the choices. He drew out of science the implications for the political and social order and produced a coherent vision of what the new community should be like.

If we are to follow Locke's example, we must first of all abstract ourselves so that we may objectively inspect all our assumptions about who we are and what we are doing. In this way, the residues of old ideology that may still be with us will be revealed, and we can set about to test their utility, relevance, and justice in the light of the real world of America today. We can also look at what new ideology is in fact already in place by virtue of the apparently irreversible behavior of our institutions—in particular, business and government—and the revelations of science about nature. Between the old and the new will be a gap, a distance which represents choice, but a choice constrained by our view of the world and its future. From these three sources—the traditional ideology, the new one emergent in experience and behavior, and our estimates of what is inexorable in the future—we can begin to develop a framework of choice, a synthesized and integrated way of defining values and fixing purposes.

By the mid-1960's in the United States, any sense of community, indeed any sense of nation, was badly shattered. As one best-seller put it, America had become "one vast, terrifying anti-community."* Like Athens in the fifth century B.C., America seemed to have lost its bearings without being able to find new ones. Our virtues had become our vices; our achievements our curse. Sales, profits, production had never been greater; but there was unease, a loss of confidence, an aimlessness, malaise. In the midst of prosperity an ominous doubt prevailed, a fear that we were moving inexorably away from old, familiar moorings into an unknown sea of storms. Public opinion polls recorded the declining confidence in our political and business leadership. The blood and roses of a dying ideology were all around.

There is a propensity at times like this to seek devils to persecute and angels to worship. But surely this is the route to torture. The fault is not with any particular individual or group of individuals; it is systemic. The crisis springs from a rupture in our social, political and economic system caused by a disintegration of the old framework by which values were made explicit and institutions legitimate.

The Route to New Definitions

In general there are two ways in which new definitions of values may come about: through the conflict of many interest groups battling at the doors of government and business; or through the

---

* Charles Reich, *The Greening of America* (New York: Random House, Inc., 1970), p. 8.

explicit reformulation of our ideology into one that is more relevant, coherent, and acceptable. We can, of course, try to do both at once. The relationship between the two can be seen in Figure 2. When an ideology is vigorous and relevant, as in China, today, interest group activity is relatively low; when the ideology is weak or in transition, interest group activity is intense, pervasive, and generally chaotic.

We are familiar with communities which have plummeted from chaos and anarchy into totalitarian order—Germany in the 1930's, for example, or Stalin's Russia. We may wish to avoid such a drastic fate. It would seem unlikely, however, that the United States can remain much longer where it is. In fact, any reasonable observation of history and current events tell us that the country is moving all the time. We have to decide how far it shall move, according to what criteria, with what degree of personal and organizational freedom, and so on. We might say, for example, that Point D would be most desirable.

We could trust in the workings of interest groups to move us down the line. This indeed is the preferred American way: a vast

FIGURE 2

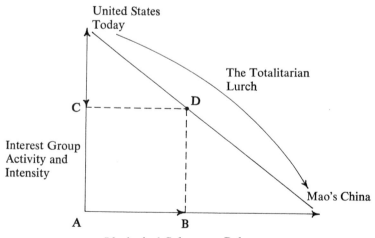

pulling and hauling—sometimes heroic, sometimes obscene—of ecologists, industrialists, unions, black power, brown power, the women's movement, ITT, U.S. Steel, Con Ed, the milk lobby, Ralph Nader, Daniel Ellsberg, Martha Mitchell, and Eric Sevareid, all battling it out in the legislatures, the state houses, the White House, the courts, the presidential campaigns, and the streets. It may not be desirable (or possible) to curtail this grand tradition, but it is clear that it is costly, time-consuming, and corrupting. Furthermore, there is reason to doubt whether such activities by themselves will be sufficient, and indeed whether, if we rely on them alone, we shall not be necessarily inviting some form of dictatorship to make the decisions which must be made.

The transformation can be greatly facilitated, it would seem, if our traditional processes were accompanied at least by an attempt to redefine explicitly our ideology and to make it more relevant to what is actually happening and what appears necessary. Then we might move more easily on the horizontal line to Point B and on the vertical to Point C.

The process of ideological formulation itself, of course, requires that the activities of interest groups be preserved if we are to retain anything like the freedom that we have cherished and avoid totalitarianism. But this process can be greatly expedited through explicit ideological analysis and clarification. John Locke did not make up a new theory of society; he observed, synthesized, and explained the chaos of change in his time, revealing issues and choices, and presenting a cohesive view of the new community aborning in his time. The implementation of his vision was, of course, a problem for generations of politicians, businessmen, and interest groups. We badly need a contemporary Locke, not to mention political leaders of the sort he helped.

With this viewpoint we can understand that the shocks and uncertainties, the fears and the doubts, which the chairman of General Motors and others around us today feel are not usefully seen as reactions to villainies or as an unrelated series of ad hoc crises. They are symptoms of a systemic change. The task is to understand the change as a whole, to see the interrelationships and to clear our minds of any old assumptions which may hinder this perception and thus distort our response to it.

As Henry Ford II put it, "the terms of the contract between industry and society are changing." Industry has succeeded, he said, by making a specialty of meeting a variety of consumer desires. "How much freedom business will retain in the closing decades of this century depends on the quality of management's response to the changing expectations of the public." It depends on management's ability to separate the inexorable from those areas where there is choice, and on its ability to inspect basic assumptions. The question is who decides what "the public" needs and how?

Ford continued: "We have to ask ourselves, what do people want that they didn't want before, and how can we get a competitive edge by offering them more of what they really want? We have to think more like entrepreneurs and innovators, and less like administrators and problem solvers."* But much of the innovation required lies in fundamental assumptions about legitimacy, authority, community need, the role of the state, and the context of science and technology. Three essential steps can be outlined here:

ONE, we must understand as fully as possible the extent to which the traditional ideology has lost its coherence, relevance, and acceptability. At the same time, we must free ourselves of the hold which it has on our perception and decisionmaking.

TWO, we must be clear in our minds about what new ideology seems to be taking its place as a result of the remorseless workings of history, and then identify the points where we still have choice.

THREE, we must then analyze the alternatives which this transformation leaves open to us, both for the internal organization of our institutions and for the relationships between our institutions and the communities they affect.

---

* Henry Ford II, "Business, the Environment and the Quality of Life," address at Harvard Business School, Boston, Dec. 2, 1969.

CHAPTER **6** From Individualism
to Communitarianism

The first of Locke's five components is the idea of individualism, with its companion notions of equality and contract. Recalling my definition of ideology as the framework of ideas by which values are defined and made explicit in the real world, "individualism" refers to the fact that the nature of society is essentially atomistic (the community being no more than the sum of the individuals in it) and also is concerned with the individual's attainment of such values as justice, self-fulfillment, and self-respect. "Equality" in the traditional ideology has meant equality in the eyes of the law and equality of opportunity for each individual. And "contract" has been used in its most individualistic sense, as a device for tying two individuals together, not in its social sense, as in Rousseau, for relating the individual to the larger community.

The American community is now in the throes of a transition from this old atomistic idea of individualism to a new organic, collective idea which I shall call communitarianism. The ideological satellites of individualism—contract and individual equality—are likewise giving way to the communitarian notions of consensus and of organizational adaptation to inequality. Unfortunately, the old is clearer than the new, but the signs of transition are obvious.

A poignant example was the case of Simas Kudirka, the Lithuanian radio operator who, seeking asylum, jumped from a Soviet trawler to the deck of the U.S. Coast Guard cutter *Vigilant* in December of 1970. The Coast Guard was so mired in bureaucratic rules that its loyalty to one of the absolutes of the traditional ideology flagged. The seamen acted like men from a civilization that had lost its moorings: they gave Kudirka back to his pursuers.

The Russians suffered no such doubts. They beat Kudirka sense-less and tied him up in a blanket.*

As bureaucracy has eroded individualism, so have social and economic inequities. In consciously designing a society in which the individual is accorded maximum freedom, we have deceived ourselves into supposing that the individuals who live in it will in fact be free. There may be a thousand Americans who could sing as well as Caruso, and would want to, if such an idea could seri-ously enter their heads; but they will never sing, for reasons that are social or economic. In the social context, they are not free— they will not fulfill themselves. "The fundamental mistake made by all those who choose weak methods of control is to assume that the balance of control is left to the individual, when in fact, it is left to other conditions," B. F. Skinner rightly notes. The other conditions, being unplanned, are accidental and thus often obscure and hard to handle. "When practices are concealed or disguised, countercontrol is made difficult; it is not clear from whom one is to escape or whom one is to attack."** Thus we find ourselves in a time of aimless flailing, aware that our freedom is diminishing but uncertain as to the identity of the tyrant or how to depose him.

Then, too, the demographic consequences of our economic activity have produced residential and industrial structures of life and work within the confines of which autonomous man finds little fulfillment. The industrial work place is in fact intensely communi-tarian, but we are reluctant to plan it as such because of our lin-gering affection for the individualism of the contract. The city neighborhood is likewise plainly a community, but we are reluctant to plan it as such because of our suspicion of governmental au-thority and of a political process dominated by interest groups, access to which is in many cases restricted and obscure. The places where we live have thus evolved into forms that frustrate our tradi-tional conceptions of the individual and how he achieves fulfill-ment and happiness; at the same time new conceptions are vague and inadequate and new forms are thus untried.

---

* Kudirka was imprisoned for treason. In 1974, the irony was intensified: he was returned to the United States after it turned out that he was in fact an American citizen, being the son of a Brooklyn-born woman who had been taken to Lithuania as a child.

** B. F. Skinner, *Beyond Freedom and Dignity* (New York: Alfred A. Knopf, Inc., 1971), p. 94.

Finally, decisionmaking by committee and the requirement for consensus in large corporations has placed in question the old virtue of self-reliance. Perhaps this is why so many Harvard Business School graduates, as Dean Fouraker remarked, have as their heroes the managers of the past for whom the old idea of individualism was "rugged," simple, and pure. Perhaps it is also why they so often prefer to work in small, entrepreneurial undertakings which, being clearly owned, are plainly property and thus clearly legitimate, with managers sure of their authority. Most managers of such enterprises doubtless adhere to the old creed. But what creed guides the big businessmen? How are they to be made legitimate, their tasks attractive to the best of the young? We shall return to this later, but it is important to note here that there are two distinct components in what too often we monolithically term "business"—one more or less consistent with the old ideology, and one searching for the new. The ideological conception of management differs between them.

Much has been written to suggest that the idea of success and even of work itself is growing obsolete. This is a dangerous and foolish misconception. The problem lies in the relationship between the terms and conditions of work in America today, on the one hand, and the definition of the values, fulfillment, and self-respect, on the other. The old relationship—or bridgework, as we have called it—through which those values used to be defined and made explicit in the real world no longer functions. A new one is being shaped, but the process is confused and takes time.

The results of the transition are well known. Daniel Yankelovich, for example, has found a marked decline in the willingness of young people to accept traditional authority. In 1968, 56 per cent of students surveyed had no objection to being "bossed around" on the job. By 1971, however, only one student out of three (36 per cent) was willing to submit to such authority. Yankelovich also found a shift in the notion that "Hard work will always pay off," from affirmation by 69 per cent in 1968 to only 39 per cent in 1971.* The problem does not lie with work or authority per se, however, but rather with the purpose and meaning of work, the legitimacy of authority, and the possibility of self-respect within

---

* Daniel Yankelovich, *Work in America: Report of the Special Task Force to the Secretary of Health, Education and Welfare* (Cambridge, Mass.: The M.I.T. Press, 1972), p. 44.

the work context. Whereas once self-respect could be had within the bounds of traditional individualism and its conceptions of autonomous man, this is no longer the case. Self-respect lies in one's relationship to a whole; work within that relationship is inseparable from it. Incentives also have changed. Money and matter are still unquestionably incentives,* but with the coming of the communitarian right to income and survival, both have lost some of their motive force.

The monumental problem confronting young people—as well as the not-so-young—is that there is no clear ideological delineation within which they can understand this transition. Young people, for example, tend to hanker after the traditional notion of individualism. Sometimes they go to absurd or even suicidal lengths to recover it. At the same time, they feel the need for new, communitarian norms to govern income distribution, inheritances, health care, and so on. They feel, but cannot quite comprehend, the contradiction between these two drives. Neither schools, parents, business, nor the political order are very helpful to them in explaining this transition or in teaching the way to adaptation. The result is too often a turning off or turning inward, a self-centeredness conditioned by the sense of futility and powerlessness to change. They withdraw from that which they cannot affect. As one twenty-year-old youth put it after returning from the Watkins Glen music festival: "We would rather live comfortable lives than struggle constantly for distant alien goals."**

The thoughts of Hegel on labor are particularly useful here. Labor—or work—is for him, if properly conceived, always creative, never merely utilitarian. It is, "always intentional, not instinctual: it represents man's power to create his own world."† The more specialized labor becomes, the more efficient, but the further it is removed from the immediate fulfillment of the producer:

Man thus achieves ever-greater comfort at the price of ever-greater abstraction and alienation in the process of production itself: "His labor and his possessions are not what they are for him, but what they

---

* It's a rare young person who doesn't want to earn money for a car.
** Ben Horowitz, "Counterculture Surfaces Again at Watkins Glen Festival," Boston *Globe*, Aug. 3, 1973, p. 20.
† Shlomo Avineri, "Labor, Alienation, and Social Classes in Hegel's *Realphilosophie*," *Philosophy and Public Affairs* 1 (Fall 1971): 103.

are for all. The satisfaction of needs is a universal dependence of all on all; there disappears for everyone the security and the knowledge that his work is immediately adequate to his particular needs; *his* particular needs become universal."

And automation is no help:

By processing nature through a multitude of machines, he does not abolish the necessity of his own labor (in the sense of creative fulfill-ment); he only pushes it further on, removes it from nature and ceases to relate to it in a live way. Instead, he flees from this negative livingness, and that work which is left to him becomes itself machine-like.*

For Hegel, the way out finally comes through the state, which shall cultivate "the reintegration of the self into itself as a universal being after economic life has particularized and atomized it and made its activity into an abstraction."

Here, of course, is the rub. We know that the state has com-mitted heinous crimes against humanity in the name of Hegel's "reintegration." It would be more desirable, presumably, if we could find a more pluralistic, more sensitive, and less centralized mode of integration.

The Restoration of Meaning

Individuals have lost their self-sufficiency; they are, as Hegel foresaw, dependent upon a complex collection of institutions, pub-lic and private, of which they are either servants or members.** We are servants of the law, of the needs of the community, of gov-ernment. We are members of business organizations; the rights of membership in determining the individual's relationship to the corporate whole are superseding those of the contract. These rights are becoming a matter of consensus rather than contract.

The passage from the notion of status which characterized the medieval ideology to that of individual freedom based on contract was a glorious one, but the idea of contract has been inexorably obstructed by several factors.

---

* Hegel, *Realphilosophie I*, as quoted in Avineri, *ibid.*, pp. 104 and 106.
** See Sir Geoffrey Vickers, "The Demands of a Mixed Economy," *The Wharton Quarterly*, Spring 1971; p. 6 and elsewhere for an interesting discussion of this point.

First, the individualistic contract cannot confer any real freedom of choice on those who must sell their labor or die. It was this failure which caused individual workers in the early days of the automobile industry to suppress their individualism and band together to collectivize the contract. And today even the collective contract is being replaced in many corporations by the consensual ideas of "participation," which appear to serve better the needs of the whole and its members.

There is a cause-and-effect relationship between the failure of the contract and the rise of the communitarian right which now virtually guarantees every American the right to survive. Even when prosperity abounds and poverty declines, the welfare roles increase; in 1973, about one out of five New Yorkers was on welfare. It was a Republican president who in 1969 proposed a guaranteed income, which was endorsed by some of the nation's leading businessmen and nearly enacted into law.*

In the second place, the contract is unable to generate the demand or regulate the supply of those goods which can only be collectively chosen and provided.** The allocation of such limited vital resources as water, air, fuels, energy, land, and even housing entails trade-offs and choices that the community must make as a whole. In 1971 and 1972, a number of oil and natural gas companies were unable to fulfill their contractual obligations. The old language of "force majeure" clauses, lifting the obligations of contract because of acts of God, piracy, and the like, seemed strangely antique and inadequate. By 1974, it was worse: soaring prices, shortages of materials, and strong demand produced a crop of broken contracts.† The community—the nation and the world—had simply failed to decide how it was going to deploy essential resources which had suddenly become scarce. Companies caught by this indecision could do little but wait for some new consensus to be shaped.

Finally, a community organized around the idea of contract cannot confer on all of its members an assured and acceptable status. It is, for example, now an aim of Equal Employment legis-

---

* Daniel P. Moynihan, *The Politics of a Guaranteed Income* (New York: Random House, Inc., 1973), pp. 56–7.
** Vickers, *op. cit.*, p. 6.
† Ralph E. Winter, "Many Contracts Now Aren't Worth the Paper They're Printed On," *Wall Street Journal*, March 26, 1974.

lation to assure that all organizations have a "fair" representation of minority group members and women, reflecting the community around them. This is a far cry from the old individualistic notion of equal opportunity; it is a stipulation of equality of result. The bitter trade union opposition to this policy emphasizes its discord with the idea of contract.

Let us consider several of these factors further, and try to clarify the ideas of communitarianism, consensus, and group equality.

There is a growing recognition within corporations that something is wrong with the traditional contractual arrangements. In a variety of ways, the idea of consensus is competing to replace or at least diminish the idea of contract as the basis for labor-management relations. In the steel industry, this has taken the form of a consensual merger at the top of the labor and management hierarchies, a no-strike pledge on the part of the union, and an agreement with management to submit to compulsory arbitration.

It is instructive to note the importance of a crisis—sharp increases in foreign imports—in causing this consensual merger. Crisis is a singularly effective means of changing structures. It would seem that a high premium should be placed upon the earliest and most precise definition of crisis in order that least crisis can afford maximum change. This is a cardinal function of education at a time of transition.

The steel industry's move to consensus, of course, does not directly touch the work relationships of the vast bulk of managers and workers. Thus it must be asked whether a consensus worked out at the top will be acceptable below and whether the motivational problems of workers will be resolved.

It is apparent that many workers feel withdrawal pains as the old ideology fades. This is especially true in large manufacturing establishments. A young man in Lordstown, Ohio, say, is brought up to believe in the old idea of fulfillment. Parents, schooling, and TV tell him of the virtues of independence, self-reliance, initiative, and the rest. When it comes time to seek work, he looks around and sees few options. Theoretically, he is a free man; but in practice he does not feel very free.* He goes to work on an assembly line, joins the United Automobile Workers, and thus becomes a member of two huge bureaucracies—General Motors, let us say,

---

* Skinner, *op. cit.,* p. 94.

and the union. He submits to two authorities, the company and the union. The management of the company is theoretically legitimized by the idea of property and the management of the union by democratic participation. But the erosion of the idea of property has placed management's legitimacy in doubt and the worker has had increasing concerns about the democratic validity of his union.

The connection between these two questionable authorities is theoretically legitimized by the collective contract, which given the traditional individualistic nature of the contract is almost a contradiction in terms. But the contract no longer seems able to embrace all of the worker's needs, especially those that arise from the discrepancy between the organization of his work place and his childhood expectations of individual fulfillment.

Alienation has become a hackneyed word, but it is reasonably precise to describe the worker's feelings. He is an alien. He is perhaps prepared to withstand the pain of alienation if he is well enough paid. But in recent years we have seen that regardless of pay increases, numbers of workers are unwilling to accept things as they are. They may erupt physically, sabotaging and wrecking whatever is nearest at hand. They may swell the Friday and Monday absentee lists and take to the hills, TV, or drugs. "For many, the traditional motivations of job security, money rewards and opportunity for personal advancement are proving insufficient," says Malcolm Denise, vice president of Ford.*

The effect on corporations is negative, especially when the work force at Toyota is behaving quite differently. At shift time in Japan, we are told, the day workers urge the night workers on to greater and greater productivity and when the company has had some great success, employees gather in the courtyard to cheer and sing. Japanese ideology continues to afford a high degree of consensus.

Several alternatives are open to us here. We could attempt to recover the old days and somehow make the contract work as the individualistic device it was meant to be, redesigning our huge corporations according to the traditional ideology. But this does not seem either feasible or desirable. General Motors and other corporations could pick up and go to Brazil or Asia, where the

---

* Malcolm Denise, speech to Ford management, November 1969.

concern with survival is sufficient to sustain traditional organizational forms. This is possible, of course, and indeed to some extent is already happening. It could result in America becoming a service-oriented, capital-intensive island in a manufacturing and labor-intensive archipelago, which might work if we could be sure of getting our money back in the face of rising nationalism. It also raises serious questions about leisure and what happens to displaced manufacturing workers. A third alternative would be to do as Nixon did in 1971, erect trade walls to protect U.S. industry from more productive foreign enterprise. This constitutes preserving a decaying system, paying the price in inflation. A final alternative is to do two things simultaneously, both of which are enormously complex and difficult.

First, we have to re-educate American youth to the fact that individual fulfillment comes about as the result of participating in an organic social process. Those who are fulfilled today are so because they are part of a whole in which they can make full use of their competence and capabilities. They have a sense of power and influence in that whole. They are motivated to use their imaginations and initiative to contribute to making it better. In such circumstances they work hard and have self-respect. As more than a hundred studies made during the past twenty years show, what workers want most "is to become masters of their immediate environments and to feel that their work and they themselves are important—the twin ingredients of self-esteem."*

The fact remains that before an individual can master his environment, he must comprehend it as a whole. He must also have confidence that its institutions are susceptible to change, that they are not the inhuman, incomprehensible constructs at the gates of which he can only patiently wait like Kafka's benighted characters. And he must see the relationships between critical categories of knowledge: the sciences, politics, the economy, social forces, and culture.

Second, we must redesign our work places according to this new idea of individual fulfillment through community. A corporation is, after all, nothing more than a collection of men and machines, taking matter in, processing it, and putting it out. Theoretically, we can assemble it however we choose. To organize work accord-

---

* Yankelovich, *op. cit.,* p. 13.

ing to the communitarian idea, we need to build throughout the enterprise a sense of participation in the decisions that affect the whole. The idea of consensus will then move in to replace the idea of contract.

The transition to such a communitarian ethic would also help to resolve the problem of management's authority; its legitimacy would derive from a consensus of the whole rather than from a collection of mythical shareholder owners. As investors, the shareholders would doubtless be better off as well, because the corporation would presumably be more efficient, its work force more productive, and its management more effective.

A number of companies are experimenting with just such redesign, although it is doubtful that they are sensitive to the ideological significance of what they are doing. This insensitivity can lead to misjudgments and hence failure. The automobile companies, for example, are engaged in various efforts at "organizational development," "job enrichment," and the like. These bottom-up efforts are designed to give the worker a greater sense of participation in the whole: a team of workers makes an entire bus, for example. They are also aimed at giving him a greater degree of responsibility for the design and organization of work and thus a greater sense of fulfillment. These activities are often handled by the vice president of personnel and his staff, which generally includes men trained in the behavioral sciences, whence the tone of many of these experiments derives. Such efforts are somewhat suspect because they are tentative and experimental, because they are oriented to the individual as well as to the organization, and because they clearly present a threat to the old contractual institutions.

Union leaders have criticized these efforts as "élitist nonsense," paternalistic attempts to divide the workers from the union. Job enrichment is just "a stop watch in sheep's clothing," says William Winpisinger, general vice president of the International Association of Machinists: "The better the wage, the greater the job satisfaction. There is no better cure for 'blue collar blues.' "* Both George Morris, Jr., vice president in charge of industrial relations at GM, and Leonard Woodcock of the UAW seem to attribute the "aliena-

---

* Byron E. Calame, "Wary Labor Eyes Job Enrichment," *Wall Street Journal*, Feb. 26, 1973.

tion" problem to academics who do not know what they are talking about.* Such a turn of events is not surprising if one considers what is happening ideologically. It is perfectly natural that bureaucratic interests associated with the contract—both in management and in unions—will resent and oppose attempts to erode the contract in favor of consensus.

Equally, there will be a natural tendency on the part of relatively new and insecure personnel men to try to sneak the new ways into the company without disturbing the old secure contractual forms; but "sneaking" may lead to failure or disruption because the old forms are exactly what must give way. The situation is comparable to what happened in the 1930's, when the old ideas of property and management rights were threatened by unionization and the collective contract. What the union organizers did to established management forty years ago is akin to what the ideologies of renewed humanism are beginning to do to both the management and union establishment today. In the 1930's, managerial blindness to what was transpiring meant that the transition was needlessly bloody, disruptive, and wasteful. Today, however, union management is threatened as well, which makes the transition even more difficult, particularly if a corporation chooses to take the bottom-up approach of the auto industry as opposed to the top-down approach of the steel industry.

The notion of consensus not only threatens management and union interests associated with the contract; it also suggests a massive change in the managerial hierarchy and in the source of management's authority. One of the more extreme consensual models in the United States is that developed by a pet food subsidiary of General Foods in Topeka, Kansas. This is a new plant with no union. Its designers deliberately set out to build a community in which all workers would have a sense of identity; in which each would have maximal capacity for personal growth; where managers would derive their authority from the consent of all; and where individual fulfillment would come from a sense of contribution to and control over a community, and not from competitive individualism. They organized the work force into self-managed teams which are given collective responsibility for large parts of the production process. Individual assignments were

---

* *Newsweek,* March 26, 1973, p. 82.

made by the teams themselves, following a consensus-making procedure, in the light of the capabilities and needs of individual workers. There was a deliberate attempt to break down division of labor and specialization: an employee's pay increases were geared to his mastering an increasing number and variety of jobs, first in his team and then in the plant as a whole. "In effect, team members are paid for learning more and more aspects of the total manufacturing system."* After two years of operation the Topeka experiment showed signs of success, including high productivity and profitability. Similar successes with comparable experiments have been reported by Procter & Gamble in one of its newer plants, and by a number of European companies, especially Norsk-Hydro, a Norwegian manufacturer of fertilizer and chemicals, and Saab-Scandia and Volvo, two Swedish automobile manufacturers.** One of the most extensive experiments of this sort is being conducted in Peru, where the new "industrial communities" law provides for eventual 50 per cent ownership of all business firms by the workers.

Note the radicality of the Topeka model and others like it. They suggest that a corporate collective works better when the legitimacy and thus the authority of managers derives from the managed. In this sense, these so-called "organization development" experiments represent an important convergence between the specialized search of behavioral scientists, on the one hand, and a major ideological trend, on the other. The search is for a way to increase workers' motivation and productivity; the trend is toward communitarianism, consensus, and rights of membership, and away from individualism, contract, and property rights. The full significance of these experiments is missed if they are seen only in terms of the search and not in terms of the total convergence. What might seem to be only a minor change in personnel policies is here revealed as a radical and comprehensive change in basic structures, promising certain benefits but also entailing possible dangers, of which both management and workers ought to be aware.

The first is a threat to equality and fairness inherent in the move from contract to consensus. Each team at the Topeka factory is

---

* Richard E. Walton, "How to Counter Alienation in the Plant," *Harvard Business Review,* November–December 1972, p. 75.
** *Ibid.,* pp. 79 and 80.

responsible for selecting, that is, hiring, replacements. Teams presumably will select those who "get along" well with the group. This means that those who do not fit in may be excluded. Equality as an idea is strongly associated with individualism; it is threatened by communitarianism unless the community defines explicit norms to protect it. Collectivism can be dehumanizing on any scale.

Second, in considering whether to extend the Topeka experiment to other plants where there may be unions, management may fail to understand fully that consensus is a radically different conception from contract and that careful adjustments must be made. Old bureaucracies and hierarchies have grown up on both sides of the contract, their loyalty to it strengthened by self-interest. Then, too, the consensus-making mechanisms which are so familiar to other cultures such as the Japanese are strange to Americans. Without persistence and careful education on all sides—without, in short, acculturation—consensual efforts such as those at Topeka may flourish for a while but then erode before the resilience of the old ideas and their institutional remnants.

Finally, the Topeka experiment constitutes a threat to the traditional conception of management rights and hierarchy. Indeed, the managers' very jobs are at stake, if subordinates are to decide who the managers are. And what is to happen to the myth of shareholder ownership and the theoretical tasks of the board of directors?

The full implications of such innovations can only be understood when considered in relation to the traditional ideology which once made business legitimate. Nonetheless, they have an ideological striking force we cannot ignore. Forty years ago, John Dewey put it concisely:

The only form of enduring social organization that is now possible is one in which the new forces of productivity are cooperatively controlled and used in the interest of effective liberty and the cultural development of the individuals that constitute society. Such a society cannot be established by an unplanned and external convergence of the actions of separate individuals, each of whom is bent on personal private advantage.*

---

* John Dewey, *Liberalism and Social Action* (New York: Capricorn Books, 1963), p. 54.

Whether we make the transition from contract to consensus comfortably may well depend on whether the good of the corporation and the community as a whole will outweigh the needs and desires of existing managers for power and prestige. The change that confronts them will be as difficult as the change that confronted the traditional Roman administrators forced to accept Christianity.

Redefining Equality

I have already pointed out that the old ideas of individualism and contract have been inextricably bound in Lockean thought to the old idea of equality. It follows then that the old idea of equality must change also, and so indeed it has. Daniel Bell must be credited with having perceived the change first and John Rawls with proceeding consequently to the definition of a new theory of justice.* In fact, if anyone deserves the title of a modern Locke, it seems to me that it is Rawls, who in his *Theory of Justice* has formulated a new bridge between "justice" and the modern reality of Western civilization. He utilizes the conceptions of contract and equality, but in a most non-Lockean way. For Rawls, both become communitarian—ideas for attaining and measuring a good community, and for defining the place and behavior of individuals in that community.

Bell demonstrates the change in the old idea of equality by analyzing the civil rights legislation of the 1960's. The initial intention of this legislation and of the Executive Orders which accompanied it was to guarantee equality of opportunity for each individual by eliminating discrimination. This was consistent with Lockean thought. But the practical objective was not being reached. So, since the early 1970's, the principle has changed in law and practice from equality of opportunity to the radical conception of equality of representation or result.** Blacks, Chicanos, and women are now to be employed as a matter of right, according to their numbers and presumed qualifications: that is, if there are

---

* Daniel Bell, "On Meritocracy and Equality," *The Public Interest,* Fall 1972, p. 29; and John Rawls, *A Theory of Justice* (Cambridge, Mass.: Belknap Press, 1971). I do not mean to imply that Rawls relied on Bell's perception. He probably proceeded quite independently.

** Bell, *op cit.,* p. 37.

a certain number of female college graduates in a corporation or in the community upon which the corporation draws for labor, for example, there must be a comparable representation of women in the corporate hierarchy. Thus what had been an individual opportunity right ten years ago has now become a communitarian principle. A "good" organization must have a specific representational profile. As Bell has pointed out:

The liberal and radical attack on discrimination was based on its denial of a justly earned place to a person on the basis of an unjust group attribute. That person was judged—and excluded—because he was a member of a particular group. But now it is being demanded that one must have a place primarily because one possesses a particular group attribute.*

An entirely new definition of equality has developed: "*equality of result*—in income, status and power—for all men [and women] in society."**

The implications of this shift for business are, of course, far-reaching. A good example of the new definition in action is the recent discrimination case at American Telephone and Telegraph.† In 1970, AT&T was seeking a 9 per cent increase in long-distance telephone rates from the Federal Communications Commission. Lawyers from the government's Equal Employment Opportunity Commission persuaded the FCC not to act on the request until the company changed its policies regarding women and minority employees. The EEOC regarded those policies as de facto discrimination. The EEOC, however, did not proceed along the traditional arguments of equality of opportunity for each individual. Instead, it argued that discrimination in AT&T had become "institutionalized," that it was a systemic problem in the company. The aim of the EEOC's young lawyers was clearly equality of result by whatever necessary means; they were applying a new criterion for the definition of "good community."††

Their suit was successful in terms of the adjusted definition of equality. The company upgraded 50,000 women and 6,600 mi-

---

 * *Ibid.,* p. 38.   ** *Ibid.,* p. 40.

 † Harvey D. Shapiro, "Women on the Line, Men at the Switchboard," *The New York Times Magazine,* May 20, 1973, pp. 26, 73–91; *Business Week,* June 8, 1974, p. 28.

 †† The leader of the EEOC team was David Copus, a thirty-one-year-old Harvard Law School graduate and former Peace Corps volunteer in India. AT&T was his first case.

nority group workers and, perhaps most significantly, hired 4,000 men as operators and clerical workers, to fill jobs traditionally held by women. By 1974, AT&T had agreed to provide $75 million as compensation for groups that the government said had been victims of discrimination. Some 1,500 female college graduates who had held managerial jobs between 1965 and 1971 but who were, according to the government, kept out of certain training programs received $850,000; 500 switchroom helpers at Michigan Bell got $500,000; and 3,000 women in craft jobs received up to $10,000 each. These three groups were awarded back pay not because they had been discriminated against as individuals, but because they "may have been" paid less than men doing equal or comparable work. A fourth group was named in the ruling—it comprised the women who had been consigned to "female" jobs and minority group males in menial job categories. Since it was simply not feasible to indemnify this huge group, the government took a symbolic approach. The first 10,000 women and minority group males who had transferred into craft jobs and held them successfully for six months received a lump-sum payment to "compensate them for the delay in transferring." Thousands of supervising and management employees also benefited from the action. Finally, the company agreed to use an elaborate system of goals and timetables for the employment of women and minority groups in the future, to ensure fair representation.

In this ruling we see the community imposing by decree a wholesale definition of what a good organization should look like. This is a far cry from previous civil rights cases that revolved around the old notion of equality of opportunity, where an individual was required to bring an action showing that he or she had been clearly discriminated against. The company treated the whole affair as though there had been some terrible misunderstanding—as though it had never intended to do any "wrong." The fact, of course, is that the fundamental rules of the game had changed. "Wrong" had changed in meaning; the underlying idea of individualism had been replaced; and a new definition of the value we call justice was at hand.

The union for its part felt equally abused and injured. The Communications Workers of America, representing 600,000 Bell System employees, realized that the consensual basis of the ruling as well as its terms were threats to the sanctity and validity of the collective contract and sought to delay its implementation in Federal Court, arguing that it trespassed on the union's right to bargain with the company over seniority and promotion policies. Again, the irony of the management-union alignment is strong. (One cannot help but recall the nineteenth-century mill owners who complained that child labor legislation violated their sacred right to contract for the skills of twelve-year-old girls.)

In a similar more recent case, General Motors signed a consent decree promising to make efforts in good faith to hire 20 per cent women and 80 per cent men for production and assembly jobs at its St. Louis plant.*

And so it is unjust, today, for a company to employ and promote solely on the basis of present potential or ability; it must consider demographics, sexual identity, minority representation, and a host of other social and political factors as well. Equally, a union can no longer count on the traditional contractual notions of seniority. Instead, it also must consider a similar host of political and social factors as they bear upon the organization as a whole. How is a company to weigh all the factors? If it waits for government action, it will sail into a morass of retroactive punishment. How is a union to decide its priorities for pressuring management? It does not know. Indeed, it would seem that government is doing the significant pressuring at the moment, with both management and unions in retreat. It appears that both are to consider the same economic, political, and social factors and come up with a consensus, limiting what negotiating efforts they may undertake to the settlement of details. Whether that impression is entirely correct or not, both groups clearly need a new vision of what they are and are not supposed to do. The time has come to look at the general terms and conditions of the concept of justice as it is being redefined.

Justice as Fairness

Implicit in this redefinition of equality and in the new ideology of which it is a part lies a distrust of merit as a justification for

---

* *Business Week,* May 26, 1973, p. 30.

individuals' different achievements. The development of merit is too closely tied to matters of economic, political, and social advantage, practically speaking. Meritocracy is seen as a way the rich stay rich, the intelligent pass on their intelligence, and the more equal retain their control over the less equal. Christopher Jencks, for example, in his controversial study, found that inequality, seemed to depend upon varieties of luck and on-the-job competence that are only moderately related to family background, schooling, or scores on standardized tests. He concluded that if we are going to have equality of result,

we will have to change the rules of the game so as to reduce the rewards of competitive success and the costs of failure. Instead of trying to make everybody equally lucky or equally good at his job, we will have to devise "insurance" systems which neutralize the effects of luck, and income sharing systems which break the link between vocational success and living standards.*

If we are to have such equality of result, then we shall need "an entirely new political agenda," as Bell notes, and a new philosophical foundation for it. John Rawls envisages a communal society in which "justice" is defined as fairness and considered the highest value. Justice as fairness rests initially on two principles, which bear repeating: the first concerns the liberties of citizenship, the Bill of Rights, and so on; the second, social and economic inequalities, the distribution of wealth and power, and the legitimacy of authority:

First: each person is to have an equal right to the most extensive basic liberty compatible with a similar liberty for others.
Second: social and economic inequalities are to be arranged so that they are both (a) reasonably expected to be for everyone's advantage, and (b) attached to positions and offices open to all.* *

Rawls stipulates that the first of these principles takes priority over the second. That is,

a departure from the institutions of equal liberty required by the first principle cannot be justified by, or compensated for, by greater social and economic advantages. The distribution of wealth and income, and

---

* Christopher Jencks, *Inequality: A Reassessment of the Effect of Family and Schooling in America,* as quoted in Bell, *op. cit.,* p. 47.
* * Rawls, *op. cit.,* p. 60.

the hierarchies of authority, must be consistent with both the liberties of equal citizenship and equality of opportunity.*

Here we have the juridical framework to make a communal organization, such as the Topeka pet food plant, "fair."

The critical phrases in the second principle are "to everyone's advantage" and "open to all." By "open to all," Rawls means first that those who have ability and drive are entitled to what they have earned. But he goes further to take account of social contingencies and unfairness:

> In all sectors of society there should be roughly equal prospects of culture and achievement for everyone similarly motivated and endowed. . . .
> Chances to acquire cultural knowledge and skills should not depend upon one's class position, and so the school system, whether public or private, should be designed to even out class barriers.**

In addition, he finds it necessary to even out natural advantages in order to ensure equality and fairness:

> There is no more reason to permit the distribution of income and wealth to be settled by the distribution of natural assets than by historical and social fortune. . . . The extent to which natural capacities develop and reach fruition is affected by all kinds of social conditions and class attitudes. Even the willingness to make an effort, to try, and so to be deserving in the ordinary sense is itself dependent upon happy family and social circumstances. It is impossible in practice to secure equal chances of achievement and culture for those similarly endowed, and therefore we may want to adopt a principle which recognizes this fact and also mitigates the arbitrary effects of the natural lottery. . . .†

If one cannot equalize opportunity, in other words, one must recognize the inequalities and make sure that the social structure adapts to these discrepancies among its members. Rawls acknowledges that no one deserves natural gifts or merits a more favorable starting place in society,†† but he recognizes that it is neither possible nor necessarily desirable to eliminate these distinctions. We do not, after all, want to put lead belts around the speedy. But fortunately:

> There is another way to deal with them [distinctions]. The basic structure [the corporation, for example] can be arranged so that these

---

* *Ibid.*, p. 61. ** *Ibid.*, p. 73. † *Ibid.*, p. 74. †† *Ibid.*, p. 102.

contingencies work for the good of the least fortunate. Thus we are led to the difference principle if we wish to set up the social system so that no one gains or loses from his arbitrary place in the distribution of natural assets or his initial position in society without giving or receiving compensating advantages in return. . . . The naturally advantaged are not to gain merely because they are more gifted, but only to cover the costs of training and education and for using their endowments in ways that help the less fortunate as well.*

Thus we move from the meaning of "open to all" to that of "everyone's advantage." Rawls notes that this phrase can be defined in terms of either a principle of efficiency or a principle of difference. The efficiency principle is familiar from traditional utilitarianism—an efficient system is one in which it is impossible to change an existing allocation of goods or utilities so as to make some persons better off without at the same time making some other persons worse off. This principle offends Rawls's sense of communitary justice because it concerns only a net social balance and is indifferent to individual fairness. "The fault of the utilitarian doctrine," he says, "is that it mistakes impersonality for impartiality."** The difference principle, on the other hand, states that if some persons are to be better off, the less advantaged are also to be better off: "The intuitive idea is that the social order is not to establish and secure the more attractive prospects of those better off unless doing so is to the advantage of those less fortunate."†

Rawls then states his general conception of social justice as follows: "All social primary goods—liberty and opportunity, income and wealth, and the bases of self-respect—are to be distributed equally unless an unequal distribution of any or all of these goods is to the advantage of the least favored."††

Rawls's justice as fairness doctrine is, of course, radically different from the traditional ideology's definition of justice in terms of individual rights, guaranteed by property rights, governed through competition within a limited state. It speaks rather in communitarian terms wherein there are proscribed rights of membership in a good social organization. His way is not necessarily less democratic, however. The difference principle sees to that.

---

* *Ibid.,* pp. 102 and 101.   ** *Ibid.,* p. 190.   † *Ibid.,* p. 75.
†† *Ibid.,* p. 303.

In Bell's opinion, the new ideology inherent in Rawls's political philosophy "will go far to shape the last part of the 20th century as the doctrines of Locke and Smith molded the 19th." This is entirely consistent with my own speculation. Of course, we are left with a number of loose ends, to say the least. There are the problems of measuring and defining "advantaged" and "disadvantaged," "fairness" and "unfairness"; of who decides and how; of who should be helped first; and of degree of disparity. How much difference should there be, for example, between the income, power, and prestige of the chairman of the board and an assembly line worker, and who should decide, using what criteria? Bell notes that the extremes of difference in pay in a business corporation are about 20:1, in a hospital about 10:1, and in a university about 5:1. What is fair? The answers, of course, depend upon authority, and authority in turn upon legitimacy; they will emerge as the future unfolds.

In general terms it seems likely, however, that these questions will increasingly be answered by a consensus of the relevant whole. The General Foods plant in Topeka will decide for itself the income ratios of its various employees. If the plant there follows the pattern of worker self-management in Yugoslavia, the employees will find that they have to pay the going rate for good management. The management-worker pay differentials, however, may well decrease from their present standard. The plant is, of course, part of a larger whole, in this case the community of Topeka; and the least advantaged members of the Topeka community would have to be borne in mind (following Rawls's reasoning) when the workers consider the organization and operation of the plant. Some may argue that just such an effort is today being pioneered by such business-led organizations as the Urban Coalition and the National Alliance of Business. What Rawls and the new ideology would prescribe, however, is considerably broader and more compelling. That is, the community as a whole which is affected by a particular plant would be expected to consider the total set of relationships between plant and community. The plant, and its corporation, would thus become an inseparable part of the larger communal whole.

This outcome would fulfill a condition of the new ideology, for both the plant itself and the people within it would enjoy a new measure of self-respect. Self-respect demands an integrated social and political order to give meaning to work, and a group of related institutions that affords everyone the opportunity to make the most of himself for the good of the whole. To be sure, these goals require extraordinary leadership and extraordinary individuals to provide it, but it is also critical that each institution, especially those of the political order, have clear functions. I shall return to this point when I discuss the role of the state in Chapter 9. Here let us just say that the individual and communal tragedies of Watergate emphasize the vulnerability of the individual when the power and importance of the group is great. Unless communitarianism and the notion of individual fulfillment as a part of a group is accompanied by a rigorous code of individual responsibility, a respect for the rights of the individual, strict protection for the whistle blower, and regard for the independent thinker, then we are more than likely to drift into Orwell's world of Doublethink, where organizational loyalty compels the individual to hold two contradictory beliefs simultaneously. It is tempting to wish the group away, to seek in old-time individualism a way out, but this would be sheer delusion. The group is with us; we are bound to live in a world of ever-increasing complexity where big organizations are essential; only conscious safeguards explicitly drawn can guarantee the value of self-respect in the new ideology.

The call to communitarianism, this search for fulfillment and self-respect within organic social processes, is rooted in a basic primitive impulse and shaped today by dynamics that in other times have been called religious. To understand and develop this idea, we should distinguish several historical stages in Western society, at each of which the definition of the individual and his fulfillment has been sharply different.*

First was the inescapable submissiveness imposed by the tribal life of the Germanic hordes which burst upon Europe toward the end of antiquity. The individual stood or fell with the group. It was in that world of the Dark Ages that the early Christian conception of the *person* emerged, the first light of individualism. But

---

* Karl Mannheim, *Man and Society in an Age of Reconstruction* (New York: Harcourt, Brace & Co., 1940), pp. 68-70.

the individual was inseparable from his role in life; man existed not in his individuality and singularity, but in his communion with others. This idea became institutionalized in the great religious and feudal constructions of medievalism. These institutions eventually drifted away from the ideology, as we have seen, and fell apart.

Second came the world of possessive, competitive individualism, which exploded during the seventeenth century in protest against the feudal communitarian models. As Mannheim puts it, "Society was not the result of a preconceived plan but developed from a chance integration of many antagonistic activities."*

Third is the stage which is forming around us now. Increasingly, individuals are being forced to renounce their private interests and to subordinate themselves to the interests of larger social units. Some have suggested that we are returning to a form of the early Christian ideology. This may be true, but so much has happened to man's consciousness between the first millennium and now that the hypothesis seems tenuous to me. It *is* true that we confront the same question that our medieval forebears did: How does one organize and direct a communitarian society and still provide for the self-respect of each individual member in the community? This question is difficult to grasp. As we have seen, man and society and the ideological framework which connects them are neither static nor disjointed; they are part of a continuous process, hard to catch and harder still to hold. "We are not stuff that abides, but patterns that perpetuate themselves; whirlpools of water in an ever-flowing river."** Or as Ervin Laszlo says in rather more functional terms:

Man is, in the final analysis, a coordinating interface system in the multilevel hierarchy of nature. . . . We are faced with the following variables: increasing communication—hence determination—on the macrolevel of sociocultural systems, great differentiation among individual aptitudes and potentials, and the value of individual and human fulfillment. Our humanistic goal is to enhance individual fulfillment in an increasingly deterministic multilevel society composed of greatly differentiated individuals.†

---

* *Ibid.,* p. 69.
** Norbert Wiener, *The Human Use of Human Beings* (New York: Avon Books, 1954).
† Ervin Laszlo, *The Systems View of the World* (New York: George Braziller, Inc., 1972), pp. 79 and 116.

The good and just organization is not one that provides equality of opportunity so much as one that adapts itself to the natural, inevitable inequalities of all its members.

Two ethics emerge: an ecological ethic, which is necessary if man is to avoid the destruction of the fragile biosphere within which he is encased; and a self-realization or self-fulfillment ethic, which allows each human being to develop his vital powers to the fullest extent. The two must be combined if we are to reach the optimal forms of social and community organizations and to specify clearly the relationship of individuals as members of those organizations. Both take us back to the spirit of early Judeo-Christian thought and to Eastern concepts of the oneness of the human race and the harmony of man in communion with nature. This connection is important because any successful transformation must build upon the past, recognizing long-lived principles, and synthesizing what is treasured now with what is required by the future.

Inherent in the transformation in which we are engaged there is an evolutionary thrust toward a wider, more extensive consciousness, a heightened sense of biological interrelation, a more far-reaching awareness of the relationships among people and between people and institutions—of wholes within wholes, part of a planetary whole, and beyond. This growing organic quality of man's awareness is an essential if mystical part of the new ideology, standing in sharp contrast with the atomistic, mechanistic interpretations of the recent past. Because of it, we are in critical need of religious assistance to provide ways in which to understand this open-ended set of mysteries which goes well beyond the powers of science. It is doubtful whether man can live with the coldly objective fact that, in the words of Jacques Monod, "he is alone in the indifferent immensity of the universe, whence he has emerged by chance."*

The religious among us are reminiscent of the bishops of the Middle Ages. William Irwin Thompson, that poetic prophet of our times, calls them institutions by themselves, as St. Thomas was. He points to archetypal figures—Nader, Buckminster Fuller, Herman Kahn, Timothy Leary (I'm not sure about him), Ivan Illich, and Paola Soleri, quoting their remarkable achievements, and the "colossal scale of media society" that has enabled them to become

---

* Interview in *The New York Times,* March 15, 1971.

free and rise above the old structures of American corporate life. His mystic vision is that:

As (these) people walk out of the old containers, the anarchic energy released will stimulate the economy in a host of unforeseen ways. . . . The solution to all our problems, or to any of them, is not going to come from General Motors, the Communist party or M.I.T.; it will come from the changes wrought by the new artistic capitalism of the individual as an institution.*

There is something hopeful and exciting in Thompson's projection. It resembles that of Jean-François Revel, the French leftist philosopher who contends that the revolution of the twentieth century is going on in America—and only here—as the result of the openness of our society and its propensity to generate a continuous stream of innovators who form important followings.** But Thompson's hopes may be somewhat utopian and insufficient. The individuals he mentions are important and can have considerable impact, given the continued freedom of the media. Their importance, however, is comparable to that of the Old Testament prophets or the medieval saints. Nader, for example, has done enormous good by helping us to perceive the illegitimacy of the large public corporation. In seeking to arouse stockholders to their responsibilities as property owners, he dramatized the fact that they neither are nor want to be owners, that the corporation is no longer property. Yet his suggestion that stockholders should want to be owners and that their annual meetings should be legislatures for the control of corporations was both naïve and impractical. The structure is going to change, but not in the ways Nader has proposed.

Nevertheless, if we are moving back into a new form of medievalism, some of these men may well be among the bishops. Each stands for an organic order that can embrace individual differences. The pope himself (who after all is something of "an individual as institution") has provided some useful advice:

The Christian who wishes to live his faith in a political activity which he thinks of as service cannot without contradicting himself adhere

---

* *The New York Times,* "Resurrection of Man," Dec. 31, 1971, and Jan. 1, 1972.
** Jean-François Revel, *Without Marx or Jesus* (Garden City, N.Y.: Doubleday & Co., Inc., 1970).

... to the liberal ideology which believes it exalts individual freedom by withdrawing it from every limitation, by stimulating it through exclusive seeking of interest and power, and by considering social solidarities as more or less automatic consequences of individual initiatives, not as an aim and a major criterion of the value of the social organization.*

In spite of the pending transformation of which these men are symptoms, it is plain that the old brand of individualism is highly resilient. There are roughly 35 million handguns in America, about 1 for every 1.4 families. A person is murdered with a handgun every 58 minutes (in England it happens every seven and a half weeks).** And yet we still seem incapable of enacting effective gun control legislation. Many otherwise intelligent Americans cling to the old notion that the right to bear arms is their basic right as individuals, a firm safeguard of democracy. Nothing demonstrates the power of ideology more persuasively; the application of reason surely reveals that in our cities today the very right to bear arms is among the most potent threats to the existence of the individual, let alone his rights.

In much of the thought, rhetoric, and action about the "social responsibility" of business, signs of the old ideology remain. There is still a disposition to suppose that American business can solve the social and socio-technological problems of our time. The opinion is heard that if business "wanted" to, if it were "socially responsible," it could effectively address the problems which plague our major cities, such as poverty, housing, unemployment, and even transportation and education; it could wipe out the blight of pollution; it could even set about the establishment of a new world order through the workings of multinational enterprises.† Business, it is said, is engaged in a war with the evils of our time, a war that it must win.†† "The new demand," says Peter Drucker, "is for business to *make* social values and beliefs, *create* freedom for the individual, and *altogether produce* the good society [emphasis

---

* Apostolic Letter by Pope Paul VI on Marxism and liberalism, *The New York Times,* May 15, 1971.
** Nathan Cobb, "Handguns in Great Britain," Boston *Globe,* Aug. 12, 1973.
† See Frank Tannenbaum, "The Survival of the Fittest," *Journal of World Business,* March–April 1968.
†† See "The War that Business Must Win," *Business Week,* Nov. 1, 1969.

added]."* Oddly enough, this call is echoed by governmental leaders, businessmen, liberals, conservatives, and bomb-throwing extremists, all of whom reflect the traditional American myth that business is virtually omnipotent.

For its part, business says that it is ready to do what it can to respond to the call. This is understandable. The quality of life in our society is obviously connected to the interests of business. If business neglects it, the penalty is high in terms of public outcry and government reaction. Business cannot sell to a sick society. Businessmen are mindful of their consciences and their image— improvements in the quality of life may offer new and rewarding business opportunities.** The haymaker in this string of arguments is that historically business has responded to various national calls for help efficiently and effectively; indeed, the techniques and system of American management are among our most renowned achievements. The demand that business apply itself to problems which government is finding it increasingly difficult to comprehend or affect is not only understandable, but profoundly appealing to traditional Lockean thought—including that of corporate leaders themselves—on the limited role of government and the glorification of the individual, his initiative, and his property.

But it is also absurd. Corporations, whatever else they may be, are not purveyors of social assistance. The danger is that they will make an oversimplified response to this siren call, which will spell disaster. Businessmen and the technical experts under their command are frequently unprepared to deal with political questions, and the community is unwilling to relinquish such authority to them. Some enthusiasts for the business solution point to the immense and successful efforts that corporations mounted to meet the crises of our wars; but the analogy between business action to improve the quality of life and business participation in a war effort is imprecise and misleading. In a war, at least one like World War II, the political and ideological cast within which all operations take place is clearly set out by the government and accepted by the community. Purposes and priorities are explicit:

---

* Peter F. Drucker, "Business and the Quality of Life," in Peter F. Drucker, ed., *Preparing Tomorrow's Business Leaders Today* (Englewood Cliffs, N.J.: Prentice-Hall, Inc., 1969), p. 77.
** *Ibid.,* pp. 78–9.

the production of guns, tanks, bullets, and airplanes to be used for the conquest of the enemy, the capture of a place. Business participation in such an activity is, of course, politically and ideologically simple, as it is in the space program; it works harmoniously within a structured setting to meet explicit objectives.*

If the United States is currently involved in a war to remake our domestic society, then the prerequisites for its successful conduct are the definition of the purpose of the struggle, and the establishment of goals and criteria for measuring victory. When such a political or ideological framework is in place, business can work efficiently within it. But for unelected businessmen to suppose that they can erect such a framework suggests anarchy. They have neither the right nor the competence to do so.

Business as Saviour?

This truth is particularly relevant when the authority of government is in question, as it is today. When a senator or a cabinet officer comes to business and says, "The job of transforming our cities is yours. Use the great genius of American business," it is hard for business to reply, "No, my friend. That is your job; we can only help when you have given us the specifications. What will be the direction, speed and design—the ideological basis—of the transformation? You are the politician. You are the elected ruler of the community. You are the sovereign state. You speak for the people; you have to do your job first." Still, that is the answer business must give. Otherwise, government will be further distracted from its task, its authority further undermined, its power more dissipated; perhaps most important, its planning processes will be weakened and delayed. Hence, if the politician speaks as a somewhat Lockean pragmatist, as he has above, the businessman must answer him as an anti-Lockean who recognizes the need for a new ideology.

It is worth pointing out here how far around the circle of irony we have traveled in the last thousand years. In A.D. 1000, the

---

* Of course, the case of the Viet Nam war is different. The purposes of the war and the political structure which the government set up to execute it were neither clear nor acceptable to large portions of the community. Business participation in this effort was correspondingly messy.

healthy mechanisms of politics and society in Western Europe denied honor and merit, sometimes even living space, to business as a concern in its own right; now our social and political orders have proceeded so far toward bankruptcy that they look to the economic sector all too often as the fountainhead of all solutions. Where once it was legitimate to question whether the economic order had any creative force at all, the other orders are now questioning whether sufficient creative force to solve our ills can be mustered from any source other than economic man in collectivity, in the form of the corporation. Business would seem to have worked its way up from the harness to the driver's seat. Small wonder, indeed, that medieval conceptions seem to be re-emerging, even if in transmuted form.

For the question whether the economic sector can take the lead can be decisively answered in the negative. Three varied examples of the failures that occur when business is flattered into responding to the siren call on its own are instructive here because they indicate the genuinely great potential of business to help in these areas, even if it cannot be expected to do the driving for us.

In Urban Black Communities

A varied and rapid assortment of unplanned changes is taking place today in our cities, resulting from the natural play of a wide variety of forces: the flow of jobs, the yearning of individuals for a better neighborhood, the working of the community, and so forth. Professor David L. Birch has been using census data to measure what actually has been going on. He sees a process at work wherein the central portions of many older cities are slowly emptying of blacks, who are going to the suburbs, where jobs are more plentiful and the living better. The neighborhoods they are abandoning are becoming sites for high-cost office and apartment buildings.

Such a process does not happen quickly or uniformly. In many cases the poorest, most hopeless, and least skilled are left behind in desperate need of motivation and organization, of hope, mobility, and power. How is their future to be planned? There are other critical questions of justice involved. Who, for example, should benefit from the rapid rise in land value resulting from this transformation—the city or the state, rich whites, poor blacks, or the black community as a whole? Overall arises the general question: In planning the transformation of our cities, do we harmonize all activities with natural demographic flows; do we resist these flows; or do we disregard them, opting for short-term, pragmatic responses to crises as they emerge?

The last is the traditional response, and it is filled with danger. In response to the turmoil in the ghettos in 1965 and 1966, large corporations established a number of plants in black areas of major cities, creating perhaps 8,000 new jobs. This action lay athwart the natural flow which Birch has projected, being aimed implicitly at keeping blacks in the ghettos rather than helping them out. Some of these plants have failed; others are in extreme difficulty, falling far short of both their economic and social goals. Investment in such plants has been small and companies may be willing to charge them off to "social responsibility." The operations, may, however, prove not even to have been socially beneficial if they retard more effective long-term community development.

Another example of pseudo-Lockean pragmatism in disappointing action is the Urban Coalition, a nationwide organization of businessmen and community leaders established to improve urban life, especially for blacks. Motivated by the noblest of Lockean individualistic concepts, the Coalition has failed to benefit the black community in many cities where it has made the attempt. In some, Boston in particular, the Coalition was apparently unaware that the black problem was one of power and that, consistent with the American way, power cannot be bestowed—it must be won. Winning comes through organization for participation in the process of interest group pluralism. The organization of urban blacks is an enormously difficult task. Short of leadership, lacking in trust, confidence, and hope, convinced of their weakness and vulnerability, urban blacks in America require unusually high levels of agitation before they achieve the necessary motivation for organization. In many instances, too, the Coalition found itself at loggerheads with those who were fostering this necessary agitation. Unable to perceive the nature of the required political process, its white leadership was repelled, embittered, and defeated.

Again, the encouragement of "black capitalism" through undernourished, underplanned governmental programs aimed at helping individual blacks to own and operate ghetto business (a clearly

Lockean notion) has also been disappointing. Probably there is no part of America in which it is harder to run an effective, profitable business than the black communities of our cities. Is this where we should encourage relatively inexperienced and rare black managers to try their hands? Perhaps the better course would be to find ways in which black businesses can gain access to white markets, where money and opportunities are more prevalent. More analysis, more planning, a broader vision, and a better ideology are needed to provide the answers.

Government at the federal, state, city, and eventually at the regional levels has the capacity for such analysis and planning, which business does not and cannot have. It is urgent that government now perform its task. In so doing, business can encourage and assist it. The Committee for Economic Development (itself an unusual agency for business-government planning) spoke of the need to modernize local government:

> The bewildering multiplicity of small, piecemeal, duplicative, overlapping local jurisdictions cannot cope with the staggering difficulties encountered in managing modern urban affairs. The fiscal effects of duplicative suburban separatism create great difficulty in provision of costly central city services benefiting the whole urbanized area. If local governments are to function effectively in metropolitan areas, they must have sufficient size and authority to plan, administer, and provide significant financial support for solutions to area-wide problems.*

Commenting on the education difficulties of our country, the CED stated: "The schooling of deprived minorities in the slums and ghettos and in many poor rural areas has been a tragic failure and one that will not be corrected without a major revolution in the objectives, methods, and organization of the schools."** The proposal has been put forward by both businessmen and black militants that education should be made competitive and turned over to private business.† Perhaps, but before such a step is taken, a sequence of profound political and ideological decisions must be made. Who, for example, will decide education policies in ten years, and how? Clearly, our present policies cannot be main-

---

* Committee for Economic Development, *Modernizing Local Government to Secure a Balanced Federalism,* New York, July 1966, p. 44.
** Committee for Economic Development, *Innovation in Education: New Directions for the American School,* New York, July 1968, p. 12.
† Drucker, ed., *op. cit.,* pp. 75–6.

tained even that long; change in the field is too rapid. If business moves haphazardly into the "education business," thus removing some pressure from government to do what the CED says it must, the results will be chaotic and disappointing, possibly highly destructive.

Had our ideology sprung more from Mill, Burke, Rousseau, or Hegel than from Locke, we might at this point readily assert that government has the responsibility and should have the capacity to perform the task of community analysis and planning, as well as of determining priorities and allocating resources accordingly; we should contend that this is not a job that the unelected leaders of business can or should undertake. We might then argue as to what levels of government would be most usefully involved—federal, state, city, or some new regional form—and how these agencies should be organized for the task. Being Lockeans, however, albeit unwitting and semi-pragmatic ones, we are puzzled by the very first stage. We are semi-consciously and inexplicitly bent on limiting the role of government, on keeping it haphazard in the hope that an unplanned collection of pragmatic public and private actions will somehow pull us out of our troubles as they always have before, leaving our Lockeanism more or less intact.

In the Ecology Crisis

The ecological crisis of which we are becoming chaotically aware involves a network of values; to sort them out requires rigorous criteria for the good community. "Ours is an age," writes Lewis Mumford, "in which the increasingly automatic processes of production and urban expansion have displaced the human goals they are supposed to serve. Quantitative production has become . . . the only imperative goal."* Consider the by-products of achieving this goal: the waste that many industries are spreading over lakes, rivers, swamps; the noxious fumes from automobiles and factories; the hot water from nuclear power stations, and the nuclear wastes themselves. A 1970 *Fortune* survey of 250 top business executives revealed an understandably equivocal reaction to the problem of environmental pollution. Businessmen knew they

---

* Lewis Mumford, *The City in History* (New York: Harcourt, Brace & World, Inc., 1961), p. 570.

must do something, but they were not sure what. They were vaguely aware that business alone could not possibly cope with the problem and thus were willing to acknowledge the necessity for governmental initiative and leadership to "set the standards, regulate all activities pertaining to the environment, and help finance the job with tax incentives." On the other hand, they were individually concerned lest government action "sap their financial vigor," and deeply uncertain about the legitimacy and capacity of government to regulate all activities pertaining to the environment.* They were justified in this uncertainty because the traditional ideology and its companion political syndromes have left government singularly unprepared for the job.

But there should have been no doubt about the urgency of government preparing itself to take on the job as it inevitably has had to do. The innumerable costs and benefits inherent in the formulation of environmental policy can only be weighed and measured by the community as a whole through government. The question is whether government will make the trade-offs wisely and comprehensively or unwisely, without regard for the full range of possible effects.

A failure to see clearly the governmental function in ecological policy and a lingering disposition to leave it to business can have expensive consequences for business itself. This is very apt to lead to haphazard and needlessly extreme governmental action in response to ad hoc crises and pressure from interest groups. Such a failure also tends to deprive government of much technical and managerial assistance that business could usefully provide.

In Rapid Transit

In the early 1960's Mark Cresap, then president of Westinghouse Electric Corporation, heard a speech by President Kennedy about urban transportation, which commented on the evils of automobile traffic and pollution, the need for low-cost urban transit to move men from home to job, and so on. He responded to the presidential call for help, doing so, we must suppose, with the expectation of profit. His response became concrete when Patrick

---

* Robert S. Diamond, "What Business Thinks: The *Fortune* 500–Yankelovich Survey," *Fortune*, February 1970, pp. 118–19.

J. Cusick, Jr., executive director of the Pittsburgh Regional Planning Association, challenged local industry—including Westinghouse—to provide a modern transit system that could effectively compete with the automobile and reduce rush-hour traffic.* Funds were allocated to design an urban transit system to be called "Transit Expressway," which would be useful for medium-sized cities like Pittsburgh.

The Expressway, to be constructed overhead in the median strip or alongside automobile expressways, would offer fast, frequent, safe, and comfortable service at minimum cost. Four different groups combined to put up $5 million for a test and demonstration in Pittsburgh: the Federal Housing and Home Finance Agency (now HUD), the Port Authority of Allegheny County, the Pennsylvania State Department of Commerce, and Westinghouse. As it turned out, the cost was considerably more than estimated, but Westinghouse, convinced that it had a good idea for meeting a grave national problem, made up the difference. The test went well. The demonstration showed that Transit Expressway was indeed a relatively flexible way to meet the transportation needs of medium-sized cities.

The company found mayors and transit authorities in other cities generally enthusiastic, but they were not the real customers. "The consultant to the authority is normally the real customer, and it's a rare consultant who will take a risk on an innovative system," said John McNulty, Westinghouse marketing manager. "The architects and city planners will accept the risk but they don't have the influence." He also encountered problems with bidding procedures; it seemed necessary to interest other companies in inventing transit systems so as to provide competition, or else turn Transit Expressway over to some sort of public body. Furthermore, with cities depending on dwindling real-estate taxes for revenue, it became apparent that federal funds would be necessary and the federal government was neither organized nor prepared to consider such funding. Finally, there was the powerful highway and gasoline lobby to be reckoned with—not exactly

---

* This account is drawn from a Harvard Business School case: *Westinghouse Electric Corporation (A)*, EA-R 527; Christopher G. Russell under the supervision of Professor John D. Glover and Professor Thomas C. Raymond, copyright © 1969 by the President and Fellows of Harvard College.

friendly to the scheme. Westinghouse came to learn that there was some truth in Andrew Carnegie's warning that "Pioneering don't pay." It persevered, however, and has sold several systems for use in airports. Meanwhile, the problem of urban transit gets worse.

As of this writing, Transit Expressway stands as a noble experiment which has cost Westinghouse a lot of money. It is not employed in any city; it is not solving the problems it was supposed to solve. Government has slowly increased funds for rapid transit, but much of the money has gone to aerospace companies, hard hit by the Viet Nam cutback. Therefore the technology of TE has in many ways been passed by. Further, it remains true that any community's transportation system is an integral part of its patterns of life, work, and physical layout. Transportation is but one part of a large and complex whole. Transit Expressway presupposed plans where there were none.

One cannot but admire the individualistic motivation of Westinghouse; on the other hand, money and time appear to have been wasted because the company was operating under a set of assumptions that were invalid in the environments it was proposing to serve. Business cannot proceed with confidence and utility until a community lays out its planning framework. Nor can it meet the transformational needs of this country until political leadership provides the necessary ideology and structure. There is danger to business itself, to the community, and to government in expecting it to do so.

CHAPTER 7 From the Rights
of Property to Those of Community
Membership

The transition from the idea of property rights to that of the rights of membership imposes constraints upon the central economic institution of our time—the great corporation—and suggests a variety of options for its redesign. There is naturally a close association between the effects of this transition and those of the transition from individualism discussed in the previous chapter.

The Lockean ideology attached supreme importance to property rights as a means to fulfilling the values of survival, justice, and self-respect. We have seen that by the term "property," Locke meant both body and estate, and that by "estate" he meant essentially land or clearly owned artifacts; and that he regarded the sole role of the state as being the protection of property, a man's body and estate. He was speaking for a clientele who owned property and were anxious to keep it from the king. For them, property was the means to political and economic independence, the guarantor of freedom. Those who did not own property, those who had sold even their bodies through wage labor, were so deprived of independence as to be incapable of voting freely and, therefore, were made ineligible to vote. In early America, property was widely diffused—nearly everyone had a reasonable chance to own some. (Slaves were, of course, excepted, being property themselves. In fact, slavery was justified in part because of the enormous power of property rights as an idea in America.)

After a period in which the corporation was seen as the creation of a legislature for the fulfillment of a specific community need, the idea of individual property rights came to make the corporation legitimate. Time and again this right was used to protect the corporation as an individual against the intervention of the state. And although the ownership of the corporation became more and more diffused until it was nothing but a myth, the idea of property was maintained, its unreality ignored in the name of efficiency and growth.* Today, the concept of private property when applied to the large public corporation is so obscure as to be nearly useless for legitimization. At the same time, uncertainty about the definition of efficiency and the acceptability of growth deprive these two notions of their old force.

The beginning of the disintegration of the idea of property rights in America can be set in the year 1877, when Chief Justice Morrison R. Waite found in *Munn* v. *Illinois*** that property "affected with a public interest" ceases to be purely private. Waite employed this concept to justify state regulation of rates charged by a private warehouse. The doctrine was taken further in 1934 in *Nebbia* v. *New York*,† when the Supreme Court found that the state could intervene whenever the public needed protection in the name of community need. It is hard to improve on the much earlier statement of the problem of private property rights versus the public interest made by Chief Justice Shaw in Massachusetts in 1839:

It is difficult, perhaps impossible, to lay down any general rule, that would precisely define the power of the government in the acknowledged right of eminent domain. It must be large and liberal, so as to meet the public exigencies, and it must be so limited and constrained, as to secure effectually the rights of citizens; and it must depend, in some instances, upon the nature of the exigencies as they arise, and the circumstances of individual cases.††

The continuing disintegration of property rights as a legitimizing idea today is rooted in two factors: the changes that have come about in the nature of the American community (Shaw's "public

---

* James Willard Hurst, *The Legitimacy of the Business Corporation in the Law of the United States, 1780–1970* (Charlottesville: The University Press of Virginia, 1970), pp. 234–53.

** *Munn* v. *Illinois,* 94 U.S. 113 (1877).

† *Nebbia* v. *New York,* 291 U.S. 502 (1934).

†† J. Shaw, *per curiam, Boston Water Power Co.* v. *Boston and Worcester Railroad,* 23 Pick, 360 (1839). Quoted in Harry N. Scheiber, "The Road to *Munn*: Eminent Domain and the Concept of Public Purpose in the State Courts," *Perspectives in American History,* vol. v, (1971): 399.

exigencies"), and the continued dispersion of "ownership" of some 2,000 large publicly held corporations which account for something like 70–80 per cent of the nation's corporate assets.* As the right to property gives way, a new idea is taking its place— the communitarian right of all members to survival, to income, to health, education, green space, natural beauty, and so on. It is not that the right to property need be abolished or that it is evil. It can continue to be appropriate in some settings, including most of the nation's several million small and clearly proprietary enterprises. But it has lost its dominant place as the prime guarantor and arbiter of human rights. In particular, it has lost its utility with respect to the large nonproprietary corporation.

The transformation is observable in several key areas. In the first place, technology has opened access to new sectors of our universe in which the traditional notions of property rights and ownership are simply irrelevant. Outer space and the seabed, for example, are defined by international law as "the common province of mankind" and "the common heritage of mankind," respectively.** No person, no corporation, no state may own these areas. They belong to all; they are of "the commons."

In the second place, scarce resources are coming to be placed in the public domain. We are increasingly aware of the scarcity of vital commodities: clean air to breathe, pure water to drink, fertile soil, natural beauty, fuel for energy, and perhaps food to eat. In the name of survival, these resources are moving inexorably beyond property into a new cradle of legitimacy composed of two

---

  * In 1968, the United States contained about 1.6 million profit-seeking corporations. Forty-three % of those possessed assets of less than $50,000 and 94% had assets of less than $1 million. On the other hand, 1,900 companies, constituting 0.13% of the corporate population, had assets of $100 million or more and held about 60% of total corporate assets. This concentration of assets in large publicly owned firms whose shares are traded on the stock exchanges has been increasing steadily since World War II. Neil Jacoby has estimated that 10,000 of the 1.6 million corporations have stock which is publicly traded—Neil H. Jacoby, *Corporate Power and Social Responsibility* (New York: The Macmillan Co., 1973), pp. 28, 49, and 179. Jacoby used data from *Statistics of Income: Corporation Returns 1965* (Washington, D.C.: U.S. Government Printing Office, 1965), pp. 4–5; Betty Bock, *Concentration, Oligopoly and Profit: Concept and Data* (New York: The Conference Board, 1972).
 ** Elisabeth Mann Borgese, "The Promise of Self Management," *The Center Magazine,* June 1972.

related ideas: community need, and harmony between man and nature.

Examples of this transformation in new law are abundant, none more dramatic than the National Environmental Protection Act and the Clean Air Act. In 1972, for example, a land developer began construction of a high-rise apartment building on a small plot of land near Mammoth Lake in the High Sierras of California. Residents sued to halt the construction even though it was on private land. It offended the environment, they said. The case worked its way to the California Supreme Court, and in a 6–1 decision the court ruled in favor of the residents. In consequence, state and local governments now must make environmental-impact studies and expose them to public scrutiny before they can approve private construction projects which may have a significant impact on the environment. The California decision meant that citizens can sue to halt any such project that is not accompanied by such a study. According to the attorney who represented the Mammoth Lake residents, the California court decision was "the first time that any U.S. law has given citizens the right to participate directly in private land-use decisions before they are made." A number of land development and housing companies are in a quandary about what to do. "I think they want to put the builders out of business," said Gene Meyers, executive vice president of Levitt United.*

In much the same vein a federal task force on land use, headed by Laurance S. Rockefeller, advised President Nixon in 1973 that henceforth "development rights" on private property must be regarded as resting with the community rather than with property owners:

There is a new mood in America. Increasingly, citizens are asking what urban growth will add to the quality of their lives. They are questioning the way relatively unconstrained piecemeal urbanization is changing their communities, and are rebelling against the traditional processes of government and the market place which they believe have inadequately guided development in the past. . . . They are measuring new development proposals by the extent to which environmental criteria are satisfied.**

---

* Earl C. Gottschalk, Jr., "Guarding the Land," *Wall Street Journal,* Oct. 9, 1972.

** Quoted in Gladwin Hill, "Authority to Develop Land Is Termed a Public Right," *The New York Times,* May 30, 1973.

Even with declining fertility rates, the report said, the nation's population will keep growing until well into the twenty-first century. It put present growth at the rate of 27,000 new households a week. The Constitution guarantees these families the right to move about freely, a fact that caused the task force to raise some long-range questions. May not the "new mood" force this attribute of individualism to change, in the face of community need? May it not be necessary for every level of government, covering every locality, to plan its growth, to provide for open space, proper housing, and the rest? And may not this require that communities establish population ceilings? Specifically, the report urged that all levels of government engage in buying up land for public uses and adopt strict regulations governing the use of privately held land. It observed that the states have the power to do this, "but must overcome a tradition of inactivity."

The strength of this tradition cannot be underestimated. Colorado Springs, for example, is a heavenly place nestled beneath the majesty of the Rocky Mountains on the edge of the Great Plains. Recently, its population has been growing by leaps and bounds, with industrial sprawl marring its perimeters. Youths abound, and there is insufficient work for them to do; vandalism is high. The community is running out of water and inversion makes the air foul on certain days. It is turning from heaven into hell before the stricken eyes of its business and civic leaders. I spoke to those leaders in 1972 about their ideology, which is as near to pure Lockeanism as one is likely to find in America today. They heard me out and shuffled silently from the hall. Later, in the hotel bar, I met the city manager who had heard the speech. He told me, "You're right. We have to plan as a community, but every time I suggest it, they call me a socialist or something worse." Others from the hall joined us in the bar. Relaxed, they lamented their plight, the waywardness of their children, the decline of what they had held dear. I made my speech again; this time the ideological barriers were more permeable. Since then, even Colorado Springs has begun to plan—its Lockeanism eroded by crisis.

In April 1974, the Environmental Protection Agency, acting under the National Environmental Protection Act, moved indirectly to limit the population size of Ocean County, New Jersey. An official of the EPA said, "We intend to do this all over the country." The EPA ruled that the national pollution standards set by the act required a total population of no more than 250,000 in sixteen municipalities of the county. It sought to enforce this ruling by refusing to grant the Ocean County Sewage Authority either the required discharge permit or federal funds to build a system which would serve a larger population.*

In the third place, mass urbanization has undermined the traditional theory of private domain. The old ideas simply fade, slowly but surely, as increasing numbers of people pay rent in vast complexes where ownership guarantees none of the political, social, and economic independence described by Locke and formerly provided by the family farm or business. The old idea of property is powerless to prevent the deterioration of low-cost housing blocs; already the federal government owns large tracts of faltering or abandoned inner-city housing. In 1972, for example, the Department of Housing and Urban Development found itself the reluctant owner of 5,000 single-family homes in Detroit's wasteland; the situation is as bad in other cities.** Cities and neighborhoods within cities are communities, and can only function if they are treated as such. But this requires entirely different ideological foundations, an entirely new collective consciousness.

In the fourth place, there has been a shift in the nature and function of work and in the means that workers have to fulfillment and self-respect. Of primary importance here is the fact that virtually all members of the American community now have at least a theoretical right that would have been unthinkable as recently as fifty years ago: the right, in effect, to survive. Along with this go other rights of community membership—to a minimum income, to health services, even to entertainment as in public television. (And further rights derive from membership in certain communities, such as IBM or AT&T, Oregon or Los Angeles.) The definition of survival has now become disconnected from work, being guaranteed by the community.

This has several important implications for the idea of property

---

* U.S. Environmental Protection Agency, Region II, "Conclusions and Recommendations on the Central Service Area Sewage Project of Ocean County, New Jersey," April 1974.
** John Herbers, "U.S. Now Big Landlord in Decaying Inner City," *The New York Times,* Jan. 2, 1972.

rights. The right to survive as a right of membership is obviously more important than property rights. And the idea of one's body being one's property, which was so central to Lockean individualistic thought, loses force.

Other factors have eroded the old notion of labor as a man's use of his own body. Today, labor increasingly means skill, knowledge, education, and organization. These are not owned by anybody; they are the product of the community. Further, as Robert L. Heilbroner has put it: "In the advanced capitalist nations, new elites based on science and technology are gradually displacing the older elites based on wealth."* At the same time, other wealth-producing factors such as resources and capital are becoming less clearly "owned" and of decreasing importance compared with the intangibles of knowledge and organization.

The ascendancy of community-created labor resources, coupled with the communitarian guarantee of survival and the decline in the legitimacy of property rights—and thus in the old basis of managerial authority—is having profound organizational effects. There need be no top or bottom in the managerial hierarchy; there must merely be a gradient of different skills and roles. Authority can derive from a variety of sources, which may have nothing to do with property—the managers of the Topeka pet food factory derive it to a great extent, as we saw, from those beneath them. And because the number, size, and importance of organizations (particularly the corporation) are growing, the terms of membership in those organizations are of increasing concern. Once, private ownership of his labor conferred a degree of individual independence upon a worker, even if it was only his body that he owned. But the worker today is increasingly compelled to function in a large organization in which any rights he may have depend upon his locus there and upon his dedication to the organization's goals.

Charles Reich has stated the dilemma well:

When status and relationships to organizations replace private property, the result is a change in the degree of independent sovereignty enjoyed by the individual. Private property gave each person a domain in which he could be independent, and it enabled him to tell the rest of the world to go fly a kite. But a person whose "property" consists of

---

* Robert L. Heilbroner in *The New York Times Magazine,* as quoted in John K. Galbraith, *Economics and the Public Purpose* (Boston: Houghton Mifflin Co., 1973), p. 81.

a position in an organization is tied to the fate of the organization; if the organization goes down he goes with it.*

This redefinition of property plays havoc with some profoundly traditional notions of individual incentive and responsibility. As Aristotle wrote:

that which is common to the greatest number has the least care bestowed upon it. Every one thinks chiefly of his own, hardly at all of the common interest, and only when he is himself concerned as an individual. For besides other considerations, everybody is more inclined to neglect the duty which he expects another to fulfil; as in families many attendants are often less useful than a few.**

Western man has seemed to husband best that which is his. Furthermore, we derive important psychological satisfaction from owning something, even though it be but a knick-knack. Surely this trait in our culture will not wither soon; nonetheless, we must adjust it to the new concept of place in the communitarian order.

Other cultures have succeeded in reaching a solution here. In Japan, for example, the common interest has always been placed above that of the individual. Indeed, the individual achieves fulfillment only insofar as he contributes to his family, to his village, to the greater Japan. Centuries of cultural development and environmental adaptation have created this ideology—if a break in the dike around your rice paddy causes a flood in mine, our individual interests become inseparable from our common interest and the latter must prevail. Tightly delimited in resources, the Japanese have consequently produced a radically different ideology and radically different institutions from the United States or the West in general. As we move into an era of communitarianism, we can see that these institutions are functioning in many ways more effectively than ours. The role of the state and its relationship to business, for example, have given Japan a substantial edge in its strategic planning in the world economy. But the difficulty of moving away from our Western bias is as great as the seeming inevitability of such a movement.

Finally, the 2,000 or so largest corporations in America, which control most of the nation's corporate assets, have over the years

---

* Charles Reich, *The Greening of America* (New York: Random House, Inc., 1970), p. 111.
** Aristotle, *Politics,* Book II, 1261b, in Benjamin Jowett, *The Politics of Aristotle* (Oxford, England: The Clarendon Press, 1885), p. 30.

detached themselves from the old idea of property. Even while managers cling to it for legitimacy, what authority they have derives from their place in a hierarchy of uncertain legitimacy. Since large corporations have obvious potential power and influence, this uncertainty renders them vulnerable to charges of abuse and conspiracy. Whether or not their power and influence are in fact abusive or conspiratorial, their estrangement from the old bases of legitimacy makes them suspect. The problem is heightened when the community is unclear or inexplicit about what it expects of corporations.

Myth has it that a share of General Motors, for example, is philosophically as important as a share in the ownership of the corporation. The myth, however, is empty of reality. A share of GM is nothing more than a claim on income and is generally disposed of if a share of IBM pays more. The claim that the shareholders elect the board of directors which in turn controls the "hired hands" of management is vapid. Myles Mace, in his study of corporate boards of directors, quotes one typical executive vice president:

Management creates policies. We decide what course we are going to paddle our canoe in. We tell our directors the direction of the company and the reasons for it. Theoretically, the board has a right of veto, but they never exercise it. . . . We communicate with them. But they are in no position to challenge what we propose to do.*

So management appoints the board and the board endorses management in a mystical, self-perpetuating process, which albeit efficient, is plainly illegitimate.** We were willing to live with the illegitimacy as long as efficiency and growth were of overriding importance, but now that other factors have called into question the previously uncounted costs of growth, our willingness is evaporating. The individual components of corporate America—what Galbraith calls the planning system—are too large and powerful to be left to themselves; and collectively, in the complexes these

---

* Myles L. Mace, "The President and the Board of Directors," *Harvard Business Review,* March–April 1972, p. 41.
** The fact that the courts are holding directors increasingly liable for the sins of managers does not really help the legitimacy problem, even though it has probably increased the wariness of directors. The amount of liability insurance sold to directors and officers has increased from practically nothing to more than $1 billion—"The Law: Trouble for the Top," *Forbes,* Sept. 1, 1968, p. 23.

organizations have formed with each other and in the economic sectors they dominate, they have become political forces to be reckoned with on the very largest scale. No one can doubt that the intentions of the utility industry, the oil industry, the automobile industry, and the communications industry have become matters of national concern politically and socially, as well as economically. Yet although in fact these are vast industrial complexes, the terms in which they regard themselves are frequently individualistic and proprietary.

Even in the equity markets that serve these industries, the trend from the individual to the collective is apparent and sweeping. Investors in the equity markets, theoretically the owners of the corporations, are increasingly unidentifiable as individuals to whom the ownership of corporations could conceivably be attached. "Like the curator of the National Zoo," said G. Bradford Cook, when he retired as chairman of the Securities and Exchange Commission, "I feel constrained to warn: The individual investor has acquired the status of an endangered species."* The place of the individual investor has been taken by huge organizations whose ownership is also extremely obscure: mutual funds, insurance companies, pension funds, and bank trust departments. Whereas such groups accounted for only 35 per cent of the dollar value of New York Stock Exchange trading volume in 1963, the percentage is well over 70 today. This development has changed and perhaps profoundly threatened capital market structures; John C. Whitehead, a Goldman, Sachs partner, asserts that institutional dominance has endangered the market's valuation capability and demolished its liquidity: "We can look forward in another decade to complete dominance of our markets and of our corporations by a relatively small handful of institutions—the kind of industrial society that currently exists in Europe and Japan."**

This phenomenon of gigantism is having an interesting side

---

* *Business Week,* June 2, 1973, pp. 58 and 59.

** In Japan, equity capital is rarely more than 25% of the corporation's total capitalization. Management controls companies with virtually no interference from stockholders. Ultimate control lies with the company's bank. The bank has no vote, but the company's dependence on the bank gives it what a Japanese manager once described as the "power of irresistible persuasion." Banks in turn are heavily influenced by government. See Peter F. Drucker, "Global Management," *Challenge to Leadership* (New York: The Free Press, 1973), p. 240.

effect on the innovation and enterprise which historically have been the handmaidens of the traditional ideology. Because the big institutions show market interest in relatively few stocks, newer and smaller companies are finding it increasingly difficult to go public at all. The vulnerability of our system to the acquisitiveness of the giants can be sensed in the example of Morgan Guaranty, which in 1972 owned more common stock than any other institution on earth—$2 billion worth of IBM, $1.1 billion of Kodak, and $500 million or more of Avon, Sears, and Xerox.*

Taken together, all these factors have thoroughly confused our original notions of the role of the publicly held corporation and eroded its legitimacy. Ideologically, it has become a mere collection of persons and matter with considerable potential power— political and social as well as economic—floating dangerously in a philosophic limbo. If it survives, as it probably will, it has to be made legitimate. The only questions are how and by whom. The issues surrounding these questions fall into two categories:

ONE, those having to do with the external relationships between the corporate collective and the communities which it affects.

TWO, those having to do with the internal structure of the organization and thus with managerial authority and collective discipline.

Corporate Legitimacy: The External Criteria

About the external relationships of the large corporation Donald S. MacNaughton, chairman and chief executive of the Prudential Insurance Company of America, wrote perceptively:

Although the corporation is really not private property in the traditional sense, we continue to think of it in those terms. Moreover, we articulate such views and so tend to create a schism between ourselves and the public, which sees the corporation in a much broader sense. . . .

The managers are not owners, nor do they have the right to behave as though the prerogatives of ownership and property rights have been delegated to them because they were elected by stockholders.

---

* *Business Week*, June 2, 1973, p. 59.

Just as we are reluctant to abandon the property rights fiction, we are equally reluctant to forego the erroneous belief that our franchise was somehow ordained by God, through the people, for our benefit. We are plagued by this false residue of a distant past. . . .

It was not God, but the people who granted us permission to function, and not for our benefit, but for the public's—by the people and for the people.*

The problem is that the American community did in fact say that the corporation as property was ordained by God to function as it saw fit, competitively, with as little government direction as possible. This was considered the best way to the public interest.

Today, things are different. "The sense of identity between the self-interest of the corporation and the public interest has been replaced by a sense of incongruence," writes Daniel Bell.** But the people—that is, the American community—lack the means, the mechanisms, and the ideological certainty to derive new criteria for the corporate franchise, its rights, duties, and relationships to the communities it affects. "Each of us, individually, may see the consequences of an indicated action, but lacking a social mechanism to assess it, we become helpless, drift, and thereby accelerate it."†

The insensitivity of managers generally to the transition we face was never more plain than in the testimony of oil company executives before the Senate subcommittee investigating their activities in 1974. The executives, relying on the old idea of property rights, were unwilling to tell the Congress about their pricing policies and appeared to be reluctant to disclose how much oil they had stashed away in various places—pipelines, tankers, or storage facilities. They were resentful that their property rights were not respected. The government, mindful that the oil shortage was clearly inconsistent with community need, reacted in a variety of ways.

The Federal Trade Commission issued a complaint, also bitterly resented by the industry, seeking to break up the eight major oil companies in the name of the old ideas of property and competition as embodied in the antitrust laws—a Lockean response.

---

* Donald S. MacNaughton, "A Responsible Business," *New York State Bar Journal,* April 1972, pp. 161–2.

** Daniel Bell, *The Coming of Post-Industrial Society: A Venture in Social Forecasting* (New York: Basic Books, Inc., 1973), p. 272. See also pp. 271, 293, and 281–3.

† *Ibid.,* p. 283.

The FTC charged that since 1950, "these companies had maintained and reinforced a noncompetitive market structure in the
refining of crude oil into petroleum products. . . ." This they were
able to do as a result of their size, power, and integration. The
FTC found that the companies had been cooperating in a variety
of anti-competitive ways, not the least of which was "influencing
legislation" by collusive lobbying. As a result, many small, independent oil refiners and marketers had been hurt.*

The Treasury Department refuted the FTC's arguments, adding
that even if the oil companies' behavior was anti-competitive under
the law, the national interest—community need—required the
economies of scale and efficiencies which resulted from size and
integration.** Implicit in the Treasury Department's statement was
the assumption that if the market place did not ensure conformity
by the oil companies with the national interest, then some sort of
governmental regulatory procedures could be used as a supplement.

At about the same time, Senator Adlai Stevenson came forward
with an alternative suggestion for forcing the oil industry into
harmony with the national interest—a Federal Oil and Gas Company, whose primary task would be "to explore for, develop and
produce the large deposits of oil and natural gas on lands owned
by the Federal Government."† Stevenson's proposal was ideologically radical, even though historically by no means new. Utilizing the charter route, he proposed the creation of an institution
specifically to fulfill an unmet community need. Senator Henry
Jackson, following a similar route, advocated federal chartering of
major oil companies with government representation on the board
of directors.

Given this state of affairs, what is the likely evolution of events
and what perceptions might oil company managers usefully
have? To start with, the concept of property rights is a thin reed

---

* *Preliminary Federal Trade Commission Staff Report on Its Investigation of the Petroleum Industry* (Washington, D.C.: U.S. Government
Printing Office, 1973).

** See *Department of the Treasury Staff Analysis of the FTC Staff Report
on Its Investigation of the Petroleum Industry, July 2, 1973, Printed at
the Request of Senator Henry M. Jackson, Chairman, Committee on
Interior and Insular Affairs, United State Senate* (Washington, D.C.:
U.S. Government Printing Office, 1973), pp. 5–67.

† U.S. Congress, Senate, *Proceedings and Debates,* 93rd Cong., 1st sess.,
Nov. 7, 1973, *Congressional Record* 119:170.

on which to rest the legitimacy of these huge multinational entities. Their "owners" are obscure, and they are handling what for the time being is a necessity of life. To carry out their function efficiently, they must be big and they must have power which is inconsistent with the antitrust laws and the old idea of competition. Uncontrolled by either owners or market forces, regulation by government and control through a new charter remain as methods of ensuring that the companies are harmonious with the public interest. The vital interest of the managers of American oil companies thus comes down to this: What purpose and function does the community want them to serve? Theoretically, the answer could be spelled out and enforced through regulation, yet it might be far better done either through a revision of the several existing corporate charters or through some new charter. The ideological preconceptions of the oil company managers may well have prevented them from even seeing this option clearly.

A new franchise will be designed; American oil companies will conform. This may prove so distasteful that they will struggle to detach themselves from America and seek a transnational home, a world charter. But in one way or another, the American community will insist upon legitimate institutions to provide it with oil.

There is still some choice about the form which the new corporate franchise will take. In the meantime, a good deal of experimentation is inevitable in seeking to define community need and the relationship of the corporation to that need. Such experimentation can be extremely wasteful if it is confused by old myth and ideology.

In the example of Westinghouse's Transportation Division and the Transit Expressway cited in the previous chapter, we can see the dangers of experimentalism in constructing the franchise. Westinghouse accepted a serious challenge and its engineers attacked the problem much as they would that of going to the moon. They designed a packaged system to meet the transportation needs of some twenty communities. But these communities were all on earth, and they were all very different. There was no NASA to plan the process. The cities were poor; the national government uncertain; mass transit was for somebody else. Transit Expressway could not fit into such a setting. The company had to abandon it as a solution to urban transportation problems and sell it to several airports instead; meanwhile our cities continue to strangle in traffic. No end of business "social responsibility" will do; communities must decide what they want to be and where they want to go—and then, as with our passage to the moon, business and government can help them get there.

A couple of additional examples—of the present predicament of the utility industry and of the problem of designing "clean" investment portfolios—will make clearer the ways in which the new franchises are likely to evolve.

Consolidated Edison, like other electric utilities in America, began in the mid-1960's to have difficulty providing power for the 9 million or so people it served in and around New York City. Originally assembled in the 1930's by a group of powerful financiers who saw profit in making one company out of a welter of power and light enterprises, Con Ed from the outset encountered community antagonism. But its political and financial clout was sufficient to overcome those who would curb its independence. Its managers' guiding principles, which they held with religious zeal, were those of private property and the limited state. As time went by, however, the company was increasingly enmeshed by regulation. This came from many different sources rather than from a single government agency, partly because the power industry had purposely sought in the name of property rights to keep its governmental interface weak, divided, and off balance. The state set Con Ed's rates, the city taxed its revenues, the Federal Power Commission had something to say about its non-nuclear facilities, the Atomic Energy Commission licensed its nuclear plants, and a variety of local governments as well as a swarm of interest groups concerned with everything from the beauties of the Hudson River to the sex life of the shad sought to affect or limit its capacity to build new generating facilities. In spite of the fact that the company has been well managed since the coming of Charles Luce as chief executive in 1968, its rate of return to shareholders has been the lowest in the industry, and brownouts and blackouts plagued its customers.

The fact is that the company has been unable to build sufficient generating capacity. And the reason for this is that the political order by which the company is bound has been unable to make the necessary trade-offs between the costs and the benefits of adequate electric power. Like a great dinosaur, Con Ed wallows in its swamp, being bitten to death by smaller animals. There is only one way out—the political order must intervene and plan, in answer to the questions: How much power is needed? At what price? Where should generating facilities be built? And what technologically is the safest and most efficient source of power? Such planning has to be regional, national, and international in scope, for the needs of the northeast must be considered simultaneously with those of New York; generating systems reach across the country and into Canada; Con Ed regularly buys power from the TVA and Quebec; and so on.

Such intervention, however, is exactly what the electric utility industry has regularly and systematically opposed with great success. The old idea of property has prevented it from seeing its only path to survival. Fearful of "nationalization" of its "private" property and rights, it avoided taking the initiatives to urge that degree of community planning which is essential to avoid total government takeover in the long run. Sooner or later, power generation in America must be taken from the hands of individual companies and placed within some regional framework.

I do not suggest that the new generating complexes need be government-owned or -operated. They could better be federally chartered as regional corporations, sustained by private investment as well as by government subsidy, servicing a variety of local power distribution and marketing companies. Under such a scheme, Con Ed would become a marketing company, its generating capacity a part of a new regional corporation. If the company and others like it were to move sooner rather than later to encourage government to design such a system, the chances are that it could make a better deal for its investors. Unfortunately, it has been inhibited from clear vision by the resilience of the traditional ideology, specifically the idea of property as well as the companion notion of the limited state. If the crisis provoked by the company's inadequacy is great enough, of course, it could lose all it has at a single blow. Such an eventuality would not be good for its investors, its consumers, or the community in general.

As a result of its astigmatism, Con Ed (and companies like it) has consistently made unrealistic choices about how its franchise is to be clarified. Historically, it has preferred to suppose that it can make the essential trade-offs between electric power and environmental quality itself, for example, by communicating with its customers in full-page ads and the like; but in the last decade, it has become clear that it lacks the authority to play a role in such a process. It has lost credibility—the old legitimacy is no longer valid. Con Ed is powerless. It lies at the mercy of interest groups who, acting through the courts, have endeavored to clarify its franchise. Thus the Scenic Hudson Preservation Society, whose members include wealthy and influential inhabitants of the banks of the Hudson River, delayed the construction of a pumped storage generating station at Cornwall for eight years, arguing that it would abominate a beautiful mountain, Storm King.* The interest group method of franchise clarification is time-consuming, chaotic, and wasteful, just as uncoordinated government regulation and ill-considered business initiatives are; but, of course, it does preserve some important freedom—at least for those who belong to the interest group. There is, however, some question whether the Bedford-Stuyvesant resident cares as much about the beauty of Storm King as he does about lower electric bills and heat on a cold night. Excessive reliance on interest groups, as noted earlier, can prove unjust and unsuccessful.

In May 1974, after failing to pay its stockholders their annual dividend, Con Ed finally, symbolically and in practice, acknowledged that it could not live as private property any more. Consequently, *in extremis* it went to the state of New York and pleaded to have two of its generating plants taken over. The state reluctantly complied. "Con Ed is out of the equity market, and New York State is in the power business—forever," moaned Donald C. Cook, chairman of the American Electric Power Company. In fact, however, crisis had made Con Ed stronger than it had been in many decades. The State had moved to clarify the company's political environment; a new partnership was in the making.

Corporations are likely increasingly to seek government intervention to neaten up the corporate context. For many, this is the only alternative left. It is also filled with the risk of inefficiency and waste, and of even more sinister possibilities such as "corporate statism" and fascism. Later, I shall have more to say about the role of the state and the possibilities for political rejuvenation. For the present, it is enough to stress that finding the right formula for increased state intervention in the operations and context of business is perhaps the most critical domestic issue we face. Further-

---

* Pumped storage generation, incidentally, causes no air pollution and probably no water pollution.

more, of the three ways in which government has historically ordered business compliance with the public interest—ensuring competition in an open market place, regulating specific activities for specific ends, and the corporate charter—it would appear that the most basic and most neglected of these, the corporate charter, will receive increased attention in framing this formula.

A final example demonstrates the unwillingness of powerful interest groups to trust government to define the criteria by which business can relate to the communities it affects, and these groups' insistence on nongovernment action. On April 21, 1972, thirty-four black students of Harvard University, members or supporters of the Pan-African Liberation Committee, seized the university's venerable Massachusetts Hall, which houses the offices of the president and other officials. Their action was in protest against Harvard's refusal to sell its 680,000 shares of Gulf Oil, 0.3 per cent of those outstanding. Gulf, the protestors charged, was contributing to black oppression in the Portuguese colony of Angola. Harvard, Gulf's largest university stockholder, agreed to obtain, and did in fact obtain, a promise from the company's management to disclose information about its operations in Angola. Harvard sent a representative to Angola to investigate the charges against Gulf. After reading the representative's report, President Derek Bok said he "was revolted by the colonialism of the Portuguese government in Angola" and "offended by the policies of our own government which indirectly served to strengthen the Portuguese rule in Angola."* But Harvard did not sell its shares. The students remained in Massachusetts Hall for seven days, and then departed peacefully.

In an earlier time, it is likely that the matter would have been conceived quite differently. First, most Americans who cared would have been confident that there was an embassy and a CIA in Angola capable of identifying the good guys and the bad guys; and that if some American company was helping the bad guys, the government would do something—invoke the Trading with the Enemy Act, for example, as we did in the case of Cuba, China, and other of our "enemies." In 1972, such a representation would have been plainly farcical, especially to a group of idealistic young black militants. Not only did they have no confidence whatsoever

---

* Derek Bok, statement, April 23, 1972.

in the U.S. government's judgment about who was good and bad in Angola; they had no confidence that they, as an interest group, could make the slightest impact on the American government's position, or indeed that they could even get a respectable hearing. For those blacks, the American government and Gulf were locked together behind an impenetrable barrier. Quite understandably, they followed the fashion of the times to make the biggest stink they could; they exploited the myth of shareholder ownership and the vulnerability of universities to internal attack in order to make a symbolic gesture which they hoped might help their friends in Angola. In so doing they underscored the profound distrust which important segments of the American community have of their government and their capacity to influence it.

Second, these students demonstrated the impotence of property rights as a means of controlling corporations. Harvard was caught in a plainly exasperating position. Nathan Pusey, the previous president, had said that, "the fundamental investment policy of Harvard . . . is to maximize over a long period of time the support which our endowment affords to the University's pursuit of learning."* He argued, significantly, that Harvard lacked the freedom of individual investors, who are not trustees of other people's money. Such a position clearly meant that Harvard felt itself unable to exercise any responsibility of ownership. Derek Bok, on the other hand, acknowledged some responsibility of ownership, pressing Gulf's management to attend to the problem of blacks in Angola and to disclose more information about its operations. Further, he sent a representative of Harvard to investigate on the spot. But although the spirit was willing, there is no evidence that Harvard had much influence with the hired hands at Gulf.

Another aspect of this story is worth noting. Subsequently, the Harvard Corporation established an alumni-faculty-student Advisory Committee on Shareholder Responsibility, which, together with a subcommittee of the Corporation, has been considering proxy resolutions that will attempt to guide the management of companies in which Harvard owns stock regarding operations in South Africa, military contracting, the peacetime conversion of defense industries, and political contributions. The establishment

---

* *The Gazette,* March 10, 1972, p. 4.

of this Advisory Committee raises the question: Can we realistically expect shareholders adequately to control huge corporations in these important areas of activity? Undoubtedly, shareholders have a responsibility until some better way comes along, but it is apparent that they are a weak reed to rely upon. As we have seen, the power of shareholders to influence management has been curtailed, partly by circumstances of growth and partly as a deliberate strategy by management itself. The Securities and Exchange Commission and state chartering rules, too, particularly those of Delaware, have over the years tended to insulate management from shareholders. Shareholders are an awkward constituency to say the least, diverse and dispersed, for the most part unwilling and unable to take on the functions of the corporate legislature.

Furthermore, the relationships between large corporations and the communities they affect are far too important to be left to shareholders. American corporate activity, whether in Africa or at home, concerns the American community in general and indeed many elements of the world community. It does not seem sensible to conclude that because someone has a share of GM or General Electric, he has any more right than anyone else to govern that corporation's community relationship. The issue thus comes back either to the regulation of the corporation or to its initial chartering. Logically, that chartering and that regulation should be by the largest community affected, which means either the United States or some international governmental agency. Here is the rub, of course. There is no such international agency—the pride of national sovereignties has seen to that—and the idea of the limited state, plus America's distrust of its government at this juncture, has prevented federal chartering within the United States. Like the national corporation, the multinational corporation is in a dangerous limbo.

In sum, the following steps appear to be called for: the creation of international chartering and control procedures; the federal chartering of all large U.S. corporations that are not clearly owned (say, those that trade their shares on the stock exchanges); and the renovation of the American political order so as to re-create confidence in government.

As Daniel Bell points out, the heart of the whole question of the external relationships of corporations is the question of the nature of the corporation itself: "Is the corporation primarily an instrument of 'owners'—legally, the stockholders—or is it an autonomous enterprise which, despite its particular history, has become or should become an instrument for service to society in a system of pluralist powers?"* The services the corporation could render, given its power and flexibility, are unquestionable. Yet it has outrun its rationale; ownership is purely a legal fiction; and it clings to the old rationale because it is unable to formulate or countenance another. Even profit, a red flag for some, is not really part of this central issue. As a measure of efficiency, profit is ideologically neutral. The real debate deals with the definition of profit, the costs that are to be charged against it, the criteria for its distribution, and the community effects of the processes on which its production depends. These are issues beyond the capacity of the corporation to decide; Professor Milton Friedman, among others, has said that all a corporation should do is to maximize profits.** This is fine as far as it goes, but it avoids the critical contextual issues and is dangerous in its complacency.

While the corporation is clearly capable of rendering certain services to society under political guidance, it can do so naturally only at certain social costs. The Western world has become quite proficient at measuring economic goods, but we are grossly unprepared to measure social goods and conversely social costs. We lack the necessary information, the knowledge, the trade-off mechanisms, and the ideology. While in the United States many linger with the individualistic and proprietary illusion that corporations can decide upon and create a good community through some form of self-audit, this is pure illusion. Unelected business managers neither can nor should assume such a function. The authority for defining community need rests with government. The implementation of that definition, on the other hand, can well be assigned to business in the name of both efficiency and economy. A clear distinction between authority and efficiency will serve the interests of government, business, and the community as a whole.

---

* Daniel Bell, "Corporations and Conscience: The Issues," *Sloan Management Review*, Fall 1971, p. 8.
** Milton Friedman, "The Social Responsibility of Business Is to Increase Its Profits," *The New York Times Magazine*, Sept. 13, 1970.

Corporate Legitimacy: The Internal Criteria

Having considered the criteria that would validate and legitimize the corporation's interaction with its external environment, let us now look at the criteria for the internal organization of the corporate collective. We must start with the general idea of the good community. As America shifts away from individualism and its companion ideas of contract and property toward some form of communitarianism, it must move with the greatest care, fully mindful of the inhumanity with which such tendencies have historically been contaminated: Hitler's Germany, Stalin's Russia, Orwell's *1984*. Inherent in much that I have said about the external controls of corporations is the specter of stifling centralized statism, which threatens our criteria for a good community. To keep this specter disembodied requires vigilant attention.

Presumably, we shall wish to decentralize power and control among smaller communities as far as is consistent with the good of the larger community. Such decentralization depends, of course, upon the internal legitimacy of smaller communities; that is, corporations and their factories can maintain power and control over themselves only if they are so constructed internally as to be legitimate in the eyes of all their members and the external community. The deterioration of management rights, as we have seen, is due to the corporation's departure from its traditional legitimizing ideas, the failure of those ideas to meet the exigencies of existing reality, and the failure of the community as a whole to agree upon a new set of legitimizing ideas. Internal legitimacy is also essential to the corporation's authority to conduct its affairs. Any activity requires leadership, any leadership authority, and any authority legitimacy.

First, we must distinguish again between the 2,000 or so giant corporations whose shares are publicly traded and the 1.5 million or more which are clearly owned by their managers; and we must eliminate once and for all the fiction of shareholder ownership with respect to the first group. Let us clearly divorce ownership from the various sources of financing of these publicly held corporations, whether those sources be individual shareholders, equity holding institutions, banks, or the retained earnings of the corporation itself. Investment in one of these corporations then becomes an investment, nothing more nor less. And the board of directors ceases to represent investors, which in most cases it does not do anyway, but instead becomes mindful of their interests simply as sources of financing. The board will also see to it that the corporation obeys the law.

This done, the broad terms of the governance of the corporation must be stipulated in its charter from the community. Among other things, this document must state how directors and managers are to be chosen, and to what extent and in what manner legitimacy shall derive from the community on the one hand, and from the general corporate membership—that is, all the employees —on the other. Since the corporations under consideration are for the most part at least national in scope, this charter must emanate from the national community; eventually, a procedure for world chartering will unquestionably be needed also.

It would seem desirable to leave the charter as liberal and flexible as possible, providing the corporation with the maximum opportunity for innovation and invention while at the same time ensuring that it can be sufficiently mobile to stay in harmony with the goals of the various communities it affects. Perhaps the charter might specify that the community shall identify certain categories of representation for board membership, but it would seem preferable to leave that membership as much as possible to the decision of the corporate collective itself.

The options for internal organization can perhaps best be seen if we review the evolution of corporate organization and consider where the trends are leading. First is the traditional Lockean model which characterized American corporations around the turn of the century and still works well for the corner grocery store (see Figure 3). Property rights and ownership are clear and natural. The owner-manager derives obvious authority from these rights and he contracts for the labor of individual workers who do his bidding. The second model, representing the collectivization of the corporation, evolved during the 1930's (see Figure 4). Property rights had become diluted and ownership separated from management; at the same time, team management replaced the individual manager, and managing became increasingly professional and bureaucratic. Workers similarly submerged their individualism into an organization to consolidate their power to influence their relationship with the corporation. Thus, the contract changed from a purely individualistic device connecting an individual worker with an authoritative manager to a collective instrument connecting two large bureaucracies to each other. It also became a means of sharing or democratizing the control of the corporation. The negotiation of the precise terms of the sharing, however, has become a more or less continuous bargaining process. Model 3 (see Figure 5), a consensual as opposed to a contractual and adversarial construct, is evolving out of the deterioration of Model 2. In sum, the causes of that deterioration, with which Model 3 presumably must cope, are these:

Confusion concerning the legitimacy of management and the means by which it derives authority;

The growing inability of union bureaucracies to embrace satisfactorily the new needs of individuals for fulfillment;

The inability of the contract as a device to assure each member of the corporate community a satisfactory status in the whole.

The impetus for this evolution in America derives from decreased productivity and increased costs in the face of competition from more productive systems at home and abroad; and also to some extent from an instinct for survival on the part of existing management and union bureaucracies.

There are countless variations on Figure 5. One represents a top-down consensus, as it were, in which the old contract is maintained but in a less important role. For example, in the U.S. steel industry, union and management have drawn together at the top out of a heightened sense of mutuality of interest in the face of foreign competition. This variation is characterized by the no-strike pledge and compulsory arbitration (see Model 3a).

Extending this variation, management may derive its authority increasingly from the union in a process which the Germans refer to as co-determination, which brings us to the second variation of Figure 5 (see Model 3b). In the German system, corporate management is divided between two boards, a supervisory board and a managing board. The supervisory board elects the members of the managing board, which is the executive arm of the corporation. In the coal, iron, and steel industries, worker representatives comprise one-half of the supervisory board and hold a veto power over the designation of the director of labor on the managing board. In other industries, worker representation is limited to one-

FIGURE 3

Model 1

```
┌─────────────┐
│  God/Nature │
└─────────────┘
┌─────────────────┐
│ Rights of Property │
└─────────────────┘
    ┌──────────────────┐
    │ OWNER / MANAGER  │   *He decides*
    └──────────────────┘
         C O N T R A C T S        *the terms which*
┌────────┐ ┌────────┐ ┌────────┐ ┌────────┐
│ Worker │ │ Worker │ │ Worker │ │ Worker │   *they can*
└────────┘ └────────┘ └────────┘ └────────┘   *accept*
                                               *or reject.*
```

FIGURE 4

Model 2

```
┌──────────────┐    Collective    ┌───────┐
│  MANAGEMENT  │──── Contract ────│ UNION │
└──────────────┘                  └───────┘
```

FIGURE 5

Model 3a

```
┌────────────┐
│ ARBITRATOR │
└────────────┘ \    *Consensus*
                \  ╭─────────────────────╮
                 ( MANAGEMENT—UNION       )
                  ╰─────────────────────╯
        *Mutuality of Interest*
```

Model 3b

```
╭──────────────────────────────────────────────────────────╮
( MANAGEMENT/UNION—MANAGEMENT—UNION )
╰──────────────────────────────────────────────────────────╯
```

Model 3c

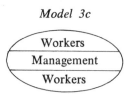

third of the members of the supervisory board. The European Common Market Commission has proposed that all European-chartered companies, including U.S. subsidiaries in the nine Common Market nations, accept the German model.* This system appears to have worked well in Germany, where the level of labor strife is a good deal below that of other industrial nations.

A third variation of the consensual form is more threatening to existing management and union bureaucracies and to the idea of the contract. It is characterized by company control resting with all employees of the corporation—management's authority derives from the workers (see Model 3c). The Topeka pet food plant of General Foods is an embryonic example of this model in the United States. Of all Western countries, Yugoslavia has had the most experience with this form. The control of productive enterprises by workers' councils elected by all employees began in Yugoslavia in the early 1950's as a fundamental part of Tito's effort to decentralize the nation's political and economic system among that country's radically diverse ethnic and religious groups. Today, in a very real sense, workers' "self-management" is a linchpin upon which the Yugoslav polity depends; it is not a peripheral exercise designed to improve worker motivation. One of its most remarkable effects has been to reduce significantly state influence in the management of enterprise. Indeed, discussions between American and Yugoslav managers at the Harvard Business School have led both to wonder whether there is not greater intervention in the United States than in Yugoslavia.**

The membership of the Yugoslavian workers' council—it may vary from 15 in a small company to 120 in a large one—is elected by secret ballot for a two-year term by all members of the corporation.† This council is clearly separate from the trade union,

---

* Philip L. Blumberg, "Reflections on Proposals for Corporate Reform Through Change in the Composition of the Board of Directors: 'Special Interests' or 'Public Directors,'" *Boston University Law Review,* vol. 53, no. 3, May 1973, pp. 559 and 560.
** Harvard Business School Advanced Management Program, Business and Ideology course, July 1973.
† W. J. Burt, "Workers' Participation in Management in Yugoslavia," International Institute for Labour Studies (Geneva, Switzerland), *Bulletin No. 9* (1972): 130–9; based on a study by Dr. D. Gorupic and I. Paj of the Ekonomiski Institut, Zagreb, and other published studies.

which everyone has a right to join, and its function is quite different from that of a union in contractual/adversarial systems. The
union appears to resemble a personnel department in a U.S. plant,
a "transmission belt" to ensure the fulfillment of norms. The council elects the company director after a public invitation for applica-
tions for a four-year term (he may be fired before his term is up
in accordance with statutes and procedures which the council is
empowered to draw up). The director participates in the work of
the council but has no vote. The other functions of the council
include drafting rules for the enterprise; preparing development
plans and programs; dividing the net after-tax income, and allocating it as the members see fit to capital for reinvestment, welfare
payments, and workers' income. In 1968, half the members of the
councils were highly skilled workers. Only 15 per cent held positions in trade unions or the Yugoslav Communist Party.*

Although at first workers' councils changed managers frequently,
as time has passed, the workers have become aware that their self-
interest is inexorably tied to effective, disciplined, authoritative,
and capable management, and the turnover has reduced sharply
as a result. Now, "once management is elected, it has influence
and authority."** Indeed, Milovan Djilas, that gadfly of Yugoslavia's "new class," asserts that the Yugoslav system is positively
oppressive. He protests the lack of freedom of trade unions and
contends that there is more freedom and social justice in Sweden,
France, Austria, Great Britain, and "even the United States of
America" than in his own country.† But the system appears to
have the general support of workers, even though there are frequent short strikes (not led by trade unions). Has workers' self-
management been effective? It is hard to say. Yugoslavia's per
capita income rose from $100 in 1939 to $600 in 1968, and the
nation's productivity index climbed from 100 in 1963 to 126 in
1968.†† Certainly, if one takes the example of the Yugoslav conglomerate Energoinvest, the system seems to have worked remarkably well.

A writer in *Fortune* called Energoinvest "one of the most am-

---

* *Ibid.,* pp. 141, 135, and 148. ** *Ibid.,* p. 164.
  † Milovan Djilas, "The Slow Strangulation of the Socialist Working
  Class," *Business and Society Review/Innovation,* Summer 1973, pp.
  5–7.
†† Burt, *op. cit.,* pp. 167, 156–7.

bitious, arresting, edifying, and important conglomerates the business world has ever sprouted."* Expanding at the rate of more than 20 per cent a year, Energoinvest employs some 22,000 people in making a wide variety of electrical, processing, and other machinery. It maintains sales offices in thirty-two countries, grosses about $160 million, and spends some $6 million a year on research, development, and scholarships. The conglomerate embraces forty-one units and has paid high fees to American management consultants to ensure that they are efficiently organized. It sells its products in highly competitive markets—refinery equipment in America, cranes to Krupp in Germany, and electrical equipment in British Columbia, where it beat out stiff Japanese competition.** In 1970, 40 per cent of the company's revenue came from exports.

Each of Energoinvest's forty-one affiliates is free to depart from the conglomerate whenever its council decides to do so. The company, therefore, has to make each affiliate much better off within the federation than it would be alone. Further, it is occasionally desirable that the company attract a new affiliate; the pitch to prospective groups goes something like this: "We ask you to adhere to our basic program, and charge you 4 to 6 per cent of your gross, depending on the kind of products you make. We have access to money, support all kinds of expertise, and can help you export in a way that nobody else can. If we cannot boost your profits in a couple of years, you are free to withdraw from our group."†

Wages and salaries at Energoinvest come out of the residue after all fixed expenses have been paid and agreed-upon amounts set aside for such social and community needs as housing and new plant and equipment. Thus, wage payments vary from unit to unit from month to month. Each worker, including the director, Emerik Blum, is rated by points which depend upon his education, seniority, function, and performance. At the end of the month, the value of each point is determined. Workers generally earn between 1,000 and 2,000 dinars a month; a plant manager may get 3,500 and Blum gets around 5,700.†† Some highly skilled senior tech-

---

* Gilbert Burck, "A Socialist Enterprise that Acts Like a Fierce Capitalist Competitor," *Fortune*, January 1972, p. 82.

** *Ibid.*, p. 126.   † *Ibid.*

†† *Ibid.*, p. 86; a dinar equals about U.S. $.066.

nicians may make more than a plant manager. In this system, then, pay is not necessarily related to function or authority, but rather to some agreed-upon measure of one's contribution to the whole enterprise.

A variation of the Yugoslav model was introduced into Peru in 1972 and reportedly has improved worker motivation and production. Peru's Industrial Community Law provides that each year 15 per cent of the net income of every corporation shall be set aside to buy shares of common stock in the name of the employees until they own 50 per cent of the company. Employees elect directors of the company according to their percentage of ownership. Within ten to fifteen years, it is estimated that Peru's corporations will in effect be owned and controlled by the employees. The bitterest opponents of this law were the trade union leaders, who resisted the destruction of the collective contract. The government of Peru deported those trade unionists who were unwilling to cooperate.

We can be quite sure that neither the Peruvian nor the Yugoslav model is trouble-free; it may or may not make workers happy, it may or may not be efficient. But both exemplify a perfectly logical process, an alternative from the one used in the American corporation for endowing managers with the authority and means of direction they need in order to function. It suggests a different basis of legitimacy from that of property rights deriving from shareholders. If an alternative of this kind were to turn out to be more profitable, as some experience suggests it might conceivably do, then the issue from a shareholder's point of view might come down to whether he wants more return on investment or an illusion of ownership. Put this way, the shareholder's response would seem obvious.

From the point of view of American managers and trade unions, the Yugoslavian or the Peruvian approach is, of course, a shock. Many U.S. managements and union bureaucracies would undoubtedly be seriously shaken up if the principles of Energoinvest were to come to America. On the other hand, the authority of managers and unions in many U.S. corporations is unsettled; no amount of hymn-singing about property rights and the collective contract is going to make it solid.

The Lordstown Phenomenon

In the previous chapter, we discussed the individual's self-respect in the context of individualism and contract. Now we turn to self-respect as it relates to issues of authority and legitimacy, by looking at a rather microscopic, although representative, problem in GM's Vega assembly plant at Lordstown, Ohio. This was reported in a remarkable series of interviews by Bennett Kremen of *The New York Times.**

In 1972, there was a highly publicized strike by Lordstown's young work force. Kremen visited the plant a year and a half later to spend a week talking to the workers, prepared to find that a good deal of the publicity associated with the 1972 strike had been cooked up by journalists and academicians, much as some company and union spokesmen had indicated. He found that, if anything, the situation had worsened. Five thousand grievances had piled up and hundreds more were sure to come.** The problem was not money; no amount of money would reduce the tension that threatened to explode again in this plant. The problem, the workers told Kremen, was working conditions. To get a more specific understanding of what they meant, let us listen to their own words, starting with those of Joe Alfona, absentee replacement operator:

Well, like all men when they used to work, they had a specific job to do. They told them to shovel 100 tons of coal within X amount of time, and that's what they did. And they left them alone.

But like now they tell you, "Put in 10 screws," and you do it. Then a couple of weeks later they say, "Put in 15," and next they say, "Well, we don't need you no more, give it to the next man."

From day to day, you don't know what your job's going to be. They always either add to your job or take a man off. I mean management's word is no good. They guarantee you—they write to the union—that this is the settlement on the job, this is the way it's going

---

* Bennett Kremen, "Lordstown—Searching for a Better Way of Work," *The New York Times,* Sept. 9, 1973.
** Lest it be assumed that only blue-collar workers are feeling the pangs of dissatisfaction and illegitimacy, a survey of 2,821 executives conducted by the American Management Association in 1973 revealed that 52% of supervisory managers "found their work, at best, unsatisfying." Less than 30% were able to say they had "never been expected to compromise personal principles to conform to organizational standards"—*Wall Street Journal,* May 29, 1973, p. 1.

to run—103 cars an hour, and we're the only ones in the world could do that pace. Know what I mean?

They agree that so many men are going to do so many things, period! Fine, the union will buy that because they negotiated it. Two weeks later management comes down and says, "Hey, listen, let's add something else to that guy." They don't even tell the union. And management says, if you don't do it, they'll throw you out, which they do. No problem. Zap! away you go.

GEORGE BRAYNOR, union committeeman, material department:
I'd like to say something to that. What he says is correct, and we're not getting any backing from the international union in Detroit. No backing whatsoever. They came down in the strike in '72 and sold us out, and they're selling us this year, too.

AL ALLI, committeeman, trim department:
That is right—they won't give us a strike letter [authorization] or nothing.

QUESTION: Do you people want to strike?

GENERAL: Yeah!

The most vexing issue, it turned out, was an obscure one referred to as "doubling up." Kremen found that workers, all on their own, and without the permission or aid of either the company or the union, were handling their jobs on the assembly line in teams. The same amount of work was being done, and the workers said the product was superior in quality, but they were doubling their speed and relieving each other in relays, so that each man would work fast for half an hour and then take a half hour off, during which he could chat, get a drink of water, or "call a chick." This apparently had never been done before. When management discovered "doubling up," workers were punished. The union pretended that the practice did not exist. Kremen's interview continues:

QUESTION: The company . . . says that if you double up the quality is going to go down.

ROBERT DICKERSON, committeeman:
They're wrong.

SEVERAL: No way.

QUESTION: You have any evidence they're wrong?

ALLI: Damn right. We had better quality when they doubled up.

QUESTION: How do you know?

ALFONA: The audit tickets.

QUESTION: What are audit tickets?

ALFONA: They come down there with the corporation and they check X amount of jobs, like maybe 10 out of 100. And they check the tickets, the repair tickets which were inspected. And they see how much repair was done to this car before it hit the end of the line.

DICKERSON: It's an inspection ticket.

ALFONA: Right, it's a rating. Like if so many repairs were on this ticket within the 10 jobs per 100 it was a good audit. But if more repairs were on it, that means that the quality was bad in certain areas. And they could detect which areas.

QUESTION: So you're saying that during the doubling up the quality, in terms of audit tickets, does not go down or does go down?

ALFONA: It goes up. I can prove it to you, because I work the line, see. And we used to double up in tail lights. It's a four-man operation —you do every other car, two people do every other car.

QUESTION: A half-hour on, a half-hour off?

ALFONA: Right. I got thrown out of the plant for a week over this issue.

QUESTION: Are the 5,000 grievances related to a lot of this?

ALFONA: Absolutely. Two people would usually stay right there if something should happen—if the gun broke down, or if I missed a screw, I'd call my partner, who was sitting down. "Hey, catch that before it goes down to the repair station." He'd jump up, put the screw in for me. No repair. I got the next car behind me.

I'm working, working, working. If something else should happen, if I fell in the hole and missed a job, I call my sidekick again. He catches it, repairs it. It's never marked on the ticket. You get 100 percent, perfect. Because we don't want no problems, you know what I mean? We're doing a good job. And I defy you to find somebody who's doubling up disciplined for bad work!

QUESTION: Would you say that that system was *a redesign of assembly line methods?* [Emphasis added.]

DENNIS MC GEE, committeeman, first shift:

Definitely. There's no question about it.

QUESTION: This is an astounding thing if it's true. It's an absolutely amazing thing. If you, by *doing it your own way produce the same quality and the same amount through your doubling, then you have redesigned the assembly line.* [Emphasis added.] Does that make sense?

DAVE MC GARVEY, rank and file:

You have to double up and break the boredom to get an immediate feed-back from your job, because the only gratification you get is a paycheck once a week, and that's too long to go without any kind of gratification from the job.

QUESTION: Well, management's argument is this: If you stay on the line and do a full hour's pace—a day's work for a day's pay— meaning you stand there and take the standard breaks as worked out in your negotiations, you should be able to do more work. You should be able to produce more at the end of the day.

But you were telling me the other night that in the eight-hour day, if you did it that way, the boredom would begin to affect the quality before the day was over. That, with the doubling up, you break the boredom, and when you get back to it, you work harder.

DENNIS LAWRENCE, committeeman, body shop:
What their (management's) reasoning is against doubling up—and the only answer I can get out of them—is basic quality. But where is your quality? Where do you show me that your quality went down?

Then they come and say, "*Well, it's our plant.*" But this idea of doubling up where you put a man on for eight hours and—after he learns that job, gets set in his ways, he no longer pays any attention to what he's doing because it's automatic—bang, bang, bang.

It is "our plant," says management. The workers are suggesting that it might work better if it were their plant. This is plainly a frightening suggestion, perhaps even more frightening than those advanced in the 1930's, when the erosion of property rights and the collectivization of the contract hit the automobile industry with such force and violence.

QUESTION: So why would the company have anything against doubling up?

MC GEE: This is what I just realized. Honest to God, I believe right now that they're *so goddamned scared* of doubling up because every job that people double up on the final line, they took that man away, they took him away, every single man.

QUESTION: But despite all the hassle with their clamping down and the 5,000 grievances in the last six months, you manage to double up.

SEVERAL: Oh, yes.

MC GARVEY: Even if they say don't double up, what do you do—it's not as good as doubling up the way we normally do it—but we'll hang on the car and we'll stand there while the other guy does it. And the minute somebody comes around, we'll just put our hand in the car. We'll just play the game with them.

And they get tired of harassing us because they keep checking like bird dogs. And every time they look we're over there. Yeah, we're doing the job—but we're not really. Just to play the game.

ALFONA: You know, there were instances out there where foremen on the floor actually paid guys to double up. They paid them.

QUESTION: Why?

MC GEE: Because they want the area to run smooth. That's why.

ALFONA: They turned their backs on it. You're not allowed to double up. In other words, the foreman says, "I'm going to go over to the next line for a couple of hours." Normally the guys know what they mean, and they'll do a good job for that foreman.

Then when this foreman turns to the general foreman, he tells the general foreman, "Well, my area is running perfect." Sure, because his guys are doubling up. If he had four guys working in this one spot at the normal pace eight hours, without doubling up, he's going to get less good work out of them. Even if the guys don't want to sabotage.

QUESTION: You mean the foreman knows that?

GENERAL: Right.

ALFONA: He says, "To hell with it. I'm going to walk over to the other line and get a Coca-Cola," because he wants the productivity and the quality.

QUESTION: Do a lot of foremen do this?

GENERAL: Quite a few.

QUESTION: You know, you read all these articles about humanizing the work place, and boredom. And I was beginning to think it was an invention of journalists myself. Now, according to what you're telling me, you've gone way beyond that. It's what they're trying to do at Volvo—redesign the line. Chrysler claims it's doing this in one of its experimental plants. And here you are doing it almost unconsciously in a highly productive plant.

ALFONA: I'd explain it to the people on the outside very simply, about Lordstown and the doubling up situation. They should think about themselves at work not at Lordstown but some other place— either in an office or in a steel mill. If they say, "Gee, I'd like to go and get a drink of water," and they go. Now I might be on the line, and my break doesn't come for four hours. What am I going to do?

I'd also tell people on the outside, "Listen, if you had a job paying $4 an hour, you and your buddy, and you're each going to carry a package"—I bring it down to very easy words so the average man can understand—"You're going to get paid $4 an hour to each carry a package up the steps and down.

"Well, isn't it a little easier for you to break your back and carry two packages up and down for half an hour and your buddy resting, and then let him take over and you rest your back. If you want to go get your drink of water or go call your chick, you get the simple freedom to go, see?

"And then they understand it a little bit more. I mean, they say, 'Hey, yeah, that makes life a little easier.' That's all we want."

Let us assume that the procedure which these workers have invented and are carrying out (apparently with the passive acceptance of the foremen) is, as they say, producing an equally good automobile, with less absenteeism, fewer ulcers, and happier workers. The issue then becomes one of authority. Do workers have a right to design the work place or does management? The traditional manager would have said quite emphatically that it was management's right because it was his property. Management cannot answer so today. Furthermore, even if it could, it might well not be in its own interest or that of investors for it to do so. Great corporations can go broke protecting the principles of property rights and contract, as some did in an earlier era protecting the contract from collectivization by unions. Noble as actions on behalf of principles may be, a rational man would seem bound at least to inspect any principle which might provoke such drastic results for all concerned.

It would appear that as the new ideology takes effect, legitimizing what in fact is in many places already occurring, institutions will need to find ways to base the internal authority of their managers (as well as the external) on a more solid foundation than that of property rights. Responsibility, essential to the health of an organization, can only proceed from definite social arrangements which are rooted in a process that is plainly legitimate. These arrangements can be autocratically dictated according to some religious creed as in Pharaoh's Egypt, Hitler's Germany, or the sweatshops of the nineteenth century; or they can be more democratically arrived at. The ideology which is upon us, unfortunately, could make room for either course. Presumably, we would prefer the more democratic approach in deference to the finer elements of the traditional ideology we may hope to sustain.

The new structures may follow many varied designs. But taken as a whole, they will probably involve an arrangement whereby all the members of an organization participate in formulating or ratifying the rules by which its different members can most effectively participate in its governance. Some decisions may be best made at the top and ratified below, after procedures for consensus-making have been devised and installed. Other decisions may well be better made at lower levels by smaller groups. Here we would be wise to study the experience of those who have gone before us in this direction: Japan, Yugoslavia, Peru, and some European organizations.

There are also tactical problems in either disposing of or in some way providing for the ruptured structures of the status quo. In a time of transition this is a crucial managerial task. It calls for the utmost selflessness, an unadulterated concern for the good of the whole organization, and for preservation of vital purposes and functions, rather than for the perpetuation of any special hierarchical form. The manager must be prepared to deny even himself and his authority if the new criteria for legitimacy require it.

It is difficult to recall in history a society which has made a transition of this sort peacefully and efficiently. The United States seems to be doing it better than most, partly because of the openness, flexibility, and strength of the political and legal institutions which grew from the old ideology. But we have a long way to go, and it is probably only realistic to expect mounting crisis. Again, it is the crucial task of managers to perceive crisis for what it is early and to use it to educate themselves and those around them about what their real choices are.

CHAPTER 8 From Consumer Desire
to Community Need

The problem which large corporations pose to the American community is not principally their power. The problem is the community's uncertainty about the purposes to which that power should be put; in other words, how to combat a major lack of focus.

The third tenet of the old ideology held in effect that virtually any corporate activity which survived competitively in the market place, satisfying individual consumers, was per se acceptable. The beauty of this idea was that it required no explicit definition of community need, that need being represented by what individual consumers would buy. Such a notion fitted neatly with the old conceptions of individualism and property, as well as with the idea of the limited state: to the extent that competition to satisfy consumers was the control on property, there was no need for planning by the community.

As the old idea of competition began to erode in the face of rising community needs which were clearly distinct from consumer desires, regulation of corporate activity became necessary. Our ideological traditions, however, ensured that such regulation was generally unaccompanied by planning. Regulation without planning has been cumbersome, corrupt, and ineffective.

Great corporations, from ITT to the oil companies, have contributed to the erosion, arguing that the old competitive notions of the antitrust laws should not be imposed upon them. They are in business to promote the national interest and they appeal to government for relief and assistance on this basis. They ask the President to judge them in terms of their return to the nation's treasury and their contribution to the national welfare. They say, in effect, "We are partners with you, Mr. President, in the design and development of the national interest." But who is the senior partner? And what the nature of the partnership?

Having followed the transitions of individualism and property rights to some of their logical conclusions, we now turn to the idea of controlling the uses of property through consumer desire.

The old belief was that the uses of property are best controlled through competition among individual proprietors, each seeking maximum gain by bidding to satisfy individual desires in an open market place. This has become increasingly irrelevant to important segments of the American economy. In its place arises the notion that community *need* is in many instances clear and distinct from consumer *desire* and that it is this need—formulated by methods often still to be determined—that must be the arbiter of property use.

Individual proprietors, of course, will continue to compete in the foreseeable future. But their power and influence have been greatly diminished by a relative handful of giant collective enterprises whose size and efficiency have given them unprecedented control over both costs and prices, and whose persuasive capabilities allow them to influence not only private consumers but also government in its roles as both consumer and regulator. Attempts to weaken these collectives through application of the old idea of competition embodied in the antitrust laws have for the most part failed. This failure represents a defeat of the old ideology, and many, therefore, treat these giant corporations as sinners who have violated the conventional rules. The companies are chastised in much the way their individualistic forebears were by the medieval Church, an ironic turn of events since these huge increasingly transnational collectives are comparable to medieval institutions in other respects also.

The attack against them derives from two quite separate sets of notions: the old ideas of individualism, property, and competition; and new ideas of world order and justice.

Even as we castigate the corporations, we recognize that their departure from the traditional norms has been in response to, or at least in line with, many community expectations for more things with which to live "the good life." The organizational efficiency of the large transnational corporation is, for example, clearly necessary to the development of the world's resources and the fulfillment of world needs. And we know that there is something foolish in the suggestion, reminiscent of the dogmatism of medieval bishops, that the large corporations should be rent asunder in order that they be remade to fit the traditional ideology. Breaking up IBM and others like it might relieve them of guilt, but it would clearly handicap the American community in its competition with other communities.

In 1945, Judge Learned Hand eloquently articulated the old idea in finding the Aluminum Company of America guilty of monopolization:

> Great industrial consolidations are inherently undesirable, regardless of their economic results. In the debate in Congress Senator Sherman himself . . . showed that among the purposes of Congress in 1890 was a desire to put an end to great aggregations of capital partly because of the helplessness of the individual before them. . . .
>
> Throughout the history of these [antitrust] statutes it has been constantly assumed that one of their purposes was to perpetuate and preserve, for its own sake and in spite of possible cost, an organization of industry in small units which can effectively compete with each other.

Nothing compelled Alcoa, he said, to keep doubling and redoubling its capacity, so pre-empting the production of aluminum from all competitors.*

The declining ability of the antitrust laws to fulfill what Hand said was their purpose is an important spur to the passion that rules Ralph Nader, perhaps the ablest and most constructive of the critics. "Where is the free-enterprise system?" he cries. "I'm trying to find it."** Markets are controlled, he says, by shared monopolies, or oligopolies, with a handful of large corporations dominating each of the main lines of American industrial endeavor: General Motors, Ford, and Chrysler, for example, in automobiles; Goodyear, Goodrich, Firestone, and Uniroyal in tires; and Procter &

---

* Nothing, we might note, except the logical extension in the name of efficiency and growth of the ideas of property and individualism which here, as Hand found, collided with the idea of competition—*United States* v. *Aluminum Company of America*, 148 F–2J 416 (1945), reviewing 44 F. Supp. 97.

** Richard Armstrong, "The Passion That Rules Ralph Nader," *Fortune*, May 1971, p. 219.

Gamble, Lever Brothers, and Colgate-Palmolive in soaps and detergents. In effect, these groupings represent closed systems, surrounded by barriers which effectively preclude the intrusion of new competitive enterprises. They exploit the consumer, Nader holds, by keeping prices high and waging a kind of psychological warfare through advertising which spreads deceit and false values; competition, such as it is, has become focused on frills and superficialities —style changes and promotional deals—instead of economy, durability, and safety.*

Nader is saying, in other words, that competition to satisfy consumers is not only insufficient to fulfill community need; it is contrary to it. The fact that consumers in the 1960's were not eager to buy either safer or less polluting cars did not mean the community did not need them. Due partly to Nader's efforts, as we have seen, the community has spoken through legislation asserting a new definition of its needs. Since the passage of the National Traffic and Motor Vehicle Safety Act in 1966, some 40 million automobiles have been recalled for safety reasons, about half the number of all vehicles, foreign and domestic, sold in America during that period. Subsequently, according to calculations by the National Highway Traffic Safety Administration, the death rate per passenger mile has declined to such an extent that by the end of 1972 more than 46,000 drivers, passengers, and pedestrians had been saved from death on the road.**

Yet the corrective thrust Nader represents, which appears to be the only one operating with significant power, is limited. His replacement for competition as a guarantor of community need is a mixture of collective action on many fronts: citizen alertness and organization for attack as consumers, shareholders, and voters; the invigoration of government regulatory agencies, free of the pressures of interest groups; and the federal chartering of large corporations to make clear and uniform the standards of competition, shareholder rights, and requirements for disclosing corporate information.† Ideologically, the effectiveness of these proposals depends upon a rising sense of community, a new and independent role for the state, the assignment of Congress as the principal vehicle for the formation of a national sense of priorities, and a

---

* Thomas Whiteside, "A Countervailing Force—I," *The New Yorker,* Oct. 8, 1973, p. 74.
** *Ibid.,* p. 67.   † *Ibid.,* p. 90.

coherent vision within which plans can be laid. Nader's is indeed a hopeful program, displaying great confidence in the capacity of democratic action both within and outside government. Admirable as it is, however, it lacks completeness.

The replacement of consumer desire as a controlling idea in those areas where it no longer works means that we must examine two related but separate questions which have evolved in my discussion thus far.

Legitimacy and Control

The first question concerns the legitimacy of the large corporation. The causes of illegitimacy were discussed in the two previous chapters. There are a variety of ways in which it can be set right: shareholder democracy, participation by all corporate members in decisions affecting the whole, co-determination, various forms of state intervention, and so on.

The second concerns the criteria for and means of controlling the legitimized corporation's relationship to the various communities it affects. These communities vary widely in their purposes and needs. They include the neighborhood in which a factory is located, the city, the state, the region, the nation, and increasingly, of course, the world itself.

Although the issues of legitimacy and control are clearly related, it is important to keep them distinct. If the internal legitimacy of the corporation is clear and acceptable to the community in general, then the community is presumably apt to allow the corporation greater control over its own activities. Recalling the three means of controlling corporate activity so as to ensure its consistency with the public interest—atomistic competition, regulation, and the corporate charter—it will be seen that each of these relates somewhat differently to the matter of legitimacy. The charter is the most basic instrument of control. To the extent that the very purpose of the corporation and its most fundamental community relationships are in question, then both corporate legitimacy and control would require attention to the charter, which is in effect the corporation's birth certificate and reason for being. In cases where corporate purpose and activity are less important to the community as a whole—that is, where they relate more to individual consumer desire—the charter can be less important as a control instrument and more can be left to a combination of competition and regulation. The intricacies of interplay between these three forms of control and their relationship to corporate legitimacy need careful analysis.

Neglect of the distinction between legitimacy and control can lead to absurdities. It is clearly impossible for the stockholders of General Motors to control that company, yet Nader and Campaign GM sought to return them to exactly that role. Other difficulties that arise from neglecting the distinction can best be seen in John Kenneth Galbraith's elegant account of what is wrong with the American economy. He is worth discussing at some length because the spirit of his recommendations, radical as they may seem to the business sector, is close to the spirit of the times, and because he has made certain fallacious but highly instructive deductions.

The Galbraithian Analysis

Galbraith starts with a useful distinction between the two quite different productive systems which have evolved in the American economy, the planning system, composed of several thousand corporate giants which have a dominant effect on the American economy; and the market system, whose members are many millions of small privately owned and managed undertakings.*

As Hand, Nader, and Galbraith have confirmed, the companies of the market system continue to draw legitimacy from the traditional ideology; the companies of the planning system, however, do not. On the other hand, according to Galbraith, while those in the market system may cherish and believe in their independence, this independence is in fact a myth, one that is giving way before the relentless pressures of the planning system. For example, small business is far more dependent on diminishing sources of equity capital than the large firms, which can reinvest their earnings; small firms are thus particularly vulnerable to the regulation of borrowing and to other determinations of government. At the same time, they have little influence generally speaking on government. As an interest group, the market system lacks the economic weight and power of the planning system. Furthermore, the market

---

* John K. Galbraith, *Economics and the Public Purpose* (Boston: Houghton Mifflin Co., 1973), pp. 44–81.

system is increasingly dependent upon the planning system as a source for what it buys and as a buyer of what it makes; and the terms of trade between the two increasingly favor the more powerful planning system.* As the service sector of the economy increases, we like to suppose, more opportunities for small enterprise will evolve and thus the market system will be strengthened. Nonetheless, the laundry must buy its soap from Procter & Gamble and the restaurant its flour from General Foods. Thus the market system, Galbraith says, has in many ways become the subsidiary of the planning system.

He paints a complementary picture of the planning system. Competitive pricing in the market place, for example, is of decreasing importance as a regulator of the planning system, even though it continues to operate on the market system. Prices in the planning system are less important "than the energy, guile or resourcefulness with which the firm persuades the consumer or the government to want what it produces or by which it eliminates the possibility of choice."** The planning system's decisions about the use of resources therefore no longer necessarily reflect the decisions of consumers. Consumption in effect can be manipulated.† The planning system further protects its prices, says Galbraith, by "a convention" against price cutting out of respect for the "community of interest" of the members of the planning system. Prices are set so "that they are consistent with the need to persuade the consumer."††

On the cost side, companies in the planning system also enjoy advantages. They can influence costs in ways which most components of the market system cannot. They can and do, for example, integrate backwards, extending their control over their sources of supply and seeking out alternative sources all over the world.‡ They can also pass increases in costs on to the consumer,

---

* *Ibid.*, pp. 45, 46, 51.   ** *Ibid.*, pp. 111, 112.   † *Ibid.*, pp. 137, 140.
†† *Ibid.*, pp. 115, 116.
‡ The Federal Trade Commission in August 1973, for example, alleged that at least since 1950 eight oil companies, individually and with each other, have "maintained and reinforced a non-competitive market structure . . . and have used various practices which control and limit the supply of crude oil to independent refiners and potential entrants into refining." Their capacity to do this, the complaint said, derived from their vertical integration, which gave them a dominating role in exporting, producing, transporting, refining, and retailing petroleum products.

whether such increases are caused by environmental regulation, wage increases, or scarcity of resources.

So, says Galbraith, the planning system can control prices, costs, and consumer demand, and even exert exceptional influence over the state through the process of interest group pluralism. An example is the power of the highway lobby—including automobile companies, oil companies, public works departments, construction companies, and all their employees, friends, and relations. Also, there is a "bureaucratic symbiosis" between government and the firms of the planning system that contributes to a "tendency to reciprocal support," between, for example, the Atomic Energy Commission and its suppliers, and between the Department of Defense and its.

In its international manifestation, the scope of the planning system threatens the very sovereignty of the nation-state and invites the formation of a supranational control mechanism. Galbraith points out that what has been called the American challenge in both Europe and the Third World is not truly American at all; it is the challenge of the modern planning system. For the time being, more American corporations are prepared for international operations than those of other countries; but this is undoubtedly a temporary phenomenon.* And the small components of the market system are becoming increasingly snared in the transnational web of the planning system, in some cases disastrously. If making widgets is cheaper in Hong Kong than in Podunk, the small businessman in the latter may well find himself absorbed by the giant which can reach the former.

The antitrust laws, which have been around for sixty years or more, "present no threat to the power or autonomy of the technostructure," says Galbraith.** Those who demand their enforcement are diverting their energies "into channels that are safely futile." And he goes on to note that it is impossible to conceive of the government making the antitrust laws effective because "a government cannot proclaim half of the economic system illegal." If these laws worked as they are supposed to work, it would only make matters worse. Corporate "competence would be lowered to the level of the market system. Policy unrelated to reality ends in absurdity."†

---

* Galbraith, *op. cit.*, pp. 169, 170.
** *Ibid.*, p. 121.   † *Ibid.*, pp. 216–17.

In essence, Galbraith says, America's huge corporations—the planning system—have outstripped the controls of competition; they are no longer under the sway of their shareholders; they have commandeered the state; they have run wild, like "rogue elephants" in the forest, to borrow Raymond Vernon's felicitous phrase. In fact, the planning system's extraordinary capacity to deploy power has led us to serious problems of priority that we seem unable to resolve. Where its power has been persuasive, things exist in abundance: automobiles, toasters, and cosmetics. Where it has not, we are in short supply: housing, medical care, and mass transit.*

So much for the problem. What of Galbraith's remedy? It comes in a three-step "theory of reform": We must emancipate ourselves, intellectually and emotionally, from the control of the planning system. Each individual, especially each educator, must examine what is truly worthwhile, free of the corruption of advertising and the conventions of materialistic, male-oriented success.**

Such a cultural cleansing on the popular level would allow the state to emancipate itself from the control of the planning system; we could achieve "the retrieval of the state for the public purpose." And then, says Galbraith, the emancipated state must "enhance radically the power and competence of the market system" to improve its bargaining power and to reduce its exploitation of the planning system. In his view, this entails the exemption of small business from the antitrust laws, and the direct government regulation of prices and production in the market system. The emancipated state must also discipline the purposes of the planning system, "making these serve, not define, the public interest." This involves converting "fully mature corporations" and others doing more than half of their business with the government into public corporations—the government buying up their stock and appointing management.†

Finally, "the economy must be managed. The problem is not to manage one economy but two—one that is subject to the market and one that is planned by its constituent firms." This requires permanent pervasive wage and price controls, government regulation of production, strong encouragement of the development of

---

* *Ibid.*, pp. 198–200. ** *Ibid.*, pp. 215–16, 225–30.
† *Ibid.*, pp. 221, 256–7, 272, 285.

trade union organization (especially in the market system), extension of and a major increase in the minimum wage, some careful tariff protection for the market system, and government support for the educational, capital, and technical needs of the market system.*

This is necessarily a very sketchy outline of Galbraith's "socialist imperative," and I apologize to him for any imperfections in my summary of his views. I am not an economist and may have missed some of the important nuances of his argument. Nevertheless, it appears that his analysis and prescription deserve serious criticism—and not only from economists.

Some of Galbraith's analysis is plainly true and his recommendations are consistent with the transformation of American ideology: he proposes a model of change that clearly would take us from the old Lockean days to a new communitarian base. It is plausible in that sense and, therefore, must be taken seriously. It represents a real possibility given the inexorable flow of things.

It also exemplifies, however, the sort of stultifyingly inefficient solution to which American society is today peculiarly vulnerable; it demonstrates the ease with which we could lurch into a system of centralized, authoritarian, and possibly barbarous statism. It alerts us to the urgency of devising other (but no less radical) alternatives that offer a better chance of meeting the needs of the American community effectively while allowing for individual fulfillment within a humane system.

Galbraith's error, if one can define it as such, is that he has seized upon the illegitimacy of the large corporation—its departure from the ideas of both property and competition—and blames it for the inability of the political order to define and meet community needs. Implicit in his argument is the assumption that the planning system is a monolithic entity, willfully and malevolently seducing government away from the urgent tasks of planning and control. His remedy, like Nader's, is somehow to awaken the citizenry to this conspiracy and thus to produce an emancipated political order which will then legitimize (through takeover) and control American corporations. He has apparently failed to perceive that the problems of legitimacy and of control are, while related, quite separate.

* *Ibid.,* pp. 222, 257–60.

Galbraith has certainly demonstrated the illegitimacy of the large public corporation, its departure both from the ideas of property and ownership and from the restraints of competition. He has defined the excesses and abuses of interest group pressures upon the state, and has also amply demonstrated that the state as it presently exists is unable to project the vision the nation needs, to fix the priorities, and to initiate and guide the planning. He has thus delineated the two critical flaws: (a) the declining legitimacy of the corporation, and (b) the incapacity of the state and of our governing process to define community need so as to be able to control the relationship of the corporation to it. But then he has connected the two, making the corporation the principal cause of the difficulties of the state. This is easy and tempting, because the corporation is so vulnerable philosophically. But the failures of our political order cannot be blamed on the corporation. In fact, it would be more precise to put it the other way round: the current plight of our corporations is the result of an inadequate state.

In seeking to deal with both sets of problems simultaneously through state ownership and intervention, Galbraith has produced an unwieldy solution which probably would succeed with neither. He is surely right in stressing that we must liberate ourselves from a variety of traditional beliefs. When he says, however, that our traditional beliefs "are derived not from ourselves but from the planning system," he is oversimplifying.* In fact, our long-held beliefs in individualism, property, competition, and the limited state predate the planning system and have been flouted by it. He is also right in claiming that the hedonistic effects of advertising can largely be blamed upon the planning system; but he fails to note that these calls to luxury and leisure have tended to subvert the notions of hard work and thrift, the maintenance of which he likewise attributes to the planning system.**

In general, we can cheer his call for increased self-consciousness and independent judgment, and for resistance to "social conditioning."† Like St. Francis or Thomas Aquinas, he demands a cleansing of the spirit in the face of institutional corruption, which is fine. There is also, however, an element of the romantic individualist seeking the promise of the Enlightenment—an anachronism in an age of huge organizations, urban complexity, and mani-

---

* *Ibid.*, p. 225.   ** *Ibid.*, p. 224.   † *Ibid.*, p. 227.

fold interdependence. This is the Pied Piper leading us to disaster. Not only is such a notion inconsistent with Galbraith's own vision of America; it is irrelevant to whatever America most Americans are likely to find. A change in beliefs is coming about, but not in the direction of old-time individualism, however appealing that might be. The change is toward a new communitarianism; and the new legitimacy will be characterized first and foremost by that.

Galbraith himself acknowledges that the huge corporate collectives will not willingly be broken up, nor will the equally huge bureaucracies of government. (In fact, he would make the latter even bigger.) But, as I have already pointed out, large organizations are likely to be bent to new definitions of individual fulfillment in conformity with various new criteria of legitimacy. If corporate legitimacy is achieved by some series of changes in corporations' internal structures, Galbraith's argument on behalf of state ownership for purposes of legitimacy loses force. In Yugoslavia, for instance, state ownership was abolished in favor of more pluralistic forms of ownership centered on corporate community control. That Galbraith ignores such a possibility may be due to his partiality for and confidence in trade unions—which, of course, depend upon the old contractual organizational form.

The task is to make the huge organizations with which we must live consistent with individual fulfillment and community need. The search must be far wider than Galbraith's, the solutions more delicate, the analysis more precise.

As to his insistence that we emancipate the state from the talons of the planning system, here he does not seem to have made his case. A hypothesized malevolence of the planning system cannot be blamed for the inadequacy of the state. That inadequacy arises from many sources, none more important than a lingering affection for the Lockean notion of "the limited state." This idea has been particularly pervasive in those places where it counts, among the handful of rural congressmen who historically have controlled the committees of Congress and who have been singularly beyond the reach of great corporations.

Of course, the inadequacy also arises from our reliance on interest groups; and these, Galbraith claims, are now dominated by the planning system. But in recent years we have seen the emergence of a range of interest groups sufficiently broad and diffuse to allow the government to fix virtually whatever priorities it liked—if it had the confidence, the authority, and the will to do so. Certainly, the enactment of the National Environmental Protection Act and related legislation and the formation of the Environmental Protection Agency cannot be said to reflect the malicious influence of the planning system. And although the highway lobby opposed allocating government resources to mass transit, an increasingly powerful lobby has been supporting such a move. Corporations have been aligned on both sides. The problem is that community planning, particularly at the local level, is so underdeveloped that we are not sure what needs to be done in the transportation field. This is not so much the fault of corporations as of an antique and inadequate political structure—of lack of focus.

There is mounting evidence that the planning system is neither monolithic nor necessarily opposed to government's fixing the priorities and doing the planning that Galbraith rightly advises is so urgently needed. Whatever the rhetoric of some of its more ritualistic spokesmen, it would seem that the planning system would increasingly relish a little more government planning, a little more objective decisionmaking about where this country should go. According to Daniel Moynihan, the corporate leaders of the planning system were the most effective in prodding President Nixon to propose his Family Assistance Plan (a proposal, incidentally, which Galbraith liked). The plan was defeated in Congress by a combination of traditional ideologists and liberals who felt the minimum proposed was not big enough. In the energy field, admittedly, the nation's oil companies and utilities have been woefully slow to realize the necessity of an energy plan. Greater federal intervention to resolve the tangle of difficulties is doubtless necessary, but the problem lies more with the state itself than with the pressures upon it. If we recall the difficulties of Con Ed, New York's energy needs are in urgent need of planning at all stages of government, especially the federal level, to sort out the trade-offs involved. From the top of the Empire State Building on a clear day you can see some 1,400 political jurisdictions. Con Ed cannot help itself because it no longer has either legitimacy or power.

Increased planning and control by the federal government in the national interest is essential. Federally chartered regional corporations for the production of power may well be necessary. These must have the full authority of government in order to assure an expeditious resolution of the intensely controversial questions concerned with power production technology, the siting of power stations, and the allocation of financial resources to build new plants. In this situation, both questions of legitimacy and control require a governmental presence. But *ownership* may not be the most effective way of providing either. Government has a critical role in coordinating, planning, and fixing priorities. It may or may not have a role in providing legitimacy—it will certainly have increasing responsibilities for control.

In attempting to carry out these responsibilities, the government would not be so much the prisoner of the corporations of the planning system as of its own conception of itself. Hobbled by the idea of the limited state, it has grown enormous and unwieldy while becoming less focused, less authoritative, and less efficient. Bureaucratic symbiosis between large corporations and governmental agencies also is a problem, as Nader and Galbraith rightly note, but it is not the heart of the matter. Galbraith uses the examples of the Supersonic Transport and the Lockheed loan to prove the evils of symbiosis, but these examples are weak and anachronistic. The SST was punctured by the thrust of the most powerful component of the new ideology—the requirement for harmony between man and nature—and its failure is a rather persuasive example of effective redefinition of community need by the state. As for Lockheed, Galbraith suggests that the government underwrote the $250 million loan to keep the company from bankruptcy as a result of Lockheed's conspiratorial influence on the Defense Department. But Deputy Defense Secretary David Packard testified before the Senate that it really didn't make much difference to him whether Lockheed went bankrupt or not.* The company's contracts with the government would be filled anyway. It was Secretary of the Treasury John Connally who pushed the loan guarantee in response to pressure from a score of banks which had already loaned the company many millions and which would have sustained substantial losses in the event of bankruptcy.

The issue raised by the Lockheed case is whether or not public policy will allow huge corporations to die when they fail to produce

---

* Testimony before the Senate Currency Committee, as quoted in Fred L. Zimmerman, "Lockheed Rescue Seems Headed for Trouble in Congress: Packard's Backing Lukewarm," *Wall Street Journal,* June 10, 1971.

efficiently. It would seem objectively healthy to ensure that this could happen, assuming that careful provision is made for the social and economic dislocation such a death entails, and also assuming that a smooth transition could be managed to transform the cadaver into something new and ideologically viable. If Lockheed were owned by the government, as Galbraith suggests it ought to be, the chances of such a transition would appear to be remote indeed. It is hard to conceive of any single step which would tend to make a large American corporation more rigid than governmental ownership.

An excellent specific example of the kind of planning responsibility that the state ought to accept is provided, once again, by the urban rapid transit conundrum. And here again the problem does not stem from the companies of the planning system, who are arrayed on all sides of the issues. GM makes buses as well as cars; Westinghouse tried hard to find customers for its Transit Expressway; many aerospace companies are now in the transit business. The problem is that local communities are not equipped to decide what their needs are and what they want to become.

In sum, the lack of definition of community need is much more a result of historic attitudes toward government and by government than of dirty work on the part of the planning system. For the state to take over the corporations of the planning system would solve nothing, except perhaps their legitimacy problems. Certainly, state ownership is a time-tested device for making an organization legitimate. But it is a sociopolitical antique, as doubtful in effect as it is simple in formulation. Given the problems which currently trouble American industry it seems highly doubtful whether government takeover would produce any solutions. In fact, without a very substantial renovation in the political process, so providing government with more authority than it now has, such a takeover would probably make corporations less legitimate and increase their problems. In any case, there are a number of alternative ways to legitimize our large corporations, as we saw in the previous chapter.

Galbraith's prescriptions for the market system, where he says competition continues to work relatively well, are difficult to comprehend. He argues that there is virtue in protecting the small, innovative, and relatively flexible components of this system, but one cannot escape the feeling that they would wither quickly in his embrace. Exempting them from the antitrust laws, abolishing competition, regulating prices and production, encouraging trade union growth, and increasing the minimum wage, taken together, would do one or both of two things: force the market system with increasing speed into the planning system through merger and acquisition; put many small businesses out of existence.

In the planning system, problems of legitimacy, Galbraith says, are reflected in such injustices in the corporate hierarchy as salary differentials. The head of General Motors gets fifty times the wages of the typical assembly line worker. This discrepancy, he notes, is justified by ideas which have lost meaning—property, ownership, and competition. Income differentials should be narrowed. He invites the attention of trade unions to these and similar inequities, but recognizes that it is unlikely they will do much about them. He comes, therefore, to the necessity for government control of all wages (including those of the executives) and prices,* and to the ownership by government of "fully mature" corporations and of those doing more than half their business with government. Mixed in with this recommendation is the implicit notion that the move would not only make corporations more legitimate, but would also provide more effectively for the control of the relationship between corporations and the communities they affect.

This is only true, however, if the community is clear about the purposes of control. Then control can be ensured in a variety of ways other than ownership; it can be specified in the charter, or imposed through regulation. (Incidentally, Soviet paper companies and European government-owned utilities are major polluters.)

Furthermore, there is a critical problem of *level* of control which Galbraith fails to address at all. General Motors affects many communities from Flint, Detroit, and Lordstown in the United States to Brazil and Germany. All these communities have rights and interests in controlling its impact. Nationalizing GM would presume that the U.S. government is the most appropriate controller, and tend to centralize and rigidify control in that nation. This would seem a foolish thing to do when the needs for increasing local community consciousness and control as well as international control are quite apparent.

The real question (which Galbraith does not treat) is: What

---

* Galbraith, *op cit.*, pp. 264, 266, 268, 270.

are to be the criteria for and means of controlling large bureaucratic entities, whether corporate or governmental? Galbraith merely pushes our problems from one inadequately controlled bureaucracy to another. The focus of inquiry must be the control of institutions at the appropriate level, and this can only be resolved when there is a clear conception of community purpose.

Great corporations, it must be remembered, are obviously meeting some community needs. While Galbraith is rightly complaining about the ones they ignore, still the Soviets, the Arabs, the Brazilians, and others are inviting corporations into their countries to do all manner of things, from laying pipe to building automobiles. This indicates another difficulty with Galbraith's formulation which others have noted. In concentrating on the capacity of the planning system to control the market, he has underestimated the capacity of the system's corporate members to adapt quickly and effectively to genuine changes in market needs. This capacity cannot be dismissed out of hand with the allegation that the planning system controls the market and thus its needs. It surely is more complex than that. The sale by Bechtel, Incorporated, of pipeline technology to Saudi Arabia is not a function of the planning system's ubiquitous powers so much as it is of Bechtel's competitive edge.* It would seem that our real challenge is to design a system of controls that will enhance the responsiveness of planning system companies to community need, thereby capitalizing on the demonstrated capacity of these companies to get things done.

Bruce Scott postulates the evolution of increasingly diversified collectives constantly probing the world's market places for new opportunities, sensitive to but not dominating those market places.** He argues that it would be most unfortunate if the United States hobbled the ability of its enterprises to play this game. Instead, he wants government incentives to encourage U.S. corporations "to diversify (even by acquisition) so they do not wind up like the meat packers, the coal companies, the railroads, and the other lumbering colossi who have allowed themselves to be bypassed by the industrial system."† He also wants to sharpen the

---

* *The New York Times,* Oct. 7, 1973.
** Bruce R. Scott, "The Industrial State: Old Myths and New Realities," *Harvard Business Review,* March–April 1973, pp. 133–48.
† *Ibid.,* p. 146.

regulatory capacities of the market mechanism—for example, by instituting progressive taxation on polluters so that they pay for it "by the pound." "The alternative," Scott writes, "is to allow economists to substitute their energy and planning skills for those of the modern corporation. I question whether they are equal to the task."*

But Scott seems to ignore the problems of legitimacy which Galbraith emphasizes. ITT is surely amply diversified, and it does have enormous power over costs, prices, the state, and the market place. Much of this power is no longer legitimized by any ideology; certainly, it is inconsistent with the old, and the new is not yet clear. Galbraith presumably would nationalize ITT to make it legitimate. This might satisfy some Americans, but it wouldn't help other countries. And there is real question whether adequate controls would result.

Galbraith's error, like that of many other specialists, is in failing to see current institutional flaws in the context of ideological deterioration. Such error leads to a vagueness of perception and confusion of issues—for example, of legitimacy and control, of the role of the nation-state, and the function of economic institutions. But in addition to the many truths within his thought, his error is also most useful in that it provides a valuable lesson for the American corporate manager: When you become illegitimate, you tend to be blamed for everything.

The Priority: Defining the Community's Need

In considering the ideological transition from the idea of competition to satisfy consumer desire to that of community need, it is important to identify as precisely as we can those areas and circumstances in which the old idea of competition and the "free

---

* Neil Jacoby, like Scott, argues that competition is not all that dead. In *Corporate Power and Social Responsibility* (New York: The Macmillan Co., 1973), he talks about "a multi-vectored dynamic model of competition," pp. 138–40, in which there is extensive competition in product design and quality, technology, services, warranties, credit terms, as well as between new products and old ones, and those which are foreign and domestic, etc. However, it appears still valid to assert that in many areas competition as traditionally understood and embodied in the American antitrust laws is giving way as a workable control in the face of new definitions of community need.

market" can continue to render useful service. The process we are discussing is, after all, a transition. Although it has been going on for a long time, it will continue for much longer before it can be called complete. I am not engaged in utopianism—indeed, one of the purposes of this analysis is to avoid utopianism and the dangers and disappointments it breeds. The task is to discern as best we can the utility in the old so that we retain its most effective and just aspects, recognizing that we would be stupid to reduce efficiency without a gain in justice.

Where competition fails as a means of ensuring that productive activity conforms to the public interest, we can consider the utility of the other alternatives—regulation by government, by the corporate charter itself, or by both.

Competition in a free market has some plainly attractive features. It provides a way for consumers to signal clearly what they want. Businesses intent upon maximizing profits can then produce what individuals really want; and naturally they are encouraged to do so at the least cost. At the same time, the suppliers of the factors of production—labor, capital, and raw materials—are induced to sell these to businesses in such a way as to command the highest price. And in the end, resources are allocated efficiently. There are many areas where this system works well and where its absence leads to inefficiency and perhaps injustice. A manager from the Soviet Union once complained to me in anguish of the warehouses full of shoes that he was supposed to sell but no one wanted to buy.

The real world has placed a variety of obstacles in the way of this simple atomistic model of the competitive market. Production in many industries is highly concentrated within a few firms, which are governed by various conventions that effectively preclude the entrance of competitors. Public policy has attempted to keep the market competitive through the antitrust laws and other incentives and penalties. Furthermore, imperfections in the market mechanism have arisen through lack of market information or false or deceptive information, as in advertising, so that consumers may find themselves at the mercy of producers. Public policy has sought to remedy this failure through regulation. Finally, business policy may not conform to the expectations of the market mechanism. As Richard A. Musgrave has put it, "Instead of adjusting prices and outputs so as to maximize profits, they may follow other goals such as maximizing market shares, economic power or growth, or they may aim at securing a targeted rate of return."*

In spite of these difficulties, it would seem likely that in many areas of the American economy the market mechanism properly supported by government regulation can continue to work. But there is an increasing array of problems with which the market mechanism cannot cope, and where action by the political order is necessary and inevitable, sooner or later, in one form or another. Efficient as the market mechanism may be as an allocator, it cannot solve problems of distribution of resources or income. It cannot resolve how many people are going to be rich or poor, healthy or sick, educated or ignorant.**

These problems have to do with the evolving definition of community needs and preferences as opposed to individual desires. The actions required by the political order include planning the design of a coherent set of community purposes, an acceptable vision, as it were, and creating a framework within which implementation of those plans can be assured. For the construction of this framework we can theoretically select from a wide variety of procedures ranging from guidance, to tax rewards and punishments, to direct regulation, to changes in the corporate form and charter. For example, the market mechanism can perhaps never cope effectively with certain public needs that are clearly urgent today—for transport, communications, electric power—and we have long recognized that a single enterprise or a few are better able to provide such services. Regulation has been necessary to control pricing and quality of service. In some instances, such as the Tennessee Valley Authority and the Communications Satellite Corporation (COMSAT), we have followed the charter route with either governmental or nongovernmental financing.

A principal cause of market mechanism failure *vis-à-vis* community need has been the proliferation of costs and benefits which are external to the production and consumption system. There are an increasing number of situations today in which the community pays an unacceptable price for private actions. Since the business

---

* I am deeply indebted here to Professor Musgrave for his thoughtful paper *Social Goods and Social Bads,* published by the Harvard Business School as a case for classroom discussion (3–371–344, BP 1009).

** *Ibid.,* pp. 4 and 5.

firm traditionally has considered only its private costs, such externals as air and water pollution have gone unpaid for. The
product is now supplied at too low a price, output grows to exceed
the efficient level, and the community as a whole suffers. Now we
are confronted with the need of somehow incorporating into the
market system the costs of externals, so that the true price of a
product is paid.* This is no small matter when the costs of air
pollution, for example, can be estimated at $16 billion for one
year, and inflation is rampant.**

In addition to ecological factors, there are also a mounting
number of other community needs which are not conveniently
covered by the competitive market. Musgrave uses as examples
the benefits from a lighthouse, an uncrowded road, national defense installations, public health facilities—and we can think of
many more.† The political order must decide the costs and the
benefits, the trade-offs associated with these needs. The political
process here serves as a substitute for competition in the market
place. The necessary function of the political process in this regard
is purely the designation of community preference. The means by
which this preference is filled are a separate matter. Goods and
services can be produced and furnished by the government free of
charge or for a price; they can be contracted for by government
from private concerns, or assured through a variety of rewards
and punishments. Thus there is no necessary connection between
the definition of community needs and preferences by the political
order on the one hand, and state ownership of the means of production or the size of government on the other.†† It is possible
that the better government is at defining community needs, the less
requirement there will be for it to engage itself in meeting those
needs.

Ideally speaking, then, we should be seeking the most efficient
and most just way of meeting community needs once these have
been defined by the political order. It is in this search that we risk

---

  * *Ibid.*, p. 8.
  ** Ralph Nader in "Profiles" by Thomas Whiteside, *The New Yorker*,
    Oct. 15, 1973, p. 47.
  † Musgrave, *op. cit.*, pp. 10, 11. General Motors demonstrated the fact
    that many community needs don't sell when it tried to market pollution-
    reducing kits to motorists in Phoenix, Arizona, in 1971. There were
    528 buyers out of a possible 334,000—Jacoby, *op cit.*, pp. 215–16.
  †† Musgrave, *op. cit.*, pp. 12, 13.

being hindered by the lingering effects of the old ideology. To be fully effective in our perceptions and judgments, we need to examine carefully all those assumptions which generally have been taken for granted. For example, clean air and pure water are high-priority needs. The most efficient way to develop the necessary technology to achieve them and the procedures for economically introducing them might include a concerted effort by various industrial combinations. Such a combination and coordination would, however, run afoul of antitrust legislation. In addition, strict enforcement of the antitrust laws to prohibit such cooperation could reduce competition still further because the rich and powerful company, with research and development capacity to spare, would doubtless win out over its poorer rivals. Thus the old idea of competition can hinder both our perception of the problem and our judgment as to how to resolve it.

The community must know what it wants to do and where it wants to go. If there is one characteristic of Japan that impresses the world, it is the ability of the Japanese community to know its purposes. For the past hundred years, Japan has concentrated on industrial growth. Lately, it has become alerted to the deterioration of its physical environment and with surprising speed has allocated large amounts of money to clean things up, to restructure and redesign its economic activity—this in spite of its crushing oil bill. Japanese efficiency in defining community need, however, has not resulted in exceptionally big government, or state ownership, or even massive state intervention.

The United States must develop some such capability. During World War II, the requirements were clear because the crisis was intense. Companies in the rubber industry, for example, were allowed to cooperate in order to produce synthetic rubber; traditional notions of competition were set aside. More recently, many companies shared their knowledge in order to put a man on the moon.

If we are truly concerned about improving the ability of our economy to compete in world markets, we should organize the economy accordingly. We should add up our competitive strengths and weaknesses in the world and proceed to make the most of the strengths and rearrange the weaknesses. This, of course, is exactly what the Japanese have been doing since World War II. If, for example, computer technology were considered to be one of our strong points in exporting, then we should develop the very best computers at the lowest possible cost. Such a decision might result in a rationalization of the American computer industry, but it probably would not bring about a large-scale effort to break up IBM.

Our purposes, our definitions of community need are not at this stage sufficiently powerful to overcome traditional ideology. This is not the fault of business or of government. It is the result of living with an ideology that no longer makes sense.

The Steel Industry

In 1971, the American steel industry was in severe trouble. Profits were down, costs were up, and foreign imports were cutting increasingly deeply into domestic markets. A few years later, the industry was healthier because of the booming U.S. economy and the willingness of both labor and management to give up some of their power and autonomy in favor of a higher degree of consensuality. But the industry's future remains uncertain. Hendrik S. Houthakker, as a member of the President's Council of Economic Advisers, was reported to have said that the United States steel industry in its present form could not survive. "We need a steel industry of some size, but not necessarily the present size. The national security argument doesn't leave you with a very big industry. National security wouldn't be impaired if the backs of refrigerators were made from imported steel."[*]

"The government and the industry have to get together and decide what their goal is," added Roger S. Ahlbrandt, president of Allegheny Ludlum Industries.[**]

Some say America must do what it does best and cheapest, fitting its strengths to the world economy. This was indeed our haphazard strategy in the mid-1970's, and it resulted in America's largest exports being agricultural products and natural resources. Our place in the world has indeed been tending toward that of an oversized "banana republic," presumably not the optimum role for the United States in the world economy.

What are some of the factors which the government and the steel industry would have to consider if they did get together to

---

[*] *Business Week,* May 15, 1971, p. 95.
[**] *Ibid.,* p. 94.

decide upon a goal? The first is ideologically ironic. The U.S. steel industry was spared the bombs of World War II which destroyed much of the steel-making capacity of Japan and Germany, but it also was thus denied access to large amounts of capital which the conquerors contributed to Europe and Japan to rebuild their steel industries anew. In many ways it became technologically backward. To obtain capital to modernize and thus meet the competition of foreign factories, the U.S. steel industry had to compete for funds in the stock market, following the traditional ideology.* The hidden premise of our system here is that if the industry cannot successfully compete for funds among individual investors it should go out of business (recalling the Lockheed loan issue). The community's goal regarding a steel industry thus would be determined through the natural processes of stock market competition.

The second factor is closely related to the first. To compete in the stock market for the funds it needed for modernization, the steel industry had to show high profits. In order to do this, it needed to charge relatively high prices; it refused to lower prices to meet foreign competition in the U.S. market place. But the Japanese were prepared to sell steel at lower profits to obtain a share of the market, thus violating one of the rules upon which the working of the market mechanism depends. In consequence, between 1960 and 1968, when steel imports made their deepest inroads, U.S. steel industry profit margins averaged 5.4 per cent and the iron and steel price index went *up* 5 per cent!** The unwillingness of American steel to compete on price had ideological overtones, as Edwin H. Gott, chairman of U.S. Steel Corporation, indicates: "We're different. It's not part of our way of life in this country."

Walter Adams, the University of Michigan economist, contends that foreign steel producers gained 20 per cent of the domestic market in the 1960's because "the American steel industry handed it to them with its suicidal pricing policies."† If Adams is right, then Gott's peculiar aversion to price competition is the villain. Gott would doubtless blame his problems on the necessity to

---

* The industry is financed with about 80% equity funds and 20% loans from banks. In Japan, the figures are the other way around.

** *Business Week,* May 15, 1971, p. 92.

† *Ibid.,* p. 92.

show a profit so as to attract equity capital as well as to borrow.

How should American industry get its money? Putting the same point another way, do we decide what we need as a community and then provide the money for it? Or do we finance only what will float competitively in the traditional money markets? The Japanese, of course, are quite clear on this point. In the 1950's the Japanese government, together with Japan's business collectives, decided that the good of the community lay in mobilizing certain industrial complexes for expansion into world markets; they proceeded to launch a well-orchestrated attack. They took a long rather than a short view—profits were incidental to market share. Many Americans regarded this as "unfair." Obviously, it all depends on how we define "fairness," which in turn depends on our ideology.

There are two approaches to the problem of the steel industry. The first was suggested by Donald F. Turner of the Harvard Law School; the second hinted at by Peter G. Peterson when he was assistant to President Nixon for foreign trade. Turner advocated breaking up the largest steel companies and creating new and independent firms—a measure that "should increase the frequency of independent pricing and, hopefully, increase the pace of innovations, which some feel has been rather slow." He felt that the U.S. steel industry suffers from too much concentration.*

While Turner tended to rely on traditional notions of competition, Peterson advocated moving more in the Japanese direction, setting the antitrust laws aside and designing the American steel industry in whatever way is necessary to maximize its strengths and improve its position in the world economy.**

My own guess is that we shall tend toward the Peterson approach, in which case the steel industry will become more dependent upon debt financing, with funds increasingly allocated in conformance with some master plan.

This raises a final set of critical factors: What will be the criteria for such a plan? And how will it be made legitimate? Once again, we are back to the familiar alternatives. Interest groups may do

---

* Donald F. Turner, "The Principles of American Anti-Trust Law," *International and Comparative Law Quarterly,* separate publication No. 6 (London: The British Institute of International and Comparative Law, 1963): 8 and 9.

** Peter G. Peterson, *The United States in the Changing World Economy* vol. 1 (Washington, D.C.: U.S. Government Printing Office, 1971).

it, with the most powerful calling the shots. It may be the work of an increasingly authoritarian state. It may emerge as the result of a consensus in which a host of new ideas are synthesized and brought together for balancing. Or it may be the result of outright clashes in the face of mounting crises caused by high unemployment and depression.

If we decide that, as Houthakker suggested, we do need a steel industry but a different, smaller one, we must clarify a variety of cloudy implications which follow from that decision. We must organize the new industry in the most effective form possible, which might mean some kind of combination allowing a high degree of cooperation among the several industry components. In such a case, the old idea of competition would have to be seriously altered, and the antitrust laws set aside. Allocations of funds for research and development would have to be increased; this would require a government decision, which could only be made in the light of other calls for funds for energy, health, transportation, and the like.

Thus, if community need is to replace effectively the already eroded idea of competition in determining the future nature of the American steel industry, the community must have an overall plan in which all needs and resources are somehow integrated. The issue of whether or not the steel industry of the future is owned by government is relatively superfluous. Only when we have decided what that industry should be—what need it should fill—can we decide how it is to be made legitimate internally and controlled externally. Among the options requiring careful exploration, it is by no means clear that enforced nationalization is the best.

Of the three devices which can be employed to ensure that business conforms to the public interest—competition, regulation, and the corporate charter—it would seem that the third is the most appropriate for the steel industry. The design of a new steel industry would indeed require a new conception of the corporate charter, which undoubtedly should be federal until the day when it might become transnational.

Much the same reasoning can be applied, as I have suggested, to the oil industry. In fact, the words of Elbert H. Gary when he was chairman of U.S. Steel Corporation in 1912 seem peculiarly relevant to Exxon and the rest today: "I would be very glad if we knew exactly where we stand, if we could be free from danger, trouble and criticism."* It appears that the United States would scarcely benefit from breaking up the oil companies in the name of the antitrust laws, or through cumbersome and fragmented regulation. In addition to domestic questions cited earlier, the issue has a variety of international aspects, such as bargaining with oil-producing countries, and so on. Ecuador has oil, but it is also the world's largest producer of bananas. It is possible that if America wanted Ecuador's oil, it would be helpful to take its bananas too. This is hard for an oil company on its own to arrange. Clearly, the purposes of the large integrated oil companies and the terms on which the American community will allow them to exist must be redefined. This would best be done through their charter, a federal charter, designed to give the companies maximum freedom but also to ensure that they respond to national needs and priorities. Oil corporation managers may well be harming the interests of their institutions, even inviting nationalization, by refusing to think in terms of charter reformation. It is both a matter of legitimacy and control.

American Telephone and Telegraph also has an interesting charter problem. For many years it served the community and its shareholders well as a monopoly, safely cradled in regulation. Recently, the Federal Communications Commission decided to open it up to competition, allowing small, innovative companies to skim off some of AT&T's cream by competing in various forms of direct communication. AT&T's capacity to retaliate was curbed by the Justice Department employing the antitrust laws. In fact, in 1974 the Department sought with Lockean ardor to break the company up. The corporation was thus caught in a squeeze between competition and regulation. It argued that it could no longer meet the community's needs unless it got relief. To provide telephone service to the remote Maine farmer at the same price as urban dwellers meant that it needed access to higher profits. If these were being eroded by competition, something would have to give. The issue is clearly a charter issue: What does the American community want AT&T to be? A new charter is required, but

---

* *Business Week,* March 23, 1974, p. 47.

one suspects that company lawyers and management, conditioned to debate in the old context are loath to seek it.

One component of any complete plan for meeting community needs must ensure the control of waste from manufacturing. Our planet is indeed a closed system. Air and water are no longer free commodities. The force of this has become visible in a growing network of environmental laws at various government levels. These laws in turn spawn a number of regulations which are burdensome, unpredictable, and subject to frequent change.

Implicit in current procedures is the old notion that anyone can start a corporation for virtually any purpose. Environmental regulation is then imposed uncertainly and unevenly on going concerns, in some instances requiring them to make costly changes. Would it not be better to state at the beginning in the original charter that the corporation shall not pollute? Two options might be offered to a firm: either it pays a resource rehabilitation tax to match the costs of recovering all its product and making that product ecologically acceptable, or it is obliged to take back its product from the customer when the customer is through with it.

Such stipulations would force manufacturers to consider their operations as part of a total system from the outset. They would then have an important incentive to plan so as to make full use of the total product, including substances previously considered waste. They would be encouraged to think in terms of what Jordan Baruch calls "a manufacturing-demanufacturing loop."* This is a way to "internalize the costs and benefits of manufacturing. Also, new opportunities for business would be created. Chemical companies would be encouraged to remember that today's waste is tomorrow's synthetic rubber. Power companies could become producers of sulfuric acid from sulfate, or the hub of a whole industry complex built around the complete demanufacturing of all waste. Business more than government has the skills to devise the most economical procedures for resource rehabilitation, but it cannot develop these without an explicit declaration of need by the community.

Baruch offers the example of the junked automobile. Currently, it is considered a waste product of the automobile industry; yet

---

* Jordan Baruch, "Demanufacturing—Threat and Opportunity for Manufacturers," *Innovation*, March 1972, p. 3.

that industry has much of the competence required to reclaim the value of the defunct car, and furthermore, the transportation and administrative system necessary to such reclamation. He suggests that the automobile company's responsibility for its waste output is inherent in its right to exist. In effect, the government would say: "If you do not dispose of your waste in a way that is harmless to society, we shall contract with a separate organization to do so and pass the cost of that disposal on to you in the form of a direct tax."*

Such a procedure could introduce new economies and efficiencies into our system. The manufacturer, after all, has several advantages in taking on the tasks of demanufacturing. His costs are apt to be less because he is intimately familiar with his product; moreover, he can probably gain some advantages from the large scale of his operations. He stands to benefit from the value of his demanufactured product. And, perhaps most important, he can arrange his manufacturing process so that it facilitates the demanufacturing process.** Those wastes with which the manufacturer could not economically cope could be demanufactured by large semi-public utilities established initially with government capital. These corporations could be multinational, taking advantage of the needs of less developed countries for much that developed countries consider waste—used engines are a case in point.

Such a scheme would require a nationwide focus; business cannot move effectively until such planning exists. Again, the nationalization of business is irrelevant to the task. If the plan is put into operation, a wide variety of corporate forms can be designed to fill its needs effectively and competitively. In the examples given, the most appropriate mechanism for ensuring business accordance with the plan—with the public interest—is the charter itself.

Government Regulation

Government regulation of business without sufficient planning generally has disappointing results. Unless the regulators are confident of the direction in which they are moving, which ordinarily in this country they are not, those being regulated can impose their own directions with comparative ease. The trouble with

---

* *Ibid.*, p. 4.   ** *Ibid.*

regulation in the United States, however, has not been so much that industry has conquered the regulators as that the regulators lacked a clear and continuing perception of the community purpose for which they were working.

There are, of course, clear examples of manipulating industry influence—for example, the import quotas and tax-depletion allowances by which the government has subsidized the oil industry. The Civil Aeronautics Board has not allowed the formation of a new trunk airline since it was created in 1938. The Federal Power Commission, however, can hardly be called the tool of the natural gas producers. For a number of years it set wellhead gas prices considerably below what the industry desired and probably below what the public interest required. In that case, the regulators were unaware of the workings of the energy supply system in the United States; there was no plan; they had no direction. Regulation was piecemeal and futile. Again, if the Interstate Commerce Commission was once dominated by the railroads, it certainly is not today. In James Q. Wilson's words:

So generous has that agency been to the chief rivals of the railroads, the truckers and barge lines, that today the rail industry favors deregulation altogether. . . . Whether a commission does or does not serve the ends of industry is much less important than whether it serves the correct ends, and these may or may not be what the industry wants.*

In evaluating government regulation as a means of ensuring behavior consistent with the public interest, it is essential to recall how the practice of regulation evolved within the workings of the traditional ideology. Corporations were held to be good as long as they were efficient economic machines that satisfied their consumers' desires. Occasionally they created problems, some of which industry perceived and some of which only the surrounding community recognized. Regulatory commissions, variously constituted,

---

* James Q. Wilson, "The Dead Hand of Regulation," *The Public Interest,* Fall 1971, pp. 47 and 41. Perhaps the most succinct criticism of the ICC was that of Ralph Nader's Center for the Study of Responsive Law, which after a lengthy study of the commission called it "an elephant's graveyard of political hacks." The study argues persuasively that given the absence of any conception of overall need by the ICC, the country and the consumer would be better off if it were abolished and the breezes of competition allowed to blow—*The New York Times,* March 17, 1970, p. 67.

sprang up around such problems. The Federal Power Commission, for example, emerged originally to cope with difficulties having to do with water. Even today it by no means embraces all the issues having to do with electric power. The least significant thing about the FPC is its control by industry; the most significant thing is that it has neither the right nor the means to frame a policy regarding energy in the United States. After reading all 1,041 pages in Volume 42 of the Federal Power Commission Reports, Professor Paul MacAvoy of M.I.T. was unable "to find any consistent policy preference concealed in their bureaucratic and ponderous language. . . . The net effects of the FPC's actions often are clear, but whether they are intended and if so, on what grounds, is not clear."*

The electric power industry is partly to blame for the FPC's inadequacies. Like many industries conditioned by the traditional notion of the limited state, the electric utilities have supposed that any government policy, any overall plan, is worse than none. Only recently has "the energy crisis" caused utility executives to inspect their assumptions on this score.

Where the purposes of regulation are clear, as in the case of pure food and drugs, it appears that regulators have been somewhat more successful, although here too there is inevitable controversy as to how much purity the community needs.**

The extent to which competition can continue as a workable idea to control the uses of property remains debatable. There is similarly room for valid argument over the nature and effects of regulation and the form which the corporate charter should most appropriately take. There is little doubt, however, that before adequate answers can be obtained about these matters, there must be a substantial improvement in the capacity of our political processes to define community needs, to set directions, and to fix priorities. This brings us to the role of the state, to the departures from the Lockean notion of the limited state which have already occurred, and to the options that exist for future development.

---

* Quoted in Wilson, *op. cit.,* p. 48.
** For an interesting study of the effects of regulation, see William A. Jordan, "Producer Protection, Prior Market Structure and the Effects of Government Regulation," *The Journal of Law and Economics,* University of Chicago Law School, No. 15 (April 1972): 151–76.

CHAPTER 9 The State as Planner

The American state no longer seems to have any real choice between planning and not planning. It will either choose to plan well and comprehensively, or badly and haphazardly. If the second, there is likely to be chaos, resulting inevitably in more crisis, which in turn will cause an inexorable demand for more planning plus more coercion. Should the crisis prove great enough, and democratic processes not appear capable of dealing with it, there will be a natural call for dictatorial measures. The state has already begun to accept these facts, yet the transition has been most reluctantly admitted. Even as government has become increasingly pervasive, finally moving away from its theoretically minimal role, its leaders and others cling to the old idea of the limited state. President Nixon invariably ended his most interventionary speeches with prayerful rhetoric citing loyalty to the "cherished values," which generally turned out to be the traditional ideology.* And even as he proposed the Family Assistance Plan to provide a guaranteed income to all, he told the Chamber of Commerce, "If we were to underwrite everybody's income, we would be undermining everybody's character."** As with great corporations, government has departed radically from the idea upon which it traditionally relied for legitimacy, and no comparable new idea has been substituted. The result has been an erosion of trust and authority.

The effects of lingering with the old ideology have been perverse.

---

* See, for example, his address of Sept. 9, 1971, in which he announced wage and price controls—*The New York Times,* Sept. 10, 1971, p. 20.
** Address, April 26, 1971.

Today, for example, the United States, for all its Lockean protestations, has one of the world's largest governments. It has grown substantially faster than the economy. Federal government spending increased from 5 per cent of the gross national product in 1930 to about 26 per cent in 1973. Expenditures directed by all levels of government increased from 15 per cent of the gross national income to nearly 40 per cent during the same period.* The costs of government have risen similarly, from $3 billion in 1913 to $400 billion in the mid-1970's. Taxes were 32 per cent of gross national product in 1973. (In Japan they were 21 per cent.)** And with growth has come enormous proliferation, layer upon layer of diffusion employing a total of some 13 million people— more than the total employment of all durable goods manufacturing industries. As government has grown, so it has lost focus. It has become very big while remaining dutifully limited in its capacity to plan coherently. This is not accidental; it is how we want it, the natural result of our adherence to the old ideology.

Multiple forces will unquestionably accelerate the transition of government from its old role to the new one—that of comprehensive planner. First is the general context of scarcity of vital resources. At the moment, there is a scarcity of energy fuels; soon it will be metals, water, and more. Second, this context of scarcity is dominated by large and complicated corporations, traditionally oriented toward economic ends, which require enormous quantities of these resources in order to operate. And, third, these corporations are intertwined with the political, societal, and cultural life of many communities, but the old explanations, the old legitimizers are but tattered shreds on the powerful new bodies of these sprawling corporate forms. As we have seen, such organizations, while immensely powerful, lack authority. Their justification is controversial because there is no framework of ideas to help us judge, criticize, or reform them. At issue are their relationships to one another, to their individual memberships, and to the communities which they affect nationally and globally.

State planning can take two forms: the kind we have generally practiced, and the kind toward which we are inexorably tending.

---

* C. Jackson Grayson, Jr., "Let's Get Back to the Competitive Market System," *Harvard Business Review,* November–December 1973, p. 109.

** Paul Samuelson, *Economics* (New York: McGraw-Hill Book Co., Inc., 1973), p. 149.

The first emanates from the old conception of the state's role—planning that is largely the product of the interplay of interest groups. This can only be tactical, shortsighted, and short-lived at best, for it arises out of the conflicts of self-interested powerholders who merely seek relatively short-range profit or protection. The state, unwilling to accept planning overtly but forced to accomplish some anyway, does so surreptitiously, responding to the desires of whatever collection of interests strikes its nerves the hardest. The result—whether taken in terms of the economy, or energy, clean air, and pure water—is a patchwork of superficiality, uncertain, unsystematic, and frequently unjust. It is inadequate to the needs we face. If we persist in it, we will experience mounting chaos and divisive crisis that will threaten the very existence of democracy, inviting authoritarianism in the name of coherence.

The second form of planning we have known only in time of war, as in World War II. A virtue of such a war is that it is unifying; it provides an ideological surrogate, a set of clear-cut ends toward which coherent planning can aim. This form of planning is integral and holistic; it is long-range; it emanates from the leadership, initiative, and vision of the state itself.

Can we achieve such planning without the crisis of war or one equally appalling? And if so, can we preserve what is noblest and best of the old ideology—the rights of the individual, his liberty and self-respect—in the face of the obvious threat to those rights? Can we maintain an open society, allowing for the free expression of views and for the maximum participation of all in the decisions which affect their lives?

The answers to these questions lie in the speed and precision with which we can identify and comprehend the manifold crises which are upon us and construct the political mechanisms capable of dealing with them. I shall first review the capabilities of our present political mechanisms to perform integral planning and then make a number of suggestions as to how they might be transformed and strengthened.

Planning in America: An Unintegrated Response to Crises

As we have seen, the tension between the Hamiltonian planners and the Jeffersonian Lockeans was resolved early in the

nineteenth century by the emergence of a clear sense of partnership between business and government, in order to tame the wilderness and develop the nation's resources. By the end of the
century, laissez-faire extremism had pretty well undermined any
legitimacy this compromise may have had. The administrations of
Theodore Roosevelt and Woodrow Wilson were marked by tendencies toward a clear-cut planning role for the state, and during
the Great Depression drastic departure from the old ideology occurred. But the departures were pragmatic, deliberately unaccompanied by any explicit ideological change.

The year 1929 found the American government with a puny
collection of administrative services, altogether a minor element in
American life. With the agony of the Depression came the demand
that government do something. The New Deal succeeded in establishing the notion that the problems of the nation could be dealt
with one by one through the creation of a random collection of
agencies and commissions. Respectful of the traditional ideology,
it also established the idea that the most desirable relationship between those agencies and commissions was one of fierce competition, each vying through fair means or foul for presidential favor
and congressional appropriations. The New Deal did not, however,
establish authoritative integrated planning as a proper function of
government. There were many reasons for this failure: the fren-
zied rush with which emergency measures had to be taken in the
"First 100 Days"; Roosevelt's eagerness to avoid an ideological
confrontation, on practical grounds; and the unfamiliarity of
America (as compared to France and England, for example) with
a prestigious, professional, and authoritative government service
capable of planning, and this country's consequent reluctance to
create or accept such a service.*

As a result, we now find ourselves confronted with newer, more
complex, and more intense versions of the same difficulties the
New Deal planners sought to solve in the thirties. The past thirty-

---

* Louis Hartz in *The Liberal Tradition in America* (New York: Harcourt, Brace & World, Inc., 1955), p. 263, notes that Roosevelt "did
not need to leave Locke openly" because he did not need "to spell out
any real philosophy at all." A consummate pragmatist, Roosevelt was
happy to let the ideologically significant—and controversial—parts of
his program go by the board. "The TVA . . . was the only full instance of public ownership, and the rationalization of this . . . was in
terms of the inspiration it gave to private initiative" (p. 267).

five or forty years have been a strange ideological interlude, during which we have been able to avoid the divisive issues raised by such New Deal intellectuals as Berle, Means, Tugwell, and Dewey. Our ideological conscience during this time has been distracted for the most part by the unifying presence of "enemies" abroad who quite conveniently, in their cruel totalitarianism, made Locke's libertarianism appear particularly appealing. Viet Nam marked the traumatic end of that era. Now we are awake again, and as we wipe the sleep from our eyes, we can dimly see that the great ideological issues perceived but never dealt with by the New Deal are still with us. Indeed, they are even more urgent, but the difference is that as yet we lack a unifying crisis as a lever to action, a lever that the New Deal had at hand with the Great Depression. It is remarkable how contemporary the tenets of the New Deal sound today:

that the technological revolution had rendered bigness inevitable; that competition could no longer be relied on to protect social interests; that large units were an opportunity to be seized rather than a danger to be fought; and that the formula for stability in the new society must be combination and co-operation under enlarged federal authority.*

Two creations of the New Deal deserve special attention because they represent our nearest approach to integral peacetime planning. One was the National Recovery Administration (NRA), which was born in 1933 and died in 1935, when the Supreme Court declared it unconstitutional. The other was the Reconstruction Finance Corporation (RFC). Begun in 1932 in the last days of Herbert Hoover, the RFC became the largest lender in the United States for some twenty years before it was abolished in 1953 under the shadow of political corruption.**

During the three years following 1929, the national income of the United States dropped from $90 billion to $40 billion; the industrial output index declined from 110 to 58; 15 million workers were unemployed.† The NRA was established to administer the National Industrial Recovery Act of 1933, a piece of legislation designed to stimulate economic recovery by increasing em-

---

* Arthur Schlesinger, Jr., *The Coming of the New Deal* (Boston: Houghton Mifflin Co., 1959), p. 170.
** Clair Wilcox, *Public Policies Toward Business* (Homewood, Ill.: Richard D. Irwin, Inc., 1971), pp. 679 and 499.
† *Ibid.*, p. 671.

ployment, raising wages, and thereby increasing consumption. To do this, it sought to establish maximum working hours, minimum wages, union recognition, and collective bargaining. So that businessmen could pay higher wages, they were to be protected against price cutting, and for this purpose the idea of competition as embodied in the antitrust laws was to be set aside. To implement this scheme (which incidentally bears an embryonic resemblance to Galbraith's proposals),* the NRA established codes of "fair competition" industry-by-industry that stipulated wages, hours, and prices.

Significantly, the actual NRA program emerged from organized labor and organized business. Labor wanted wage and hour regulations and union recognition; business wanted liberation from the antitrust laws and nationwide "coordination of production and consumption," to quote Gerard Swope, president of the General Electric Corporation. "The time has come," said Henry J. Harriman, then president of the United States Chamber of Commerce, "when we should ease up on these [antitrust] laws and, under proper governmental supervision, allow manufacturers and people in trade to agree among themselves on these basic conditions of a fair price for the commodity, a fair wage, and a fair dividend."** More than 2 million employers agreed with the basic concept and signed onto the program while the industry codes were being worked out. Cooperating businesses displayed the Blue Eagle on their wares, and consumers were invited to boycott those who did not. Significantly, it was business which was in the forefront of this radical change. Like ITT and other such companies today, business had become restless in the bonds of the old ideology.

The draft codes were drawn up by various trade associations in negotiation with labor unions and submitted to NRA officials. Then they were submitted to two advisory boards, one representing labor and industry, and the other the consumers. If industry and labor agreed, the codes were approved. (Consumer representatives might have objected, but their protests were ignored, since consumers at that time had little power as an interest group.) The 874 approved codes controlled sales, prices, markets, production, capacity, and the channels of distribution. In the name of competition, they required adherence to practices that the courts had

---

* See Chap. 8 of this text.   ** Wilcox, *op. cit.,* p. 672.

held to be unfair: "Industry by industry, they were designed by a majority to curb the competitive propensities of an obstreperous minority," writes Clair Wilcox. "Item by item, they copied the pattern of the European cartel." Further, the codes were administered by "authorities" whose membership was chosen principally by the trade associations. Thus the government virtually delegated to trade associations many of its powers, including, in some cases, the power to tax.* Business and government were partners, but it appeared that business was the senior partner.

The NRA failed when it became apparent that the trade associations had abused the power the government had abandoned to them. Despite Roosevelt's pleas, prices rose; consumers complained, as did "competitive" businesses whose interests had been restrained by the codes. The President appointed an investigative committee, which finally denounced the whole system as "monopoly sustained by government" and "a regimented organization for exploitation."** On May 27, 1935, the Supreme Court declared the NRA to be an unconstitutional invasion of intrastate commerce and an unconstitutional delegation of legislative power.†

It is generally agreed that the NRA was a failure. Business, when given the power to organize itself efficiently in the public interest, proceeded to commit economic suicide, pricing itself out of markets and forcing consumers to turn to substitutes.

Two lessons could be drawn from the NRA experience. Some might say we had best remain within the confines of the old ideology and never try such a stunt again. Others might argue that since we need to organize business differently and plan strategically as a nation, we must do it consciously, recognizing that if we are going to put aside one ideology, we had better make sure that another is in place to give support and power essential to reorganization. For example, let us say that ITT is right: that in order for it to compete effectively in the world it must be big and strong at home, regardless of domestic competitive considerations, and that for such a purpose the antitrust laws should be watered down. In this matter, as in others—the efficient disposal of solid waste, an economical telephone system, the maintenance of a steel industry sufficient to our needs—business and government must be seen as partners in the design and development of the public in-

---

* *Ibid.*, pp. 673–4. ** *Ibid.*, p. 679.
† *Schechter* v. *U.S. 495* (1935), in Wilcox, *ibid.*

terest. Then it becomes crucial to clarify who is the senior partner. There must be a clear and legitimate procedure for defining the community needs that ITT shall fill. Is this to be a political process, with government responsible for initiation, information gathering, analysis, and coordination? Or is it to be a commercial and economic process, initiated and coordinated by business and other interest groups? Plainly, the lesson of the NRA is that if there is to be a plan, government must play a central and dominant role in the definition of the public interest and the plan's formulation.

Furthermore, a national plan had best take into account the complete array of relevant factors. Keeping down the price of natural gas in the late 1960's exacerbated our energy problems; it did not contribute to a plan for their resolution. At the same time, it appears that insufficient planning and/or inadequate regulation of the oil companies was a significant factor in our fuel crisis. If our government is to be capable of planning coherently, it must have the authority and information it now lacks. In large part this lack is the result of the legitimacy problem: we do not yet officially acknowledge that it is the role of the state to plan.

Far more successful than the NRA was the New Deal's development of the Reconstruction Finance Corporation (RFC). This agency was created on a temporary basis in 1932 to provide capital to such essential institutions as railroads, banks, and insurance companies. Its life was extended repeatedly and its powers enlarged; during the war, it provided funds for the procurement of strategic materials and emergency construction of industrial facilities. In 1949, the Hoover Commission found that its record during the Depression and World War II had been highly satisfactory,* but by 1953 the quality of its management had apparently deteriorated—it was charged with making bad loans on the basis of political favoritism and was abolished.** At that time it had suffered defaults on only 1 per cent of its loans, and had paid the Treasury more than $1 billion. Its remaining assets were valued at $700 million.

---

* Commission on Organization of the Executive Branch of Government, *Task Force on Lending Agencies* (Washington, D.C.: U.S. Government Printing Office, 1949), pp. 21–2, as cited by Wilcox, *op. cit.,* p. 499.
** Wilcox, *ibid.,* p. 499.

Conceptually, the RFC represented an instrument for planning the allocation of the nation's capital resources. Today, considering the impending capital shortages in the face of the increasing capital needs of such industries as transportation, communications, and electric power, one wonders whether the intervention of government will not again be necessary, to ensure that resources are allocated to community need. Similarly, one wonders whether the problems of converting major industries from one function to another in the public interest will not require financing of a sort that will be commercially unobtainable.

In 1974, the nation found it difficult to finance many of its vital functions. Government was restricting the overall money supply in order to restrain inflation; the stock market was failing to attract needed equity capital; interest rates on loans were at record highs; utility bond ratings had deteriorated. Capital thus being scarce, there was a problem of allocation. Who was going to decide how capital would be raised and where it would go? Either this could be left to private institutions, such as banks and large insurance companies, or some form of government intervention could be arranged. If government intervention, again there were two choices: the haphazard rescue of selected institutions from the waves of bankruptcy at the last minute, or—following the example of the RFC and Europe and Japan—intervention as part of a national planning process. It is important to note in this connection that the RFC was successful so long as the criteria which it employed for determining the public interest were made clear by crisis; but when the criteria became fuzzy, corruption and illegitimacy set in, and the agency lost its purpose and its life.

The Dangers of Ambivalence

The experience of the New Deal and subsequent political events exemplifies Samuel P. Huntington's observation that power in America is fragmented much as it was in Elizabethan England— the England from which Locke descended and which in many respects he was describing.* Not only is power deliberately diffused among the three separate branches of government, which jealously guard their boundaries; but also within each of these

---

* Samuel P. Huntington, *Political Order in Changing Societies* (New Haven, Conn.: Yale University Press, 1968), pp. 98–121.

branches, power is dispersed among competing groups and interests. Our Presidents, like Tudor kings, have had the continuing task of creating some unity and simplicity out of enormous diversity and complexity. This is the way our Constitution was written. As Walter Bagehot put it: "The English constitution . . . is framed on the principle of choosing a single sovereign authority, and making it good: the American, upon the principle of having many sovereign authorities, and hoping that their multitude may atone for their inferiority."*

Unlike the federal administrative processes of other modern governments, ours have worked to disaggregate public power instead of making it more coherent, as the example of the NRA demonstrates. Our federal ability to control the mighty has weakened; its vulnerability to control by them has increased. To give one example, on March 12, 1971, Secretary of Agriculture Clifford Hardin announced that the price which the government pays to support the price of basic milk would remain at $4.66 per 100 pounds. On March 25, Secretary Hardin reversed himself, announcing a price increase to $4.93. As the *Wall Street Journal* described it:

During the 13 days between the governmental "no" and "yes" a classic sequence of interest group pluralism unfolded. In Congress and the White House the Dairy Lobby pressed its purpose. Two million dollars found its way to President Nixon's campaign committee.**

Two years after the event, William A. Powell, president of Mid-America Dairymen, Incorporated, wrote: "I have become increasingly aware that the sincere and soft voice of the dairy farmer is no match for the jingle of hard currencies put in the campaign funds of the politicians by the vegetable-fat interests, labor, oil, steel, airlines and others."† By way of further explanation, Mr. Powell wrote as follows to a farmer in Cameron, Missouri:

On March 23, 1971, along with nine other dairy farmers, I sat in the Cabinet Room of the White House, across the table from the President

---

* *The English Constitution* (London: Oxford World's Classics, 1949), p. 202, as quoted in Huntington, *ibid.*, p. 111.
** *Wall Street Journal,* Nov. 5, 1973; Frank Wright, "The Dairy Lobby Buys the Cream of the Congress," *Washington Monthly,* May 1971, p. 17.
† Letter dated June 7, 1973, as quoted in *Wall Street Journal, op. cit.*

of the United States, and heard him compliment the dairymen on . . . our involvement in politics. He said, "You people are my friends and I appreciate it." Two days later an order came . . . increasing the support price for milk.*

The Watergate investigations revealed that this was only one among many examples of interest group pluralism in which high government officials squeezed the vassals for payment into the king's purse in return for presumed favors. Where just controls for the public good ought to prevail, government power is instead exploited by the wealth and influence of the interest group and by the private ambition of the politicians. The "explanation" of those involved—that this is the way it has always been done, that this is how America works—is in a sense accurate, but at the same time plainly deficient. Creating government policy and action through interest group pluralism may have been acceptable when government was a relatively small and limited part of American life and when those who counted were usually members of one or another interest group. But the reality of America has changed; interest group pluralism and the limited state no longer make justice explicit. Thus both have lost legitimacy.

Shortly after his visit with the dairymen, Mr. Nixon, confident of his electoral victory, said: "It is time that good, decent people stopped letting themselves be bulldozed by anybody who presumes to be the self-righteous moral judge of our society." This speech, incidentally, was one of quite a number given by Nixon that extolled the virtues of the traditional ideology of individualism, hard work, and the rest. It was aimed at those "self-righteous" communitarians who, like the Supreme Court, felt that the integration of blacks and whites in schools was a good thing. But there is indeed some evidence that the people are in a mood to resist the bulldozing of those interest groups who have traditionally held sway, whether it be the dairy interests, the highway lobby, or individual potentates. There is an increasing sense that the conflicting tensions of interest groups constitute insufficient due process and threaten desirable democratic procedures. We can expect that additional formal procedures will be introduced to deal with environmental pollution, the organization and priorities of scientific and technological research, the design of new and

---

* *Ibid.* ** Address, Oct. 21, 1972.

better total communities, the control and distribution of population, and the like. Inevitably, society itself is consolidating a planning role for government.

This emergent role carries its own threats to the notions of self-respect, efficiency, and individual liberty. Consequently, many citizens are understandably reluctant to move at all. But if movement is already under way and its continuation inevitable, aimless foot-dragging only makes it inefficient, wasteful, even illegitimate. How can the individual be protected against the necessarily increasing power of a necessarily active state? The answer can only lie in new, improved methods of democratic participation and control over the processes of government. Otherwise, either the liberty of our citizens will be unjustly diminished and their self-respect threatened, or we shall sacrifice the efficient working of our social and economic system and invite depression and all that goes with it. We shall degenerate or atrophy unless we can find ways to renovate our political order, invigorate its procedures, and increase our capacity for participation in it. We must make its task more explicit and its workings more open. The collaboration of all private groups is essential, but this should not be covert. Instead of attempting to take the politics out of our problems, we must recognize that our problems are for the most part essentially political. Rather than planning our political future in back offices (or Oval Offices), we must do it out in the main lobby.

Ideological Schizophrenia

There is considerable evidence that the need for comprehensive and authoritative state planning is recognized, in theory, by a wide range of American opinion, especially big business. But the endorsement is generally for "planning" in the abstract; as soon as it drifts toward reality, the myths and structures of the old ideology intervene. Our leaders are no longer merely ambivalent in their formulations; they seem to suffer from downright ideological schizophrenia. At certain levels of objectivity and rationality, they cannot help but see the necessity for a new role for the state and acknowledge that the passage from the old belief in the limited state is inseparably connected with departure from the old ideas of individualism, property, and competition. Yet, at the same time, such leaders cannot accept the transition subjectively; they persist in trying to legitimize the new in the language of the old. The result is predictable—confusion, hypocrisy, paralysis, and the danger that those treasured rights and liberties of the individual which we yearn to safeguard will be trampled down through mere clumsiness.

Richard Nixon was a particularly good example of this ideological schizophrenia. Early in his administration, he called on a group of wise men to divine a set of national goals. This was by no means the first time that a President had attempted such an exercise and the lessons of the past were not auspicious, but, as Mr. Nixon said, "We can no longer afford to approach the longer-range future haphazardly."* The report of the group did not provide many answers, but it did shed light on the planning problem. The wise men told the President they could not recommend any goals until he and the political order which he led answered some questions. And these questions, they emphasized, had no pragmatic answers. They concerned the definition of a good community—they were inherently ideological. Until the political order answered them, there could be no goals. The questions included: Should we limit our population size, and if so, how? Should we redistribute our population, and if so, how? How clean do we want our water, how pure our air? What is the purpose of education, whom should it serve, and how? What is the purpose of science, and to what extent should it be allowed to proceed unguided by the government? The group stressed the desirability of shifting from "a reactive mode of dealing with problems that have forced themselves on us to an anticipatory mode in which we either attempt to prevent their occurrence or are prepared to deal with them as they emerge."** Inherent in this proposed shift were a transition from a pragmatic code to an ideological one and a new role for the state.

Similarly in 1970, the President's Task Force on Economic Growth told him:

. . . government was never simply the protector of a free enterprise system. It also managed the public domain, developed transportation, encouraged infant industries, established monetary institutions, insti-

---

* Report of the National Goals Research Staff, *Toward Balanced Growth: Quantity with Quality* (Washington, D.C.: U.S. Government Printing Office, 1970), p. 31.

** *Ibid.*, pp. 28–31.

tuted a social security system, and undertook a host of other functions required to meet the opportunities and problems of urbanizing, industrializing society.

The Task Force, composed of six business leaders, five scholars, and two labor leaders, went on to urge government planning in the following areas: "Social costs of production and consumption," the use of "technology to serve human needs," the level and distribution of population, the preservation of the physical and social environment, and "growth for greater human well-being." A couple of sample sentences show the radical implications of the Force's report: "The United States needs a population policy for long-term economic progress." And "Dispersion of population should be sought." In other words, the government should be thinking about how many people America should have and where they ought to live. Shall we regulate family size? Won't we need ceilings on community population size? Hadn't we best consider curbs on mobility? And again: "We believe that a stable dollar is attainable under conditions of full employment."* But, in order to achieve full employment, the Task Force called for the collection of substantial new information, much of which must come from business and some of which business has been reluctant to supply. If we are to have effective manpower planning, government must have access, for example, to the expansion and contraction plans of all major U.S. employers. With this knowledge, which it has never been able to obtain, it could, as the Task Force advises, plan the fit between jobs and workers more effectively. In fact, a stable

---

* *Report of the Task Force on Economic Growth* (Washington, D.C.: U.S. Government Printing Office, 1970) (0–383–637), pp. 1, 11–12, 18. The Task Force members were: Neil Jacoby, Chairman, Professor of Business and Economic Policy, University of California at Los Angeles; Moses Abramovitz, Professor of Economics, Stanford University; Atherton Bean, Chairman of the Executive Committee, International Milling Co.; Henry T. Bodman, Chairman of the Board, National Bank of Detroit; Emilio G. Collado, Executive Vice President, Standard Oil Co. of New Jersey; Edward F. Denison, Senior Fellow, The Brookings Institution; Nathaniel Goldfinger, Director, Department of Research, AFL-CIO; Alan Greenspan, Chairman of the Board, Townsend-Greenspan & Co., Inc.; Walter E. Hoadley, Executive Vice President, Bank of America; John W. Kendrick, Professor of Economics, George Washington University, Senior Staff Member, National Bureau of Economic Research; Lee W. Minton, International President, Glass Bottle Blowers Association of the United States and Canada, AFL-CIO; Eli Shapiro, Sylvan Coleman Professor of Financial Management, Harvard University; Lynn Townsend, Chairman of the Board, Chrysler Corp.

dollar and full employment require unprecedented levels of government planning.

Herbert Stein, then chairman of the President's Council of Economic Advisers (incidentally, the nearest thing we have to a national planning group), acknowledged in 1974, however reluctantly, that America might "need an economic planning agency like the Japanese or the French." It is plain that such an agency would have to be comprehensive, alert to the relationships between wages, prices, employment, resource allocation, energy, communications, transportation, the position of America in the world economy, and more.*

In 1970, President Nixon himself appeared to perceive clearly the necessity for governmental planning, vision-setting, and coordination. "The critical question," he said in his State of the Union Message, "is not whether we will grow, but how we will use that growth. . . . At heart, the issue is the effectiveness of government." And, he continued, "As a people, we [have] had too many visions—and too little vision."** The following year he proposed a governmental reorganization more radical than anything suggested since 1789. After "a long, dark night of the American spirit . . . we are ready," Mr. Nixon said, "for the lift of a driving dream." The need was "not simply for more new programs in the old framework, but to change the framework of government itself—to reform the entire structure of American government so we can make it fully responsive to the needs and the wishes of the American people."†

The President recommended first telescoping the seven existing federal departments into four new ones, to increase the unity and decisionmaking capacity of the central government in Washington and to enhance executive planning capacity. Second, he sought to disperse the federal government's power by sharing its revenues with state and local governments. Under this scheme, Washington was to set out broad guidelines for the nation on such matters as welfare, hunger, pollution, transportation, and equality of opportunity; the localities were to decide on the specific means of implementation.

Nixon's governmental reorganization and many of the broad

---

* See *Business Week,* Jan. 5, 1974, p. 26.
** State of the Union Address, Jan. 22, 1970.
† State of the Union Address, Jan. 22, 1971.

guidelines failed to materialize—the idea was strangled as Senate Majority Leader Mike Mansfield predicted by "a combination of lobbies the like of which the Congress has never seen." "It's not only impossible, it's unthinkable," argued Rubin Johnson of the National Farmers Union, referring to the proposed abolition of "the farmers' " Department of Agriculture.* Revenue sharing and decentralization had more success, because most interest groups favored them, but the concepts produced little in the way of a national vision. Mr. Nixon abandoned his proposal for a guaranteed income and later sought to sabotage one of the most promising experiments in decentralization, the Community Action Program, by abolishing its parent agency, the Office of Economic Opportunity.

Thus, in one connected action, he succeeded in angering the congressional liberals by withdrawing federal pressure on behalf of the poor and in worrying the conservatives by flouting the will of Congress and seeking to build executive power. Instead of the unity and "vision" Nixon sought, he evoked "visions" more plentiful and an even more disintegrated government. But after the President's re-election in 1972, he was determined that the White House should set direction and priorities for the nation, whatever Congress might choose to say. He placed his loyal agents in the various departments and agencies; he strengthened the lines of control from the Office of Management and Budget and the White House; and he impounded funds appropriated by Congress for programs he did not like. In short, like Charles II, he set out to assert the power of the executive against the forces of the legislature.** Congress became increasingly alarmed and, against a backdrop of looming scandal, the partisans within it joined forces in the name of Lockean principles. For a time the national hero was Sam Ervin, whose eloquent soliloquies were pure Locke. We sought refuge, in other words, in our tattered ideological security blanket instead of tackling the issue of the power of the executive, a power which is immense, necessary, and ideologically out of control.

Mr. Nixon's cause, which in many ways was the essential and inevitable one of improving government focus and effectiveness,

---

* *Wall Street Journal,* Jan. 25, 1971.
** Aram Bakshian, presidential speechwriter, actually sought to help his master by comparing him to Charles II in *The New York Times,* op. ed. page, June 12, 1973.

failed for two reasons. The first, of course, was just plain old ordinary corruption. But also the President was apparently blind to what he was doing ideologically. Unaware of the radicality of his proposals, he was unable to explain them properly and to persuade Congress effectively, and so he finally resorted to futile arrogance. His ideological schizophrenia showed clearly in his repeated, almost psalmlike incantations of the traditional ideology from which in many ways he was seeking to depart. "The new American majority," he said in 1972, "believes that each person should have more of the say in how he lives his own life, how he spends his paycheck, how he brings up his children."* True as this may be, Nixon himself at other times seemed to appreciate fully that the freedom he extolled depended, as Hegel noted long ago, on "the recognition of necessity." Without definite arrangements to ensure survival and justice, there will be ruin; hence the clear-cut need for rules and coercion with respect to our use of land, air, water, and other vital resources.

The President's belated and hesitant response to the shortage of energy resources was another sign of his schizophrenia. The gigantic dimensions and implications of the crisis were obvious. Business, so often in the forefront of ideological change in America, had for some time been calling for energetic and comprehensive government planning. John G. McLean, chief executive officer of Continental Oil Company, was among the first to suggest "a single, high-energy agency in our government to develop a comprehensive national energy policy and to coordinate all our national efforts relating to energy matters."** If we were to take Carroll Wilson's sensible advice, such an agency would have "authority to over-ride obstacles in regard to land acquisition, siting, environmental impact, and other areas as necessary to carry out the program." It would need a financial handmaiden like the RFC to provide funds for such facilities as superports, oil storage facilities, offshore oil production, tankers, coal gasification plants, and various pipelines.†

Nixon's response, like Gerald Ford's after him, was ambivalent.

---

* Quoted in Robert Semple, *The New York Times,* Oct. 22, 1972.
** John G. McLean, "The United States Energy Outlook and Its Implications for National Policy," *Remarks at the World Affairs Council,* Pittsburgh, Sept. 21, 1972, p. 10.
† Carroll Wilson, "A Plan for Energy Independence," *Foreign Affairs,* July 1973.

He recognized the need for real energy controls and simultaneously advocated leaving such controls essentially to the voluntary actions of individuals, a procedure that would almost certainly reward the chiselers and punish the suckers who observed the presidential appeal.

Where the vital needs of the community are concerned and the common good involved, each individual's freedom requires rules based upon necessity. The crucial task of leadership at this juncture is to make this fact clear. President Nixon obscured it.* One can only wonder why he did not, in his hour of critical need, take advantage of widespread support and public awareness to deal with the energy matter properly. Why did he not use the relatively mild crisis in the winter of 1973 to alert us to the serious scarcities of all resources which our country faces? That crisis could have been a means to educate the American people to the fact that the allocation of vital resources can no longer be left to individual decision. Again, why did he not explain that the freedom of the individual to "live his own life" and "spend his paycheck" is inexorably circumscribed by iron limitations, and justice and survival require these to be designed by all of us working as a community through our governmental processes? One can only guess that he was misled by vestiges of the old ideology which he neither recognized nor understood. Perhaps this confusion was reinforced by a desire, as others have suggested, to let the course of events in the energy area distract national attention from the immensity of the whole body of his problems. In any case, his strange ambivalence is dramatic. Few Presidents have recognized more explicitly the need for stronger and more effective government; few have shown themselves less capable in achieving it.

President Nixon's failure may result in a fruitless reversion to tradition, or in a welcome reformation in which the powers of the executive are more precisely defined and fused with those of Congress to permit effective planning. Glorious as the idea of separation of power between the legislative and the executive may have been historically, it cries out for attention and modification; we have neither the time nor the need for aimless battling between the two. Our problems urgently require a joint planning mechan-

---

* For an excellent discussion of the problems of "the commons," see Garrett Hardin, "The Tragedy of the Commons," *Science,* Dec. 13, 1968, pp. 1243–8.

ism, such as the Council of Economic Advisors was initially intended to be. Hopefully, our political leaders will design new forms of legislative-executive collaboration so that executive planning will have democratic support and legislative planning be susceptible to execution. A significant step in this direction was taken in June 1974, when Congress passed a bill revolutionizing the way in which government plans federal spending and taxation. This bill provides for a fusion of legislative and executive power, allowing Congress for the first time to participate in the overall shaping of the federal budget, which is after all the focal point of much of our national endeavor. Until now the budget process has been loose and fragmented, much of it proceeding out of control behind closed doors where special interests could cause wild distortions damaging to the public interest. Oddly enough, the new bill bears a strong resemblance to the budget procedures proposed in the Full Employment Bill of 1945 some thirty years ago. This proposal, designed to prevent a recurrence of the Great Depression, was eviscerated in the name of the old ideology and became the much weaker Employment Act of 1946 that established the Council of Economic Advisers.

Nixon's ambivalence was as much a threat to individual rights and liberty as it was a hindrance to effective government. Indeed, we have already glimpsed at some of the vile possibilities inherent in this movement toward a more authoritative and focused state. In his interview with Garnett D. Horner, for example, Nixon said (the transcript was checked by the White House for "accuracy"), "The average American is just like the child in the family."* If so, the implication is he must be protected from subversive ideas, and especially from those dangerous TV programs. Clay T. Whitehead, director of the White House Office of Telecommunications Policy, followed up with an explicit warning: "Station managers and network officials who fail to act to correct imbalance or consistent bias in the networks—or who acquiesce by silence—can only be considered willing participants, to be held fully accountable . . . at license renewal time."** That is, although the individual should have more to say about how he lives his own life, the government must protect him from opinions of which the White House disapproves. Thought control—no less and no more.

---

* *The New York Times,* Nov. 10, 1972.
** *The New York Times,* Dec. 19, 1972.

The Reactionary Impulse

In the last chapter, we followed Galbraith down the path of centralized and highly bureaucratic state socialism. In this chapter, we have seen the necessity for a careful and deliberate adjustment of the legislative-executive balance to permit government planning on an appropriately large scale and in an ideologically and morally acceptable fashion. Let us now turn to C. Jackson Grayson, Jr., who believes we may already have moved too far toward a controlled economy and who argues that we can and must reverse our evolution toward communitarianism, in the economic sphere at least. Grayson's thinking is important for an obvious reason. If he is correct—if we can return to the Lockean condition—then we need not wrack ourselves with the problems of analyzing and documenting the new ideology, nor need we struggle to mold a communitarian society that is tight against the corrosive fluids of totalitarianism. Further, Grayson's viewpoint is that of many conservatives; and it is not uneducated, for he has held the responsibility for price planning in our present economy, being for a time head of the Price Commission in President Nixon's Economic Stabilization Program, Phase II.* Significantly, like Galbraith, he confirms the transition which we have been describing:

I am personally convinced that our economic system is steadily shifting from a private enterprise, free-market economy to one that is centrally directed and under public control. . . . Call it what you will—managed capitalism, socialism, a planned economy, a postindustrial state—the end result will be the virtual elimination of the free-market system as we know it. There will be no signposts or traffic lights. We will simply shift over to another kind of system.

He does not foresee Galbraith's public ownership, but he does predict increasing public control:

General Motors will not die; but neither will it remain a capitalistically motivated and directed enterprise. Rather, it will operate as an organization, designed to implement *public* economic, political, and social policy.**

And he notes that much of the impetus for this transition is coming from business leaders, as well as from representatives of labor and the public at large, springing from business's desire to

---

* Grayson left the government to become Dean of the School of Business Administration of Southern Methodist University in Dallas, Texas.

** Grayson, *op. cit.,* pp. 103–4.

insulate itself against the unpredictabilities of economic change and to ensure bureaucratic security against the vagaries of competition. Grayson quotes as evidence a number of letters from businessmen which he received as head of the Price Commission, noting that they prefer regulation to the problems posed by freedom.*

It is clear that wage-price controls interfere with the sensitivity of the market system. Where prices are artificially depressed, there are shortages, as with natural gas; where wages are artificially depressed, there are also shortages of skills and workers generally. "We live in a world of scarce resources," Grayson observes, "and, as much as some would like to repeal the laws of supply and demand, it can't be done." In his view resources will be allocated, if not by the market, then by business-labor monopolies or government regulation and control. If the latter, then it is inevitable that businessmen will tend to pay more attention to the regulatory process than to the perfection of their function, for, as Grayson quotes one executive saying, "We know that all of our sophisticated analysis and planning can be wiped out in the blink of a Washington controller's eye."**

Grayson views the transition with horror, and says we must turn back. He contends that it is impossible for central planning to be as efficient and effective as the market place in allocating resources, however uncoordinated and messy the latter may be: "The trade-offs in our extremely large and highly interdependent economy are too complex to be done efficiently on a centralized basis." And, he asks, "Who would supply the value judgments for the operations of such a system?" But while we are moving in the wrong direction, he says, we are very near the point of no return.†

So far so good. Now let us look at why he wants to return and how he proposes to do it.

His belief in the market system, he says, rests not on "blind faith in an ideology" but on three reasons:

1. The United States free-market, private-enterprise system "has produced the highest standard of living in history and has demonstrated a remarkable ability to adapt to changing conditions."

2. "The principles of democracy and personal freedom are most compatible with a decentralized market system."

---

* *Ibid.,* p. 105.   ** *Ibid.,* p. 107.   † *Ibid.,* p. 109.

3. His experience with price controls has convinced him that "billions of daily market decisions by the public" provide a better method of resources allocation.*

Needless to say, Grayson is being ideological in that he measures standards of living inferentially solely in economic terms, not by "quality of life"; and he apparently also prefers an individualistic, atomistic, and proprietary society to an organic, communitarian one. In any case, these are the reasons why he wants us to retrogress.

Grayson's ideas on how we can do this are less clearly stated. First, he says that he deeply believes in social equity. He would, therefore, maintain and presumably extend social legislation that "protects the unprotected" and provides for the more equitable distribution of wealth. He appears to be saying that the state has a legitimate role in ensuring survival and health and income, a role it has been developing during the last forty years; these should not be left to the vagaries of individualistic, proprietary competition in the market place.** Grayson thus acknowledges the role of the state in making a rather critical trade-off or value judgment —one which, as we have seen, impinges upon the five "essential features" of the free market system which he would continue: "the price system, private ownership, collective bargaining, the profit motive, and freedom of entry."†

Second, following the free trade suggestions of Peter Peterson discussed earlier, he would reduce regulations that interfere with foreign competition, such as subsidies, quotas, and tariffs. This leads him to a conception of the United States in the world economy wherein the nation plays to its strengths and adjusts to its weaknesses. It also foresees a modification of the antitrust laws at home to allow for more effective competition abroad. Thus he appears to agree with the ITT syndrome: "If we are going to compete effectively in the world, we must be big and strong at home. We are partners with government in the development of the national interest." This concept inevitably requires a high order of governmental planning, so that our leadership can identify and coalesce "strengths" and adjust for "weaknesses." But, Grayson says, we need even stricter enforcement of the antitrust laws to preserve competition.†† His self-contradictions between ends and means are mounting.

---

* *Ibid.*, p. 110.   ** *Ibid.*   † *Ibid.*, p. 112.   †† *Ibid.*, p. 111.

Third, he suggests structural reform of government to make it more efficient. In particular, he calls for the creation of a new Department of Economic Affairs—part of Nixon's "Driving Dream." The new department (which would include Transportation, Commerce, Labor, the Small Business Administration, and others) would unify and centralize economic policy formulation, making possible "an integrated and consistent program." But it is inconceivable that such an entity could do its job without a rather comprehensive plan. The free market is not going to solve mass transit problems any more than it will solve energy shortages. So we are back to the planning he earlier discarded as impractical. Instead Grayson proposes a greater political involvement by business and labor leaders and increased "public advocacy of all views about our economic system." He urges those believing in "the private enterprise system" to sing out. There are several other suggestions, but I shall conclude with just one more: "Business and labor must work together to shore up our lagging productivity, particularly as we shift to a more service-oriented, and hence lower productivity, economy."*

Grayson suggests that we institute a private-sector productivity institute like those in Japan, Germany, and Israel, but this raises a welter of interesting conflicts with the traditional ideology he wants to preserve. Businesses conspiring together to raise productivity would almost certainly affront the antitrust laws. As I noted in Chapter 6, procedures to increase worker motivation and productivity increasingly threaten our traditional principles of collective bargaining and private ownership, two of Grayson's "essential features." Certainly, the experience and experimentation in the three countries he mentions raise serious issues for traditional American theory.

I do not mean to pick a fight with Grayson. It is rather that, like Galbraith, he has put forward an articulate and thoughtful formulation of the transition in conventional terms, sliding back and forth as it were in the traditional ruts. As a result, his perception of the connection between the elements he analyzes is obscured and his resulting recommendations lack comprehensiveness and are flawed and contradictory.

No one can deny the virtues of the market system for the al-

---

* *Ibid.,* pp. 111–12.

location of certain resources at certain times in certain places. At the same time, it is apparent that changes in the real world—the recognition of a general scarcity of vital resources, questions about the legitimacy of the institutions which convert and exploit them—have produced a radical rupture in the traditional workings of the market system and require unprecedented levels of comprehensive planning by government. If we are to save the virtues of price competition, we shall need a most careful analysis of where it works and where it does not. If we are to save the virtues of democracy and personal freedom, again the most careful analysis of where they are effective and safe and where they are a pretentious delusion is essential.

The fact is that the new planning role of the state is virtually upon us, but its ideological underpinnings are still missing. Without them it will lack legitimacy and will tend to be misunderstood, mishandled, and totally inadequate.

Reorganization for Planning

Reactionary impulses notwithstanding, we can fairly predict that government control of the economic and social life of our increasingly complex community will increase. We can also predict that an increasingly important part of its task will be the definition of the public interest and the resolution of trade-offs among competing community needs. This task becomes more urgent as the old definitions of values, based upon conceptions of "natural" rights, become weaker. Further, a growing number of trade-offs will necessarily be made in the name of a community that is larger than the nation; transnational governmental forms will become essential.

So far, I have used the terms "state" and "government" almost interchangeably, but now it is necessary to distinguish between them. I shall define "the state" as the institution that retains the ultimate power and authority in society.* "Government" then refers to a group of public persons and organizations that exerts

---

* See Max Weber, *Economy and Society,* edited by G. Roth and C. Wittich (New York: Bedminster, 1968), p. 54; ref. Severyn T. Bruyn, "Notes on the Contradictions of Modern Business," *Sociological Inquiry* 42 (Spring 1972):132.

this power and authority according to a set of laws and rules. Government is therefore part of the state in the sense that it derives legitimacy from it; but government also may be quite separate from the state, as with Church government or corporate government, for example. One can therefore imagine a whole range of governmental forms, spread out on a spectrum of proximity to and distance from the hub of the state itself, carrying out its various public functions through a number of structures: centralized and decentralized, coercive and voluntary, rigid and flexible. I call this range the "centralization spectrum."

Further, I have assumed that the old connective tissue of our former ideology will exert its natural influence on the evolution of the new—specifically, that because of the lingering influence of the Lockean style, we shall find that the governmental forms that seem most desirable to us in the future will be those forms on the spectrum that are as decentralized, as voluntary, and as flexible as possible. If this assumption is correct, then the challenge of planning specific actions for renewal becomes one of designing governmental forms for defining needs and resolving trade-offs, given that our preference as a people is for plurality and individual freedom, but also recognizing that freedom depends upon the recognition of necessity. These predictions may presently represent wishful thinking, but since the wishes are rooted in a still resilient and powerful ideology, they also represent realistic thinking.

Let me begin by sketching the course of our reorganization for comprehensive planning. Such governmental planning, carried out at many levels and backed by the state, will become increasingly necessary and—because of the crisis—will gradually be supported by public consensus; it will then begin to prove effective. This process will be both impeded and assisted by universities and other such institutions—impeded by those who insist upon employing the traditional specialized disciplines to examine individual aspects of the environment; assisted by the increasing number of academic integrators who are developing new techniques for analyzing and understanding whole systems. It will be greatly helped by the modern technologists, whose work allows us to gather and analyze huge quantities of information. High-resolution and infra-red photography from an earth satellite can produce instantaneous information about all forms of construction which we have never possessed before, and computer simulation techniques are now at least theoretically capable of modeling the behavior of whole environments, from neighborhoods to the world, and so predicting future behavior. Perhaps most important, the new methods for quick access to data allow for speedy correction of such predictive models which, of course, can never be perfect. The towns of Houston, Texas, and New Haven, Connecticut, the Department of Housing and Urban Development, and many large corporations are now using such planning techniques on one scale or another. Such an expansion of planning capability can push us either way on the centralization spectrum. Ideally, it will also help us to form more refined judgments as to which policies are best dealt with centrally and which can best be handled by smaller, more dispersed units.

Two factors relating to decentralization and to the control of decentralized government require particular attention. First, what we today call decentralization—revenue sharing, and so on—is in many ways not decentralization at all; it is simply disarray. Local policies and operations can only be sound if they are integral parts of a national policy framework. Whether one considers energy, education, housing, or transportation, there is a greater or lesser need for decentralized control and conversely a lesser or greater need for a national framework.

Second, decentralization has historically been exploited by local powerholders to resist change. Under such circumstances, it has been necessary for those who want to alter the status quo to call in the power of the more distant, better-insulated national government. This pattern cannot be erased, but it can be lessened. A central government that knows its mind can detect and measure local activities far better than before, because of the technological factors mentioned above; it can consequently strengthen resistance where helpful. Furthermore, taking the predictions I outline here as a package, one can project a greater sense of community consciousness into the decentralized unit and a wider participation by its members in the decisions affecting control and direction. Even though participation per se is no guarantee of democratic control, it would seem worth encouraging as a means of ensuring community well-being and protecting liberty. Participation renders a bureaucracy less chilling, more open, and part of the community it was designed to serve instead of separate from it. Too many bureaucracies today seem to operate, in Theodore Levitt's words, as sealed continuums [that] "can only be shaken out of their respectable impassiveness by confrontation and force."*

I envisage a relatively small, highly focused national government, authorized for and capable of comprehensive long-range planning, and empowered to collect and allocate virtually all the nation's tax revenue according to general criteria set nationally. At the same time, there might be a large number of regional communities, some comprising several states and others small neighborhoods. These divisions might or might not have relevance to existing political boundaries. One cannot help but wonder, for example, whether Rhode Island makes sense as a geographic entity or why there should be two Dakotas. Political division of the country would follow planning needs and capabilities. The implementation of planning goals should be as near to the local level as possible.

It is easy to imagine the upheaval of existing structures which even this simple and brief description entails: the abolition of much of the federal government structure, leaving what remains authoritative and powerful; the elimination of many states and their replacement by regional governments that would take on part of the administrative apparatus displaced from Washington; and the reduction of many of the redundant city, town, and county structures.

Federal Chartering and Community Control

Among the functions of the central government will clearly be the chartering of the 2,000 or so large publicly held corporations which affect the life of the entire country. This charter—not the ideas of property and ownership—would be the fundamental legitimizer of the corporation. It would establish that Exxon, for example, is not an individual with rights of privacy but a public collective chartered by the community to serve certain functions, and that all its activities are susceptible to public inspection. The corporate charter should stipulate certain conditions of legitimacy and set forth general rules of corporate organization and conduct. Most important, it should detail the information that the corporation is required to disclose regularly. This should include arrangements made with foreign governments, internal and external cost/

---

* Theodore Levitt, *The Third Sector: New Tactics for a Responsive Society* (New York: AMACOM, 1973) p. 22.

benefit accounting, productivity information, costs of externalities such as pollution, and forecasts about growth, contraction, and other major corporate changes.*

The national charter should be relatively brief, general, and flexible, enabling corporations to invent and to experiment as far as possible. It should also leave room for supplementary legitimization by the various communities which the corporation affects and by the internal membership of the corporation. The corporation must be seen as a part of the several communities it touches, and essential to the design and development of the communities in which it is actually located; the charter must consider it an integral part of the political, economic, social, and cultural life of each such community, one that affects its housing patterns, transportation system, educational needs, and more. Through the charter itself, therefore, the community must have a fundamental say in the corporation's being. Consider the difficulty Xerox Corporation encountered in moving its headquarters into Greenwich, Connecticut. In 1969, Xerox set up a dummy corporation, the Pacific Development Company, and through a West Coast real-estate firm proceeded to buy up 104 acres in the town. The company had no illusions that "it could just walk into town," but was unprepared for three years of wrangling and being forced to locate elsewhere. Yet Xerox is among the most community-sensitive of U.S. companies; it is clean; its buildings are well designed. What held up its move was both an ideological confusion concerning the fit between

---

* The disclosure problem is evident in the experience of the Council on Economic Priorities, a research group which seeks to bring corporate activities to public attention. In 1973, it sought to evaluate sixteen pharmaceutical companies with respect to the safety and efficacy of their products and their research productivity. CEP sent a four-page questionnaire to the companies inquiring about product line, relations with the Food and Drug Administration, research activities, and promotion activities. One company cooperated fully; the others less so. The vice president of public affairs of one of the companies with more than $500 million in sales explained his refusal to cooperate on the grounds that a public corporation has no more responsibility to the public than does a private individual. "How would you feel if someone came up to your door and asked what your income was and what your husband earns?" he asked. He was, of course, reflecting the traditional ideology. It seems likely, however, that there will be a change—huge, multimillion-dollar, nonproprietary collectives cannot for long sustain the fiction of individuality. See the *Economic Priorities Report,* "In Whose Hands?", August–November 1973, pp. 25 and 26.

the purposes and functions of Xerox and those of the Greenwich community and the inadequacies in the planning mechanisms by which the Greenwich community designs its future. These procedures are at present weak and untried, and there is confusion. In some cities, influential banks decide the community's future, directing the flow of mortgage money out of one neighborhood and into another—a practice called "redlining" which understandably evokes the wrath of those in abandoned neighborhoods. In others, neighborhood groups and associations have had some success in planning with City Hall. In Ocean County, New Jersey, as we saw, the Environmental Protection Agency has indirectly sought to specify population size in sixteen municipalities. In Oregon, under the leadership of Governor Tom McCall, the entire state appears to have had an unusually clear vision of what it wants to be—pretty much like it was—which means population control and rigorous environmental protection.

For the time being, openness may be the most important requirement to ensure the fullest expression of many experimental forces and the free play of a wide variety of model builders. Their way can be smoothed and their utility enhanced, however, by a general consciousness of ideological transition so that a new consensus ensues before anarchy invites authoritarian control.

The conduct of the corporate community will likewise benefit increasingly from the participation of all its members. The way should be left open for a wide variety of forms and experiments in governance to achieve this participation. This will entail a loosening of the rigidities of the National Labor Relations Act and other rules and regulations rooted in the old notion of contract.

Although legitimacy, both national and communal, will be provided for by the charter, as well as by internal corporate by-laws, and although certain controls will emanate from these legitimizing devices, additional controls on the corporation will, as now, spring from other sources—principally regulations to meet the exigencies of changing times and the forces of competition. It seems likely that the existing plethora of regulations on corporations could be reduced by a more orderly and responsive chartering procedure. It also seems likely that the antitrust laws will have to be substantially revised to cope with the needs of the United States in the world economy, as well as to allow for collaborative ventures by corporations to meet pressing needs at home. In short, community need will become the dominant principle of control. Over-all, there could well be *less* government intervention in corporate activities than there is now.

Conventional competition and other parts of the traditional ideology will still flourish for the host of small clearly owned cor-porations—Galbraith's market system—and careful efforts should be made to distinguish this more traditional part of business from the more radical forms. Market system businesses should be chartered locally or regionally where they operate.

Collective bargaining in large corporations will diminish in importance as the contract between workers and employers de-creases in significance. It will be replaced by consensual mecha-nisms, both within the corporation and between the corporation and the communities it affects. Collective bargaining will also be weakened as the increasing interdependence of economic and tech-nological systems makes work stoppages less acceptable in either the private or the public sector. Concomitantly, there will be rising demands for a guaranteed income and a more equal distribution of wealth. One might expect limits on executive salaries and severe strictures on inheritance rights.

Inasmuch as large corporations will no longer be considered property but rather nationally chartered, community-oriented col-lectives, their shareholders will no longer be considered owners but merely investors whose rights are safeguarded by law like those of other providers of corporate funds, such as banks and in-vestment institutions. This simpler and clearer identity will mean that corporate boards of directors may be made into more legiti-mate, more useful instruments. Certain general stipulations re-garding their composition might be contained in the federal charter, but it would be more desirable to leave sufficient leeway so that representatives of workers or various communities might be in-cluded on boards, where appropriate, as part of the general con-sensual mechanism. The capital needs of the corporation might be assisted by federal planning mechanisms, as I suggested earlier.

Finally, whatever is done nationally to legitimize and control the corporation will have to take account of the increasing pres-sures and needs for transnational controls. The transnational busi-ness corporation itself was an outgrowth of the nation-state, but it is becoming increasingly different from it, serving separate func-tions. It is possible for strong transnational business organizations and strong national governments to exist side by side; nevertheless, transnational organizations are sure to have a revolutionary impact on the current national structures. Samuel Huntington says,

Today man's capacities for organization are outrunning the nation-state system. Internationalism is a dead end. Only organizations that are disinterested in sovereignty can transcend it. For the immediate future a central focus of world politics will be on the coexistence of and interaction between transnational organizations and the nation-state.*

This brief projection of what the new role of the state entails is as filled with possible danger as it is rich with opportunity. A more authoritative state naturally brings the possibility of repression, conformity, and stifling bureaucracy. But the state we have now is surely far from ideal. One does not have to be a utopian to imagine a better-ordered society, one in which values are more explicitly defined and more readily attainable. Part of the purpose of ideological analysis is to discover as nearly as possible the direction in which a society is moving; to encourage an inspection of old assumptions; and to allow the comparison of those assumptions with current directions so as to minimize dangers and make the most of opportunities.

Business Can Help

Corporations can and should play an important part in encouraging the state and the various levels of government to assume their new role. They have a clear interest in doing so, depending as they do upon an orderly and purposeful community. And they have much useful knowledge and skill. But the dangers inherent in corporate collaboration need to be carefully understood, as do the Lockean inhibitions which can retard and distort it. Some of these have been alluded to in Chapter 6, but they need emphasis.

The first danger is that of totalitarianism. We hear repeated many times, especially by businessmen, variations of the simplistic notion that all ills are caused by the state and that somehow, if its heavy hand could be withered, good would follow. This is not surprising; anarchism, after all, represents, as Carl Friedrich noted,

---

* Samuel P. Huntington, "Transnational Organizations in World Politics," *World Politics*, April 1973, pp. 365 and 368.

"the high point of Western individualism and in a sense its reduc-tio ad absurdum."* Historically, anarchism seems almost inevit-ably to evoke totalitarianism, so it is essential to the maintenance of democracy and maximum individual liberty to avoid it. This requires first, the recognition that government has a job, and sec-ond, the precise definition of what that job is. "Government's job is not business, and business's job is not government," Levitt has written. "And unless these functions are resolutely separated in all respects, they are eventually combined in every respect. In the end the danger is not that government will run business, or that business will run government, but rather that the two of them will coalesce . . . into a single power, unopposed and unopposable."**

The second, related danger lies in the inexplicit assignment of rights and competencies between government and business. There is a tendency to suppose that business can solve the social and technological problems of our time. Failure to see the limitations in this supposition will retard solutions, undermine the integrity and effectiveness of government, and impair the efficiency and profitability of business.

The matter of right is clearly raised, for example, when one hears businessmen talking about "competing with government" to provide better education. George Champion, former chairman of the board of Chase Manhattan Bank, suggested that business "must do its part" to make the most of new teaching and learning ma-chines, providing not only the "hardware" but also the "software" (the thoughts) to feed into the machines. "Otherwise government will move into still another vacuum, and its influence will be further extended."† The implication here is that education cannot be en-trusted to government, but it can be entrusted to business. This is a tempting doctrine, given the inadequacy of the political frame-work around our public schools; but do we really want to remove our school system from its democratic foundations and turn it over to unelected corporate leaders?

In the wake of the 1967 summer riots, the Michigan Bell Tele-

---

* Carl J. Friedrich, "The Anarchist Controversy Over Violence," *Zeit-schrift für Politik* (Cologne: Carl Heymanns Verlag WG, 1972), p. 168.
** Theodore Levitt, "The Dangers of Social Responsibility," *Harvard Busi-ness Review,* September–October, 1958, p. 47.
† George Champion, "Creative Competition," *Harvard Business Review,* May–June 1967, pp. 64–5.

phone Company announced that it would "adopt" Detroit's Northern High School. It would provide instructors, equipment, and teaching materials to "enrich" the regular teaching program. William M. Day, the president of Michigan Bell, when asked why he wanted to do this, said that he felt it was important "to help prepare the students for the business world. We think we can make a real difference in pupil attitudes."*

Plainly, there is a question here of who has the right to shape the attitudes of young minds.

David Rockefeller has said that "corporations must develop more effective tools for measuring the social, as well as economic, costs and benefits of their actions."** In this connection, he has taken admirable leadership in many efforts to improve the life of poor blacks in greater New York. But such efforts raise matters of right and competence. Who is going to decide what should happen to black communities? Who is going to determine what is socially beneficial? Must not any such determination lie with the community and its political order? If so, then we must ask: How can that political order be affected, persuaded, or moved?

We must acknowledge that government has the responsibility and should have the capacity to perform the task of community analysis and planning, as well as of determining priorities and allocating resources accordingly. This is not something that the unelected leaders of business can or should undertake. We may argue as to what level of government would be most useful— federal, state, city, or some new regional form—and how it should be organized for the task. Being Lockeans, however, we tend to be puzzled at the first stage. We are semi-consciously and inexplicitly bent on limiting the role of government, on keeping it haphazard, in the hope that an unplanned collection of pragmatic actions, both public and private, will somehow pull us out of our troubles as they always have before, leaving our Lockeanism more or less intact.

Adherence to the old notions can be very expensive for business. I know of a small paper company located beside one of New

---

* *Business Week,* Feb. 3, 1968, p. 121, as quoted in Hazel Henderson, "Should Business Tackle Society's Problems?", *Harvard Business Review,* July–August 1968, p. 79.

** David Rockefeller, "The Essential Quest for the Middle Way," *The New York Times,* March 23, 1973, op. ed. page.

England's more putrid streams. Several years ago on Earth Day the company's president "got religion," as it were, and decided he was going to clean up his effluent. He invested $2.5 million and six months later was bankrupt. The river was no cleaner because some seventeen other companies upstream were not so moved.

I asked the president: "What lessons did you learn?"

"Well, I guess I learned that in this life we must be prepared to make material sacrifices for spiritual ends."

"But," I said, "the river is no cleaner."

"Oh, I know that. But I think that the other companies will learn from my example and follow my lead." It was as though his monumental goodness would somehow ooze osmotically upstream.

"Did it occur to you," I asked, "to go to the state, or maybe the several states involved, or perhaps even to Washington to the EPA and seek strict enforcement of uniform standards so that when you went clean, everybody would go clean, and the river would run clear?"

"Oh, no, no, we can't get government into this thing. This is a job private enterprise can do alone. This is a war that business must win."

Business obviously has an enormous role to play in the renovation of America, but it is crucial that that role be clear. Confusion will leave the problems of our time unsolved, contribute to anarchy, and thus eventually to the danger of authoritarianism if not outright totalitarianism. This is not to suggest that business can afford to sit by complacently until government acts. There is too much at stake and government is itself too much imbued with the old notions.

Corporations must, therefore, take the lead in pressing government to do the planning needed to create the framework for change—the framework within which business can then make its own enormous contribution. And much can be done in this regard at local and regional levels.* If New York business is concerned about the health and safety of its backyard (which it is), the proper course is for it to stimulate and assist the political order of the entire region—the relevant whole—to make the necessary

---

* A good example of such action is Quaker Oats Company insisting that Danville, Illinois, pass a fair housing code before it agreed to locate a plant there—*Business Week,* March 6, 1971, p. 59.

decisions and trade-offs and then work to implement those decisions. The acceptability of business as a partner in community
design and development will be increased when the questions of
legitimacy discussed earlier have been resolved and its relationship
to the several communities which it affects clarified.

The transition we are witnessing is removing economic activity—
that is, business—from its transcendent role in American life and
compelling its integration with the political and social order.

Just as there are dangers in this transition to communitarianism,
so there are manifold opportunities to master such hitherto un-
tractable dilemmas as unemployment. This seems to be less and
less responsive to general economic conditions—the country in
general may boom along, but increasing numbers of workers are
left behind. As a result, when pressure mounts to ensure full employment, we feel impelled to drive the economy at full steam; but
ironically we are apt to witness soaring inflation without any comparable dent in unemployment.

The problem is structural, to begin with. It may assume a
geographical shape—an unemployed coal miner in the Appalachian
hills or a displaced fisherman in Gloucester, Massachusetts, will be
unemployed, more than likely, in good times and bad. On a deeper
level, the problem is one of ignorance and insufficient planning
capability. Alone among the industrialized nations, the United
States has no clear or current data about who the unemployed are
or what job vacancies exist nationally; we simply have no national
employment service with which every worker must register his
skills and desires and every employer his vacancies and needs.
There are several reasons for this. Business does not want to provide government with the data; private employment agencies oppose and have successfully obstructed any coherent national
agency or plan; and government has never really considered full
employment a top priority. It has thought of it as pleasant to have,
all other things being equal.*

It is often maintained that if we can go to the moon, we can
arrange for full employment. This is true, but it assumes an
ideological shift from the old notion of the role of the state to the
new. Once that transition has been made, it would be a relatively
straightforward matter to plan a better fit between workers and

---

* See the preamble to the Employment Act of 1946.

their skills and jobs. Government at a national level, for example, could know that Company A was planning to expand and Company B to contract. Incentives, or coercion, could persuade Company A to locate its new plants in the vicinity of Company B, and the government could provide A with a training subsidy so that some of B's employees could be trained in the new skills necessary. Today, governmental programs are training people badly for jobs that do not exist. The shift to communitarianism offers an opportunity to resolve such a dilemma. In the future, a person should be trained for a specific job he is sure of having.

Further, with the new ideology firmly in place, we can as a people develop a higher sense of coherence and the state will consequently gain in both authority and focus. As I have suggested, this change could bring about a reduction in the size of government and a decrease in the occasions of its intervention. Intervention by the state, after all, is in many ways a sign of failure on the part of the organization being "helped." The government intervened in the affairs of the Penn Central because the company failed structurally; and it is intervening with various components of the energy industry for the same reason. If we improve our structures—that is, make them more inherently legitimate and clarify their aims— the need for intervention ought to decline.

Similarly, we have big government today largely because we have unfocused government, layer upon layer added to deal with problems as they come along. As the state's responsibility and competence to plan becomes generally accepted both by government and the public, there is no reason why the state should necessarily increase its operations. In fact, proper planning would tend to assign implementation to whatever organization was most effective and efficient. The Japanese government, for example, can be relatively small because it has considerable authority and focus; it performs economically because there is a high degree of consensus in Japanese society. It is not considered either interventionary or particularly arbitrary (see the Appendix). If, on the other hand, Japanese ideology and the consensus beneath it were to break down, the government would probably become both larger and more obnoxious.

Also, as America becomes more conscious of its new ideology and as we render it more precise, it should be possible to limit the functions of the state to the planning and control which only it can do, dispersing implementation among a wide variety of organizations along the centralization spectrum—that is, distant from direct state control. In this way the size of what we now call government would be reduced, the functions of government being allocated to the most effective organizations. Such a trend is already visible in the increasing number of partly governmental, partly private organizations that perform a wide variety of public tasks. Kenneth Boulding calls such organizations "intersects":

> They are not quite government, although they are usually the result of some kind of government action. They are not quite business, although they perform many business functions. They are not quite educational or charitable organizations either, though they may also perform some of these functions. They frequently occupy "cracks" or interstices in the organizational structure of society.*

These organizations are for-profit or not-for-profit or not-for-very-much-profit. They are partly regulatory and partly operational; partly coercive and partly not. In a sense, they are buffers between parts of society where discontinuity has produced frictions and gaps; the Denver Regional Transit District, for example, brings together city and state planners as well as land developers and other private interests to plan and coordinate land use.** Other forms include the Bay Area Rapid Transit Authority in San Francisco, the Port of New York Authority, and the Tennessee Valley Authority. The Federal Reserve System is probably the oldest and largest of intersects, a federal organization chartered by Congress but operating independently of both the legislature and the executive. A good example of a modern "buffer" intersect is COMSAT, which occupies, as Boulding puts it, "a certain social space between 82 nations, AT&T, ITT, and all their prospective customers."† It is in effect a vehicle for the commercial utilization of satellites, allowing a wide range of government and private organizations to work together.

The number and prominence of such organizations is bound to increase. In the energy field, for example, I have suggested the need for federally chartered regional corporations to coordinate and plan the production of electric power.

---

* Kenneth Boulding, "Intersects: The Peculiar Organizations," *Challenge to Leadership,* The Conference Board (New York: The Free Press, 1973), p. 179.
** *Ibid,* p. 181.   † *Ibid.,* p. 187.

Chartered by different levels of government, they could serve as the means for comprehensive, integrated planning, and for the development of areas ranging from a single ghetto to a multination region. They could be designed to attack a wide variety of problems—energy, housing, waste disposal, pollution, population control—which now lie awkwardly beyond the reach of either government or business. The responsibilities of the state with regard to such organizations—as Franklin Lindsay, the president of Itek Corporation, has pointed out—would seem to be a major share of the initial financing, overall planning, and public accountability; the responsibilities of such an organization's managerial and business talent would seem to be operations, research and development, and marketing and distribution of the intersect's products and services to customers.* The lines of responsibility could be easily drawn, in other words, within the traditional vocabularies of American business and American government, but the entities themselves would enjoy a greater reach than that of business or government acting alone.

In addition, from the point of view of traditional business, these organizations could serve the critical function of providing a public market, a buyer as it were for goods and services designed to meet a community need rather than a consumer desire. Recalling the Westinghouse experience with Transit Expressway, one can see how extremely useful it would have been if an intersect could have created customers for Westinghouse, acting partly as federal planner and partly as consultant to the cities that needed the innovation. And recalling the possibilities of more efficient and economical recycling of manufacturing waste, we can envisage that the largest public problems might be resolved by the design of appropriate intersects between the political order and conventional business.

A New Political Movement

The vital tasks for this society are to recognize the ideological meaning of the changes that have already occurred in the real

---

* Franklin A. Lindsay, "Management and the Total Environment," *Columbia Journal of World Business,* January–February 1970, pp. 21 and 22.

world; to understand precisely how far we have come from the traditional notions to which we have so ardently adhered; to work toward the formulation of a new, coherent, and generally acceptable ideology to take the place of the old; and to restructure and rearrange our institutions accordingly. This is a revolutionary task, but one that cannot be avoided.

The decisions about the course we take will be made in the political arena, not in corporate boardrooms or university classrooms, important as these are and will continue to be. The workings of the transformation will be totally embraced by and infused with politics. The challenge, then, is a political one: How best do we call forth and mobilize the leadership required? How best do we formulate the vision upon which that leadership must stand and perform its work.

The two major parties of the United States do not seem adequate on either count. The leaders of the two parties—those who might conceivably be nominated for President—are either ideologically retarded or so fragmented in their vision that they cannot comprehend what is happening to America as a whole. Consequently, it is a fair guess that more than half of American voters do not seriously regard themselves as members of either party. In short, our political parties are incoherent. A new political movement is essential. Such a movement must clarify the transformation of American ideology through thought, argument, and debate; it must set forth the programmatic consequences for the nation and its institutions; it must put forward a new vision and formulate the means of moving toward that vision. It may or may not become a political party; that is a tactical question, which depends in part upon the ability of the movement to influence or capture one of the existing parties. My guess, however, is that it will need to be a party—at least for a time—if only because such a force must be national in scope, based upon a foundation of ideas such as those which I have roughly described here as the new ideology.

Plainly, the application of the new ideology will differ in emphasis and application in different regions of the country. Colorado is not New York. But my experience in Colorado Springs suggests that every day the nation's regions are finding they have more in common.* The procedure should begin with the drafting of a com-

---

* See Chapter 7, p. 202.

prehensive national statement, both ideological and programmatic. This statement should then be debated by broadly representative groups of people in the fifty states, who should change and amend it in the light of their interests and perspective. A national convention of all groups could then be held to draft a new national statement. Note that no charismatic leader is required so far, although one might expect that the convention would produce a leadership that commands the respect and loyalty of the movement. At that point the movement would have acquired the capability of becoming a party.

The core of the new movement will doubtless be those groups who have most knowledge: scientists, planners, researchers, and thoughtful people who perceive and understand the transformation around us, however dimly. Businessmen will be important, not for the conventional reasons of their wealth or political influence but because of their particular knowledge; they are in the vanguard of the transition, feeling its pinches, sensing its sometimes dreadful inexorability, and mindful of the contracting options ahead. It will also require the participation of those with political skills—generalists, who are tactically aware of environmental patterns and sensitive to the practicalities of change.

The process I have described is inherently one of controversy. Many interests would feel threatened. It need not, however, be angry or divisive; in fact, it should provide the means to coherence. Fifty years ago Lord Keynes wrote:

Half the copybook wisdom of our statesmen is based on assumptions which were at one time true, or partly true, but are now less and less true day by day. We have to invent new wisdom for a new age. And in the meantime we must, if we are to do any good, appear unorthodox, troublesome, dangerous, disobedient to them that begat us.*

As Keynes implied, one of the most important functions of politics and politicians in such a time of transition is to clarify the facts of change, and to sort out the contradictions between those facts and existing political structures and leadership. I have already mentioned Richard Nixon's inadequacy in this regard. George McGovern had a similar difficulty, although in an entirely different form.

---

* John Maynard Keynes, "Am I a Liberal?" (1925), in *Essays in Persuasion* (London: Macmillan and Co., Ltd., 1931), p. 337.

In his 1972 preconvention speeches, Senator McGovern committed himself both to the traditional ideology and to the new one. He never resolved the contradiction, and after the Democratic Convention consequently lost almost everything. On the one hand, he spoke out for old-time individualism, for the little guy against the big organizations of both government and business. This commitment sprang from his South Dakota background—deeply rooted in rural America—and aroused the enthusiasm of many who also found George Wallace appealing. Ideologically, this stance was profoundly conservative. On the other hand, McGovern also dedicated himself to a new society, one with rigid new communitarian norms for income distribution, inheritance, health care, and the like. In this regard, he was ideologically radical.

There was a plain contradiction between his definitions of individual fulfillment, and of the roles of property, competition, and the state. This contradiction did not trouble McGovern before the Democratic Convention, partly because his youthful followers were as insensitive to it as he was. After the convention, however, he encountered the main lines of institutional America and his contradictory positions lost him votes right and left. The big labor organizations, for example, found his rural populism alarming. And many who fancied the old-time ideology regarded his communitarianism as downright dangerous.

McGovern's fate provides a valuable lesson for the designers of the new political movement. The contradiction between old and new must be recognized, clarified, and dealt with. Let us imagine what McGovern *might* have said: "There is no American more aware than I of the glories of our heritage—the freedom and liberty of the individual. We have bled and died to protect his rights and his dignity, and so may it always be. But at the same time we cannot ignore the fact that America today is changing, and changing rapidly. We are a community of large, complex organizations. These are essential to the large, complex tasks we face at home and in the world; they are not going to wither away. Community need requires us to create new definitions of the old values of survival, justice, and self-respect, and so ensure that in the real world of America's institutions those values are perpetuated, not stifled." And so on. McGovern still might not have won but he would certainly have done more good, because he would have clarified instead of having confused the essential issues.

The ability to clarify is a signally important characteristic for the leadership of the new political movement. The radical changes with which it is concerned will, of course, appear threatening to countless structures of the status quo, and gaining allies from among those structures is critically important to the movement's success. Those allies will be the more ready to go along with the movement if they are convinced that the structures of which they are a part are crumbling, that they and their institutions are indeed in the midst of a crisis. Crisis is peculiarly educational in this regard, but only if it is clearly understood. Also, if we are to avoid bloodshed and waste, the sooner the crisis is properly identified and explained, the sooner it will have the desired effect on the status quo. The trick is to use minimum crisis in order to effect maximum change—the mark of a good political leader, as it is of an effective manager. The leadership of the new movement must fully understand the political functioning of crisis.

Further, the clarification of crisis is important in rendering it a unifying rather than a divisive force. For example, violence in black communities in the late 1960's had two effects, one useful and one not so useful. On the positive side, it prodded the white Establishment into a variety of actions which, taken together, spelled change: the Civil Rights Act, Equal Employment Opportunity legislation, and the like. On the negative side, it infuriated and divided large sections of the white community, who solidified their resistance to the blacks' acquisition of more power and to their integration into the white community through such means as school busing. Leadership, black and white, failed to make the crisis clear.

Whether or not any new political movement coalesces depends upon the strengths of the aspirations of the whole community—upon the visceral hopes of millions of Americans. We are gravely threatened by despair and the apathy that goes with it. Like the old man in Kafka's *The Trial*, many have sunk into unhealthy resignation in the face of the massive bureaucratic structures of our political and economic order. They sit patiently waiting for the gates to open and justice to be done. Such passivity is disguised hopelessness. Others are looking for a return to the past, to the comfort and familiarity of the traditional ideology. They, too, are essentially hopeless. The hope upon which the new political movement will be based is best described by Erich Fromm:

To hope means to be ready at every moment for that which is not yet born, and yet not to become desperate if there is no birth in our lifetimes. . . . Those whose hope is weak settle down for comfort or for violence; those whose hope is strong see and cherish all signs of new life and are ready at every moment to help the birth of that which is ready to be born.*

* Erich Fromm, *The Revolution of Hope* (New York: Harper & Row, 1968), p. 9.

CHAPTER **10** The Organization
of Knowledge: From the Parts to
the Whole

It may be helpful at this point to map the paths of thought along
which we have traveled. We began in the ancient Mediterranean
world, where we observed a static order enshrined in the concept
of an empire. Economic activity emerged as a useful but suspect
and unintegrated endeavor, by and large cut short by the collapse
of the Roman world. A thousand years later, when a separate
economic sector began to appear within the structure of the
medieval world, once again it was not integrated into the main
fabric of the society—it was weakly institutionalized and legitimized. True, it was able to hold its own, after a fashion, but
chiefly only in locations of potential flux, the cities and the towns.
As it grew, unblessed and unintegrated, it exacerbated the decay
which had already begun to infect the institutions of medieval
society. Since that society could generate no theory to legitimate
the emergent energy and power of commerce and business, this
"third estate" grew by any means it could. Eventually it was cap-
tured within the statist mercantilism and centralization of the
continent on the one hand, and joined with the science, epistom-
ology, and political and legal constructions of post-Tudor England
on the other.

In that joining there was a paradox. The Lockean paradigm
works well so long as the acquisitive urges of individuals can be
accommodated with an endless stream of resources—as they
were, at first, in the English maritime expansion, and later in the
virgin richness of the New World. But while the paradigm may
work under such circumstances, a political collective of possessive
and acquisitive individuals with only limited resources and a weak

state must have recourse to non-Lockean measures to maintain economic activity, civic progress, and social order. In our history, these measures have been explicitly corporate and only inexplicitly and weakly statist. The imperatives of community overtake even Economic Man, eventually; and this is precisely what has happened in America.

The device of the corporation, by which America consolidated elements of power to undertake the large tasks of its early days, has now outgrown its simple origins; it has become a thing in itself and an end to itself, and thus has outgrown its legitimacy and controllability, if not its potential utility. Industrialization helped to drive the wedge between economic realities and Lockean political theory. Interest groups of all kinds have grown and intensified their activity, and the society has fragmented itself, not into atomistic individuals but rather into institutional communalities of every description, corporate and otherwise, although principally corporate. Our government, for its part, has never been given fiat to rule, but only to adjust and to regulate on an ad hoc basis. Its techniques for doing that reached their zenith with the temporizations of the Roosevelt era, and also at that time government filled a certain function of holding back the rising tide of explicit communitarianism. But now we find ourselves forced to permit rational rule, through planning; and this means we must redefine the old, seemingly basic notions on which our society has been erected—the old concepts of justice and equality, of freedom, of purpose—to fit within a communitarian mode that may someday be applied with worldwide scope.

The process of redefinition has already begun. All organizations are being affected, but the central organizations—corporations (especially the large publicly held corporations) and the various levels of government—will be affected the most severely. It is now our task to perform the job that has been deferred for 2,000 years: to capture the energy and power of the commercial sector and graft it onto the community. The central institutions will all be changed by this integrative process, both in spirit and in letter. In spirit, they will be given a new legitimacy, one that satisfies the new communitarian criteria for organization and control; and in letter, they will be given a new efficacy, through coordinated planning. The ideological schizophrenia that divides us will be resolved, perhaps violently, perhaps peacefully, through a new political sensitivity embodied at least for a time in a political movement both eager and competent to build a framework out of crisis and change.

Throughout this whole development we can discern one most important fact: that the concept of the integrity and independence of the smallest unit (the atom, the individual) suddenly appeared to us as ultimately important about three hundred years ago; but that this concept seems to have yielded to that of the relative importance of the whole and of wholes within wholes—the community, the universe. Where once the attainment of human fulfillment appeared to be an individualistic process, it now is increasingly dependent upon community design. Where once we focused on the atom and the monad, we now focus on the relativity of these things within the entities of which they are parts. Where once we thought of Economic Man, we are now beginning to think in terms of global society. Our attention is shifting from the parts, now that we have passed the crest of the Lockean blip, and is turning instead toward the whole.

If we are to shift our vision successfully, obviously we must know as exactly as possible what we are doing. We cannot possibly plan such an immense undertaking, involving literally everything in the world, unless we know what is possible; then, the best alternative among the possibilities; and then, how to accomplish our goals. At present we have only glimmerings; we cannot say we know these things, in any detailed or profound way. We have some ideological notions to guide us, to be sure—the new theories I have sketched in this book, as well as the healthy residues of the old ideology which I have also tried to sift and identify. But in their present condition these are hardly sufficient guides for detailed action, far less a source of substantive solutions to specific problems. Even when the new ideology has gathered momentum and begun to solidify, we shall obviously have to turn to the whole body of our organized knowledge for specific planning. But we cannot fully trust the competence of our knowledge, were it suddenly to be confronted with the mighty task we shall set before it.

For our organized knowledge—our *science* as a whole—is itself in the midst of a serious evolutionary phase, complementary to and consonant with the ideological tranformation I have been describing. It too is outgrowing basic notions formed in the seventeenth century; this final component of the Lockean ideology is also afflicted with the ideological schizophrenia we noted in the other domains. In this final chapter I shall trace this change, this transformation, which is occurring within science itself, within the organization of our whole body of knowledge, and the effects on its institutional custodians—notably, schools and universities.

The Transformation of Science

Science includes a body of knowledge and a method of perceiving, by which it gathers and prepares knowledge for application to human affairs. This method differs with time and place. However "pure" science may be, it always proceeds within certain limits, follows certain purposes, and rests upon certain assumptions—what Thomas Kuhn called paradigms.* These paradigms are part of the ideological context of the times. The Chinese invented gunpowder and used it for religious ceremonies; the Americans created the atom bomb and dropped it on the Japanese.

When science now and again breaks with the paradigms of the past, it also moves against the traditional ideological context of which they are a part, and the old context and its institutions shudder. Copernicus may have astonished sixteenth-century Europe with his revelations about the posititon of the earth in the universe; but he shook the ideological foundations of the Western world when it was suggested that such cosmic questions no longer belonged to theory and philosophy but to systematic observation and experimentation.** The great shock wave was caused by the old scientific paradigm giving way; one ideological framework of science was replacing another.

The intensity of such a shock derives from the fact that science, construed in its broad sense, is the lens through which the quality and hardness of reality is filtered to us in each age; it is the device through which we decide what the scope and nature of our reality is going to be. In each age it admits to our minds what makes sense and excludes what does not. What makes no sense in one age, of course, may very well make sense in another. The concept of television would have seemed extrarational to the ancients (ex-

---

* See Chapter 1, p. 26.
** See Willis W. Herman, "The New Copernican Revolution," *Stanford Today,* Winter 1969.

cept perhaps to the mystics among them), although it makes perfect sense to us today; and the science of the witch and the geocentric theory of the solar system, however sensible these seemed to the medieval mind, seem nonsense to us today (once again, with the possible exception of the mystics among us).

Thus science, taken broadly as all the organized knowledge of an era and as the method by which it is gathered and set into place, tends to tell us what is real and what unreal; it suggests what is possible; it tends to condition, to define human wants, aspirations, and needs. Consequently, it leads man on by its suggestions of what can be done; and man, always ambitious, follows its leads and dictates, incorporating its potentials into his scheme of purpose and his ideology. The established and organized knowledge of each era thus colors the nature of that era. It gives a tincture and character to all its achievements. It lies at the roots of the institutions of that era, and at the roots of their behavior. Aquinas, for example, attempted to organize all the knowledge of his day around the meaning of the figure of the Christian saviour, and was largely successful. He thereby provided a canon, as vitally important in its rubrics of organization as in the substance of the knowledge organized under them, for judging what was sensible, possible, desirable, and sound—in short, for judging what was good in every act and institution of his society. The measure of his success lay in the intensity and durability of his authority, which continued for centuries after the particular filter he had perfected for viewing reality had yellowed and cracked with age. Before Aquinas, Aristotle had declared what the scientific paradigms for the perception of reality were to be, a set of constructs that held sway for a thousand years on its own, and another five hundred as revised by Aquinas. Again, in crystallizing the experimental method and its ramifications for his culture, Newton provided a scope on reality—one which, because of its peculiarly rational glass, tended to segregate all of what might be termed the religious elements of the time on the shady side of the screen. Now Einstein has given us the basic metaphor of relativity, a theory which, as we shall see, is stretching to embrace the relations of everything to every other thing, including religious phenomena.

The sequence here is significant: from Aristotelian organism to medieval organism to Newtonian atomism to modern relative organism. It appears that, in science as in society, mankind's basic reference is to the whole, and that we have pressed our English adventure toward the empirical, the objective, and the specific to the point at which we must return our attention to the whole.

Further, in the social and economic and political spheres, science itself is explicitly leading us back to the global, the integrated, the organic. To take only one familiar example: General Motors bloomed from the science of the days of its founding, through the energy of creative men from the legitimate orders of society, and for its time it was good. But now ecologists inform us that automobile exhaust is bad; the science of today is questioning in many ways the soundness of the traditional concept of GM, questioning whether it is wise to permit its untrammeled operations. It is questioning a multitude of other corporations, institutions, and agencies in the same vein. This development is a most serious indictment of our decaying ideology, for, as I have pointed out, science has a dominant voice in determining what is totem and taboo; and science—specifically the new science—is beginning to condemn institutional America.

This condemnation, it is important to note, has a moral flavor for us, the ominous sound of a religious judgment. For there is no appeal from an absolute scientific judgment. When the men of science can demonstrate "real facts" to us, we must accept them; we cannot litigate against them. True, we may not do as they advise us. Our traditional prejudices may get in the way. Or we may believe their view to be still unformed and limited; it is certainly true that scientists cannot always assemble the whole picture they would like to paint. But they are getting closer to the whole picture (one of the hallmarks of the scientific revolution that is taking place), and when they are certain, and when we are certain that they are certain, then they will assume the role of final arbiters of the possible, the acceptable, and the inevitable. To some extent they wear this mantle already, and to some extent they realize it. As Einstein put it, "In this materialistic age of ours, the serious scientific workers are the only profoundly religious people."* Only they move freely through the domain of unappealable truth;

---

* Albert Einstein, "Religion and Science," *The New York Times Magazine,* Nov. 9, 1930.

only they have godlike certainty on their side. Science is indeed the religion of today.

Just as in the seventeenth century, however—at the last great node of ideological change—the religion of the culture is in schism. As the West was split between the communitarian norms of the Roman Church and the individualist doctrines of the Reformation, so today the scientific community is divided between loyalty to the older concepts of science and a new organism of knowledge, an holistically developing science of relativity that will present us with a new filter through which to look at the universe and to judge what is real and what is not. It is to the credit of the scientific community that its ideological revolution is a little ahead of the one afflicting our society at large.

And thus we face a truly Lockean task. Locke's ideology rested squarely on Newton's science. Locke's genius lay in his ability to synthesize Newton's vision of reality with the flow of events in revolutionary England. We have a parallel task: to seek in the knowledge of the new science the basis for a new synthesis, which gathers all the components of the new ideology in a single mesh, including the new ideology of science itself.

The Old Scientific Ideology

Five powerful theories were created by the genius of Copernicus and Newton* and developed by their followers. These have domi-

---

* It is ironic that Newton's name should be identified with this ideology of science, because it is so far from where he thought he was going. He was concerned above all with a total synthesis; he was in truth a metaphysician. It is worth repeating what John Maynard Keynes said of him: "Newton was not the first of the Age of Reason. He was the last of the magicians, the last of the Babylonians and Sumerians, the last great mind which looked out on the visible and intellectual world with the same eyes as those who began to build an intellectual world rather less than 10,000 years ago. . . . Why do I call him a magician? Because he looked on the whole universe and all that is in it *as a riddle,* as a secret which could be read by applying pure thought to certain evidence, certain mystic clues which God had laid about the world to allow a sort of philosopher's treasure hunt to the esoteric brotherhood." (From "Newton the Man," in *The Royal Society, Newton Tercentenary Celebration* [1947], p. 29, as quoted in Giorgio De Santillana and Hertha von Dechend, *Hamlet's Mill* (Boston: Gambit, Inc., 1969). How far his learning fled!

nated scientific thought for the last three hundred years. They constitute an idea that is bound up in the phrase "the scientific method," which has legitimized many of our institutions, in particular those concerned with knowledge and education.

The first of the five is *specialization,* the inevitable process of fragmentation that accompanies the efficiency of division of labor. This is a necessary and powerful tool for the deep analysis of matter; it has guided our creation of the expert, the person competent to analyze man, society, and the world in one particular aspect—say, chemistry or anthropology.

The second, related theory is *reductionism,* the belief that the way to understand systems or wholes is to break them apart. If you know enough about the parts, you can put them together and understand the whole; or, to put it another way, if you concentrate on the parts, the whole will take care of itself. Understand Humpty Dumpty's organs, cells, molecules, and atoms, and you can put him together again. In combination, specialization and reductionism have produced the proliferation of "disciplines." This proliferation is accelerating. Shortly after World War II, there were about fifty-four specializations in the sciences; twenty years later there were more than nine hundred.* Our present approach to reality may be pictured as in Figure 6.

The third theory is the Newtonian belief that knowledge, to be scientific, must be *objective.* That is, it must be quantifiable; what cannot be measured presumably is not worth knowing. Although this idea began and predominated in the physical sciences, it has also come to pervade the social sciences. Sociologists, for example, busy themselves with counting and quantifying. In their pursuit of what is good, corporations insist that somehow "goodness" must be measured in a "social audit" or something of the kind.

The fourth component of traditional scientific ideology has been *rationalism.* Reason was exalted; the emotions, the intuition, spiritual perceptions were considered unscientific, the domain of mystics.

Finally, the overwhelming emphasis of science has been on physical matter. It has tended to identify reality with matter and

---

* Daniel Bell, *The Coming of Post-Industrial Society: A Venture in Social Forecasting* (New York: Basic Books, Inc., 1973), p. 187.

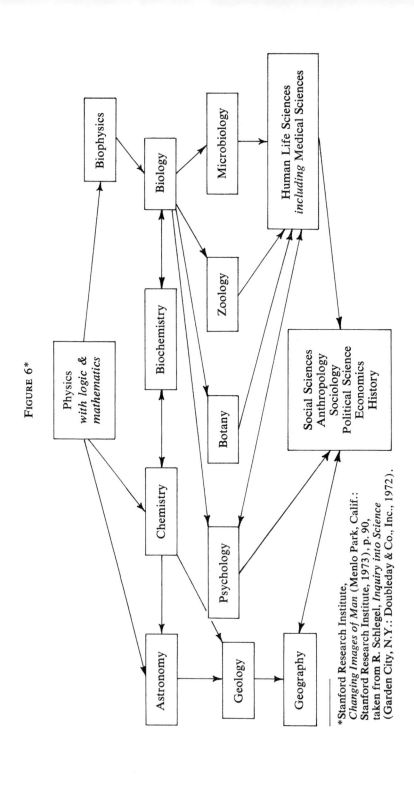

FIGURE 6*

*Stanford Research Institute, *Changing Images of Man* (Menlo Park, Calif.: Stanford Research Institute, 1973), p. 90, taken from R. Schlegel, *Inquiry into Science* (Garden City, N.Y.: Doubleday & Co., Inc., 1972).

thus to sustain *materialism*. As a consequence: "What counts is what I can feel and touch and see. If it feels nice and looks magnificent, so much the better—especially if I own it."

Plainly there has been and will continue to be great power and convenience in these old paradigms, but they have become increasingly suspect. Anachronisms have developed, inconsistencies between the concepts and the real world to which they were supposed to relate. The ideas no longer work very well.

The whole, we now know, does not take care of itself; nor is it necessarily understood or cared for through an analysis of the parts. Furthermore, the rigid bureaucracies of specialization, each with its covey of experts rewarded for knowing more and more about less and less, have constrained the outlook of science and limited the variety of frameworks with which it can approach the world and nature. The eclectic empiricist who, in the best tradition of experimentalism, sets forth to find out what is really happening in the world frequently finds himself put down by the refined and elegant constructs of the specialist. This is reminiscent of Copernicus's problems with the Church in the sixteenth century, the Church today being the economics department or some such hallowed group. What the Fathers determined then was not to be questioned; so it is with specialists now. Thus their constructs have come to obscure our vision of reality by imposing too segmented and finely divided a filter on it; the absolutes of reality—which seem to exist and operate, although we may never know them directly—are straining such constructs to the breaking point. I want to discuss two compelling examples of the failure of the old paradigms, notably of specialization and reductionism. The first has to do with the social environment and the processes of social change or "development"; and the second with the physical environment, the truths of ecology, and the facts of scarcity.

In the Social Environment

Change has been a big problem for social science.* It defies specialized analysis. Reductionism does not work in understanding

---

* See Samuel P. Huntington, "The Change to Change," *Comparative Politics* 3 (April 1971):283.

change because change is a holistic process. Take change apart
and it decomposes. Academics, therefore, have tended to throw
up their hands in dismay. Talcott Parsons flatly stated in 1951 that
"a general theory of the processes of change in social systems is
not possible in the present state of knowledge."* He might have
said, more precisely, "in the present ideology of knowledge."

In the mid-1960's I spent time with a group of students in
Veraguas Province, Panama, attempting to learn how irreversible
change takes place. Our teachers were a group of relatively radical
priests and young lay people led by a remarkable bishop, Msgr.
Marcos McGrath, later Archbishop of Panama. The bishop had
approached this province with the express purpose of trying to
change it. Veraguas was a poor and neglected bit of countryside,
whose 150,000 people were for the most part scattered among a
number of rural settlements in the unfertile hills, and where political and economic power had been concentrated in a few hands
for hundreds of years. Effecting permanent change constituted a
real challenge; but unlike the experimenters who have tried to
"develop" Brazil (mentioned in Chapter 3), the bishop and his
followers realized that the obstacles to change were all parts of
an interrelated whole, a circle, as it were, of parts each inseparably
connected. All the characteristics of the environment had to be
comprehended and weighed before change could be introduced.
An expert dealing in a specialized way with one characteristic
was inviting failure.

As in many of the Veraguases of this world, increased food production was regarded as a desirable change. Agriculture experts
were sent into the countryside with seed and fertilizer to increase
output. Once there, however, they found obstacles which had little
to do with their expertise.

First, the peasant was unwilling to change his methods. Living
on the knife edge of existence in an environment which he believed to be essentially hostile and over which he had little or no
control, he saw suicide in change. Persuasive as the expert might
have been with "demonstrations" and rational argument, there
was little trust on the part of those who by long experience had
learned that few could be relied on.

---

* Talcott Parsons, *The Social System* (New York: The Free Press, 1957),
p. 486.

Second, increased food production by itself was no real incentive. When an expert came to Veraguas and after some difficulty found a farmer who was willing to try his seed and fertilizer, other forces in the environment made his innovation essentially pointless. To be sure, his tomatoes were more bountiful, but that season the rain washed out the road up which the truck had to come to get his crop. So 30 per cent of his output rotted in the field. And when the truck came, it was the same truck as before, owned by one of the three families that controlled almost everything of value in Veraguas. The trucker, seeing the more bountiful crop, raised the price for hauling it to market; since there was no alternative, the farmer had to pay the price. The market—again, the only one, also controlled by one of the three families—compensated the farmer at the same rate as before. Even worse, the farmer feared that the neighboring landowner, a powerful man, might look at the newly blooming field and be tempted to extend his fences to enclose what previously had appeared to be of little value. If this were to happen, the farmer would have been hard put to resist—deeds of ownership were unclear, the costs of lawyers high, and the political system inclined to favor those who contributed most to it.

Even more ironically, when the expert prepared to leave, he advised the farmer that the following year he should buy the recommended seed and fertilizer; he should go to the local agricultural extension bank and get a loan for that purpose. The farmer knew, however, that the local bank had a firm policy against loaning money to poor credit risks, a category to which he had always belonged and to which he had no reason to suppose he did not still. If he wanted to borrow money, he would have to go to the local storekeeper or loan shark, and this he could not afford to do because his debt was already great. The expert left, disenchanted, convinced that the farmer lacked the entrepreneurial spirit and drive upon which "progress" depends.

The introduction of change of any kind requires recognition of and simultaneous action against all the relevant obstacles. In this case, these were political, social, economic, and cultural, having to do with land tenure, the market, credit systems, the law, and the courts. If the expert is to be useful at all, he must be integrated into a general scheme and led by a generalist who is sensitive to the interplay of all the parts.

Successful leaders of movements for change, whether in Veraguas or Manhattan, also realize that there are two fundamental prerequisites in addition to an integrated approach. These are the existence of motivation and organization among those who are to change. Let us look at another obviously "good thing"—elementary school education in Veraguas. The province was dotted with a great quantity of cinder-block school houses. It had many schoolteachers, and there were warehouses full of textbooks. All this was the product of a conviction on the part of U.S. and Panamanian "developers" that if one put school houses together with teachers and books, education would result. It was plain, however, that very little learning was taking place inside the school houses. Children would come three of four days a week, often late, stare out the window, and go home. Generally this would continue for several years and then the child would drop out. A survey of parents revealed that they regarded education as important in an abstract sense, but that in reality, they believed it would not make any difference to the lives of their children. They were convinced that no matter what a child might learn, he was not going to have any greater influence over his environment; his world was controlled by things beyond his reach and so he might as well do something useful like take lunch to his father in the field or fix the roof or tend the family pig.

When the bishop's movement had succeeded in organizing some 5,000 peasants in forty-five separate community groups and when these groups were able to exert control over land, market and credit systems, and politics, the education of the children of those 5,000 followed naturally. They were in school on time and overtime. The organization redesigned the regular curriculum; four vocational schools and a radio school were added and they flourished. There was the confidence that with education would come a real capacity to control one's life and thus a degree of self-respect. Without such motivation there can be no education. And motivation without organization is powerless; the two must go together.

Specialization impedes the accurate perception of such processes; reality escapes the narrow gaze of the typical economist, the political scientist, the anthropologist, even the theoretically broader view of the sociologist. This fact becomes tragic when, as so often happens, the specialist bullies the generalist. As a nation, America heaps admiration and respect upon the specialist. Our educational system trains him, our organizational system hires and promotes him. It is unnatural to expect that when he confronts a problem like that of Veraguas, he will refrain from viewing it through carefully formed preconceptions. Being well trained, he is apt to be persuasive and articulate and thus often imposes his distorted vision upon the generalist or manager whose essential task should be to comprehend the whole and to integrate the skills of the expert for an approach to it.

Our commitment to expertise is also remarkably wasteful. In Veraguas, for example, the overwhelming proportion of health needs can be met relatively simply; through better nutrition and a simple organization and communications network to ensure that when a man cuts his foot with his machete, someone knows about it and brings him disinfectant and a bandage so that he does not die of gangrene. Large numbers of expensively trained doctors are not necessary to solve these problems; in fact, they are superfluous. What is required is organization and authoritative leadership capable of communicating with those concerned. The message for Veraguas is simple: "Eat low-cost high-protein cereal. Brush your teeth. Boil your water. Keep clean. If you are sick, come to the clinic. Don't have too many children." The achievement of any of these changes is part of a holistic process.

In the United States, as in Veraguas, we need holistic vision. We have problems of food production, marketing, and distribution;* we have parallel problems of education; we have great need for effective health care systems. The time has come to part from the romance with specialization.

In the Physical Environment

The failure of traditional scientific ideology to anticipate or comprehend environmental degradation and the related problem of scarcity of vital resources is all too obvious. As in the social environment, so in the physical, the metaphor of the circle comes to mind. "We have broken out of the circle of life," Barry Com-

---

* David Caplovitz, for example, documented in his 1963 study of East Harlem and the Lower East Side of Manhattan that the New York poor—like those in Veraguas—are prisoners of a market and credit system in which they invariably are required to pay more—*The Poor Pay More* (New York: The Free Press, 1963).

moner writes, "converting its endless cycles into man-made, linear events. . . ."* We have succumbed to a nearly fatal illusion that through our machines, our technology, our specialization we have escaped from dependence on the natural environment. Again, the expert is peering tangentially into a void, his specialty meaningless unless connected to the circle. We are reminded that any species which has overspecialized has always become extinct, its adaptive capabilities having atrophied, and that the fundamental law of nature remains as inexorable as ever: Adapt or perish.

The problems of adaptation bring us quickly back to the institutional questions considered in previous chapters, questions of control and legitimacy, of priorities and visions. Industrial pollution is upsetting the basic balances of the fragile biosphere in which our planet is encased, and in many ways the modern city is a threat to the maintenance of life. Scarcities remind us that nothing is limitless—neither air nor water nor oil nor iron ore— and that the institutional forms and criteria by which we distribute what is scarce are in need of inspection and reform. The idea of competition to satisfy consumer desire, for example, has resulted in the growth of technologies since World War II which are most disharmonious with nature and in many cases most consumptive of energy. The big gainers have been such things as nonreturnable bottles (53,000 per cent), synthetic fibers (5,980 per cent), aluminum manufacture, air conditioners, nitrogenous fertilizer, high-powered engines, detergents—all outgrowths of linear technologies, all disruptive of nature's circle. They were the result of the scientific capability to pull nature apart for specialized purposes, without regard for the whole.**

Yet, as Commoner remarks, there is no technological necessity for such outcomes: "Ecological survival does not mean the abandonment of technology. Rather, it requires that technology be derived from a scientific analysis that is appropriate to the natural world on which technology intrudes."† A steel can rusts; an aluminum can does not. And the latter, incidentally, requires more energy to make than the former.

We can see the radical implications of the ecological imperative for the private enterprise system, given the linear sequence of

---

* Barry Commoner, *The Closing Circle* (New York: Alfred A. Knopf, Inc., 1971), p. 12.
** *Ibid.,* p. 143.   † *Ibid.,* p. 189.

investment for profit leading to new technology, which in turn affords greater productivity, the major source of profit. Yet the following facts give us room to maneuver and re-form that sequence:

ONE, profit is not the problem. Profit per se is ideologically neutral.

TWO, pollution derives from technology, which is a function of emphasis on productivity.

THREE, the vital trade-off is between the interests (profit) of the whole (society) and the interests (profit) of the individual investors.

Admittedly, the cost of retreat and reorganization will be enormous, particularly since many of the new, high-polluting technologies have greater profit rates than the older, low-polluting technologies. Further, the costs of environmental degradation and resource scarcity are already being reflected in higher costs of production, leaving a dismal array of consequences: wage reductions, further price increases, vulnerability to competition from those whose costs are lower.

The way out of these difficulties is narrow and obscure, as well as expensive. Our best and cheapest chance—perhaps our only chance—is to develop a measure of community or collective planning which is consistent with the natural principles of the biosphere. This is inconsistent with our traditional ideas. We shall have to develop and forcibly impose new technologies to cover our flanks and take all kinds of other high-handed measures; and, most importantly, we must bring ourselves to recognize that production of goods and services is merely part of a total environmental process, necessarily subservient to the good of the whole. Even if we reconcile ourselves to these measures—even if we somehow manage to provide a new political process to carry them out—we still cannot rely on the old scientific establishment to advise us on how to reach a true harmony within the biosphere. For that establishment is based on an ideology composed first and foremost of the principles of specialization and reductionism. No scientist is so presumptuous as to say, "We have the answers to the questions you are asking about man's fit into the cycles of nature. We have been studying this. We have synthesized our knowledge. Now what you must do is . . ." Focused on the entire biosphere, the lens of reality provided by the old scientific ideology has cracked.

The erosion of the old ideology of science goes part and parcel with the general transformation of ideology through which we are living. It has been noted by scientists themselves since the turn of the century. As with other facets of the transformation, the old ideas are not entirely useless; indeed, they have and will continue to have great power and force. It is just that there is more and more with which they cannot deal, while in the meantime new directions are emerging.

Toward an Organic Vision

Early in the twentieth century, the neatly ordered Newtonian world began to disintegrate. Time and space, matter and energy, the mainstays of Newton's mechanics, were the separate building blocks of his vision of reality. With these clearly in hand, one could determine the location of objects and forces and predict what and where they would be in the future. Darwin's notion of a logical and natural evolution of life lent strength to this ordered vision. But Albert Einstein ended the neat dichotomy of time and space. He suggested as well that matter and energy shared the same equation. Niels Bohr in his Principle of Complementarity held that light could be both wave and particle. And Werner Heisenberg showed that one could never know momentum and direction at the atomic level at once. Matter dematerialized and continua coalesced. Determination becomes more difficult, or, rather less cozy and less sure, in such a world.

Also the universe, instead of being a mechanistic one, was suddenly becoming a personal one, its nature depending on where one sits, so to speak. As Jacob Bronowski described it:

Einstein showed that the laws of physics are universal, that is, are formulated in the same terms by every observer, but only because he carries his own universe with him. Time as you measure it may be different from my time, mass as you measure it may be different from my mass, speed and momentum and energy may all be different; it is only the relations between them that remain the same for us both. Each of us rides his personal universe, his own travelling box of space and time, and all that they have in common is the same structure or coherence; when we formalize our experiences, they yield the same laws.*

Nothing is fixed or neat. Even the universe itself is expanding in strange and eerie ways, and it is full of wonders: quasars, pulsars, and black holes. Its "edge"—whatever that may look like—is billions of light years away. Sensible people talk of antimatter, of time flowing backwards, of negative mass, and of particles traveling faster than light. Science has put man in a universe infinitely more extraordinary and less determinable than the vision of Newton prepared him for. This universe is not made up of things, invariant atoms in space, but of a complex hierarchy of flow patterns, some small, some enormous. Objects in it can only be understood in terms of their holistic relationship to their fields of flow.** And these flow systems are constantly changing, often suddenly, not apparently as the result of the external design of some cosmic watchmaker but as the result of information and processes inherent in the flow itself, as with chromosomes in a plant. Again, everything is related to everything else and can be comprehended only so. According to John Platt, a biophysicist at the University of Michigan, "It is not entirely false or even mystical to say that in these restructurings . . . the system is 'going beyond what it knows how to do,' and the organism or individuals are in the grip of 'a power beyond themselves.' "†

In the world of politics and society, great events have this same characteristic—the Russian revolution and the American revolution, for example, and the creation of the U.S. Constitution, which was written in a few weeks. Are not the transnational corporations—IBM, Mitsubishi, Unilever, Nestle—perhaps similar flow patterns? Are they not powers beyond themselves, forcing the restructuring of nation-states and the creation of new world systems? And at the same time that population biologists and ecologists are disclosing global inexorabilities in the flow patterns that support life, geneticists, microbiologists, and brain researchers are

---

* J. Bronowski, "A Twentieth Century Image of Man," Salk Institute, as quoted in Stanford Research Institute, *op. cit.,* p. 94.

** John Platt, "Hierarchical Growth," *Bulletin of the Atomic Scientists,* November 1970, p. 2.

† *Ibid.,* p. 3.

probing the internal, psychical environment of the human being. Here too we see flows, patterns of growth and change and decay. Indeed, in general, there are fewer and fewer sectors of science about which we know nothing at all, and yet there are more and more processes—flows, if you will—in each sector that we acknowledge to be mysteries. These flows turn our attention more and more unambiguously to the unknown motive principles of the complex hierarchy of which they are elements; and even now we can dimly sense, perhaps, the awesome synthesis toward which these widely separate pursuits of knowledge are converging. It is an understatement to say that such a synthesis will posit radically different relationships between the economic and social aspects of existence and human life in its totality—it will do that and much more to boot. Will mankind have the understanding and the wisdom to deal with this new knowledge? Can we make the choices which it will present? What criteria will we use? In approaching such questions we are driven back to the need for a new ideology and inevitably, too, a new spirituality. For it seems certain that science will make mystics of us all.

Science is revealing the awful collision between growth—of population, consumption, and waste—and the limits of resources. Humanity is discovering that, like other species, it is bound by the S-curve that governs growth in any environment. It is clear that the ideology which was effective in governing man's conduct during the first part of the curve, when survival depended upon individual initiative and competition, tooth and claw, must be different from the ideology that will govern the second part of the curve, where survival requires cooperation—where, in Jonas Salk's phrase, only the wisest will survive.* The need for social, political, and above all, religious systems by which to recognize and allow for the interrelation of all things—to recognize and give consent to the laws of the whole, whatever we may discover them to be—is the inescapable conclusion of countless modern scientific studies.**

Scientific investigation of the human being is requiring new definitions of self and self-realization. Genetic engineering, cloning,

---

* Stanford Research Institute, *op. cit.*, p. 99; Jonas Salk, *The Survival of the Wisest* (New York: Harper & Row, 1973); see also Barry Commoner, *op. cit.*
** Dunella H. Meadows *et al., The Limits to Growth* (New York: Universe Books, 1972).

and the like are making the determination of human nature to some extent a matter of human choice.* We may, if we choose, be able to weed out the "bad" and duplicate the "good"—truly a godlike responsibility. Such possibilities for modifying the individual obviously demand criteria for protecting him.

No area of modern science is expanding more rapidly than that of the human brain and its functions. For example, knowledge of brain chemistry has allowed the development of a large number of mind-altering drugs. These developments led Kenneth Clark, when president of the American Psychological Association, to conclude that "We might be on the threshold of that type of scientific, biochemical intervention which could stabilize and make dominant the moral and ethical propensities of man and subordinate, if not eliminate, his negative and primitive behavioral tendencies."** Some have hypothesized the emergence of a "psychocivilized" society in which dangerous behavior in man will have been eliminated either chemically or electrically; warlike instincts or propensities to abuse nature could simply be destroyed.† This knowledge opens the way to the external control of the human being. Can we entrust such control to common law? Is this not a responsibility, rather, for a religious canon?

On the other hand, biofeedback techniques appear to provide the means by which the individual himself can control his own brain and body. As Eastern thought has long held, man can, if properly trained, exert remarkable control over such bodily functions as heart beat and blood pressure. Recent research indicates that with biofeedback training, in which a person receives precise and immediate feedback regarding a particular physiological process, he can learn to control brain functions, skin temperature, muscle tension, and more.†† Now we must ask: How should the individual use these powers? Into what forms shall he mold his self?

Such forays into the inner man have brought science increasingly into the realm of the subjective, the irrational, and the intuitional,

---

* Stanford Research Institute, *op. cit.*, p. 103.
** Kenneth Clark, "The Pathos of Power: A Psychologcial Perspective," *American Psychologist* 26 (December 1971): 1047–57.
† José M. R. Delgado, M.D., *Physical Control of the Mind: Toward a Psychocivilized Society* (New York: Harper & Row, 1969).
†† Stanford Research Institute, *op. cit.*, p. 114.

as opposed to its traditional stamping grounds, the objective and the rational. This tendency was encouraged by Heisenberg's Principle of Uncertainty, which established the fact that the subjective physical act of observation affects the object of study, thus rendering objectivity a pretense. In psychology, parallel with this, considerable evidence suggests that the expectations or motivations of investigators influence the subjects of investigation. As a result of these developments, new importance is being attached to the nature of consciousness, and scientific inquiry is increasingly extending into areas previously held to be the domain of religion and mysticism—hypnosis, dreaming, meditation, telepathy, and the like.* In such matters, the East has a long-time advantage over the West. Science, already a cult to many of its followers, seems to be accepting the techniques of cult as real, embracing them through its lens on reality. If it succeeds in integrating them into science as good and useful things, it will have validated and legitimized certain elements of religion—and such validation and legitimization are surely themselves religious functions.

In its impressive study *The Changing Images of Man*, Stanford Research Institute was led to suggest this line of thinking:

> The time is clearly ripe for a new vision, and it is natural to wonder if once again the methods of inquiry of another culture might not be strong where ours are proving weak. It may be that these methods will be found in an epistemology of the self, such as held sway in the East. . . . This is not to suggest that modern science would or should adopt totally all of the Eastern notions of consciousness, but rather that they might be fruitfully adapted and synthesized with traditional Western scientific methods to produce the next stage in man's evolutionary advance.**

Beyond the Resolution: The Alternatives Ahead

These directions in science suggest that several new ideological components are at hand:

First, in place of specialization, or rather as a counterweight to it, there is holism. This is the recognition that everything must be considered in relation to everything else; that mankind is one; that it lives on a spaceship, earth; that the resources available to it

---

* *Ibid.*, pp. 111–12, 122.   * * *Ibid.*, pp. 136, 138.

are limited; that to survive, men must become harmonious with each other and with all the rest of nature.

SECOND, complementing reductionism, there is a new appreciation of synthetic thought, a kind of synodism among the sciences. It stems from the awareness that wholes cannot necessarily be understood solely by the analysis of their parts and subsystems.

THIRD, complicating objectivity, there is the recognition that all observation, all measurement, all experience is necessarily subjective. Neither the measurer, the measure, nor the measured are absolute.

FOURTH, complementing the purity of rationalism, there is an awareness that the power and scope of objective reason are slighter than we had supposed. The subjective and the irrational have been granted status as real, and it follows that an understanding of reality cannot rely exclusively on the severely logical—one might even say, syllogistic—reasoning processes on which science has prided itself in the past. Even the understanding of oneself, both in terms of one's internal nature and one's relation to the surrounding whole, depends on varieties of consciousness which are intensely subjective, intuitional, and psychic. The concept of self-realization, now taken seriously by science, also obviously depends on such subjective consciousness.

FIFTH, complementing materialism and to an extent replacing it, there is a new tenderness for the value of the human being and humanity.

Let us assume that these new components will gel with the older concepts into a new guidance system for science. In fact, let us hope this with all our hearts, for the alternative is plainly appalling; if we simply extrapolate forward from where we are today, the knowledge and techniques of science are more than likely to land us in a Brave New World which will make Huxley's pale. We are likely to build ourselves a prison to end all prisons. The sequence of events is all too easy to predict: the inexorable, empirical, rational drift; an ever-increasing centralization of power into the hands of a specialized élite capable of manipulating unlimited numbers of people; the people themselves, neatly engineered, pulled together into burgeoning concentrations for surveillance and control.

If, on the other hand, we are consciously seeking to make explicit the new ideology and designing new institutions to fit, we may achieve a much more benign alternative. Dr. Glen T. Seaborg, when chairman of the AEC, expressed his optimism concisely:

What we are seeing today in the anguish over environmental feedback and the piling of crisis upon crisis, is not a forecast of doom. It is the birth pangs of a new world—the period of struggle in which we are making the physical transition from man to mankind.

This organic mankind must learn to exist as an integral and contributing part of the earth that up to now supported it unquestionably. This can only be achieved by the formulation and application of a whole new scientific outlook and new ecological-technological relationship.*

Strangely enough, it is perhaps appropriate to begin a discussion of the impact of this reformulation with religious institutions. We can envisage the coming together of the two great pillars of Western civilization, science and religion, in a synthesis that accounts for the oneness of things and for the harmony of man with nature. This spells change for Judeo-Christian traditions as they have evolved in the last three hundred years. Tending to divide mankind within itself and to separate it from nature, Western religion needs to learn from Eastern thought. "Behold but One in all things," wrote the Hindu poet, Kabir. And the Upanishads assert, "An invisible and subtle essence is the Spirit of the whole Universe. That is Reality. That is Truth. Thou art that." The primary task of religion may well be to inculcate an understanding of this enormous fact. In a sense, it lies at the heart of the early Judeo-Christian concept of "the brotherhood of man," but that concept has tended to be forgotten in the possessive individualism of the Protestant ethic.** Religion will also have to reawaken its respect for mystery. The new revelations of science surely remind us of the limitations of reason and of the necessity for recognizing the transcendental mystery of things if man is to be fully conscious and self-fulfilled.

---

* Glen T. Seaborg, quoted in Bayard Webster, "Seaborg Links Survival of Man to Science's Success or Failure," *The New York Times*, May 3, 1970, p. 30.

** It is interesting to note the surprising popularity of the television show, *Kung Fu,* in which Caine, a communitarian holist incanting Oriental truths, makes mincemeat of the John Wayne types. I recall especially one show in which Caine, gently loving some little chicks, explained to a frontiersman the joy of oneness with nature, elucidating the necessity of community in a chaotic world. Is it conceivable that such a story would have sold soap or whatever ten years ago?

Political institutions will undoubtedly bear the brunt of the transition. They will of necessity have to rely increasingly on the specialized and holistic skills of "knowledge élites." But knowledge will be too awesome and too powerful to be safely concentrated. Great care will need to be taken to preserve openness, divergent thought, and maximum participation in political decisions at all levels. Never will diversity have been so essential, but it will necessarily be diversity within a conscious plan, the product of a planned, explicit balance between what is rational and empirical and what intuitive, what is manipulative and what an individual right, what is utilitarian and what aesthetic. China offers a helpful illustration here. Probably the most important expression of political participation in China, says Rensselaer W. Lee III, is in the technical sphere—"the mass application of creative intelligence to improving the nation's productive capacity." Chinese ideology "opposes the concentration of technical control in the hands of a few . . . 'experts,' " so that China's people can have "a sense of being masters rather than appendages of their technological environment." A model villain in Chinese life is the "bourgeois expert."*

In community planning, the most important future element may be based not so much on reason as on those subtle realms of consciousness which transcend rationality. In older times, the sovereign was never without his seer, his oracle, or his "fool." We may be able to extend the seer's vision mechanically and deepen his rational understanding scientifically; but the synthesizing power of his intuition, itself perhaps heightened by scientific technique, will be of inestimable value.

Attempts to exalt chauvinistic considerations at the expense of world order (or national order or local order) will fly in the face of reality. Corporations, governments, and economic institutions will become integral parts of a variety of communities, from the neighborhood to the world. Further, the new ideology of consciousness seems to support internally, the extension of consensual forms and procedures in the place of the old hierarchical, con-

---

* Rensselaer W. Lee III, "The Politics of Technology in Communist China," *Comparative Politics*, January 1973, pp. 237–9; based on a paper delivered at the Social Science Research Council Conference on Ideology and Politics in China; Santa Fe, New Mexico, August 1971.

tractual forms. And business itself will be selling systematic performance within integral wholes—health systems (as in Health Maintenance Organizations), transportation systems, housing systems, sewage systems, community-wide air purification and solid waste disposal systems, versatile public recreational systems, and so on.

The Special Problem of Education

For educational institutions the change in the ideology of science is especially crucial. Education in America is rooted firmly in the old paradigm. As such, it is increasingly deficient in providing the young person with what he needs to cope with a changing environment. The child is taught about a series of matters which, for the most part, are unrelated to one another and to the world as he finds it. He is not provided with any sort of framework within which to order or derive meaning from the information he gets. He is not helped to understand the great integral transition in the midst of which he must live and die.

Together with the idea of scientific specialization, this lack of structure has produced an educational system unable to train minds to understand the interrelationships between things, to grasp the whole. As Alfred North Whitehead remarked, "It . . . [produces] minds in a groove. Each profession makes progress, but it is progress in its own groove." We have replaced the celibacy of the medieval learned class with

a celibacy of the intellect which is divorced from the concrete contemplation of the complete facts. . . . [Consequently], the specialised functions of the community are performed better and more progressively, but the generalised direction lacks vision. The progressiveness in detail only adds to the danger produced by the feebleness of coordination.

In an attempt to become more concrete, education has directed itself increasingly toward the real world, but its focus is piecemeal, governed by the old abstractions and disciplinary divisions. Furthermore, in the name of rationalism, education has been guilty of a form of irrationalism. By limiting itself to what is considered rational, education halts at a particular set of abstractions, which may greatly curtail learning. Thus we are apt to miss what is important. Again, as Whitehead put it: "When you understand all about the sun and all about the atmosphere and all about the rotation of the earth, you may still miss the radiance of the sunset."*

One can see Whitehead's point by taking a brief look at the modern American college. There was a time, in the more medieval past, when the college told the incoming freshman, "We know what an educated man or woman needs to know. We will give it to you, and once you have it, you can go forth and cope." Today it says instead, "We don't know what you need to know. We assume that you do. Here is a thick catalogue. Take your choice." The college is a series of long, dark tunnels. Each represents a specialty, a field of expert knowledge which has been carefully dug over the years. The best man in each tunnel is at the end, digging a little groove in the darkness. If the student is persistent, he may find him, and if he is lucky, the expert may raise his head and mumble. The student wonders whether this is what he needs. He asks himself: Do I not need to know what ties these tunnels together? What are the implications for politics and economics of genetics and microbiology, for example? Who will help him to integrate the available information to make it useful in explaining the world around him? It is hard to say. Maybe some maverick, some wandering guru, some amateur on the fringes of things. But respectable professionals don't get their Brownie points that way. They must go to the end of the tunnels; once having made that trip, it is hard for them to come back.

The prescribed remedy for the disturbed student is to go into the world, take a year off, and through experience build his own integrative model of what is happening out there. Practical as this may be, it is an institutional cop-out, a chancy and expensive way of doing the school's work.

The situation is reminiscent of the one faced by Locke at Oxford in the seventeenth century. We can be quite sure that the philosophy department had little use for this marginal chemist, with his amateurish insights; they didn't even let his books into the library until he had been dead seventy years. And the person today who attempts a radical synthesis between the revelations of science and the changing real world will find the university environment a chilly one. There is a double danger here: first, that the vital task

---

* Alfred North Whitehead, *Science and the Modern World* (New York: The Macmillan Co., 1925), pp. 197, 282–3, 286, 289.

will be delayed; and second, that it will be left to the untrained hands of irresponsible amateurs.

The vitality of traditional academic bureaucracies does not suggest that the old structures of education will dissolve easily or quickly. Holism will be a long time coming to education, but a start has been made at some universities with the establishment of a variety of centers to which specialists come for the integrated study of problems: urban growth, pollution, world order, and so on. Out of these problem-oriented studies will hopefully come new integral curricula and forms of knowledge.

So much for colleges and universities. The problem of the school in society at the elementary level is perhaps even more serious. In a remarkable book, *The Micro-Society School: A Real World in Miniature*, George Richmond describes his experiences as a fifth-grade teacher in Brooklyn:

Mass society has generated the kind of alienation that allows neighbors to live side by side without knowing each other. It has produced a human experience that is fragmented, often ideologically and aesthetically bankrupt, an impersonal world that may be over-industrialized and over-mechanized. Together these components of modern life sum to a condition of self-alienation and estrangement from society. . . . If the student is lucky, he will graduate from school with a piecemeal understanding of how the major institutions of society operate. He will have obtained fractions of experience without having been exposed to the ideological networks that order that experience and make it coherent. He will look at the "great society" he enters as a large, unmanageable, chaotic series of stimuli that will atrophy every response he makes to them.*

The problems Richmond found in Brooklyn are very similar to those in Veraguas, and exist for very much the same reasons. The schools are disconnected from society, teaching separate packages of knowledge which the student firmly believes will make no difference whatsoever in his relationship to what he finds around him. In Veraguas, the bishop's movement convinced parents and children alike that they could cause change—that participation, power, and influence would be theirs if they had the skills. Education followed. Richmond did very much the same thing.

If primary and secondary education are to gain any kind of

---

* George Richmond, *The Micro-Society School: A Real World in Miniature* (New York: Harper & Row, 1973), pp. 265, 266.

integral value, parents, alumni, neighborhood business, and political institutions must all be brought into its processes. The child must be allowed to see, in fact, that all of these contribute to him and that he can contribute to them, that he can make a difference. This cannot be a game; it must be for real. In an earlier time, the task was easier—when, for example, the community was integrated around the farm or the factory. In each case, however dismal may have been the child's lot, he felt useful; he was part of a perceptible community. Today he is not. I do not mean to suggest that the school can abandon the basic knowledge which it now tries to impart. This knowledge is crucial. The problem is that increasingly it is not being imparted, or rather it is not being absorbed. Special efforts must, therefore, be made to trace and demonstrate the interrelationship between critical areas of knowledge and to connect that knowledge to the real world so that the child can believe that it will be useful to him. The framework which used to allow him to take it on faith has gone.

Educating the Managers

Finally, there is the crucial task of educating those who will manage our institutions through the various transitions which this book has described. The skills are in very short supply. They have been gathered by, and largely reside in, a handful of graduate schools of business administration. Implicit in this fact are the antique assumptions that management is peculiarly a business skill; that it is concerned with the organization of private economic activity, which is separate from political and social relationships; and that it is presumably less pertinent to the conduct of the nation's largest collection of institutional activity—government. These are dangerous assumptions. They tend to limit managerial training to those interested in business. They bias such training toward the specialized skills associated with business as it has existed in the past. And they cause many who will be engaged in the management of non-business institutions to be deprived of necessary training.

Further, schools of public administration generally do not train managers, focused as they are on the relatively abstract conceptualization of policy problems and only slightly concerned with the functions of the executive. The merger of business schools and public administration schools would be an excellent thing, right in step with the movement to synthesis. Clearly, the old distinctions between what is private and what is public have less and less meaning; in many areas they are merely artificial remnants of the old ideology, figments of the old notions of property, competition, and the limited state. The management problems of Consolidated Edison, the oil companies, General Electric, IBM, ITT, AT&T, savings and loan associations, and the like are as inseparably involved with public questions of community need as are those, let us say, of the TVA, COMSAT, the Port of New York Authority, and HUD. The management of garbage disposal, health systems, land use, and welfare is equally complex and in many ways quite similar to the management of the so-called private sector. There may be different measures of efficiency, different sources of capital, different allocations of profit, different problems of incentive, but these differences are closing and they do not detract from the overall similarities. Yet consolidation of the business school and the public administration school is hindered by traditional academic bureaucratization and deeply felt loyalties to old specializations. In consequence, both sets of schools are in danger of obsolescence.

This attitude will have to go. Managers will increasingly be concerned with the design and direction of whole systems oriented around a variety of community needs. The job of the manager will be to perceive and understand these systems, and to manage them using such administrative skills as marketing, finance, control, accounting, and organizational psychology. More than ever he will need to be a generalist, a person uniquely trained to integrate the specialized skills of experts so as to give purpose and direction to the whole and maintain maximum efficiency.*

He will also need to be boldly imaginative, sensitive to the changing criteria of the environment. His task increasingly will be one of transforming old institutions and building new ones. The forum in which many of his decisions will be made will be profoundly political. The task of the manager, in whatever sector he finds himself, will be to emphasize this fact, not to obscure or resist it; to assist the political order in gathering the required information and analyzing it; to give government the confidence it

---

* See Chester T. Barnard, *The Functions of the Executive* (Cambridge, Mass.: Harvard University Press, 1938), pp. 136–7.

requires to plan, respecting its objectivity and its essential independence from any special interest, mindful of its communitarian nature; and then to execute community need as efficiently as possible. The corporate manager's task also includes competing with others to serve that need.

Let us assume that the community decides there shall be no such thing as waste any more, that everything we once called waste shall in fact be only part of a circle, a point in a process; and that the whole cyclical process must be managed. It follows that science and technology must be concentrated and organized to invent the means of meeting this need most effectively. Implementation of the new scheme will strike many components of the status quo. Some institutions may die—the town dump, for example. Costs and benefits must be calculated and a legitimate system designed to do the task. A system of such scope will necessarily impinge upon many other systems in the community, as a whole within a larger whole. The task of the manager here involves perceiving those wholes and recognizing their relationships to the political order and to the social needs and activities of the community. Peter G. Peterson, speaking as chairman of Lehman Brothers in a speech to the Pacem in Terris III meeting in the winter of 1974, described the need for managers of international systems, "a new breed of public official and corporation executive, one who can relate his own specialty to the large whole, one who can switch from one area to another, and not be a narrow special-interest pleader . . . who can at all times see the *new interrelatedness of things.*"

For the years ahead the manager must see himself perhaps first and foremost as a changer, architect of a smooth transition from the traditional ideology to the new, seeking reconciliation between the status quo and what must come in the nation and the world. In this task, crisis will be an essential tool of management. When the cities burn and crime is the rule; when the lights go off and the radiator grows cold; when the air is foul and rivers run dry; when bankruptcy is imminent—then we know something is wrong, and we are prepared to change. But we seem as a nation to be very poor at anticipating crisis. All the components of the energy crisis, for example, were in place at least four years prior to the fall of 1973, but few people calculated their significance. The fragmented nature of management, both political and economic; the ideological insistence that government's role does not embrace effective planning; the momentum of great bureaucratic interests—all precluded a proper anticipation of what was at stake.

The usefulness of crisis as a stimulant to efficient change is unquestionably enhanced by perceiving crisis sooner rather than later, and in real rather than mythical terms. There is a premium, therefore, on managers' comprehending the precise nature of crisis without illusion or scapegoating. Early perception requires holistic vision. Often we perceive crisis only when an expert tells us it is at hand—which is already too late. Even in 1969 the oil companies firmly believed that prices of oil would remain stable, because economists told them so. When political forces in the Arab world in 1970 produced effective organization of the oil-producing countries, crisis followed. A skilled generalist surely could have foreseen Arab unity; he would have been swifter than a specialist in perceiving and defining the crisis.

It is common to blame crises on some familiar foe—the young, the old, blacks, whites, government, business, or labor. Perception is thus blinded and managers lose the utility of clearly defined crisis as a means to change their institutions. Although every self-respecting manager generally acknowledges the need for change abstractly—for a safe and pure environment, for an end to poverty and racism, for urban renovation, and the like—he is apt to harden up when change threatens the structure which he manages, and becomes positively antagonistic when it threatens an idea he has conventionally used to define values.

Irreversible, permanent structural changes have already occurred in America which have undermined some cherished ideological assumptions. In many instances, business itself has spurred them on. In the pursuit of increased productivity, the General Foods factory in Topeka is now organized around non-Lockean definitions of individual fulfillment and managerial authority—each derives from the whole through a consensual process. If headquarters intends to extend this experiment to other plants and perhaps even to itself, it must understand why the effects would be so profoundly disruptive to traditional union and management structures. Is management's function to perpetuate a certain technostructure, or is it to serve the best interests of the community which surrounds and depends upon General Foods? If the answer is the latter, managers must be prepared for radical, structural change which will not only erode their "prerogatives" but may put a number of them out of work.

And when I say "prepared" I don't mean dug in behind the barricades ready to fight. The introduction of change should be a primary order of work, not so much out of any sense of nobility—although this is not unimportant—as out of an awareness of the requirements of survival and justice.

Once the manager has joined the side of change and survival, he will require a clear perception of how an engine of change works. First, as I have noted, its task is a holistic one, addressing the system to be changed as a whole. Next, it must be capable of producing motivation and organization for change. Generally speaking, it must begin its activities with agitation; that is, education about a precise need—often born out of crisis—for purposes of motivating and organizing.

Further, a successful engine of change must have five characteristics. First, *authority*: when the leader speaks, he must be believed and trusted. It is noteworthy that for this reason religious figures are often involved in the early phases of change. Then too the leader must have the *ability to communicate* with—talk the language of—the most remote element he is trying to affect. Third, he must have *access to power*, in order to bring to bear the resources required for change at the appropriate time. Fourth, he must be capable of providing *protection* to the forces of change against the inevitable retaliation of the status quo. And finally he must have *competence,* that special ability to integrate the skills of experts conscious of the nature of the whole system in which the change is occurring.* We must educate men and women in considerable numbers to become such engines of change. Much is at stake. From now on, good management will be measured by the levels of waste and violence in society; by the quality and standard of life in our communities; and by the creativity and self-respect of our people.

There is, of course, no good reason to suppose that the next 5,000 years are going to be any better or worse than the last. That really is not the point. Earlier on, I quoted Norbert Wiener: "We

---

* See G. C. Lodge, *Engines of Change* (New York: Alfred A. Knopf, Inc., 1970), Chap. 6.

are not stuff that abides, but patterns that perpetuate themselves; whirlpools of water in an ever-flowing river."* Many of us can be concerned only with the small bits and pieces of progress. The process may be, as Jacques Monod has said, chiefly the product of chance and necessity;** but it is clear that mankind also has some choice. Western civilization has moved more or less unconsciously through a series of ideological frameworks, each building upon the one that went before. Institutions and behavior have adapted to the flow. Some adaptations have been hideous to behold, others glorious. The West is in the throes of another of its great adaptations. This time we can have the choice for glory, if we will but be aware.

---

* Wiener, *The Human Use of Human Beings* (New York: Avon Books, 1954).

** Jacques Monrod, *Chance and Necessity: An Essay on the Natural Philosophy of Modern Biology*, translated from the French by Austryn Wainhouse (New York: Vintage Books, 1972).

Appendix
Index

On the Japanese Ideology*

This note attempts to describe the Japanese counterparts of the five components of traditional American ideology outlined in Chapter 1. In this way it seeks to provide an insight into contemporary Japanese thought.

The Relationship Between the Individual and Society

UNITED STATES—Individualism, equality, and contract.

JAPAN—The place of the individual in society is given by the nature of things, as in a family.

Before a Japanese recognizes himself as an individual, he tends to define his relationship with others and his position in a group. "I am the second son of my family," "I am a first-year pupil in teacher A's class, in elementary school X." This recognition has two parts: first, of the group with which the individual identifies himself; second, of his position and role in that group.

Such recognition is not necessarily hierarchical; rather, it is a consciousness of the order of things emanating from a certain view of life and the world. It leads the Japanese to regard human beings not as single individuals but as groups of creatures inevitably interrelated and dependent on one another, accentuating the interdependence of human relations. Nobody thinks that interdependence is better or worse than independence; but since it is obvious that one cannot live alone, interdependence is a fact of

---

* This note was prepared by Masatake Ushiro, MBA 1974, with the collaboration of the author.

nature. (It is important to note that in human relations and human goodness, Japanese tend to be rational and pragmatic. In matters concerning truth and beauty, they tend to be nonrational.)

Equality is desirable always. But it seems that the fact that persons belong to the same group or share common feelings is more important than the notion of equality. Japanese admit the fact of inequality; it is given; it is natural. Human relations do not depend upon equality so much as upon sharing common feelings and understandings. The shared experience expressed as the comrades who shared food from the same bowl can be the strongest lifelong tie among people, regardless of their further attainment in the society. "One of the same" is more important than "equal."

As for the idea of contract, legally it is almost the same as in the West. In practice, however, it differs a good deal. Very often articles of the contract are not carried out as stated. An unstated common recognition of "the way things are," arising out of face-to-face relationships, frequently plays a more important role, especially in critical situations.

The contract is not so much an objective matter as a subjective arrangement between persons. Again, the basic human relationship in Japan arises, not through the contract but rather from spontaneous or given relationships, as within a family.

The Treatment of Property

UNITED STATES—Property rights as the fundamental guarantor of individual rights.

JAPAN—Legally, the same as in the United States, but the practice is very different.

The Japanese conception of property is deeply rooted in history and tradition. It arises from the traditional family structure and from the historical development of business in the last one hundred years or so.

Traditionally, landed property did not belong to the individual. As in the medieval West, it belonged to feudal lords. As feudalism broke down, the rights to the uses of property came to belong to the village or the family. Within the family, property rights were held by the father, who was the family chief, and he always passed his position and rights to his first son. However, the family chief was not normally allowed to sell his property since he was not so much its owner as a consignee; that is, property was passed to him by his ancestors for caretaking: he was not to use it up or dispose of it. He was entitled to keep it, protect it, improve it, and pass it along to his descendants. Property was thus owned by a family but not by any single generation or individual.

This idea relates to the concept of the Japanese business enterprise today. The firm in a real sense is felt to be the property of all its members, including those who hold its equity and debt and, increasingly, the people generally. The employee of a Japanese firm refers to "my company." He says, "I am a member of Company X." He belongs to the Company X family, even though he may have no right to represent Company X officially. And he feels proud of this sense of membership. I remember my father, who is a managing director of a medium-sized printing company, saying that the members of his company were excited and proud when they moved from an old, shabby-looking building into a new one. He said that the employees were saying in their heart: "Look! I am a member of this growing company." This is not only a spiritual matter. Given the lifelong employment system, the prosperity of "his" company guarantees the employee's well-being in the future.

The lack of an individualistic concept of property also means that today there is a feeling of mass or public ownership of Japan's large business firms. The growth rate of Japanese business since World War II could never have been generated by internal means. Stock is widely dispersed among many stockholders, who are very often banks, insurance companies, and other big firms. The Japanese business today, therefore, is in a very real sense a public enterprise. This has tended to enhance the personal status of corporate management. But it is important to note that corporate leadership is not chosen by stockholders. The company president is the person who has the strongest balance of influence *inside* the corporation, among all its members, even though officially he is elected by the stockholders. Once he assumes the presidency, he plays the role of the eldest son who succeeds the family chief. He even is expected in many cases to choose his successor on retiring, unless he loses his legitimacy as the result of pressures either from within the corporation or outside. By and large, the rapid growth of the economy so far has helped these "consignee" presidents to strengthen their positions. However, outside pressures on managers are becoming increasingly important, especially where pollution is involved.

The concepts of the rights and obligations of property in Japan and the traditional United States are plainly different. In his autobiography *My Years with General Motors,* Alfred Sloan boasts about the company's ability to pay dividends even during the Depression, when many workers were laid off. For a Japanese company president, such action would be suicidal. He would be regarded as selfish and inhumane. In the event of an economic downturn, the probable sequence in Japan would be: a cut in dividends, lower management salaries, and finally, if bankruptcy were the only alternative, a lay-off of workers.

The Control of the Uses of Property

UNITED STATES—Competition in a free market to satisfy consumer desires as well as the desires of self-interested proprietors.

JAPAN—Competition to serve communal or family needs.

Until one hundred years ago, the political history of Japan had been marked by violent competition among feudal lords. Since that time, there has been factional strife among different leadership groups, seeking to draw upon traditional sources of power, but relying increasingly on the sheer ability of young men emerging from the highly competitive Japanese educational system.

Japan's educational system provides for a high degree of social mobility. A young person, regardless of his economic standing, can receive outstanding training if he passes a rigorous sequence of competitive examinations. His education is in a very real sense his ticket of admission onto the train of life, given the general expectation of lifetime employment in Japanese firms. Every youth is highly motivated to secure the best education he can, to go to the best high school and university. What he does in a few days of competitive examinations virtually decides his future. Almost all the leaders in every field—government, business, the law, social activities—consist of the graduates of a handful of famous universities. This procedure means that a poor boy can rise to great heights in Japan; it also means that there is intense competition.

Naturally, intense competition in all aspects of Japanese life, including business, follows. Firms are always struggling for a larger share of the market. And yet this competitiveness is accompanied by an equally strong sense of cooperation between business groups and of harmony within businesses. The explanation of this apparent contradiction can be found in the legend of Mori Motonari.

Mori Motonari was a famous feudal lord who lived four hundred years ago. In his old age, he was worried about the safety of his territory. Turmoil and disorder prevailed. One day he called his three sons to his bedside, gave each of them an arrow, and said, "Break it." Each did so easily. Then he gave each of them three arrows and said, "Break them." They could not. Then he said, "If you are alone, you won't be able to survive. If you cooperate together, you will prosper and protect your family."

Since Japan was first exposed to the West a hundred years ago, it has always been conscious of the threats from the outside. These threats have heightened its sense of family. Competitiveness, therefore, is subordinated to the common interest in protecting the Japanese family. The definition of "survival" in Japan embraces the whole—not Japan, Inc., but the Japanese family.

Thus, although competitiveness is an obvious trait among Japanese, competition as embodied in the American antitrust laws is not the means for controlling the uses of property. Rather, property is controlled by a transcendent sense of the value of cooperation and harmony for the good of the whole community or family. Even though it is quite legal, acquisition of one company by another tends to be regarded as somewhat immoral. To take over another company or to force it into bankruptcy is, for Japanese, comparable to burglary.

The Role of Government

UNITED STATES—The limited state; the less government the better; it is a "convenience" to protect body and property.

JAPAN—Government as supporter, coordinator, and father.

If one asked a hundred leading Japanese businessmen, "Is the Japanese government a planner and vision-setter?", eighty of them would answer, "No." They think that they are going their own way, often cooperating with one another because it is essential for their survival and prosperity. They feel that government support and coordination is useful to them. Remembering the story of Mori Motonari, the government in Japan plays the role of the father. He does not order things. He does not impose plans. He says, "If you wish to survive, cooperate instead of fighting among brothers. If you want to fight, go ahead as you like." The Japanese government cannot set any vision unless it is to everybody's advantage, unless there is a consensus among all the sons.

It is true, of course, that the government is very important and its function deeply respected. But its role is that of coordinating and reconciling different interests, developing a continuing consensus. The "vision" seemingly set by government is more often the product of discussion among political and business leaders. Those visions which have been set without such discussion are generally not carried out. Here it must be remembered that leaders of government and business come from a very similar educational background, which creates a shared understanding, a common feeling.

It is also true that in spite of its seemingly well-designed economy, Japan actually lacks the real leadership for long-range planning.* Firms tend to be concerned with shorter-term, here-and-now problems, and government cannot display real leadership without their consensus and support. The common educational background produces a sense of equality which inhibits government from imposing its plans on business. (This is a difference between France and Japan.) The present ecology problems, for example, reveal the lack of such long-range leadership in economic planning. The ecology problem is a bad omen for Japan's future, since it is a result of the remarkable progress brought about by Japanese-style planning and coordination.

It is easy to take too simplistic a view of the relationship between Japanese government and business. In its study of these relations, the U.S. Department of Commerce, for example, stresses the important role of government in the development of the Japanese economy** but fails to note the wide variations in government-

---

* "My observation is that Japanese are not too skillful as planners," said Chujiro Fujino, president of Mitsubishi Corporation, Tokyo, in a speech before the Harvard Business School Club of New York, April 11, 1973, p. 6. "In America change is something that is planned for and created by anticipating the future. By contrast, the Japanese people tend to be quite conservative and thus change for them is the result of being forced to act by something in the external environment."

** *Japan: The Government-Business Relationship,* Eugene J. Kaplan, Director, Far East Division, Bureau of International Commerce, U.S. Department of Commerce, Washington, D.C., 1972.

business relations in different industries at different times. It says, "The case studies point out instances where government-business interaction has fallen short of the mark as well as instances in which it has been immensely effective. . . ."* But the interaction is far too varied to be so formalized.

The relationship is better understood if we recognize that the government is playing the father's role. The father provides special care of "infant" industries, such as computers, which cannot help but accept it. "Young adults" like the automobile industry are essentially autonomous. Those industries which have reached "manhood" sometimes take strong positions against government —unless they are sick.

Science and Technology

UNITED STATES—Scientific specialization; experimentalism; concentration on the parts on the assumption that the whole will take care of itself.

JAPAN—Technology is the servant of the family.

Japan has long admired and absorbed Western technology, but it has resisted Western culture. The phrase *"Wakon Yosai"* expresses this notion: "Japanese spirit; Western technology." Japan is the Asian country which has been most influenced by Western technology but least influenced by Christianity.

Japanese received Western culture simply as a different one with an excellent technological development. They felt that their traditional spiritual culture worked much better for them than the Western variety. Interestingly, Japan has been more willing to accept the workable technology than the theoretical aspects of Western science. Although there are some notable attainments in the sphere of basic science, Japanese firms have generally been more eager to adopt licensed technology than to devote themselves to elaborate basic research and development. They know that in the given time and with small financial resources, the best way of keeping up with developed countries is to receive the fruits of scientific development without paying so much regard to the roots of science. Their excellence has been shown in adopting Western scientific attainments and improving them. However, now that

---

* *Ibid.,* p. 75.

Japan has become one of the world's most technologically developed countries, it must confront the problem of how to attain further development on its own feet.

The present pollution crisis in Japan is especially shocking because in a sense it represents a failure of Japanese society to properly contain technology—a violation of *Wakon Yosai*. The recognition of that fact, however, will doubtless ensure that the Japanese family cleans house with considerable expedition.

The similarities between Japanese ideology and the new American ideology are obvious; the differences are still great and will continue to be so for a long time. But there may well be an inexorable synthesis of the world ideologies underway. If we placed the great ideologies of the world on a spectrum, with the United States at one end and communitarian China at the other—and England, France, Germany, the U.S.S.R., and Japan ranged in between—we would, I believe, notice this growing synthesis. We would also incidentally be aware that Japan is ideologically much closer to China than is the Soviet Union. Amity between China and Russia is inhibited by enormous ideological obstacles. If a world ideological synthesis is occurring, the task of intellectuals must surely be to analyze and describe it so that it can function fully in designing such new world institutions as transnational corporations.

Index

A Note About the Author

GEORGE C. LODGE was born in Boston in 1927 and after two years in the Navy was graduated from Harvard College in 1950. He served as a reporter on the Boston *Herald* for four years, and from 1954 to 1961 was with the U.S. Department of Labor, first as director of information and later as assistant secretary for international affairs. In 1962 he was the Republican candidate for the U.S. Senate from Massachusetts, and then joined the faculty of the Harvard Business School, where he is now professor of business administration. He is the author of *Spearheads of Democracy: Labor in Developing Countries* and *Engines of Change: United States Interests and Revolution in Latin America,* and contributes articles to *Foreign Affairs* and the *Harvard Business Review.* Mr. Lodge is married and the father of six children.

A Note on the Type

The text of this book was set on the Linotype in a face called Times Roman, designed by Stanley Morison for *The Times* (London) and first introduced by that newspaper in 1932.

Among typographers and designers of the twentieth century, Stanley Morison has been a strong forming influence, as a typographical adviser to the English Monotype Corporation, as a director of two distinguished English publishing houses and as a writer of sensibility, erudition, and keen practical sense.

This book was composed by Maryland Linotype Composition Co., Baltimore, Maryland; printed and bound by The Book Press, Brattleboro, Vermont. Typography and binding design by Camilla Filancia